CALLING
T H E
EQUALITY
BLUFF

The ATHENE Series

An International Collection of Feminist Books

General Editors
Gloria Bowles
Renate Klein
Janice Raymond

Consulting Editor
Dale Spender

The Athene Series assumes that all those who are concerned with formulating explanations of the way the world works need to know and appreciate the significance of basic feminist principles.

The growth of feminist research has challenged almost all aspects of social organization in our culture. The Athene Series focuses on the construction of knowledge and the exclusion of women from the process—both as theorists and subjects of study—and offers innovative studies that challenge established theories and research.

On Athene—When Metis, goddess of wisdom who presided over all knowledge was pregnant with Athene, she was swallowed up by Zeus who then gave birth to Athene from his head. The original Athene is thus the parthenogenetic daughter of a strong mother and as the feminist myth goes, at the "third birth" of Athene she stops being Zeus' obedient mouthpiece and returns to her real source: the science and wisdom of womankind.

CALLING T H E EQUALITY BLUFF
WOMEN IN ISRAEL

EDITED BY

BARBARA SWIRSKI
Breirot Publishers, Tel Aviv, Israel

MARILYN P. SAFIR
University of Haifa, Haifa, Israel

PERGAMON PRESS

Member of Maxwell Macmillan Pergamon Publishing Corporation
New York • Oxford • Beijing • Frankfurt
São Paulo • Sydney • Tokyo • Toronto

Pergamon Press Offices:

U.S.A.	Pergamon Press, Inc., Maxwell House, Fairview Park, Elmsford, New York 10523, U.S.A.
U.K.	Pergamon Press plc, Headington Hill Hall, Oxford OX3 0BW, England
PEOPLE'S REPUBLIC OF CHINA	Pergamon Press, Xizhimenwai Dajie, Beijing Exhibition Centre, Beijing 100044, People's Republic of China
GERMANY	Pergamon Press GmbH, Hammerweg 6, D-6242 Kronberg, Germany
BRAZIL	Pergamon Editora Ltda, Rua Eça de Queiros, 346, CEP04011, Paraiso, São Paulo, Brazil
AUSTRALIA	Pergamon Press Australia Pty Ltd., P.O. Box 544, Potts Point N.S.W. 2011, Australia
JAPAN	Pergamon Press, 8th Floor, Matsuoka Central Building, 1-7-1 Nishishinjuku, Shinjuku-ku, Tokyo 160, Japan
CANADA	Pergamon Press Canada Ltd., Suite 271, 253 College Street, Toronto, Ontario, Canada M5T 1R5

Library of Congress Cataloging in Publication Data

Calling the equality bluff : women in Israel / edited by Barbara
Swirski and Marilyn P. Safir. -- 1st ed.
    p.   cm. -- (The Athene series)
    Includes index.
    ISBN 0-08-037471-9 -- ISBN 0-08-037472-7 (pbk.)
    1. Women--Israel--Social conditions. 2. Feminism--Israel.
I. Swirski, Barbara. II. Safir, Marilyn. III. Series.
HQ1728.5.C35 1991
305.42'095694--dc20   90-49394
                                                CIP

Printing: 1 2 3 4 5 6 7 8 9   Year: 1 2 3 4 5 6 7 8 9 0

Printed in the United States of America

The paper used in this publication meets the minimum requirements of American National Standard for Information Sciences—Permanence of Paper for Printed Library Materials, ANSI Z39.48-1984

Contents

Acknowledgments and Credits

ACKNOWLEDGMENTS

The editors would like to thank Dafna Izraeli for her contribution to the crystallization of the concept of the book.

We express our appreciation to the University of Haifa and its Research Authority for making available computer facilities and services, and to Heather Kernoff, Danielle Friedlander, and Angela Greenson for their dedication and patience with the typing of the manuscript.

We would like to thank Efraim Mizrahi for his support.

CREDITS

The credits for the Personal Dimensions are as follows:

"An Agunah Testifies on the Floor of the Knesset"—The editors wish to thank the Israel Women's Network for the translated transcript of the testimony.

"The Emergence of a Palestinian Identity"—Adapted from Bili Moskona-Lerman, "May God Watch Over Her Man," which appeared in the Hebrew daily "Ma'ariv," January 8, 1988.

"Musings of an Israeli Superwoman"—Adapted from an article that appeared in the Hebrew daily "Davar," November 28, 1986.

"Amira Dotan: Israel's First Female General"—Adapted from Abraham Rabinovich, "My Mother the General," which appeared in the English daily "The Jerusalem Post," October 24, 1988.

"It's Like Going to a Movie"—from Barbara Swirski (1987) "Israeli Women on the Assembly Line," in the Hebrew version of Annette Fuentes and Barbara Ehrenreich, WOMEN IN THE GLOBAL FACTORY, Haifa: Breirot Publishers.

"A Jewish Factory Worker Talks About Opportunities for Promotion"—from Shlomo Swirski (1981) ORIENTALS AND ASHKENAZIM IN ISRAEL: THE ETHNIC DIVISION OF LABOR. Haifa: Mahbarot L'Mehkar U'Libikoret (Hebrew).

"Violet Khoury"—Adapted from Yehuda Zur, "Violet Khoury: Volcano Extinct," which appeared in the Hebrew daily "Al Hamishmar," January 29, 1988.

"Motherhood: An Early Kibbutz Experience"—Interview by Michal Palgi, 1988.

Introduction

Israel is the meeting ground for a diverse group of women, most of whose foremothers did not come from Western industrial societies. The prestate Jewish community in Palestine was created by Zionists from Eastern Europe, the social group which, in the aftermath of the Second World War, absorbed large numbers of Jewish refugees who had survived Hitler and, in 1948, fought and won a war against their Palestinian Arab neighbors. The outcome of the 1948 war was an uneasy coexistence with a sizeable Palestinian minority, and a great influx of Jewish refugees from Arab lands. The state that emerged was modeled after Western societies.

Contemporary Israel is a welfare state with a socialist, egalitarian rhetoric, a capitalist economy, and strong religious and traditional influences. There are relatively few homeless, but unemployment (10% in June 1990) is on the increase, especially among women, and there is a growing tolerance of the phenomenon. Persons without income are eligible for unemployment compensation or welfare allocations; subsidized housing or loans are available for young marrieds; singles over the age of 36, and new immigrants (singles receiving less); basic staples have been subsidized (but these subsidies are presently in the process of being abolished); and income supplements are provided to families, in accordance with the number of dependent children, by a National Insurance Institution. The socialist ideology of settlers who became the elite of the state-in-the-making is reflected in the collective organization of most of Jewish agriculture, and in state ownership of nearly all the land and vital industries such as defense, as well as in Histadrut (National Federation of Hebrew Labor Unions) ownership of various industries and services. The egalitarian ideology of the Declaration of Independence, reflected in the relatively small wage differences that prevailed at the dawn of statehood, and the idea of the kibbutz and moshav (collective agricultural village) has been eroded, as this book will show, by legislation and bureaucratic regulations institutionalizing discrimination on the basis of gender and nationality, and the development of a capitalist economy that involves increasing wage differentials, the encouragement of private ownership of banking and industry, and incentives (including no unionization and cheap labor) offered to foreign investors. Strong religious and traditional influences, both Jewish and Islamic, find tangible expression in institutions like the family, the traditional Arab village leadership, the Rabbinate, and the Jewish religious political parties.

1

Calling the Equality Bluff: Women in Israel was designed to present readers with a broad perspective on women's experience in contemporary Israeli society and an insight into some of the institutions which have helped to shape that experience. The chapters represent scholarship by the leading experts in their fields, and most were written especially for the book. In our opinion, they represent "the state of the art" with regard to Israeli feminist concerns vis-a-vis women in Israel. As such, the book cannot claim equal or proportional representation of all social groups within Israeli society, but is, rather, a reflection of the present social structure. The groups we refer to represent national, ethnic, and religious or secular divisions. The national groups include Jews and Palestinian Arabs—Muslims, Christians, Druze and Bedouins (there are also small Armenian and Circassion communities in Israel, not represented in this volume); the ethnic groups include Ashkenazi Jews (whose origins are in Europe or English-speaking countries), Oriental Jews (whose origins are in North Africa or the Middle East), and a small minority of Ethiopian Jews (also not represented in the volume). As pointed out in Chapter 1, secular Ashkenazi Jews constitute the mainstream Israeli society. Among women, Ashkenazi Jewish women have the highest educational achievements, and this fact is reflected in their over-representation in this volume. It is axiomatic that we tend to write mainly about ourselves; thus there has been considerable research on women in the public service, the professions, academia and management, but almost no research on women employed as assembly-line workers or holding low-level office jobs. Numerous studies have been made of women running for public office, but there are hardly any on grass roots organizing. Studies on women in kibbutzim abound, but there is almost nothing about women in development towns. While we tried to include as many Israeli women as possible who identify as Palestinians, as Oriental Jews, and as religiously observant, we were not entirely successful. Five of the 40 articles were authored by, and two others are interviews with, Israeli Palestinian women living in Israel. Only two of the articles were written by women who identify and write as Oriental Jews; an effort was made to offset this imbalance by including an interview, and by devoting a chapter to, the workforce participation of Oriental Jewish women. Another failing is with regard to Jewish women who regard themselves as religiously observant, a serious shortcoming in view of the fact that such women constitute nearly 20 percent of the Jewish female population of Israel. There are two chapters written by women who identify as devout Jewesses, one of which addresses the question of religion; while other articles refer to the experience of women who belong to this community, the fact of under-representation remains. This, too, reflects the state of the art; ultra-Orthodox women do not ordinarily attend university, analyze their position in society for scholarly works, or write for feminist publications.

The volume is divided into sections, most of which focus on the unique in Israeli women's experience. The first section, *Living in a Jewish State,* shows how women's lives are affected by the fact that the state is defined as Jewish. It explores the meaning and implications of "Jewish" in the context of Israel — those included and those excluded by the definition, the implication of non-separation of religion and state for Israeli democracy, and how the fact that Judaism is the state religion affects Jewish women's experience of religion.

The second section, *Family Comes First,* reveals that contemporary Israel is a family-oriented society in which most women marry and relatively few divorce. It examines the strong heterosexual bias and the importance of children in both the Jewish and Moslem sectors of Israeli society. The experience of Palestinian women in Israel, shaped by national as well as sexual identities, is explored on both the theoretical and existential level. The interface of family and work is examined for Israeli career women.

Section three, *Society Under Siege: The Spectre of War,* reflects the fact that Israel has existed in a continuous state of tension and hostilities, with six wars in its 42 year history. Chapters in this section examine the double rhythm of women's lives, in which the public sphere constantly intrudes upon the personal. They focus on issues such as the phenomenon of military conscription for women, the institutionalization of bereavement, and women's anti-war protest activities, especially during the Intifada.

Section four, *The Work Women Do,* examines past and present trends and patterns of employment among Jewish and Palestinian women. It shows how protective legislation helped to reinforce women's workforce participation in traditional female occupations, as well as their traditional roles as caretakers of the family, and points to a current trend in the direction of equal opportunity.

Section five, *Golda Notwithstanding: Participation and Powerlessness,* shows how women have been excluded from the centers of political power and why they have not succeeded in establishing a power base of their own. The chapters examine Israel's political system, women's performance in national and local politics, and the conflicting aims of Israel's largest women's organization. They also examine anomalies such as the fact that while Arab women have even less political power than their Jewish sisters, they often function as change agents in Palestinian society in Israel.

The sixth section focuses on what has often been considered the most unique aspect of Israeli society: *Women of the Dream: The Kibbutz and Moshav.* Since these institutions have been viewed as experiments in social equality, the major research question here is why they have not achieved gender equality in the areas of work, family roles and political activity.

The seventh and last section of the book, *Feminism Israeli Style,* reviews the history of feminism in Israel and examines its implications for contemporary Israeli women. Chapters in this section point out that the prestate women's movement aimed to transform both women and society; while it fell short of these aims, it achieved suffrage for women and established women's right to work. The development of the new women's movement is critically reviewed, and issues of rape and battering examined at length.

The contributors represent different sectors of the Israeli political spectrum (with a center bias) and hold a variety of conceptions concerning feminism. They include scholars, professionals, politicians, and grassroots activists, and these categories are not mutually exclusive. All, however, share a more or less critical view of Israeli society and of women's position within it. It is our hope that the composite picture presented in this volume will give the reader valuable insights into the experience of women in Israeli society and challenge our sisters to undertake projects that will fill the gaps in both knowledge and praxis.

Barbara Swirski
Marilyn P. Safir

Section One
Living in a Jewish State

Living in a Jewish State: National, Ethnic and Religious Implications

Barbara Swirski
Marilyn P. Safir

That Israel is a Jewish state is common knowledge. What is less well known is how Israel's definition as "Jewish" affects the lives of its female citizens. In analyzing the impact of the Jewishness of the state, it is necessary to first examine what the founders meant by the notions of "Jewish" and "Jewish state."

For Israel's Zionist founders, Jewish settlement in Palestine meant establishing a refuge for a persecuted minority—the Jews of Eastern Europe. With the ascension of Tzar Alexander III in 1881, anti-Semitism, discouraged during the previous regime, became official policy, and a new, 2-year wave of pogroms broke out in Russia. Secular, educated Russian Jews, who, following the lead of Western European Jewry, had been undergoing a process of assimilation, began to reexamine their situation and seriously consider two alternatives: immigration to America or Palestine, the latter for the purpose of creating a Jewish state in the land from which the Jewish people had been exiled 1,900 years before. The idea of a Jewish state was originally formulated in 1862 in Germany, in a book entitled *Rome and Jerusalem,* written by Moses Hess, a colleague of Karl Marx. It was further developed by Leon Pinsker, a Russian Jew, in *Autoemancipation,* published in 1882. Arguing that Jews were despised because they had no home of their own, Pinsker concluded that Jews would be respected only if they acquired a territorial base. He called on Western European Jews to convene a congress to work towards that end. Pinsker's ideas found an audience among Eastern rather than Western European Jews; two writers with Orthodox Jewish backgrounds, Peretz Smolenskin and Moshe Lilienblum, further pursued the idea of a Jewish homeland, locating it in Palestine, as the ancient Jewish homeland, then part of the Ottoman empire, was called. The idea of Zionism took on concrete polit-

We wish to thank Shlomo Swirski for his comments and suggestions.

ical form with the convention of the first Zionist Congress in Basel in 1897, by Theodor Herzl. This idea was based on three assumptions: that Jewish identity was essentially national, that assimilation was impossible, and that the liberal world would aid the Jewish people in their efforts at national restoration (Hertzberg, 1969: 39).

The Jews who came to Palestine in the first wave of immigration (1882–1903) were Zionists from Eastern Europe, mainly Russia, and they established traditional farming communities on the central coast of present-day Israel. The second (1904–1914) and third (1919–1923) waves of immigration consisted primarily of socialist Zionists from Russia and Poland. Inspired by the Russian revolution of 1905, these women and men created social forms which later became the hallmark of Israel: the kibbutzim and moshavim—the cooperative farming communities; the Histadrut—National Federation of Hebrew Labor Unions; the *Shomer, Haganah* and *Palmach*—prestate military organizations; and the Representative Assembly—the predecessor of the Israeli legislature. These were all Jewish institutions; that is, they were created by Jews and for Jews. The Arabs living in Palestine were never a part of them—nor did they want to be. In fact, one of the purposes of these organizations was to protect Jewish settlers from Arab neighbors—from either physical attack or from competition in a labor market with limited job opportunities.

The Jews who settled in Palestine to escape their inferior, minority status in Europe were following a familiar pattern: every European state had its dominant nationality; the immigrants would create a new nation-state, to be dominated by Jews. Arthur Hertzburg describes this as "the most radical attempt in Jewish history to break out of the parochial molds of Jewish life in order to become part of the general history of man [sic] in the modern world" (1969: 20).

The Zionist movement understood the word "Jewish" not merely as a religious or even national category, but also as an ethnic one. Accordingly, the Law of Return, enacted after the establishment of the state, stipulated that anyone whose mother was a Jew (and who had not declared her or himself a member of another faith) or anyone who had converted to Judaism was a potential citizen of the Jewish state and therefore entitled to automatic citizenship upon immigration. For secular Jewish leaders, observance was never a criterion, and neither was belief. However, as will be seen below, the Orthodox establishment harbored a somewhat different conception of "Jewishness."

Two large groups who eventually became citizens of the Jewish state were not included in the original formulations of who the state-to-be was intended for: Palestinian Arabs and Oriental Jews. The state was established in 1948, after a military confrontation between the Jews and the Palestinian Arabs—who by then had galvanized a national movement of their own—in the course of which they were aided by a number of Arab states. The Jews won the war, most Palestinian Arabs left the country, and those who remained became a national minority. It was soon evident that the new minority would not obtain equal citizenship rights without fighting another, civil battle (which has yet to be won). A Palestinian educator described the dilemma of the Israeli Arab citizen: "In a Jewish Zionist state (as in every other state), the citizen must accept the basic ideology of the state, in order to receive his due, get ahead and realize his civil rights. In Israel, there are positions which demand a clear, Zionist allegiance; however, due to his very ascription, the Israeli Arab citizen cannot accept the ideology of the Zionist movement . . . Israeli Arabs have low social status, because in Israel the social status of the citizen is determined not only by education and professional achievements, but by the degree of identification with the central goals of Israel as a Jewish Zionist state" (Tzartsur, 1985: 479).

Following the War of Independence, Palestinian Arab lands were expropriated for Jewish settlement or military use, and the building rights of Palestinians within their own towns and villages were—and still are—severely restricted. With land confiscation, the agricultural base of the local Palestinian Arab economy was destroyed, resulting in proletarization (Rosenfeld, 1964). Today, most Palestinians live apart from Jews and attend schools belonging to a separate, state system, in which Arabic has been retained as the language of instruction. While the Declaration of Independence granted equality without regard to religion, race or gender, the ambivalence towards Arab citizens can be seen in the fact that their local governments receive much smaller allocations than Jewish local authorities. Government ministries are not oriented to serve their needs; special "Arab Departments" in the Ministries of Education, Labor, Interior and Housing operate without established budgets or long-term programs (Lustick, 1980). Until 1989, there was no religious academy in Israel for training Moslem clergy. The Jewish leadership, which identified with Western liberalism and democracy, shared the Western disdain for Arab culture, viewing it as unenlightened, that is, backward and inferior.

It should be added that for years, the Palestinians (with the exception of the Druze and Bedouin communities, who had sided with the Jews in the War of Independence) were not viewed as just any national minority, but as a potential "fifth column" on whose domination and control the survival of the state depended. Until 1966, Arab towns and villages were under military administration. One of the methods for maintaining control was the co-optation and strengthening of the traditional leadership, which for Palestinian women meant reinforcement of patriarchal control. Over the years, such patriarchal control has been reflected in a high school drop-out rate for Moslem and Druze girls, limited opportunities in the labor market, and low work force participation. It has also resulted in the maintenance of male control over female sexuality and choice of mates.

The second group that was not part of the original plan for a Jewish state are the Oriental Jews. The Zionist founders dreamed of the ingathering of all exiles, but they had in mind the Jewish majority who came from Eastern or Western Europe and who spoke Yiddish, that is, the Ashkenazim. A problem arose when Jews began immigrating en masse from the Arab countries of the Middle East and North Africa in 1948 (until 1948, Oriental Jews comprised about 15 percent of the Jewish population), for they did not look, dress, or talk like European Jews, but rather like Arabs, and their numbers (575,000) were too great for the host society (650,000) to easily absorb, especially in view of its limited resources. The attitude toward the new immigrants was ambivalent. On the one hand, they were viewed as fellow Jews who were to be assisted, assistance being thought of mainly in terms of their being "desocialized" from their Arabness and "resocialized" into a Western-oriented society, and on the other, they were regarded with the same contempt displayed towards Arabs, an attitude reminiscent of that of American WASPs towards Eastern European immigrants at the turn of the century. The fact that they spoke a language that was foreign to the immigration agencies, and that they generally did not have relatives or connections that might ease their absorption into the new society, exacerbated the situation.

Instead of becoming a part of the dominant group, the Oriental Jews were relegated to the status of a minority. Their language (English, not Arabic, became Israel's second language), history, and culture, including a large body of religious literature and expression, was ignored or rejected as inferior and irrelevant. They were directed to development towns near the borders, immigrant towns on the outskirts of cities, and cooperative farming villages, to be administered by settlement agencies or Labor party functionaries, until a new generation of Israeli-born Oriental leaders emerged in the 1980s. In retrospect, these Jews provided the cheap, manipulable manpower—and later womanpower—that enabled the Jewish state to industrialize and develop (Swirski, 1989). They became a laboring class, a position that was maintained and reproduced through the educational system (Swirski, 1990). For females, this meant low-quality education that prepared them for cleaning work or the production-line in the textile, garment, food processing, and, later, electronics industries. With the increasing supply of even cheaper labor—Palestinian women from Israel and the occupied territories, and the expansion of service industries like insurance and marketing, Oriental women moved into low-level secretarial work. In contrast to the situation with regard to the Arab population, the Jewish state's blanket negation of Oriental Jewish culture involved the loosening of patriarchal control over women and the right to work, but it also meant membership in an underclass.

Living in the Jewish state of Israel involves not only the domination of a particular national and ethnic group, but also that of a particular brand of Judaism, namely, Orthodoxy. In this book the term "Orthodox" does not refer simply to a stream of Judaism which is more traditional than Reform,

Conservative, or Reconstructionist Judaism; it also refers to a religious establishment that is actually the descendant of a protest movement against modernization. The movement developed in Western Europe at the beginning of
the 19th century, in opposition to attempts to introduce into Jewish society
changes similar to those occurring in the larger society. It was a reaction that
represented a departure from the past rather than a continuity; through the
ages, Jewish law had been flexible, and scholars had interpreted Jewish law
in accordance with the time and place of the Jewish community in question.
Thus Orthodoxy is not an extreme form of religious traditionalism, but rather
an innovation which often deviates from tradition in the direction of increased
rigidity (Samet, 1979). In Israel, this reaction is expressed in, among other
things, clear separation of the sexes within the religious educational systems
and in daily activities: in manner of dress (women wear long-sleeved blouses
or dresses, thick stockings, long skirts and wigs), in rejection of radio and television, and in reading only books and newspapers approved by religious
leaders.

   Within Orthodox Judaism various streams developed, including the ultra-
Orthodox, some of whose adherents settled in Palestine prior to the Zionist
immigration. They viewed themselves as a religious elite and were supported
by contributions from their coreligionists in the Diaspora. At the end of the
19th century and the beginning of the 20th, Orthodox Jews in Israel crystal-
lized the religious institutions, the Rabbinate, the Rabbinic courts, the yeshivas
(religious academies) and the political parties, which now constitute the religious establishment of Israel. In fact, in 1921 the Rabbinate became the first
institution of self-government of the Jewish community in Palestine (Samet,
1979).

   The religious establishment has imposed a certain degree of adherence to
Jewish law on all Jews living in Israel through an arrangement referred to as
the "status quo." This arrangement has its origin in the results of the elections
to the first Knesset in 1948, when the Mapai party, which received the largest
number of votes, but not a majority, formed a government coalition with the
National Religious Party (NRP) as one of its members. The NRP agreed to
join the coalition in exchange for a commitment to integrate Jewish law into
Israeli state law: the arrangement involved making Saturday the legal day of
rest, on which there was to be no public transportation and no movies; stipulating that every institutional kitchen observe the Jewish dietary laws; granting
Rabbinic courts jurisdiction over personal status laws, and preserving the
separateness and autonomy of the religious school systems. Giving religious
courts jurisdiction in personal matters meant that in domestic litigation women
would remain at a disadvantage; their status would be inferior at the very outset, they would not be judged by their peers (i.e., by women), and they would
have to continue to plead their cases in the framework of laws prejudicial

to females. Since that time, the NRP and other religious Zionist political parties have always been part of the government coalition, using their leverage to resist all attempts to erode the "status quo." In recent years, they have tried to extend the domain of religious law.

The "status quo" is, in effect, a compromise between socialist men and Orthodox men, at the expense of women. A similar bargain was struck between the state authorities, socialist men, and Arab religious leaders, also men. The latter agreed to cooperate with the government in return for, among other things, control over "their own" women. Thus for Moslems, Christians, and Druze (recognized as an independent religious community in 1957), matters of personal status were left to the jurisdiction of the respective religious courts. For years, state authorities did not enforce compulsory education for Moslem (including Bedouin), Christian and Druze girls (Swirski, 1990), and to this day "family-honor" murders of Arab women are treated with leniency by the Jewish legal and law-enforcement system.

Orthodox Judaism as described above is an Ashkenazi phenomenon; Oriental Jews who view themselves as religious, practice a much more tolerant and flexible form of Judaism. For example, in contrast to Ashkenazim, they may watch television on the Sabbath and send their children to either secular or religious schools (Samet, 1979). Furthermore, the religious establishment in Israel has been dominated by Ashkenazim, although in recent years religious Oriental Jews, "resocialized" by Ashkenazi Orthodox Jews, have established their own, alternative institutions, such as the "Shas" political party, in order to compete for parliamentary power and governmental allocations.

The religious establishment of Israel has generally opposed political equality for women. The vote is a case in point: in 1918, when women demanded suffrage in the new institutions of self-government, the idea was perceived as subversive to the values and way of life of traditional Jewish society, in which women were excluded from political activity. Under pressure from the veteran Orthodox Ashkenazi community (composed of members of the first wave of immigration), the Jerusalem Rabbinate issued a statement against the vote in 1919: "The law that grants voting rights to women is in absolute contradiction to the spirit of our Torah, our tradition, and our concepts of modesty . . . " (Friedman, 1979:147). At that time, the Orthodox Jewish community consisted of Zionist as well as nonZionist factions; the nonZionist factions regarded woman suffrage not only as contrary to Jewish law, but also as a dangerous step in the direction of establishing a modern nation-state, one whose society resembled "the culture of Western nations" rather than the traditional Jewish society they sought to preserve (Friedman, 1979:148). According to Friedman, during the first years of the British Mandate, woman suffrage was the most controversial subject between secular and non-Zionist Orthodox Jews in Palestine, and a test of the latter's strength. Zionist Orthodox Jews, on the other hand, were less opposed to the vote, but could not ignore the fact that the highest religious authority, the Rabbinate, opposed it (Friedman, 1979, p. 148). The two groups worked together to prevent women from receiving the vote, delaying a decision on the question of woman suffrage for several years, even causing the Representative Assembly to rescind a decision in its favor by threatening to boycott the Assembly. Women won the vote in 1925, but due to the opposition of the Orthodox parties, the national governing body did not pass a law that was binding at the local level, and women had to fight for the right to vote and be elected in each and every Jewish settlement in Palestine. The last succumbed only in 1940 (Azariyahu, 1980).

Once the vote was won, religious Jewish women had to struggle for the right to run for public office. After Israel became an independent state, the non-Zionist Orthodox political parties ceased their opposition to the state and once again formed a united front with the Zionist Orthodox parties. As a result, one of the latter, the Hapoel Hamizrahi Party, which had intended to include a woman in its list for the first Knesset elections, removed her from the slate. The women in the party revolted and formed their own, separate list (Samet, 1979). Women's participation was curtailed once again in 1978, when a coalition was formed between the National Religious Party, the successor of the Hapoel Hamizrahi Party, and Agudat Yisrael, the successor of the non-Zionist parties, for local elections, and the former once again agreed not to include women candidates in its slate (Samet, 1979). In 1989, an old scene was reenacted, when despite pressure from "Emunah," its women's section, the National Religious Party refused to place a prominent woman on its slate for the Jerusalem City Council. The woman in question, Yehudit Heubner, then formed her own list, which won a seat on the Council. While there have been a few female Knesset members from the National Religious Party, none of the religious parties gave a woman a safe spot on their slate for the last (1988) Knesset elections.

The fact that matters of personal status are under the jurisdiction of the religious courts has, as noted above, an adverse effect on women. First of all, the law as presently interpreted discriminates between Jews, on the one hand, and Christians, Moslems and Druze, on the other. While Jews can adjudicate matters concerning custody, child support, and common property in either religious or civil courts, Christians, Moslems, and Druze can only apply to their respective religious courts (with the exception noted below). This is to the disadvantage of women, because in Moslem and Druze religious law, as in Jewish religious law, women have an inferior status.

For Jews, only marriage and divorce are the exclusive domain of the religious courts. A Jewish woman cannot receive a divorce without the consent of her husband, even if she is battered or her husband is missing or insane. While a man cannot divorce a woman without her consent either, there are special conditions under which men may marry a second wife. The religious courts discriminate against women in other ways as well: for example, a man can commit adultery and eventually marry his lover, while a married woman is forbidden to ever marry her lover, and any children born from such a union are considered bastards. A bastard cannot marry another Jew unless he or she is also a bastard; neither can a bastard marry outside of the faith, as there is no provision for civil or intermarriage in Israel. Another anomaly of Jewish religious law, enforced in Rabbinic courts, is the levirate marriage: a woman whose husband dies leaving her childless must be released from her deceased husband's unmarried brother in a ceremony carried out in Rabbinic court. Often extortion payments may be involved before she gets her release.

The patriarchal nature of Moslem law *(Shari'a)* is revealed in, among others, the fact that a woman is not defined as the natural custodian of her own children. In cases of divorce, *Shari* courts generally grant women custody of young children (as they are viewed as in need of a woman's care), but when males reach the age of 7 and females the age of 9, custody reverts to the father. In such a situation, women may relinquish custody in the present so as to avoid a painful separation in the future. Moreover, pressure is often brought to bear on women by the husband's family to give up the children altogether in return for a divorce, and the courts accept extortion of this kind. Moslem law makes the man the master of the house; when a couple divorce, the woman leaves and the house and furniture remain with the man. However, it is possible for Moslems in Israel to write into the marriage contract a provision that in the event of divorce, the matter of property division is to be decided in civil rather than religious court (under civil law, a woman is entitled to half of the property accumulated in the course of the marriage). The question is how common such a provision actually is; obviously, it depends on the power of the bride's family and their willingness to invoke Israeli civil law rather than Moslem religious law.

Grounds for divorce in Moslem law are similar to those in Jewish law. While Moslem law gives the man the right to divorce his wife without her consent and without applying to the court (tyrannical divorce), Moslem courts in Israel caution men against using this right, as it runs counter to Israeli civil law and if the woman complains to the police, the man who so divorces her will be liable to criminal proceedings as well as damage claims in the civil courts. The question, again, is how many women actually register complaints and bring civil suits. Unlike Rabbinic courts, *Shari* courts may insist that where the divorce is contested, the couple submit to compulsory arbitration. In cases in which a woman's life is in danger, the religious judge may grant a divorce.

Another area in which the Jewish religious establishment in Israel has prevented Jewish women from achieving full equality is military service. The religious parties objected to women serving in the army, and the 1952 Military Service Law stipulated that women (but not men) could receive an exemption on the basis of religious belief. Further concessions were made when the right-wing Likud Party came into power in 1977 and formed a coalition with the religious parties; their agreement included the stipulation that women receive exemptions from military service on the basis of sworn statements alone, without the necessity of checking the truth of the declarations (Samet, 1979).

Finally, the fact that Israel's religious establishment is guided by an ideology that rejects gender equality has resulted in men preventing women from gaining control of their own bodies. Jewish law rejects contraception that would cause the "spilling of a man's seed"; like their Catholic sisters, Orthodox women generally use only "natural" methods of birth control. The opposition of the religious establishment is among the factors that prevented the creation of birth control clinics until quite recently. (Another factor is what is termed "the demographic problem," that is, the perceived need of Jews to reproduce in order to remain in the majority.) There is very little sex education in the schools, and birth control information is not readily available. Lately, however, the threat of AIDS is changing the picture somewhat.

Abortion is also interpreted by the Orthodox establishment as contrary to Jewish law. In 1977, a new law was passed that liberalized existing statutes against abortion by enumerating the conditions under which a woman could procure a legal hospital abortion, coverable by medical insurance plans. This was a compromise between the abortion-on-demand bill introduced by MK Marcia Freedman and the religious parties' opposition to any liberalization in the law. By the end of 1978, the clause which permitted abortion under certain "social circumstances" was repealed, as another part of the coalition agreement between the Likud and the religious parties.

Just as it opposes the participation of women in political life, Orthodox Judaism opposes the participation of women in religious life. The fact that it constitutes the religious establishment in Israel means that women who define themselves as religious are deprived of self-determination in all matters of faith. While there are a number of Reform and Conservative congregations in Israel, three led by women rabbis (new immigrants from the U.S.), they are not recognized by the religious establishment. Any attempts on the part of women to introduce innovations into religious life are vehemently opposed. This is illustrated by Women of the Wall, a group of women who broke with tradition by praying together at the Wailing Wall from their own Torah scroll, adorned in prayer shawls (considered for men only) and in voices that could be heard by the men (a woman's voice is considered lewd), and were met with violent opposition from Orthodox women as well as men. The Supreme Court upheld the women's right to pray at the wall, but while the decision was pending, religious authorities introduced a new regulation prohibiting any religious ceremony that deviated from custom or might be offensive to the prayers. The women continue to pray at the Wall, and the religious establishment continues to oppose them; in December 1989 the Rabbinate threatened to withdraw the food license of the Laromme Hotel if it did not cancel a function at which the Women of the Wall were to receive a Torah scroll from overseas supporters (even though no food was to be served) (*Jerusalem Post,* December 21, 1989). The courts refused to grant the women an injunction, and the hotel cancelled the event.

It should be noted that while Orthodox women in Israel have on a number of occasions insisted on their rights with regard to secular matters, like political activity or candidacy for political office, they have generally been unwilling to challenge the religious establishment in religious matters, like ritual or the content of religious learning. In the context of Israeli society, the demands of Women of the Wall represent unprecedented, radical demands.

Jews in Israel, including the secular majority, generally accept the domination of Orthodoxy in religious matters, perhaps because they do not perceive it as meaningful to their daily lives: religion becomes relevant only at the birth of a male child, due to the commandment of circumcision, at marriage, as the ceremony must be in accordance with Jewish law, and at death, because burial, too, follows the dictates of religious law. The monopoly of Orthodoxy has arrested the development of alternative, more moderate or modern forms of Judaism in Israel. Unlike the contemporary Jewish scene in the United States or that in Germany prior to Hitler, religion in Israel has not been an area of creative activity. The only significant change that has occurred over the years is that religion has become part of normal bourgeois family life, which includes extravagant celebrations to mark the few occasions on which religion is relevant, and synagogue attendance on major holidays.

For secular Jewish women, the fact that there is no separation between religion and state may be irrelevant, much in the way that the dominance of Christianity in the United States is irrelevant to a great many Christian women. But it may also be the cause of considerable suffering, in the case of women who are unable to obtain a divorce, or great inconvenience, in the case of women who desire civil marriage, intermarriage, or unions forbidden by religious law; paradoxically, it also constitutes an impediment to religious expression for women.

REFERENCES

Azariyahu, Sarah. (1980). *The union of Hebrew women for equal rights in Eretz Ysrael.* Haifa: Women's Aid Fund.

Friedman, Menachem. (1979). *Society and religion. The Non- Zionist orthodoxy in Eretz Israel 1918–1936.* Jerusalem: Yad Ben-Zvi (Hebrew).

Hertzberg, Arthur (1969). *The Zionist idea.* New York: Atheneum.

Lustick, Ian. (1980). *Arabs in the Jewish state. Israel's control of a national minority.* Austin: Texas University Press.

Rosenfeld, Henry. (1964). From peasantry to wage labor and residual peasantry: The transformation of an Arab village. In Manners, R. A. (ed.) *Process and Pattern in Culture.* Chicago: Aldine Publishing Company.

Samet, Moshe (1979) *Religion and State in Israel. Papers in Sociology.* Jerusalem: Hebrew University (Hebrew).

Swirski, Shlomo (1989) *Israel's Oriental Majority.* London: Zed Books.

Swirski, Shlomo (1990) *Education in Israel: Schooling for Inequality.* Tel Aviv: Breirot (Hebrew).

Tzartzur, Sa'ad (1985) "The Problem of the Education of a Minority Who Are Foreigners in Their Own Country." In Ackerman, W., Carmon, A. and Zucker, D. (eds.) *Education in an Evolving Society.* Tel Aviv and Jerusalem: Hakibbutz Hameuchad and Van Leer Institute (Hebrew).

The Concept of Gender Equality in a Jewish State

Frances Raday

A legal system is a mirror of the society in which it functions, reflecting different aspects of social reality at different levels of its infrastructure. Constitutional principles reflect the views of the Knesset, the courts and academia regarding the fundamental societal norms, which are to bind not only the courts but also the legislature. The courts provide a forum for a dialectic of opposing views—the plaintiff articulates his or her case, the defendant responds, and the judges determine the norm as they perceive it, each in his or her own way. This litigatory process reveals both the parameters of social activism and judicial perception of the normative consensus. In the legislative process, there is a testing of practical priorities, of the preparedness of a society not only to declare values but also to implement them. By examining women's status in these various legal forums, we can obtain an overview of the position of women in Israeli society.

CONSTITUTIONAL PRINCIPLES— ENDORSEMENT OF A PATRIARCHAL LEGAL SYSTEM

Israel's Declaration of Independence was one of the earliest constitutional documents to include sex as a group classification for the purpose of equal social and political rights. The message was clear—Israel's prestate experience of discrimination and persecution had produced a heightened sensitivity to the issue of group discrimination in the founders of the state and this included an appreciation of the need for equal treatment of women.

However, the principles of the Declaration of Independence were not subsequently ensconced in a constitution. The Women's Equal Rights Law passed in 1951 was an ordinary statute. Neither the Declaration of Independence nor the 1951 Law were interpreted as carrying constitutional authority by the Supreme Court. They remained a declaration of intent. Although the Declaration of Independence enabled the Supreme Court to introduce an impres-

18

sive range of fundamental rights into the Israeli legal system where the legislature remained silent, it did not enable the Court to override primary legislation even where it impinged on fundamental rights. The right to equality between the sexes was not recognized as "a fundamental principle" by the Supreme Court until 1987; it was then given a relativist interpretation, rather than being established as a fundamental right having constitutional priority over any other right not in the category of fundamental rights (Bagatz 153/87 *Shakdiel v. Minister for Religious Affairs et al.*, 42(2) P.D. 221; Bagatz 953/87 *Poraz v. Lahat, Major of Tel Aviv et al.*, 42(2) P.D. 309). In this situation, it would be logical to expect that a demand for a constitutional right to equality between the sexes would be high on the Israeli feminist agenda. This is not the case, and the reasons for it are not hard to find.

Every attempt to give constitutional expression to the principle of equality between the sexes has either been marked by the subordination of the principle of equality to that of commitment to certain predicates of a religious Jewish state or has failed to gain any modicum of acceptability because it did not incorporate such subordination. The significance of this priority of religious values over egalitarian values is that it incorporates and endorses a patriarchal concept of women's role in the family. The *halakhic* (Jewish law) rules of Jewish law, as well as the rules of Moslem, Druze, Bedouin and, to a lesser extent Christian law, are typical of all patriarchal legal systems in that they exclude women from full participation in the public sphere while subordinating them to male authority in the private sphere (Polan, 1982: 295).

In the public sphere, under *halakha,* women are not regarded as fully qualified to give evidence in court, and cannot be appointed as rabbis or judges. (Deuteronomy 17:6; Maimonides, *Laws of Evidence* 9:2, *Laws of Study of Torah* 1:13.) (For a recent exposition of the *halakhic* position see "Extracts from the Petition in the *Shakdiel* Case," the Newsletter of the Association for Civil Rights in Israel, No. 16, May 31 1987, where Rabbi Halevi Steinberg is quoted as giving the most recent authoritative summing up of the *halakha* on this issue: "To all functions only a man should be appointed. Hence a woman does not have the capacity to be a judge.") Since these are the norms which direct the functioning of the rabbinic courts, conferment of exclusive jurisdiction over any matter to the rabbinic courts (like the matter of marriage and divorce) subjects women to patriarchal exclusion from public life regarding the same.

In the private sphere, family life, Jewish women are subject to male predominance under the *halakha*. Although it can be said that, for the era in which it was promulgated, the *halakha* exhibited a considerably advanced sensitivity to the need to protect women against male exploitation, in modern terms it subordinates women to men in marriage. (For example, the *halakha* protected women against exploitation of their property during marriage or loss of it upon divorce: *Ketubot* 78a-30b; rape within marriage was prohibited: Maimonides, *Personal Laws* 15:17; *Shulhan Arukh,* "Orah Haim" 25:2; Rakover, *Shnaton HaMishpat HaIvri,* Vol 6–7, 295–317.) The basic concept of the marriage ceremony is "purchase" of the woman by the husband, who takes her as his wife in a unilateral ceremony (Mishna in *Kiddushin* 2a). Divorce is not a judicial act and may be achieved only in accordance with the husband's wish—until he declares that he is willing to divorce her, there is no way in which she may be released from the marriage bonds (Deuteronomy 24:1; Gittin 85a–b). Later introduction of a requirement of the wife's consent to divorce did not result in a symmetrical impediment for men and women (Ban of Rabbenu Gershom, 11th century). Women refused a divorce cannot remarry and, if they bear children from a union with another man before the divorce is given, face the severe problem of "mamzerut"—a form of bastardy applicable only to the children of adultery by a woman. (A bastard cannot marry within the Jewish community: Deuteronomy 23:3; *Shulhan Arukh,* Even HaEzer.) In contrast, for men whose wives refuse to agree to the divorce there is no problem of "mamzerut" and there are even ways in which the husband may acquire the right to remarry without a divorce (Shifman, 1984; Shereschewsky, 1984).

In 1951, the Women's Equal Rights Law was passed, under which women were to be entitled to legal equality and equal rights to carry out legal transactions. Unfortunately the Law did not have constitutional force; while it could be used to invalidate laws existing prior to its enactment, as far as subsequent legislation was concerned, it was considered merely a directive to assist in the interpretation of ambivalent primary legislation and a norm allowing invalidation of secondary legislation. Here, too, the Knesset gave expression to subordination of the principle of equality for women to *halakhic* rules on marriage and divorce: the right to equality was expressly excluded regarding all issues of "prohibition and permission to marry and divorce."

Since 1951, there have been many initiatives by members of the Knesset to introduce a Bill of Rights. However, they have almost all been marked by the same unwillingness to insist on the right of women to equality in marriage and divorce. Even in a proposed constitution drafted by a team of Tel Aviv Law Faculty members, in 1988, the issue was not squarely confronted. Their compromise was that any law which subjects a person to the rules of a religious law under which that person has chosen to marry will be constitutionally valid. This solution would not only leave existing generations of Israeli married women without the right to equality but also the vast majority of future brides who, as they marry in traditional ceremonies, will be taken to have permanently waived the right to equality in divorce or to equal enjoyment of the freedom to establish a new family. The only proposed Bill of Rights which has uncompromisingly insisted upon equality for women in the personal law is that proposed by Member of Knesset Shulamit Aloni, but her attempts have been met with a solid wall of parliamentary opposition.

THE CONSTITUTIONAL PRINCIPLE
OF EQUALITY – IN THE COURTS

Although the principles of equality for women under the Declaration of Independence and the Women's Equal Rights Law are not endowed with constitutional force, they have been applied as constitutional principles in the courts. In view of the fact that the clash between the religious personal law and the concept of equality is central to constitutional thinking in Israel, it is instructive to examine judicial developments in two separate spheres: the private sphere – the family; and the public sphere – the economic and political life of the society.

In the private sphere, the exclusion of marriage and divorce from women's constitutional right to equality, established in the Women's Equal Rights Law, has been clearly regarded by the courts as beyond challenge. Even more, the Supreme Court has not taken it upon itself to develop indirect incentives to lessen women's disadvantage under the *halakhic* rules of marriage and divorce. Thus, the Supreme Court has refused to sanction the use of punitive maintenance payments given by rabbinic courts against husbands who were unreasonably withholding a *gett* (divorce); the Court preferred to preserve the "real" purpose of maintenance payments rather than countenance extending their function to discourage abuse of the power to withhold a divorce (*Mira Solomon* v. *Moshe Solomon*) 38[4]P.D. 365).

Within the narrow limits of the residual right to equality in family life, the best that could be achieved was the removal of disqualifications incidental to married women's legal status. In the early years of the state, immediately following on the enactment of the Women's Equal Rights Law, there was intensive litigation to accomplish this goal. Little controversy appears to have accompanied cancellation of *halakhic* rules, where both parties did not expressly choose to be governed by those rules, for the purpose of equalizing women's rights in the sphere of married women's property and domicile rights (Raday, 1983).

Regarding women's equality in guardianship rights, which was expressly guaranteed in the Women's Equal Rights Law (sec. 3(a)), the courts confirmed that the various religious courts were subject to the provisions of this Law (Raday, 1983). However, the limited effectiveness of this guarantee is well illustrated by the case of Halima Bria (*Halima Bria* v. *Qadi of the Shari' a Moslem Court et al.,* [1955] 9 P.D. 1193). In that case, a widowed mother of three children who had remarried petitioned the High Court of Justice to order the Qadi of the *Shari' a* Moslem Court to desist from hearing an application to cancel her guardianship, on the basis of Moslem law. Under Moslem law, a mother who remarries ceases to be the natural guardian of her children. The application to cancel Halima Bria's guardianship had been brought by the dead father's sister. The High Court refused to grant the petition, on the grounds that the decision of the Qadi to decide the case according to "the *Shari' a* and legal aspects of the law" did not prove that the Qadi would ignore the Women's Equal Rights Law. There was disagreement between the justices as to whether the provisions of the Moslem law discriminated against women. While one of the three justices found discrimination (Justice Goitein, At 1998), a second remained silent on the issue and the third held there was no discrimination "since the question was which of two women was to be given guardianship of the child." Whatever their opinion on the issue of discrimination, all three justices agreed not to invalidate the Moslem law as a relevant consideration. The Court pointed out that under the Women's Equal Rights Law, the Qadi would be entitled to determine guardianship on the basis of the good of the child (sec. 3(b)). Only if it was proven that, in the final judgment, the Moslem courts had "intentionally ignored" the provisions of the Women's Equal Rights Law in judging the good of the child would the High Court interfere (At 1199). The Court dismissed the claim that a skillful Qadi could find ways to disguise the fact that his decision was based on religious law and not on the principles of the Women's Equal Rights Law (At 1199).

In the public sphere, women were less active in testing their rights under the existing constitutional framework. The first case to be brought before the courts was that of a man who claimed that his prosecution for refusal to serve in the army under the Women's Equal Rights Law constituted sex discrimination, since a woman who held his religious convictions would have been entitled to an exemption from army service (*Steinberg* v. *Attorney General*, [1951] 5 P.D. 1061). The Supreme Court rejected this claim, holding, amongst other things, that the Law was intended to protect women, not men.

The failure in the early 1960s of the first constitutional claim brought by a woman to enforce her right to economic equality may have helped to discourage further litigation in this sphere (*Lubinsky* v. *Pakid Ha Shuma*, [1962] 16 P.D. 304). The case in which tax authorities assessed a married woman's income from an orchard which she owned together with her husband's income from salary for income tax purposes and refused her request for separate assessment, resulted in the Supreme Court not only finding that the ruling could not be challenged because it was based on statute law but also holding that there was no sex discrimination. The Court regarded the ruling as based on principles of progressive taxation and the greater economic efficiency of combining incomes to run one household. It did not draw a conclusion of discrimination from the fact that the same ruling would not have applied had the income been from the husband's orchard and the wife's salary.

It was not until 1977 that the next litigatory attempt was made. A petition was brought before the Supreme Court by a legal apprentice. She claimed that refusal of the Law Society to reduce the length of legal apprenticeship in the case of absence for maternity leave, mandatory by statute law, in the same way as it did in that of absence for reserve military service discriminated against women (*Lifshitz Aviram* v. *Israel Lawyers' Association*, [1977] 31[1] P.D. 250). The High Court of Justice found it patently unproblematic to dismiss the petition, holding, in an uncharacteristically short decision (less than two pages long), that there were no possible grounds for finding discrimination since women as well as men serve in the army. The Court did not weigh questions of disparate impact nor did it analyze the possible analogies between absence from legal apprenticeship as a result of maternity leave and reserve service, other than making a cryptic comment that they both constituted an important service to the nation. The similarities between the two regarding legal prohibition of work and social insurance coverage of leave pay were not even raised.

An apparent breakthrough was made in 1988 in the *Shakdiel* and *Poraz* Cases. (Bagatz 153/87 *Shakdiel* v. *Minister for Religious Affairs et al.*, 42[2] P.D. 221; Bagatz 953/87 *Poraz* v. *Lahat, Major of Tel Aviv et al.*, 42[2] P.D. 309). For the first time, organizations and not only individuals were involved in petitioning the High Court of Justice on the issue of women's right to equality in the public sphere. The Civil Rights Association was counsel for the plaintiff in *Shakdiel*, while the Labor Party and Na'amat were joint petitioners in *Poraz*. For the first time, women's right to equality was recognised by the Court as a "fundamental principle" of the Israeli legal system, and for the first time, women succeeded in obtaining a remedy against discrimination in the public sphere from the Court.

Undeniably, these cases form a turning point: they signify the raising of public consciousness concerning discrimination against women in the public sphere, and they involve a normative consensus that women are entitled to equality in this sphere. However, there are grounds for some hesitation regarding the impact of the two High Court decisions on both the practical and the theoretical level.

The issue in *Shakdiel* was the decision of the Minister for Religious Affairs and a Ministerial Committee set up under the Jewish Religious Services Law of 1971 to refuse to appoint Leah Shakdiel to serve as an elected member of a local religious services council, on the grounds that she was a woman. The petition was brought against the Minister for Religious Affairs in 1987. After granting a series of requests for delays brought by the respondents, the Court finally handed down judgment in favor of the petitioner in May 1988. Shakdiel took up her position on the religious council in October 1988. Three women were voted onto the Tel Aviv religious services council in 1989.

The issue in *Poraz* was the Tel Aviv Municipal Council decision not to appoint women to the electoral board for the Tel Aviv municipal rabbi. Here the remedy granted in the High Court of Justice did indeed take effect and women are now sitting on the electoral board. However, the practical impact of the decision was not the achievement of progress towards equality but rather prevention of a deterioration in the existing situation. Prior to the decision of the Court, women had already been included in electoral boards for municipal rabbis. (For instance Vicki Strasbourg sat on the electoral board for the municipal rabbi of Beit Shemesh.)

On the theoretical level, both the decisions accorded the principle of equality for women, which they termed a fundamental principle, much less than a hegemony.

In *Shakdiel,* Justice Elon held that the principle of equality is to be "balanced against other legitimate interests of individuals or the public." Hence, he argued, "had there been a prohibition in the *halakha* against women serving on religious councils, . . . a compromise would have had to be found between the two approaches. Although the municipal council is a secular statutory body and is hence subject to secular law, it deals with *halakhic* affairs . . . and thus it would be desirable to seek ways to bridge the opposing interests" (At 242–243). Justice Barak appeared to qualify Justice Elon's view: "I want to point out that whatever the nature of this balance may be, it cannot rest on negation of the principle of equality. . . . the balancing should only be carried out if there is evidence that the public interest in the existence of religious services will be injured by giving full force to the principle of equality. Mere suspicion is not enough" (At 277).

In *Poraz,* Justice Barak does indeed carry out that very balancing process. He regards it as the duty of the Court to balance "the general principle of equality, on one hand, and particularistic interest in the appointment of an electoral board, which should be able to carry out its functions properly, on the other." Furthermore, he points out that the balancing process is, on this occasion, "horizontal not vertical . . . we do not have a situation here of a clash, in which one of the principles predominates over the other. Equality is an important principle but it is a relative principle. In the absence of constitutional intent, it does not have an absolute meaning" (At 336).

It is not easy to tell from these judgments where relativism ends and equality begins. Justice Barak goes on to assure us that, even in this horizontal balancing process, the importance of equality is central and infringement will only be permitted if there is no other way to implement the particularistic purpose which underlies a specific law. However, since he has established that there must be "mutual recognition of the importance of proper functioning of the municipal rabbi and the principle of equality," he makes it clear that the principle of equality is determinative in this case only because there is, as a matter of fact, no real barrier to the proper functioning of a municipal rabbi where women sit on the electoral board: "Justice Elon showed in the Shakdiel decision that there is no *halakhic* prohibition of participation by women in elections of functionaries to public office. It can be assumed that there are certain rabbis who think as he does and hence will be candidates for municipal rabbi" (At 337).

The Court's readiness in the above decisions to ascertain whether the inclusion of women was prohibited by the *halakha,* as a relevant issue in determining the right of women to participate in these public bodies, was misplaced. The only issue relegated to *halakhic* rather than egalitarian values by the Women's Equal Rights Law was that of marriage and divorce; the impact of the approach in *Shakdiel* and *Poraz* appears to have been to extend the statutory exception to the principle of equality in favor of the *halakha,* in a way which is contrary to the express intention of the Knesset in that Law. The judgments indicate a preparedness to tolerate the encroachment of inegalitarian *halakhic* values on areas of public life: the bodies in question were, as the Court itself stressed in both cases, public bodies set up under the secular law. The Supreme Court could have furthered the cause of equality by a decision that, until such time as the legislature expressly provided otherwise, it was to be assumed that even if the inclusion of women was contrary to *halakha,* or even if no rabbi was willing to sit with a woman in a religious council or be elected by an electoral board which included women, the legislature did not intend to condone unequal treatment of women in this sphere. In such circumstances, the solution should not be to endorse, or even express readiness to tolerate, discrimination against women but rather to regard the legislative purpose of appointing a municipal rabbi as being frustrated, just as it would have been if there were no candidates for the job of municipal rabbi or for the religious council.

In a recent hearing of a petition seeking to prevent the Ministry of Labor from funding a professional training course for the unemployed from which women were excluded, the dangers of the intrusion of *halakhic* values into the sphere of public life were further illustrated. The reason given by the Ministry of Labor for not including women was that the courses were being held in a Boys Town institution, which being a religious educational establishment, would not admit women. The Civil Rights Association and the Israel Women's Network, which represented the two women petitioners who sought admission to the course, argued that the Ministry should be required to seek nondiscriminatory alternative venues for the professional training courses which it funds. The Justices hearing the petition expressed concern for the unemployed (by definition in this case, the male unemployed) and refused to allow the petitioners even to proceed to the pleadings; they termed the petition "vexatious" and told counsel that their clients would be subject to heavy costs if they did not withdraw the petition. In 1990, in the context of the issue of equal retirement age for women, the Supreme Court gave, for the first time, a decisive, unambiguous ruling on the supremacy of the principle of equality under the Women's Equal Rights Law: ". . . where there is no *expressly* contrary provision, the courts must prefer that statutory interpretation which is consistent with the principle of equality between the sexes." (Bagatz 104/87, *Nevo v. the National Labour Court et al.*, 22.10.90)

THE KNESSET

Knesset activity regarding the issue of equality between the sexes falls into two categories: differentiation between the sexes in general regulatory legislation, and legislation which is expressly concerned with issues of women's status or equality between the sexes.

There are various areas of general regulatory legislation in which problems of sex discrimination arise as a result of the differential treatment of men and women. Such, for instance, is the situation under the National Insurance Law, where "housewives" are treated as a separate category for insurance purposes, and under the Income Tax Law, where married women are subject to criteria for tax liability different from those for married men. As has been pointed out, there is no judicial review of these statutory provisions. The only way to achieve change is through legislation reform.

In 1987, the Israel Women's Network Legal Center put forward a comprehensive program for abolition of sex discrimination under the Income Tax Law to the Sheshinsky Commission on Tax Reform. It called for an end to the attribution of a married woman's income to her husband for tax purposes, discrimination between married men and women in the allocation of tax credit and benefit points, and the registration of a married woman's tax return on her husband's name. The program was accepted by the Commission but not implemented. (Interview 1988 by Leah Inbal of Eitan Sheshinsky, *Coteret Rashit*, February 24 [Hebrew].) Efforts to achieve legislative reform have since continued with the participation of Members of Knesset (MKs) Sarah Doron and Haike Grossman, of the Citizens Rights Party and of Na' amat. At the time of writing, a bill presented by MKs Doron and Zucker, incorporating all the suggested reforms, has passed its first reading in the Knesset. A further tax reform proposed by the women's organizations has not yet been adopted in any serious legislative effort—allowing, as a tax deductible expense, costs of care for dependent family members, including children, the expenditure of which is necessary for the earning of income.

Legislation expressly concerned with specific women's issues or with equality between the sexes is concentrated in two areas: the criminal law and labor law. (Labor law is discussed in the section titled "The Work Women Do".) In criminal law, sections dealing with prostitution, rape and abortion all expressly regulate women's issues. While the laws on prostitution have not changed much over time—they are primarily concerned with prohibiting procurement of prostitutes—there have been major changes in the laws of rape and of abortion.

In one important respect, the law of rape in Israel has been extremely progressive in comparison with that of other legal systems: marital rape has never been condoned as legal. In 1981, the Supreme Court held that marital rape is prohibited in Israel: provisions of the Criminal Code which derived from British Mandatory law, and excluded marital rape, were to be interpreted in the light of Jewish law, under which marital rape was prohibited (C.A. 91/71 *Cohen* v. *State of Israel* 35[3] P.D. 281). In recent years, two amendments were made to the law of rape which improved the trial situation of rape victims. In an amendment to the Law of Evidence in 1982, the requirement of corroborative evidence of rape was abolished, leaving in its stead a requirement that a judge who convicts on the evidence of the rape victim alone give his or her reasons for doing so in the judgment (The Law of Evidence, sec. 54B). Under a 1988 amendment to the Criminal Law, (Amendment No. 22) it was provided that the Court not allow examination of the rape victim's past sexual experience, except in the event that the court considered, for reasons which it must register, that the prohibition of examination would cause a miscarriage of justice for the accused (Amendment of Civil Procedure Law [Examination of Witnesses], 1957, sec. 2A). Additionally, the definition of rape was broadened and, the prohibition of rape of a woman by her husband, already established by case law, was retained (1988 Amendment to secs. 345–360 of the Criminal Law).

Abortion was initially regulated by Section 175 of the Criminal Code, inherited from the British Mandate. It provided that the "unlawful" procurement of an abortion was a criminal offence. Abortions for the sake of saving the life of the woman or preserving her health were not considered unlawful. In 1966, an amendment was made clarifying that a woman who procured her own miscarriage was not criminally liable. In practice, the prohibition on procuring abortions was a dead letter—abortions were performed, many of them in recognized medical institutions, and prosecutions were not brought, in accordance with the declared policy of the then Attorney General Haim Cohen. In 1978, the law was amended in order to reduce the gap between prohibition and practice. Under the amended law, abortion remained prohibited unless it was performed in a recognized medical institution and there was prior authorization by a committee of two doctors and a social worker. The abortion committees could only authorize abortions on one of the grounds specified in the statute: (1) the woman was below marriage-age or over the age of 40; (2) the pregnancy resulted from a prohibited or extramarital relationship or incest; (3) the child would be born with a physical or mental defect; (4) the continuation of the pregnancy might endanger the woman's life or impair her physical or mental health; and (5) the continuation of the pregnancy would seriously damage the woman or her children because of difficult family or social circumstances (the Criminal Law secs. 315, 316, 317).

Short of recognizing the autonomy of a woman over her own body, at least until the fetus was viable, and short of recognizing her right to privacy on the issue of abortion, which had in practice been the situation for Israeli women under the legal administration of Haim Cohen, the original drafting of the circumstances in which the right to abort would be recognized was clearly liberal. In 1979, there was a regression, when a new coalition of the religious parties and the right wing Likud party repealed the "family or social circumstances" clause. Abortion committees have, however, acted liberally within the new framework. Statistics have shown that after the repeal of the "family or social circumstances" clause, there was an increase in the authorization of abortions under other clauses, which kept the overall number of authorizations at approximately the same level (Mazori, 1986). Thus once again Israeli practice appears to be more liberal than the law. Nevertheless, the further minimization of the importance of the woman's own wishes and convenience, as formal reasons for allowing abortion, signifies a deterioration in the political consensus on women's right to the equal opportunity to plan their lives socially and economically.

CONCLUSION

At the most fundamental level, the level of constitutional principle, the Israeli legal system reflects basic conflict between a conviction that the religious Jewish nature of the state does, and should, inform our concept of womanhood and a commitment to the principle of equality. In this conflict there is a clear consensus in favor of the religious Jewish nature of the state. In this context, at the level of Knesset legislation, readiness to give normative expression to the principle of equality has not extended to endorsement of women's right to equality where it impinges upon the religious Jewish nature of the state. The courts have taken a course of judicial inactivism on the constitutional issue of equality for women. With few exceptions, they have not used the options open, even in the absence of a written constitution, to challenge the supremacy of the religious Jewish nature of the state over the right to equality between the sexes. In the sphere of economic equality, the most recent decision by the Supreme Court holds out the promise of important changes through litigation. However, in order to activate a wide ranging egalitarianism in Israeli law, a change in the national consensus regarding the balance between religious values and the right to equality is indispensible.

REFERENCES

Mazori, T. (1986) "Avoiding the Abortion Law," Ma'ariv, February 21 (Hebrew).

Polan, Diane (1982) "Toward a Theory of Law and Patriarchy." In Kairys, D. (ed.). The Politics of Law. New York: Pantheon Books, 1982.

Raday, Frances (1983) "Equality of Women Under Israeli Law." Jerusalem Quarterly 27: 81, 84.

Shereschewsky, Ben Zion (1984) Family Law in Israel (3rd edition). Jerusalem: Reuven Mass 448–450 (Hebrew).

Shifman, Pinhas (1984) Family Law in Israel. Jerusalem, Sacher Institute for Legislative Research and Comparative Law, Hebrew University, 178–179 (Hebrew).

AN AGUNAH TESTIFIES ON THE
FLOOR OF THE KNESSET

(Translated by Moshe Shalvi)

An "agunah" is a Jewish woman who cannot obtain a divorce, usually because her husband, or the unmarried brother of her deceased husband, refuses to grant her release. The following testimony was given at the time of a Knesset (Parliament) hearing on the subject of Jewish women who were trapped in unhappy or violent marriages.

I was a young woman in my thirties, a mother of two young children aged 5 and 7, when in December 1968, after 15 years of a miserable marriage, I filed for divorce in the Jerusalem Rabbinic Court. My whole life was before me, and being optimistic, I though that the worst part — the decision — was behind me. My claim was just, and the divorce would soon be forthcoming. I was naive.

It was only on January 8, 1986, eighteen years later, that I received a judgment from the Rabbinic High Court in Jerusalem obliging my husband (but not compelling him) to grant me a divorce. I received this judgment thanks to the tenacity, devotion and steadfastness of my friend and attorney Tova Aduram.

My husband has been in New York for fifteen years — since January 1971. The abovementioned judgment has been sent to the U.S.A. for implementation (based upon legal precedents), and I hope that in the end I will finally manage to obtain the long hoped for divorce, even though the road still appears very long and paved with many dollars.

During the eighteen years that elapsed between the beginning of the proceedings and the handing down of the judgment, I initiated legal actions in every possible court concerning alimony, property division, child custody and various injunctions:

- Tel Aviv Magistrate's Court
- Jerusalem District Court
- Tel Aviv District Court
- Supreme Court (Jerusalem), including a number of precedent-setting appeals which law students encounter on examinations
- Main Execution Office in Jerusalem
- Jerusalem Rabbinic Court
- Tel Aviv Rabbinic Court
- Rabbinic High Court in Jerusalem

The deliberations on the divorce began in 1968, were discontinued in 1971, renewed in June 1979 and continued until January 1986, when the above judgment was handed down – nine years of deliberations. Alimony proceedings in the Jerusalem District Court, including a famous appeal to the Supreme Court, took over three years.

So it was with the other suits. I have very harsh things to say about the entire system. At every level, proceedings dragged on for years and cost me a great deal of anguish. They were replete with unfounded pleas that the court lacked the authority to deal with the matter or that my husband was ill or on Army Reserve duty, so that he could gain time. Even when the claim was obviously false, the court would accept it and postpone the hearing for months. In many instances, the new date fell during the court recess, or the lawyers had difficulty finding a suitable date for resumption of the hearing. Often hearings were cancelled for one reason or another without notice, after I had made a special trip from Tel Aviv to Jerusalem, losing a day's work. All my efforts to move the hearings to Tel Aviv were to no avail, despite the fact that I, the plaintiff, reside in Tel Aviv, and my husband, the defendant, resides in New York. Over the years, I spent many long hours awaiting my turn in court corridors, for in most instances all contestants were asked to come in the morning, even if the hearing was to take place in the afternoon. In many cases, even after the hearings were over, considerable time elapsed before the decisions of the judges were handed down, causing nervous tension and additional delay, in a complete perversion of justice.

The actual hearings were painful and in many instances insulting and degrading – when judges allowed the lawyers to probe with a crude finger into one's guts, despite the fact that the relevance of their cross examination to the point in hand was tenuous at best. I speak in general terms without going into detail or bringing specific examples, although I can back up everything I have said with solid evidence. However, I do not have the emotional stamina to relive it; moreover, this is not the place.

The best years of my life, most of my money, and much of my family's money and that of friends who have supported me all along has been wasted on these proceedings. By the time I received the judgment there was no longer any cause for rejoicing – for who knows if and when I will ever receive the divorce.

Making the Silences Speak
in the Israeli Cinema

Ella Shohat

The myth of equality fostered by Zionist discourse, in which feminism has generally been marginalized, is reflected in Israeli cinema. The Israeli film industry has not only been dominated by men but has also catered to privileged male-oriented concerns, addressing women's issues only insofar as they seem relevant to nationalist rhetoric. One can hardly speak of a feminist alternative discourse for reasons which have to do not only with the militarization of Israeli culture but also with the history of the nationalist Sabra (native-born Jew associated with European origin) ethos: the mythological Sabra, the prototype of the newly emerging Jew in Eretz Israel/Palestine, constituted the masculine antithesis of the Zionist image of the "feminine" Diaspora Jew. The Sabra was created by the immigrant generation of pioneers, who viewed their children as the hope for Jewish salvation and therefore endowed this first generation with the proud status of a kind of moral aristocracy.

In a reversed oedipalism, the Sabra was born into a vacuum in which the ideal figure was not the father but the son. Hebrew narratives were therefore premised on the absence of the Diaspora parent. The heroes—there was very little space for heroines—were celebrated as eternal children devoid of parents, as though born by spontaneous generation. Zionist parents raised their children to see themselves as historical foundlings, worthy of more dignified, romantic and powerful progenitors. The mythological Sabra, posited in genderized language as the masculine redeemer of the passive Diaspora Jew, also signified the destruction of the Diaspora Jewish entity. Incarnating the same nationalist features that oppressed the Diaspora Jew, the Sabra hero was portrayed as healthy, tanned, often with blond hair and blue eyes, presumably cleansed of all "Jewish" inferiority complexes, a kind of child of nature, confident, proud and brave. Ironically, this conception was partially influenced by Gustav Weinken and the "youth culture" fashionable in Germany at the turn of the century, especially in the German youth movement, Wandervogel (Elon, 1981). The Zionist stereotype of the Diaspora Jew as a passive victim and the Sabra as an active redeemer has subliminally perpetuated a gender-

31

ized discourse in which masculine toughness has been highly cherished, undermining the possibility of a revisionist feminist perspective.

Already during the Yishuv (the pre-1948 Jewish settlement in Palestine), the "'pioneer" genre of films such as *Sabra* (1933) suggested the superiority of Jewish over Arab society through the comparative portrayal of the status of women in the two communities (Shohat, 1989). As equal members of the collective, women pioneers are portrayed working alongside the men. They demonstrate—in accordance with a positive female stereotype—an enhanced mental capacity to continue the struggle in the face of adversity. Images of women working the land and, in later films, wielding weapons, further strengthened this egalitarian mystique. (In fact, however, even in the socialist communes, women were still largely limited to traditional roles.) In the pioneer films, female equality is directly correlated with conformity to Zionist pioneering ideals: the hard-working pioneer is portrayed as a Madonna, the hedonistic bourgeois as a whore. *Sabra*, for example, contrasts the hard-working pioneer woman who sacrifices her beauty and comfortable life in Europe with the provocatively dressed Jezebel-like woman who refuses to abandon her hedonistic ways and spends her time drinking and listening to the gramophone in the pioneers' tent. The film enforces identification with her boyfriend's puritanical censure, culminating in his final expression of contempt: "The only thing you know how to do is drink, while we go hungry. You would dance all your life, but here dancing is death."

In *They Were Ten* (1961), produced decades after the early pioneering films, the pioneer woman as Madonna is exalted, even mythologized, into the status of a veritable "great mother." The film portrays Manya, the only woman among nine men living in overcrowded conditions, as unable to find the privacy to fulfill her function as wife to her pioneer husband. An exemplar of self abnegation, she is characterized as a substitute mother who takes care of all the pioneers' needs. When one of them desires her, however, she rebuffs him, evoking an embarrassed confession of moral weakness. The only lovemaking between Manya and her husband during the film takes place outdoors and leads to her pregnancy. Fulfilling her ultimate woman-mother role of giving fruitful birth, she dies shortly thereafter, suffering the fate of the frontier woman in many "Western" films.

While pioneer women are granted few roles and little dialogue, no dialogue is accorded the Arab women who appear but briefly in the "pioneer" and post-1948 heroic-nationalist films. The few sequences with Arab women reduce their image to the exotic Orientals familiar to Western imagination. A rather improbable melange in *Sabra* features a belly dancer with a ring in her nose, a dot on her forehead, and a jar on her head, thus condensing several Third World female stereotypes. The dot on the forehead is usually associated with women from India, the ring in the nose is more common in Africa, while a jar is usually carried on the head by Arab women for practical rather than exotic-artistic purposes. The Hollywood-style "mark of the plural," to borrow Albert Memmi's terminology (1967:85), flattens a diversity of Third World cultures in an unlikely synthesis. While the belly dancer in *Sabra* leaves the screen when an Arab man signals for her to go, the equally brief appearance of a "noble" Arab woman is associated with one of the pioneers. She shyly exchanges affectionate glances with him early in the film and later succors his wound and gives him water as in the classical Biblical figure of the worthy woman.

In films such as *Rebels Against the Light* (1964) and *Sinaia* (1964), the "positive" portrayal of a "noble," "exotic," Palestinian or Bedouin woman entails her devotion to the Israeli cause. The representation of the Arab woman is, in many ways, subordinated to Romantic fascination with the "other." Arab women, as pointed out by literary critic Gershon Shaked (1983) with regard to Hebrew literature of the twenties and thirties, tend to assimilate with Jews, as though their origins were in the East but their heart in the West (i.e., as represented by Israelis). The Orient, as suggested in Edward Said's *Orientalism* (1977), is regarded as mute and powerless, available for European plunder, in complete disregard of the desires and resistance of the indigenous population. In the Israeli heroic-nationalist films, the traditional Western male fetishization of Oriental women takes the form of a virtually silent Arab woman behind whose melancholy eyes seems to lurk a desire for rescue by the Western male. The minor Arab woman character in *Sabra* is granted no dialogue, and Naima in *Rebels Against the Light* mouths only a few sorrowful words of mourning.

In *Sinaia*, the noble Bedouin mother who hides an Israeli pilot (who has bandaged her wounds) from Egyptian soldiers—even though it was his crashing airplane that caused the destruction—is marginalized within the film's narrative. The Hebrew title *Sinaia* is taken from the actual Hebrew name given to a Bedouin baby girl rescued by an Israeli pilot during the 1956 war—the inspiration for the film. Set during the same war, the film presents the Bedouin woman as an object of ethical debate between the Israeli pilot and the infantry. Although there is no room in the helicopter, the pilot insists on taking the Bedouin mother and her two small children. The infantryman argues that in wartime soldiers must have first priority. His mean-spiritedness is explained as a product of traumatic memories of Arab terror (a massacred sister) as well as the recent loss of his best friend in the war. Gradually, however, he adopts the pilot's morally superior stance, even saving the life of the woman's son from a threatening Egyptian soldier. While the Egyptian soldiers torture the Bedouin woman to extract information about the Israeli pilot, the Israeli soldiers rescue her. Here the narrative-ideological role of the Bedouin female character is to contrast the humanism of the Israelis with the barbarism of the Egyptians. The infantryman agrees to stay behind to facilitate the rescue. When the helicopter crashes, only the baby girl survives. The depiction of the Bedouin woman as almost silent, expressing, through gesture, primal emotions of motherhood and fear, forms a striking contrast with the portrayal of the Israeli soldiers' free stream of expression. Close shots emphasize the beautiful (light) eyes of the Bedouin woman, but otherwise she forms part of the desert scenery, a perfect embodiment of nature. The actress, painted dark with makeup, literalizes the notion of a Western soul beneath an Oriental surface, allowing the film to construct her as "positive," an "exotic" woman on whom an expansive and eroticized "generosity" can be projected. Arab women, in other words, can be seen as analogizing the Hebrew settlers' relations to the "alien" land and culture, via a metaphor which links the Orient and sexuality. The Middle East is subliminally conceived as fallow land awaiting ploughing, as a resistant virgin coyly awaiting to be conquered.

Like the Arab woman, the Oriental Jewish woman (also referred to as "Sephardi"—Jews who came to Israel mostly from Arab and Moslem countries, who form the majority of the Jewish population yet have been denied access to political, economic and cultural power)—is also typically denied a voice in Israeli films. In *Hill 24 Doesn't Answer* (1955), for example, the ethnic "inferiority" of the "exotic" Oriental Jewish woman is compensated for by her heroic sacrifice for the country. Set during the 1948 war, *Hill 24 Doesn't Answer* revolves around the personal stories of four (in fact three) fighters: an Irishman, an American Jew, and two Israelis, one an Ashkenazi Sabra and the other an Oriental woman, assigned to defend a strategic hill outside Jerusalem. On the way to their last mission, the three men recount, in lengthy flashbacks, the roots of their Zionist conviction and their previous combat experiences. *Hill 24 Doesn't Answer* chronicles the evolving Zionist consciousness of the protagonists and, through them, of the spectator. The device of focalizing the narrative through an ethnically (and nationally) diverse gallery of characters enables the film to maintain the facade of a democratic distribution of points of view. The merging of the three stories into the brief final episode on Hill 24 reflects the final integration of perspectives within the mold of a national collective history. A reductionist view of the Arabs as a kind of synecdoche for violence and menace is accompanied by European paternalism toward the "friendly East" of the Druze and the Oriental Jews, as epitomized in the character of the woman fighter. The only detail she provides about herself concerns her place of birth, Jerusalem, but her accent and appearance make it clear that her country of origin is Yemen. Although one of the four protagonists assigned to defend Hill 24, she is granted no episode of her own, as if she had no particular story to tell. It is up to us, therefore, to make the text's silences, and hers, speak.

Within the film's Zionist Eurocentrism, the history of Jews from the Middle East is eliminated or subordinated to the European Jewish memory. The Arab historical memory of the Yemenite Jewish woman is elided, an absence forming an integral part of her definition as one of the four Zionist heroes. The film thus reflects the official view that the Arab culture of Oriental Jews was fated for extinction, in accord with general colonialist assumptions about what were regarded as the "twilight" cultures of the East, an idea expressed by various Zionist leaders, on both the right (Ze'ev Jabotinsky and the Revisionist movement) and the "left" (David Ben-Gurion and the Labour movement). In the context of the mid-1950s, following the mass immigration of Arab Jews, the creation of a Jewish national identity came to imply the melting down of Orientals into the hegemonic Euro-Israeli culture based on the assumption of a single official, European Jewish history. It is scarcely surprising, then, that the film stages an encounter between the (Ashkenazi) Sabra man and his European history, condensed into the image of the Nazi soldier-oppressor who fights with the Egyptians against Israel, while never offering any equivalent encounter for the Yemenite woman. Not only is the Israeli-Arab political conflict projected onto an imaginary Arab-Nazi nexus, but also all other Jews are grouped, inappropriately, under the "sign of the Holocaust." The Oriental Jew does not look to her own historical roots in the East, or to those with whom her ancestors shared what was essentially a life of coexistence (i.e. the Arabs) even though the film, like Israel, is "set" in the Middle East and not in Europe. While European Jewish history is referred to in all three episodes, Asian and African Jewish history is totally excluded from representation.

Hill 24 Doesn't Answer also intimates the "price" paid by Oriental Jews for "redemption" from their "primal sin" of belonging to the Orient—the waging of war against the Arabs. The climactic United Nations decision that Hill 24 belongs to Israel—even though the four fighters do not survive to claim it—is a consequence of the Israeli flag being clasped in the hand of the dead Oriental woman. The sequence inadvertently suggests the ironic nature of her "equality" and "redemption"; through her self-sacrifice, she is accepted (as a martyr) even though, as the film implies, she has no story to tell. Her (hi)story begins here, with the Zionist act, not before it, and will only be told through the agency of male western (Jewish and non-Jewish) narrators.

In other films, western "altruism" saves the Jewish Orient from its social, moral and sexual obscurantism. In the melodrama *Fortuna* (1966), an Algerian Jewish family, from a development town near Sodom, forces their daughter Fortuna to wed a rich old man to whom she was promised at an early age, while sabotaging her love for a French engineer. The tyranny of what is presented as a typically patriarchal Oriental family leads to the heroine's death. The critique of the "inferior culture" brought from "underdeveloped" countries is reinforced by the topographical reductionism of the Orient to desert, and metaphorically, to dreariness. The desert, a frequent reference in the dialogue and a visual leitmotif throughout the film, is presented as essential to the history of these Third World Jews. The Oriental is associated with images of underdevelopment, poverty and backwardness, in implied contrast to the Sabra, generally portrayed as the very antithesis of the (Oriental) desert: an active, productive, and creative pioneer, the masculine redeemer who conquers the "feminine" wilderness. In *Fortuna,* the Orient becomes a world immersed in death, a theme emphasized by shots of circling birds of prey, and by the association of Fortuna's family with Sodom, the biblical "city of evils." The dichotomy of Orient (death) and West (life) structures the film. The Orient appears as the enemy of Eros and the partisan of Thanatos, both in the attempts to kill the French lover and in the forced marriage which indirectly leads Fortuna to her death. The West, meanwhile, is personified by the handsome Frenchman, the savior of the oppressed daughter and the bringer of technological advancement. Salvation for the Oriental woman must come from the West, or from the westernized, modern Sabra world.

The victimization of the Oriental woman by Oriental men and her implicit salvation by the western Ashkenazi world, particularly by a western man, is presented in other Israeli films as well. In *Queen of the Road* (1971), the narrative promotes an opposition between the gentle kibbutznik, who gives the protagonist, a Moroccan prostitute in Tel Aviv, warmth and affection, and the rough Oriental men, especially those of the development town in the South, who brutally rape her during her first months of pregnancy. Her involvement with the kibbutznik, her pregnancy by him, and her visit to the "enlightened" kibbutz, where she sees his well-ordered family, make her decide to give up prostitution and raise the child herself. While visiting her mother in the South of Israel, she is violently raped, leading to the birth of a retarded child. Rape, retardation, and even death, caused in these films by Oriental male mistreatment of Oriental women, stimulate a kind of rescue fantasy in the "progressive" male spectator.

A similar representation of sexual tensions between Oriental men and women is extended to the present day in the comedy *You're in the Army Now* (1985). The film recounts four weeks of boot camp training for women soldiers in the Israeli army. From the very beginning, the film develops a structural contrast between its major characters, an upper-class Sabra woman, Niva, and a development-town Oriental woman, Shula. Already in the credit sequence, the film cuts from Niva's separation from her father to Shula's separation from her family, underlining their opposing class and ethnic backgrounds. The film betrays a differential attitude towards these backgrounds, one which permeates the entire film. Whereas the camera foregrounds Niva and her handsome, protective father, revealed to be an "insider" in relation to the establishment, Shula's large family remains more or less anonymous as the camera pans over-their-shoulders to record the daughter kissing them goodbye, while she censures their overly emotional (i.e. non-Israeli) reaction to her departure. Shula is dressed in colorful, cheap clothing, while Niva is dressed in expensive, fashionable togs acquired in the boutiques of Paris and New York. (The contrast in their appearance and manner, trans-

lated into a North American context, would correspond, roughly, to the stereotypes of the refined [perhaps repressed] Wasp and the sexy Latina.) Ac-
knowledging that her situation at home is unbearable and rebelling against
the (presumably Oriental) prospect of "ending" her "life at the age of thirty
with fifty children," trapped "between the grocery store and the laundry," Shula
joins the army. Once in the army, however, she becomes the object of prejudice. Perhaps in reaction to the treatment accorded her, she runs away from
the army and encounters her Oriental boyfriend, depicted as stuttering, weak,
and unintelligent, but also good hearted. Out in the brutal Oriental world,
she finds herself forced to smoke dope and about to be raped by three Oriental men. Unable to save her, the weak and pitiful boyfriend calls Shula's
women's unit for help. The Sabra women's unit collectively perform a private
military mission to save their comrade from the Oriental sexual vultures, thus
"compensating" for their previous lack of ethnic sensitivity. In a heroic action, they release the Oriental woman and humiliate the surprised and frightened Oriental machos. The unit's patriotism is expressed in an additional act
of generosity toward the "culturally deprived" Oriental woman. With her
father's help, Niva gets the musically talented Shula into the prestigious army
entertainment troupe, while she herself gets another (equally prestigious) position in military radio. The army, metonymic of Israel and its Ashkenazi elite,
then, together save the Oriental woman from her backward, violent world
and give her the opportunity to develop her talents and resolve the sexual
conflicts presumably endemic in Oriental society, in a way that intimates a
peaceful transcendence of the ethnic, class tensions of Israeli society.

The violence of Oriental men towards Oriental women and their rescue
by the Israeli establishment or Ashkenazi men function ideologically to explain away the exploitation of Oriental women within the Israeli system—
Oriental women are the lowest paid sector within the Israeli Jewish
population—as well as the exploitation of working class Oriental men, while
at the same time eliding Ashkenazi men's oppression of Ashkenazi women.
These films reproduce the hegemonic male discourse whereby gender relations are blamed on the Orientalism of Sephardi Jews. The position of women
within Israeli society, as well as the fact that the Sabra ethos is based on
nationalist-macho ideals, are ignored.

Such a vision is at times internalized by Oriental Jews themselves, as in
Kurdania (1986), a short film made by an Oriental director. Set in a transit
camp of the 1950s, it opens with the rape of an Oriental woman by her husband. The problem is not the "realism" of the scene, but the fact that it was
created in an interpretive context in which the notion of sexual violence within
the Oriental family has been used to rationalize Euro-Israeli male power. The
rape of women has not been limited to particular classes, ethnicities and na-
tionalities, and in Israel, Ashkenazi men have raped Oriental women; there-

fore the political drift of such representations is obvious, especially consider-
ing the history of Israeli cinema, in which rape is never performed by Ashkenazi men, but always restricted to Oriental men.

More often, however, in the comic "bourekas" genre (the name derives
from a popular Oriental pastry and came to refer to comedies and melodramas
which deal with Ashkenazi-Oriental ethnic tensions), gender relations are subjected to a more implicit nationalist ideology in which young mixed couples
allegorically unite conflicting communities. Social integration is dreamed via
eroticism, and the wedding which presumably "bridges the gaps," celebrates
national-familial harmony, as expressed in the song "We are all Jews" used
in the movie Casablan (1973) or the song "To the Life of this Nation/People"
used in Salomonico (1973). Most "bourekas" films give expression to the dominant attitude that cultural differences and class distinctions will be eliminated
by the younger generation, especially through marriage. The Israeli-Arab conflict remains latent, an unspoken presence in "bourekas" films, suggested only
through the context of Jewish unity in the face of Arab animosity.

With the decline of the mythic heroic Sabra in the seventies, the new movement of personal cinema focused on sensitive, vulnerable male characters,
thus indirectly opening up some space for women protagonists. As in much
of personal cinema, My Michael (1974) focuses on alienated outsiders, this
time with female protagonists. But even the political parti pris of personal
cinema is not completely untouched by national context and Orientalist ideology. The Arab twins in My Michael, for example, presented within the woman
protagonist's stream of consciousness, serve little narrative function beyond
mirroring and metaphorizing the repressed Dionysian inner self of the protagonist and her romantic frustration with her humdrum and unimaginative
existence. In this sense, the Arab presence penetrates the hallucinatory space
of Jewish-Israeli subjectivity, but is silent as a national, political voice.

The late seventies also witnessed the emergence of women filmmakers,
who, like their male colleagues, tend to highlight themes of alienation and
the search for identity. The personal films present a closed world that is centered in the West, spurning any authentic dialogue with the East. Moreover,
the focus on women is rarely an explicitly feminist one. Depicting the world
of upper-middle class Ashkenazi women, women's personal films tend to reproduce the hegemonic national, ethnic and class perspective. For example,
A Thousand Little Kisses (1982) fosters identification with the elegant and
sophisticated bourgeois Euro-Israeli widow facing a crisis in her life. Through
the visually "precious" and sophisticated mis-en-scene and complex camera
movements, the spectator is led to identify with the "complex" world of the
widow against that of the petty, intrusive and materialistic maid, who is merely
interested in taking food and clothing from her employer and is totally insen-
sitive to the widow's emotional state. Due to their conspicuous and unnatural exclusion from a film shot in a well-known Oriental neighborhood,

Orientals (other than the maid) form a "structuring absence" in the film. *A Thousand Little Kisses* consistently maintains a hygienic and self-conscious atmosphere of artistic beauty, exploits the old local architecture of the neighborhood but eliminates almost all traces of its inhabitants.

The superficiality and passivity associated with Oriental women has been challenged in a few films made by Oriental producers, notably *The House on Chlouch Street* (1973) and *Light Out of Nowhere* (1973). In the former, the protagonist's mother, Klara, works as a housemaid, and this is one of the rare cases in Israeli cinema where the Oriental female laborer receives understanding treatment, largely through mechanisms of identification. Her portrayal contrasts with numerous Israeli films in which the maid is depicted as a symbolic ornament for the upper class and presented from the vantage point of her employers (and her producers), whether she is a marginal character or a central one. *The House on Chlouch Street* devotes most of Klara's narrative time to events in her home, showing her on her own terrain, where she is independent and even a "boss" to her children. This film's portrayal of the maid's emotional depth not only eschews all condescension, but also reinforces identification with her struggle as a widowed working mother. When Klara is first seen scrubbing the floor, the act is not presented from the employer's point of view, but from the point of view of her son, the protagonist, who intensely identifies with her feelings of shame and hurt, an identification underlined by a close shot of his face. His humiliation is exacerbated when Klara's employer, Mrs. Goldstein, enters the house, for her remarks call attention to a painful situation of dependency.

Similarly, in *Light Out of Nowhere*, the Oriental woman is significant even though she is not a central character. When, for example, establishment representatives break into an Oriental underclass neighborhood to carry out their mission—the implementation of harsh social policy—the Oriental woman is the one who expresses protest. In a sequence in which the inspectors and the police execute an order to destroy a home, the protagonist's female neighbour becomes the representative of the Oriental community, whose rebellion is expressed by the words she hurls at the authorities: "It's OK for our kids to fight the Arabs, but nobody gives a damn where they live! What does this government care! Go on, bring those *Vuzvuzim* (a pejorative for Ashkenazim) from Russia . . . ." In this period, there was large-scale immigration from the Soviet Union. The Soviet immigrants were given preferential treatment, which angered Oriental Jews, who had never been the recipients of similar governmental largesse. In *Light Out of Nowhere* and *The House on Chlouch Street*, the Oriental woman fights within the limited framework of her possibilities. Furthermore, her oppressor does not take the form of a monstrous Oriental man, but rather that of an oppressive establishment. *Light Out of Nowhere* does not ignore the macho behavior of street youths towards women; it demonstrates that Oriental women and men, whatever their differences, are nonetheless victims of the same policy. The woman's violence is presented within the context of a violent policy and, as a consequence, takes on a significance different from the stereotype of "Oriental irrationality." This woman expresses the anger and violence of a subjugated group which is first and foremost a reaction and rebellion *against* violence, the violence rooted in the asymmetries of power.

REFERENCES

Elon, Amos (1981) *The Israelis.* Jerusalem: Adam (Hebrew).
Memmi, Albert (1967) *The Colonizer and the Colonized.* Boston: Beacon Press.
Said, Edward (1977) *Orientalism.* New York: Vintage Press.
Shaked, Gershon (1983) *No Other Place.* Tel Aviv: HaKibbutz Ha'Meuchad (Hebrew).
Shohat, Ella (1989) *Israeli Cinema: East/West and the Politics of Representation.* Austin: Texas University Press.

THE EMERGENCE OF A
PALESTINIAN IDENTITY:
INTERVIEW WITH MARIAM MAR'I

(Translated by Barbara Swirski)

Mariam Mar'i was born in Acre in 1945, in a house that her father built in the 1940s. When she was 18 months old, her mother fled to Lebanon with Mariam and her 6 brothers and sisters. Her father stayed in Acre. Forty years later, Mariam is sitting in the house where she was born, with her mother, now a woman of 80. In the course of the interview, Mariam conjures up scenes from the past, a puzzle of memories, smells, colors, and feelings that explain the elements that come together in a 43-year-old educated Arab woman living in Israel in 1988.

A scene from the 1950s: "We are in a big house in Bourge el Barajne living with uncles and grandmothers. No one pays any attention to me. I'm the smallest one around, lost underfoot. The only one who gives me the time-of-day is my big brother. Every morning I wait my turn as he shaves, holding the towel for him next to the bowl. Afterwards he holds my hand as if I were a big girl. It's my own private moment. We go out into the street and he buys a banana for me. That banana makes me special and sets me apart from all the other children."

A four-year stay in Lebanon is also part of the mosaic. Her father was on the other side of the border, in Acre. For a two-year old girl, the word "father" was an abstract concept which came automatically after the word "mother." From the stories told by her sisters, she imagined a big house with land, trees and a vegetable garden. In 1954 her mother returned to Israel, taking the little children with her. One sharp memory is of waving to her big brother who had to stay behind. Afterwards, being sprayed with DDT and receiving a bag of candy from a young woman in uniform. In the end, an old man with a white *kafia* and everyone kissing his hand: father.

The Israeli "Law of Family Reunion" limited the right of return to the wife, unmarried daughters, and sons under the age of 16. Her big brother and married sisters had to remain in Lebanon, on the other side of the border. Her mother did not understand Israeli law. "Bosta," she said calmly to the little girl who wanted to hold the hand of the brother who had raised her, it meant "immigration." "We're in the first immigration, and he'll be in the second." Mariam says, "My God, how were we to know that we wouldn't see one another for 15 years."

From age 9 to 18 Mariam studied in the convent school in Acre. School was the only thing that allowed her out of the house. The convent symbolized freedom

---

Adapted from Bili Moskona-Lerman, "May God Watch Over her Man," *Maariv*, January 8, 1988.

from her father and the exactitude of tradition. She pulls out a memory with a sound: "I remember a big hall, modern music. We're standing around in couples, all girls, and the nuns are teaching us to dance the waltz, the cha-cha-cha, and the tango. Teaching us to be women. To sit upright, to cross our legs, to converse in French and English. . . ."

When she asked about her older brother, they told her that he was forbidden to cross the border. "Border," she said to herself, trying to understand the word, to make it tangible. "I thought, how could a word that doesn't even have a shape bring so many yearnings and so much suffering. The suffering spoiled relations between my mother and father. 'You deceived me!' she would yell at him, breaking a hierarchy of long tradition with one painful cry. 'I wouldn't have come back here just for you. You could have joined us there in Lebanon. I miss the children.' "

In 1965, when Arabs were given permission to live outside the old city of Acre, they rushed to see their old house, then occupied by two Jewish families. Her father went to government offices, waved his papers in front of the officials, insisted. He bought the house back for a large sum of money. "It's my land," he said. Then he turned to family matters. He looked at his daughter Mariam and thought to himself that she was learning too much. She knew how to read and write. All she needed now was a course in sewing. Mariam smelled the danger and reacted with passive resistance. She spoke to her middle brother about her desire to continue her studies. She excelled in school. She was lucky. In his wisdom, her father said to her middle brother, who was still living at home: "I'm giving you the responsibility for her. I don't understand the world she grew up in, and I don't want to do any injustice—not to her and not to myself."

"My father wanted me to wear long sleeves. I insisted on short sleeves like all the others, and I complained to my brother that in the end they would force me to wear a veil. Rather than answer, my brother said he wanted to show me something. He said that my modernity was an imitation of the Jewish woman. He took me to a kibbutz. 'Look,' he said, 'you're imitating the freedom of Jewish women. Let's take a look at what's really worth imitating.' We saw women working in the fields, in the barn, on the roads, driving a tractor. 'Imitate the freedom of their actions,' he said, 'not outward appearances. Imitate the inner freedom.' I didn't quite understand what he was trying to tell me, but the image remained in my mind."

Her father was the one who taught Mariam both the negative and the positive meanings of equality: "We were sitting around the table. My youngest brother, a 'male chauvinist,' said 'The water pitcher is missing.' Right away the women sitting on both sides of the table ran to bring him water. My father didn't say a word. The next day, during dinner, he got up abruptly from the table. My mother became nervous—what's missing? He went quietly to the shelf and brought the salt, sat down, and said to my brother: 'After we sit down at the table, we are all the same.' "

Mariam doesn't remember intimacy or physical contact. They would kiss their father's hand without coming close to his face. Her mother slept in the same room with the girls. One embarrassing memory: "We all lived by my father's clock, tiptoeing around so as not to disturb his prayers or bath or rest. One day I forgot one of my notebooks, and I ran home from school to get it. I knew that mother was sick in bed. I entered the house in a mad rush and saw my father standing beside her bed, preparing tea for her. Right away I started to stutter. We weren't supposed to run in his presence but to walk quietly. I was afraid he would scold me and I thought to myself: how come he's making tea for mother and sitting beside her bed. And mother was so embarrassed that I'd come in upon the scene that she blushed and didn't know what to do. As for my father, he didn't scold. He smiled.

"Years later I was giving a Jewish woman private lessons in Arabic. It was in her house that I saw a father bringing his daughter refreshments and she hugging and even kissing him as if it were natural. I rubbed my eyes. I realized that it was possible to act this way, and I decided that one day that's how I would act. I was already a married woman when I went to the States to study, and when I said goodbye to my father, I kissed him on the cheek. I said to myself, my God, I'm breaking this tradition as well. I was the first to dare. He kissed me back and hugged me." Tradition, Mariam says, can be broken only when both sides are ready to break with it.

Mariam graduated from high school, earned a Bachelor of Arts degree from the University of Haifa, married, had two children, and received her Master of Arts and Doctor of Philosophy degrees from American universities. Her marriage to Sami Mar'i, a professor of Educational Psychology, involved a sharp conflict between education and tradition. When they first met, Sami was an outstanding teacher. She was attracted to his intelligence, and he by her earnestness as a student and her coming to him for advice and help. The crisis that occurred later in their lives was the result not only of a conflict between a man and a woman but also one between two different cultures.

"He talked a lot about equality, but he always had to have the last word. When my own status rose and I felt that I had something to offer, I started out on my own. I remember the first time I got a telephone call from a village asking me to give a lecture. I trembled with excitement. It was the first time I'd been invited to lecture without his intervention. I ran to tell him about it, and I saw that he wasn't very happy. When I pressed him about the matter, it turned out that he didn't like the idea of my giving the 'OK' without consulting him first. I asked him whether he wanted me to tell them to wait on the phone for a moment while

I run to ask my husband. 'No,' he replied, 'tell them that you need to check it out with the family, and call back later'. 'But that's not true,' I protested."

He found her independence threatening. She decided to take a step forward. She told him she didn't feel he treated her as an equal and left the house with her daughter. Then came a barrage of letters from relatives and even strangers, young people who considered them the ideal couple, modern, educated. "How can you do this to us?" young couples would write to her, while others, traditionalists, pointed to them, with satisfaction, as an example of the failure of modern ways.

Mariam remained true to herself. They missed each other. They finally came to a decision: either they would split up or they would find a way to live together. They went to consult with a well-known psychologist in Florida. For a whole month they dealt with their resentments and frustrations. They put everything on the table, examined every problem under a magnifying glass.

He said: "At home, five women served me. With you I have to serve myself."

She: "You fashioned me as if I were a statue, like George Bernard Shaw's 'Pygmalion.' I won't let you break me."

She: "I saw him as a famous teacher, and I didn't understand that underneath he was a man with feelings of inferiority like everyone else."

Mariam leans back on the sofa. Her husband Sami died three years ago of heart disease. Now she is a widow with many memories of "bitter" love. He had told her: "Can't you understand that with all my education, I still carry the burden of a whole tradition on my shoulders. I want to be a man. And I want you to be a woman."

Mariam and Sami lived in Haifa, lectured at the University, raised two children. A family. Normalcy didn't last for long. One night there was a knock on the door and Sami Mar'i was taken in for questioning. The charge: meeting with hostile elements abroad. Within hours a group of Jews from Tel Aviv were at Mariam's house, and with the intervention of Member of Knesset Shulamit Aloni, Sami was released within a day. At one time he was considered an extremist. Mariam says, "I, too, think that a Palestinian state is the only solution to the problem. One has to negotiate with the Palestine Liberation Organization. It's the official representative. You see the PLO as we once saw Zionism."

The idea of a Palestinian state is a source of both hope and fear. Mariam has qualms about tradition, religion and extremism—Arab as well as Jewish. Concerning the uprising in the territories, she says in that soft, calm voice of hers: "I felt pride. I didn't know we had so much power. I think right now we're in a better position that you are."

Challenging the Roots of Religious Patriarchy and Shaping Identity and Community

Eveline Goodman-Thau

Religiously observant Jewish women in Israel and other parts of the world are increasingly shaking the very foundations of their tradition. In search of identity, they look to the past in an attempt to find answers for the future. The search should have been viewed by the religious establishment as a true spiritual renaissance, for Jewish tradition has always availed itself of this method. It is in the reliving of past experience and the process of integrating it into contemporary life that one becomes a part of the chain of Jewish tradition. Jewish tradition does not derive from a set of dogmas, or a fixed creed, but rather from a series of insights into human nature and the structure of the world; insights which developed gradually, often amidst anguish and crisis, out of the collective experience of the Jewish people. Jewish tradition can thus be described as the long record of the spiritual quest of a people who turned again and again to the Holy Scriptures in a constant act of self-affirmation as Jews.

Although women have been active in preserving the collective memory, their voices are absent from religious sources. The interpretation of sacred texts and subsequent rulings were made almost exclusively by men, in settings usually closed to women: houses of study, courts of law, or synagogues. Men recorded the religious laws and implemented them, wrote the prayers that make up the liturgy, and established the institutions that guide daily life.

The imbalance created by the fact that, on the one hand women played a central and active role in the community, while on the other hand they were excluded from the process of recording and interpretation, seriously distorts the picture women and men have of their role in Jewish life. Under the strictest interpretation of *halakha* (Jewish religious law), a woman is not permitted to serve as an orthodox rabbi, as a judge in a religious court, or in any official capacity in communal life. As a result, many religious women have

45

become apprehensive regarding the relation between their age-old tradition and their status in the community.

WHO IS A JEWESS?

The quest for women's identity in the Jewish tradition began in the United States, when in 1973 Rachel Adler referred to the Jewess as "The Jew Who Wasn't There." Jewish women began to feel the impact of the feminist movement, and the debate over feminism and *halakha* has since become one of the touchstones of emancipation for Jewish women the world over. One of the earliest comprehensive treatments of the subject was written by Moshe Meiselman (1978), an orthodox rabbi who refuted feminist claims and rejected any demands for change in *halakha* or ritual. In his opinion, involvement of women in religious matters had to remain within the strict confines of traditional roles for men and women.

Other Orthodox writers, such as Saul Berman (1973), accepted the challenge of feminism, but concluded that the *halakha* affirms the centrality of women's domestic role as a desirable social goal and denies anything that might jeopardize the Jewish family. Berman encouraged women to seek additional forms of expression, and he conceded that the creative religious energies of women remained a major source of untapped strength for the Jewish community as a whole. Another scholar, Eliezer Berkovitz (1976), attempted to reconcile women's rights and *halakha*. He contended that there is a higher ethos in Judaism which recognizes the equality of all human beings. Therefore, any laws that seem to contradict this principle, like those that discriminate against women, must be the product of historical circumstances, and one must search for possibilities within the *halakha* to correct such injustices. A female scholar, Blu Greenberg (1981), made an important contribution to the acceptance of feminism within *halakha;* Greenberg did not ignore the inherent tension between feminism and *halakha* but argued that both were essential for Jewish life. Another scholar, Judith Plaskow (1973, 1987, 1990), suggested a total transformation of the *halakha* to make it expressive of feminist Judaism. Judith Hauptman (1974) has been providing a much needed social history of women in the talmudic period, and Rachel Biale (1984) produced an excellent study of women's issues as they are defined in *halakhic* sources.

In Israel, scholars have recently recognized the fact that the time has come to reappraise the status of women in religious life. Numerous articles were written on the subject, as well as books, such as the three-part study of Rabbi Elyakim G. Eilinson (1974, 1984). Naomi D. Cohen (1980, 1988) has dealt extensively with questions centering around women's education, and a number of excellent collections of articles have appeared on the subject (Rosenfeld, 1980; Rappel, 1989). While much of this literature is concerned with the status of women within the religious establishment, some of it deals with *halakhic* issues connected with the legal status of women in the state of Israel, an area which affects religiously observant and secular women alike.

It is one of the ironies of the treatment of women's issues in Israel that the question "Who is a Jew?" has been much disputed, causing many government crises and recently creating division among the Jewish people in Israel and in the Diaspora. In the Hebrew language, the masculine gender may include the female. The question "Who is a Jew?" is answered by *halakha* as "one having a Jewish mother"; that is, only the biological issue is addressed. The question being asked by Jewish women today, however, is "Who is a Jewess?" This is not a problem of biological destiny, but rather one of identity, a fact that seems to have escaped *halakhists* and politicians alike. Its absence as a public issue violates the very core of Jewish religious principles, namely the premise that women and men are equally created in God's image. A new evaluation of women's (and men's) roles in the Jewish community needs to be considered in order to move beyond the current limited view of women, so that the premise of religious equality is honored and women become full members of Jewish society.

Our discussion will focus on those areas in Jewish tradition—namely worship, synagogue life, ritual and study—where the unequal status of women seriously threatens the fabric of Jewish life. At the same time, it should be borne in mind that other areas of discrimination, such as the disadvantaged position of women in marital law, which is carried over into the social sphere in matters such as income tax regulations, also have their origin in orthodox religious practice and affect all women. It must be remembered that for many centuries, religious practice shaped the nature of Jewish communities; the Israeli social order is thus inseparably linked to religious attitudes.

JEWISH TRADITION AND THE QUESTION OF EQUALITY

Jewish women can find considerable support in religious texts for their rejection of patriarchy. There is an established principle in the *halakha* that although the Torah was written in the masculine, all laws are to be observed by men and women alike: "Thou shalt not kill" applies to both. According to the *halakha*, the commandments are the blueprint for the ideal life and the attainment of holiness. The rabbinic formula for a blessing reads: "Blessed are you Lord our God, King of the universe, who had made us holy with your commandments and commanded us . . . ." The injunction to remember that we are a holy people also applies to women: "For you are a holy people" (Deut. 14:2); "Women are also included" (T.J. Kiddushin 1:7). Furthermore, the *halakha* indicates that the commandments cultivate ethical concern for fellow beings. They encompass every aspect of life, both the religious and the secular, the private interests of the individual and the public concerns of society. "The commandments were given to purify all creatures" (Tanhuma 5). "All creatures," of course, means both men and women. In its response to the divine command, which is God's call to Israel to be purified, to become "a holy nation" (Ex. 19:6), the Jewish community is drawn into an intimate spiritual relationship with God as a covenantal faith community. By performing the commandments, each person in the community is able to relate to God and attain holiness (Lev. 19:1,2), that is, to develop a Jewish identity. So we see that the principle of religious equality is necessary for the establishment of community.

Despite these and other texts, a strong patriarchy has characterized Judaism for millenia. The Jewish community was one in which men decided on the religious criteria to sanctify the differences between them and women. Separation was not used merely to attain holiness, but also as a means of domination.

THE EXCLUSION OF WOMEN

What is the religious significance of the commandments from which women were exempt according to rabbinic law, and what were the reasons for this exclusion?

Analyzing the major commandments in this category, namely: prayer and the reading and study of Torah, it becomes clear that the common denominator is that these involve obligations between "man and God." By being exempted from such obligations, women were deprived of the ability to act religiously as independent agents. Furthermore, their exclusion from these areas not only deprived them of the means of religious expression and identification, it also deprived the community of the spiritual input of half of its population. Privately women could take some of these obligations upon themselves, but the religious merit of private acts was placed in doubt by the rabbis, the result of which was social discrimination, as religious and social life are inseparately linked in Jewish tradition.

It is interesting to note that in the Bible we find no specific rules defining principles of exemption or exclusion of women and men from certain obligations. However, as Rachel Biale (1984) has shown, the rabbinic principle of obligation distinguishes two categories of obligation. The first are commandments which apply only to men or only to women. The second are commandments which, while not directly related to biological differences, are gender-based. The first category includes circumcision and laws regarding menstruation. The second includes the prohibition of multiple sexual partners for women but not for men, the requirement of three yearly pilgrimages for men but not for women, and the laws of priesthood and inheritance, which apply to men only. Whereas some might argue with regard to the first category that scripture intended to sanctify the biological characteristics of both

men and women, without placing a negative value on women's menstruation, the second category shows clear evidence of discrimination. Here biological differences are translated into male domination, and the specific
commandments maintain this domination, under the guise of "separation."

In the *Mishnah* and the *Talmud,* the differential attitude towards women
becomes more specific: "All positive commandments which are time-bound
[to be carried out at a specific time of day—E.G.T.] are binding upon men
and women" (T.B. Kiddushin, 29a). The rabbis introduced a category of time
to distinguish between the sexes, a distinction that applies not only to positive commandments; negative obligations ("Thou shalt not") are binding upon
men and women alike. In the Talmud we find many discussions as to whether
women are indeed exempt from positive time-bound commandments and examples of many obligations in this category from which women are not exempt, such as the blessing over the wine on the Sabbath (T.B. Berakhot 20a)
and eating unleavened bread on Passover (T.B. Kiddushin 34a). Some of these
exceptions have a scriptural basis; some are the result of rabbinic ruling. From
these discussions it is clear that the principle of exemption is not a general
one; it allowed men to decide when to exempt women and when not.

Rabbinic sources do not offer specific reasons for enactment of the "time"
category. Various justifications are offered, ranging from practical considerations of women's domestic role in society, to the elevation of the exemption
to the spiritual realm: men have to "sanctify time" by performing additional
commandments at specific moments in time; the activities of women in the
home are, in themselves, an "act of sanctification." It is important to note,
however, that it was men and not women who decided on the exemption,
and many commentators, such as the medieval scholar David Ben Abudarham
(Sefer Abudarham, Part III), reveal that women's religious obligations were
often sacrificed to maintain a social reality in which women were subordinate
to their husbands, not God.

JEWISH IDENTITY AS FORMED BY
TRADITIONAL MODELS

To gain a deeper understanding of the religious significance of the commandments from which women were excluded, we will now take a closer
look at prayer and public reading and the study of Torah.

Prayer

The private nature of prayer in the Jewish tradition is guaranteed by its
silence (T.B. Berakhot 31a). Every individual must pray for him or herself,
and women are therefore obligated to pray as men. However, in discussing
the obligation of prayer, the rabbis put women in the same category as minors

and slaves, all three sharing a dependent role in the religious life of the community (T.B. Berakhot 20a-20b). Although the *Shulkhan Arukh,* a later code of Jewish traditional life, obligated women to say the *Shema* prayer (since it contains the central creed of Judaism, acceptance of the "kingdom of heaven") and later commentators all ruled that women were indeed obligated to pray, women's prayer remained a private matter. The paradigm of prayer is the biblical Hannah: "And Hannah talked (to God) of what was in her heart, only her lips moved and her voice was not heard" (I Sam. 1:13). While it might be argued that women perpetuate the biblical notion of prayer, whereas men pray only by rote, and that women were better able to develop their religiosity because the *halakha* exempted them from formal duties, it cannot be denied that the exclusion of women from these obligations put them in an inferior category.

It should also be borne in mind that women are excluded from the *minyan,* or formal prayer quorum, required for communal prayer. The root of the *minyan* idea is found in the Pentateuch, where the congregation is referred to as an *edah,* a "congregation of those who bear witness." Whereas in the Bible, women are clearly a part of the *edah,* rabbis later denied them this status when it came to prayer. Contemporary demands for equal rights for women in communal worship should therefore be seen as a desire on the part of religiously observant women for reinstatement as full members of the community.

The Public Reading and Study of Torah

Public Torah reading and study are central to religious Jewish life. The Bible required that the Torah be read publicly from Deut. 1-31 once in seven years to tell the history of the people of Israel and summarize the law (Deut. 31:12). In the time of Ezra (sixth century B.C.E.), weekly readings from which women were excluded were instituted. This resulted in rabbis not obligating women to hear the weekly reading of the Torah. It was said that a woman should not read from the Torah out of "respect for the congregation" (T.B. Megillah 23a). However, we have no explanation of why the congregation would be less respected if women were to participate in public reading of the Torah. Some sources hint at the danger of sexual distraction and others at the possible shame caused to illiterate male members of the congregation. However, it is intolerable that women should be prevented from becoming full members of the community in order to protect the morals or honor of some of the male members. What began as a *halakhic* ruling to accommodate men in a certain social context ended up as the exclusion of women and the designation of public ritual as the province of men: men put themselves between God and woman.

The same discrimination can be seen in the study of the Torah. Jewish tradition connects learning and praying; a confrontation with Jewish sources is equal to an encounter with God. Although women are required to know the laws that pertain to their lives, they are not obligated to study Torah for its own sake (T.B. Kiddushin 29b). Religious education was not entrusted to women; their virtue lay elsewhere: " 'What is the merit of the woman in the Torah?' Rav asked Rabbi Hiya. And the latter answered: 'Their merit is that they take their children to their places of study and that they receive their husbands when they come home' " (T.B. Berakhot 17a). Discussions in the Talmud (Sotah 20a) center around the educational merits of teaching one's daughter Torah, but later sources *(Shulkhan Arukh)* claim that women, because of their limited understanding, might misinterpret the Torah. A distinction was made between studying Oral Law (interpretation of scripture) and studying scripture itself. The latter was permitted, the former forbidden. In my opinion, women were prevented from studying the Oral Torah in order to keep them from challenging the interpretations and legal decisions of the rabbis. Despite this limitation, Talmudic sources indicate that there were, of course, women Torah scholars. Bruriah, the wife of Rabbi Meir, was said to be a scholar in her own right. Other instances of women scholars are cited in T.B. Tan'anit 23a, Eruvin 53b and Nedarim 50a. It is only recently that *halakhic* authorities in Israel and the Diaspora have begun to consider equal religious education for women and men, contending that barring women from Torah study is not tantamount to freeing them from an obligation but rather to denying them a basic Jewish right.

In summary, rabbinic interpretations created a community in which men ruled and women were inferior. No distinction was made between the sacred and the profane, and religious status was automatically translated into social status. In contemporary times, the intellectual development of many religious women in secular areas exceeds their development in religious ones, resulting in fragmented personalities and the mechanical performance of religious duties. The fact that women cannot develop their spiritual potential points, therefore, also to a wider issue, namely the attitudes of both women and men towards divinely ordained matters. The question is not the validity of Jewish law as the word of God meant to direct one's spiritual life in His service according to male criteria, but rather whether Jewish law contains rules and guidelines for a life of spiritual growth which are meant to enrich all areas of existence.

REFLECTIONS ON SPIRITUAL
AND SOCIAL CHANGE

The challenge for women and men today is to find ways that both can participate as equal partners in a community in which the symbols for identification — be they religious or secular — enhance, rather than oppose this goal. To do this we must ask ourselves whether men's domination over women is *halakhically* based as the will of God or whether it involves a male-power base developed over the years which has decreed a subservient role for women. In other words, religious integrity demands that we ask ourselves ethical questions to deal with the injustice done to women. I think we would be underestimating the importance of the issue if we were to view it as a matter of liberation or a demand for power on the part of religious women; we are talking about the genuine desire of women to deal with a crisis of identity and to find ways of becoming authentic partners in the preservation and building of Jewish life in all its ramifications.

It is to be hoped that men will begin to realize that the positions they hold are not religiously based, but rather unethically gender-based. It is also hoped that women will demand equality not from a *halakhic* perspective, as developed by men, but as a realization of the proper intention of God's commandments. No longer can we afford to hide behind the *halakha* to maintain the dominant position men, as men, hold over women. The lack of shared creativity is very costly to Jewish life.

Judaism is, however, not only a religion; we are also a nation. For Israeli Jews, Jewish identity develops between two severe constraints: affiliation with Jews as a nation and conformity to certain religious prescriptions. As a result, some forty years after the establishment of the state (the time it took for the Jewish people to reach spiritual maturity after the exodus from Egypt), we are witnessing the most severe confrontation between religious and non-religious Jews in its entire history. Religion, which more than any other institution provides symbols for ultimate meaning, is a main topic in the *Kulturkampf* over the Jewish nature of society, a touchstone of its test for survival.

The issue of women in religious life has now become a human rights issue. For many years secular Israelis have been silent partners in this struggle. Not only did they abandon their responsibility as part of the Jewish community in a traditional sense, they also released themselves from the obligation of serving as active agents of a vibrant Jewish heritage. A change is presently taking place. Many people are beginning to realize that religion is too important an issue to be left to the rabbis, that religion does not pertain merely to religious practice but to matters such as personhood, identity, spiritual development and, above all, the soul of the nation. The monopoly held by the rabbis over the spiritual life of Israelis is becoming more and more apparent. And as it has already been pointed out, in Israel, in contrast to the situation in the Diaspora, Jewish law pertains not only to religious but also to social life. There is no clear dividing line between the "sacred" and the "profane."

A coalition is therefore needed between religious and secular forces. One positive development in this direction is that in both Israel and the Diaspora, women from all Jewish denominations are increasingly engaged in the serious study of Jewish writings and are bringing their experiences to bear on the text: an Oral Law of women is being created. Thus, while challenging the opinions of the rabbis, women remain rooted in tradition and are drawing upon its spirit. It is not enough for women to rediscover customs expressive of their religious feelings, such as *Rosh Hodesh* (New Moon) celebrations, to establish feminist prayer groups and synagogues, and to organize conferences. Jewish scholarship involves the obligation to make legal decisions for the entire community, and women must take responsibility and participate equally in this decision-making process. I would like to see secular women, too, seriously addressing the issue of Jewish tradition as a source for their identity.

For the sake of the Jewish people as a whole, women must assume spiritual roles. The paradigm of women leading in the redemptive process is found in the Talmud: "Because of the righteous women of that generation were the Jewish people taken out of Egypt" (T.B. Sotah 11b). It was women who made the exodus from Egypt, the spiritual birth of the Jewish people, possible; then, as now, they were responsible not only for their own liberation, but also for that of their people.

The basis of change is the realization that women are not asking for women's rights alone, but are deeply concerned with issues pertaining to society as a whole. Men have traditionally spoken for themselves and for women. The time has come for women to take responsibility for themselves and for men. In Judaism, the spiritual emergence of women and their search for identity is necessary if Jewish tradition is to have true relevance for future generations.

REFERENCES

Adler, Rachel (1973) "The Jew Who Wasn't There: Halakhah and the Jewish Woman." *Response*, 18.

Berkovitz, Eliezer (1976). *Crisis and Faith*. New York: Hebrew Publishing Company.

Berman, Saul (1973). "The Status of Women in Halakhic Judaism." *Tradition* 14: 2.

Biale, Rachel (1984). *Women and Jewish Law*. New York: Schocken.

Cohen, Naomi (1980). "The Education of the Girl and the Woman." In *The Education of the Girl*. Tel Aviv: Ha-Kibbutz HaDati (Hebrew).

Cohen Naomi (1988). "Women and the Study of Talmud." *Tradition* 24: 1.

Eilinson, Elyakim G. (1974, 1984). *The Woman and the Commandments*. Jerusalem: The World Zionist Organization (Hebrew).

Greenberg, Blu (1981). *On Women and Judaism: A View From Tradition*. Philadelphia: Jewish Publication Society.

Hauptman, Judith (1974). "Images of Women in the Talmud." In Radford Reuther, R. (ed.). *Religion and Sexism*. New York: Simon & Schuster.

Meiselman, Moshe (1978). *Jewish Woman in Jewish Law*. New York: Ktav Publishing House and Yeshiva University Press.

Plaskow, Judith (1973). "The Jewish Feminist: Conflict in Identities." *Response*, 18, Summer.

Plaskow, Judith (1987). "Halakhah as a Feminist Issue." *The Melton Journal*, Fall.

Plaskow, Judith (1990). *Standing Again at Sinai: Judaism From a Feminist Perspective*. San Francisco: Harper & Row.

Rappel, Dov (ed.) (1989). *The Jewish Woman in Education, the Family and Society*. Jerusalem: Dov Rappel (Hebrew).

Rosenfeld, Ben-Zion (ed.) (1980). *The Woman and Her Education*. Kfar Saba: Amana Publishers, Ulpana B'nei Akiva (Hebrew).

Section Two
Family Comes First

Religion, Tradition
and Public Policy Give
Family First Priority

Marilyn P. Safir

While Israelis characterize their country as a developed, westernized democracy that happens to be located in the Middle East, historical patriarchical influences have produced a traditional family-oriented society in which family stability is the rule in all sectors of society. Judaism has always regarded the home as the repository of Jewish tradition and values. In fact many religious holidays are considered family occasions and cannot be properly celebrated without family: Rosh Hashanah (Jewish New Year), Succouth, Chanukah, Purim, Passover and of course, the Sabbath (Friday evening). Each of these celebrations involve traditional meals and customs that demand a family context. Being with the family is so important that the Army makes every effort to release soldiers so that they will be able to spend Sabbath and holidays in the bosom of their families and there is a special army unit which tries to find "foster" families for immigrant recruits so that the young soldiers will not be alone over the holidays. Organizations of former immigrants offer the same services for singles and new immigrant families that may not have established social connections. The concept of the Jewish people as a family is readily demonstrated by this concern, which results in attempts to supply a family context for those who find themselves without one. Therefore, it was not surprising that centrality of the family is important even for teenagers — Shahar (1977) found that Jewish 18 year olds rated founding a family as the most important reason for marriage. Moreover, it is not unusual for older people whose children are grown and who are without a partner to make every effort to travel abroad for holidays such as Passover, if they have the financial means, to avoid the discomfort of being alone in Israel at this time of year.

Within the context of this background, it is not surprising that family stability is the rule, and that marriage and divorce rates are more similar to those of agrarian than to those of western society. While one scholar (Davis, 1983) has argued that family patterns in Israel are becoming more western: fewer marriages, an increasing divorce rate, and a trend in the direction of zero population growth, others (Peres and Katz, 1984) who analyzed demographic data (marriage, divorce and birth rates) over a 36 year period found that Israelis were not marrying less, but only later. They found no evidence that the proportion of never married was increasing. Moreover, they found that the divorce rate in Israel was consistently 20-25 percent that of the American rate. The same authors attribute the decrease in fertility since the early 1950s to the increase of age at first marriage, effective birth control and increasing levels of women's education. Only 5 percent of households in Israel are headed by one parent, 85 percent of them by the mother, who is either widowed or divorced. Only 2 percent of women and 4 percent of men have not married by the age of 40 (Katz and Peres, 1986). In contrast with the United States, where 20 percent of all births are out of wedlock, only 1.2 percent of all women who give birth in Israel are unmarried (Central Bureau of Statistics [C.B.S.] 1988).

The median age for first marriage for Jews is 22.8 for women and 25.9 for men; for Moslems, 20 for women and 23.9 for men; for Christians, 22.4 for women and 27.4 for men; for Druze, 18.8 for women and 23.4 for men. One out of 6 Jewish marriages, 1 out of 10 Druze marriages, and 1 out of 11 Moslem marriages end in divorce. Most Israeli Christians are Catholic and divorce is rare in this community (C.B.S. 1988).

For both Jews and Arabs, marriage is extremely important, but not enough. A childless marriage is not considered a family, and the couple are pitied. Fertility is a major concern of Israeli society. There are periodic news items in all the media of new breakthroughs in fertility treatments. A clinical psychologist who does group therapy with infertile couples stated on a popular TV program (August 21, 1989) that she estimated that over 10 percent of all Israeli couples have fertility problems, but that there is a general tabu about discussing this problem openly—fear that this may result in social stigma. She reported that such couples experience stress and guilt, and anger toward each other, their fertile friends ("are we inferior?" "what's wrong with us?") and both their families ("we are depriving them of their grandchildren"). She also reported that it was not unusual for couples to receive medical treatment for infertility for as long as 10 to 15 years. Adoption is not a real option, because very few children are available for adoption; many couples opt to adopt a child from abroad. For those groups for whom continuing the family name (blood line) is very important, adoption is not a solution. Jewish and Moslem Law both make provisions for the husband to take a second wife if his first wife is "barren," (i.e., cannot produce sons).

The total fertility rate (the average number of children a woman may bear in her lifetime) is 2.8 for Jewish families (Ashkenazis, 2.7; Israeli born, 2.8; Orientals, 3.1; 4 for kibbutz families and 6+ for extremely Orthodox families). The fertility rate for Christians is 2.6; for Druze 4.2; and for Moslems 4.6 (C.B.S. 1988).

The "demographic problem" is a public issue predating Israel's Declaration of Independence. High birth rates were seen as a means of perpetuating the Jewish people. In the 1950s, Prime Minister Ben Gurion established prizes for families with ten children or more. Articles about mothers with 12 to 14 children appeared in the media, especially around Mother's Day, which is a legal work holiday for women with children. For such an article to appear today, a woman would not only have to have many children, but be a high level professional (superwoman) as well. Birth control information has not been readily available until recent years. While modern Orthodox rabbis may permit women to employ family planning techniques, birth control is often interpreted as being contrary to Jewish law. The ultra-Orthodox do not use birth control. All women receive a special birth allowance from the National Insurance Institute, which also pays families a monthly children's allowance according to the number of children in the family, regardless of the family's income. There are special discounts for large families (defined as those with four or more children) for public child care and for summer camps, as well as municipal taxes. A national organization and political lobby exists (Zehavi) which lobbies to protect the rights and interests of large families. Zehavi has 49 chapters around the country, with a membership of 30,000 families. Housing policies are also family oriented. Long term apartment rental is practically nonexistent in Israel. Government loans and mortgages are available for families and young marrieds, who must present a wedding certificate in order to be eligible. There is very little available to singles, who must be over the age of 36 to qualify for certain government sponsored mortgages. Government policy also considers the family as a unit for taxation purposes, and the husband is considered head of household, even when the wife is the major breadwinner. This also holds true for membership in sick funds and census taking.

Most Israelis own their apartments; thus the family moves from place to place very infrequently. Even during periods of unemployment, relocating the family to another city for the sake of work is not seen as a relevant option by the majority of families. It is not unusual for a promotion to be refused if it means relocating the family. Moving from city to city is seen as a major upheaval and disruptive of extended family relationships.

Child welfare is of major concern to Israeli society. There are over 900 well-baby clinics in almost every neighborhood that provide free pre- and post-natal care for mothers, routine weigh-ins, and physical and developmental check-ups for infants. Children continue to receive vaccinations at these clinics until they begin school. In all sectors of Israeli society, social life revolves around the children. Although both the nuclear and the extended family are very child oriented, child care has been and continues to be primarily the mother's responsibility. In fact, even though early labor laws were based on the socialist idea that all women should work, the assumption was that women would work part-time. This stemmed from the fact that women were perceived as the natural caretakers of both children and the household. Far-ranging legislation was passed to protect women in their multiple roles as workers, wives and mothers: employers were prevented from firing pregnant women; nursing mothers were enabled to work an hour less without pay deductions and to take days off to care for sick children without being docked; women were granted mandatory maternity leave for three months and an additional nine months leave without pay. Most important, women who worked at least half time, were guaranteed tenure. This represented very advanced legislation for its time. However, in the 1970s these protective labor laws began to be perceived as discriminatory because they legislated the mother's responsibility for childcare. In 1988, women from across the entire political spectrum banded together for the first time to fight to change these laws in order to enable either parent, at the couple's discretion, to take responsibility for child care.

Orthodox Judaism delegates activity in the public sphere to males only. The Orthodox family is not complete until a male child is born (only a male can pray to honor his departed parents). All male infants are circumcised a week after they are born, and a large party is held in honor of the child and his parents, often catered in a hired hall, as hundreds of guests may be invited. This party takes place in secular families as well as in religious ones. A Bar Mitzvah ceremony takes place when the boy is 13, to symbolize his coming of age. The majority of secular boys, along with their Orthodox peers, prepare for months for this religious ceremony. An elaborate party is held, often with a seven-course meal, at which the boy is expected to give a speech. A typical joke about these parties is that the only thing missing is the bride. There are no equivalent religious ceremonies for girls. Contemporary families do tend to celebrate a girl's 12th birthday with a party for her friends and family, but without the fanfare described above.

The Moslem religion also requires male circumcision. This ceremony used to occur when the boy was between 7 and 13 years of age and included a large celebration, particularly for the first son or the first son born after several daughters. Today, however, circumcision takes place during infancy and without a party. For both Christians and Moslems, producing a son is crucial for continuation of the family name. Even a highly educated couple who are interested in having no more than two children feel both internal and external pressure to keep trying for a son if both children are girls. The more sons, the more power and status for the family. Sons are expected to contribute to the family income and to care for aged parents. A daughter resides with her birth family only temporarily; when she marries, she joins her husband's family. Parents are referred to by the name of the first male child, Abu (father of) Hasan or Em (mother of) Hallid. A man who only produces daughters is jokingly called Abu Banat (daughters). Oriental Jews share this tradition; the topic was the subject of a popular film (in the '70s) occasionally shown on television. However, the desirability of social and sexual equality counter these influences on a conscious level; Navah Butler-Por (1983) found that parents do not admit a preference for either sex on questionnaires, but reveal a preference for boys over girls in indepth interviews. This preference cuts across social classes, urban and rural residence, and ethnic origin (Ashkenazi and Oriental, as well as Arab and Jew).

Daycare centers exist for Jewish working mothers, subsidized mostly by the Labor Ministry and run by various women's organizations. An infant can be registered at 6 months of age and can continue in daycare until first grade. The centers are open from 7:30 a.m. to 4:00 p.m. and are viewed very positively as a childcare solution for working women. There are not enough places available to meet the demand; according to one estimate (Prime Minister's Office 1988), there is a need for a 25 percent increase. Still, preschool facilities are more readily available in Israel than in most other countries. Prekindergarten classes are held between 8 a.m. and 12 p.m. Sixty-seven percent of Jewish children begin these classes at age 2. By age 3, 92 percent and by age 4, 99 percent of all Jewish children are enrolled in kindergartens. Among Moslems, Christians and Druze, the attendance rate is about 20 percent for 3 year olds, about 40 percent for 4 year olds, and 95 percent for 5 year olds (C.B.S. 1988). These figures would probably be higher if more facilities were available.

While the socialist ideal is productive labor outside the home, the prevailing notion in Israeli society is part time work for women. If this were not so, the school day for elementary school children as well as the preschool framework, would be longer than the present 4 hours. Not only that, there are frequent school holidays in Israel, during which the children are out of school for extensive periods of time. For example, the Passover holiday is 10 days long. The children are released a week before Passover, so that the teachers (mothers) will have enough time to prepare their homes for the holiday. This creates problems for mothers who work outside of the educational system. Often when a teacher is ill, children are sent home from school since their mothers are expected to be on call. Working women have to find private, often expensive solutions if no one in the extended family can be enlisted to help out.

Dating in urban Jewish society usually begins during early adolescence within peer social groups such as Scouts or neighborhood schools, and the "date" occurs within the group. Neighborhood social groups are stable, as most Israelis move house infrequently. Children tend to remain in the same homeroom class from first through at least sixth grade, and they socialize after school. Casual dating is unusual, and when a couple forms they usually continue to date for a minimum of several months. A steady dating partner spends a lot of time with and feels at home at the partner's family. A girl who dates a boy once or twice and then dates a new boy and switches again is viewed negatively, even if there has been no sexual relationship. While this pattern is changing under the influence of American movies and TV programs, it is still not uncommon to discover couples who formed a relationship at age 14 and later married. Girls often initiate these early relationships. For Jews, the Army is an inadvertent matchmaker, bringing together young people who might not have otherwise met socially. Most Jewish marriages take place upon completion of army service.

The dating pattern for the religious Jewish girl may be similar to that described above, as there is a special Scout movement for religious children. However, she would be less likely to date a boy who was not a potential marriage partner. In the Orthodox community, peer groups develop around religious activities because boys leave the public religious school system at age 13 to study in all-male Yeshivas. The ultra-Orthodox community is concerned with the "purity" of its young women, and prior to the passage of a law stipulating the minimum age for marriage (17), it encouraged marriage at an earlier age. Dating in this community is not acceptable. A professional matchmaker may be employed, or the rabbi may make a "match," although the young woman has veto power. In a study of ultra-Orthodox residents of Mea She'arim, Simon (1978) discovered that 89 percent of women who were not already engaged, expected that their marriage would be arranged. It is not unusual in this community for parents to petition the courts to enable them to marry off their daughters at age 16. If a secular woman has no fiancee by her mid to late twenties, her family and friends also try their hand at matchmaking. Their anxiety about the chances of marriage may be related to the fact that 80 percent of women marry before age 29, or to the commonly held belief that there are far fewer eligible men than women as a result of casualties in Israel's constant wars. However, arranged marriages occur only within the most traditional "born again" or ultra-Orthodox Jews and, to a lesser extent, traditional Arab clans from the smaller villages.

In Arab society dating is less "public" than it is in Jewish communities. Modernization and westernization of the Arab family and the status of women is highest in mixed cities, followed by all-Arab towns and rural villages, due to relative anonymity, educational opportunities and the weakening of traditional social controls (Abu-Baker, 1985). It should be recognized that in the Arab communities in Israel there is a continuum, from a pattern that is very similar to that described above, to the following: teenagers meet either in coeducational schools (which they attend) in their neighborhoods, or at work. They date in the context of their social group, but their parents remain unaware of this until the attachment becomes serious. The young man then approaches the father of the young woman to ask for her hand in marriage. This is usually a formality, but if the father vetoes and family and friends cannot convince him to change his mind, his daughter will end the relationship. It has been suggested (Katz and Peres, 1986) that the military administration of

Arab settlements through 1965, actually strengthened the *hamula* (clan) and the authority of the head of the clan regarding marriage and family affairs. In rural communities, tradition and religious influence have effects similar to those in Jewish ultra-Orthodox communities. The bride's purity is an important issue, and the family is interested in their daughter's marriage at the earliest age permissible as the best possible safeguard.

The centrality of marriage in Israeli society can be gauged by the large number of professional matchmakers in the Jewish religious community, the large numbers of marriage bureaus, the endless advertisements in the personal columns in all national and local newspapers and the extensive efforts made by the kibbutzim to find spouses for their members.

In all sectors of Israeli society, a thriving industry has developed around the marriage ceremony—from beauty parlors that rent the bride her dress, do facials, apply makeup and fix her hair, to huge public and private halls that cater the wedding, to which from 300 to 1500 guests may be invited. Arab weddings often involve several large parties, the first to celebrate the engagement, a remnant of the tradition of the husband purchasing his wife from her father. Today the bride price is purely symbolic, and the young man buys his future bride gold jewelry and other presents which may be presented at a formal party. The bride's family may hold a large celebration several days before the wedding: traditionally, the purpose of this party was for the bride to formally part from her female relatives and friends; today it is an affair for the bride's family and friends as well as for the groom and his family. In addition, the groom's family has a party to welcome the bride into her new family at the time of the wedding ceremony. At a rural wedding celebration, the whole community is often invited. Traditionally, the bride would join the groom in his family home; today, young couples often establish a separate household.

Israeli families are also consumers of goods and services. While various appliances have eased domestic burdens like cooking, cleaning and washing, women are still responsible for a growing number of tasks which link the family to services outside the home. These include shopping for food and a plethora of other consumer goods which previously were not available in Israel, as well as shopping for services such as education, health, and recreation; deliveries of all sorts, including transporting or accompanying children to doctors, private teachers and hobby groups; taking in cars and appliances for repairs, paying bills, and being present at occasions such as school parties and school trips. Moreover, mother is expected to prepare and serve the major meal of the day, in accordance with the schedule of the children and spouse, who return home between 1 and 4 p.m., when banks and small businesses close. They also include a host of other tasks which have come to be known in Israel as "sidurim" (arrangements). Even tasks traditionally identified as masculine, such as banking, car repair and guarding the school ground are increasingly performed by women. Despite the fact that the majority of young women now work outside the home, most social arrangements are organized on the assumption that women are still full-time homemakers.

While women may not perform all boundary spanning tasks themselves, they bear responsibility for these tasks. When they can be performed outside "normal" working hours, husbands are more likely to share in the activity. For example, where stores remain open evenings and teachers invite parents to events scheduled late in the day, men are more likely to participate than otherwise. Even when husbands play an active role in domestic tasks, however, they are rarely full partners in managing the home. The situation is sustained by sex socialization. The man is presently being encouraged "to give her a hand," that is, to share the work but not to share the responsibility. The difference is significant. Responsibility requires psychological involvement even if one is not doing the work. It engages the person in planning, supervising, and finding alternative solutions when plans fall through.

When children enter army service, the result is more often an intensification of mothering rather than an "empty nest." Family life revolves around children who are in basic training. Social plans are not made until parents know whether their child will be home for the Sabbath. When the soldier does come home, he or she brings all the laundry which must be washed and ironed between Friday afternoon and early Sunday morning. Parents are expected to "spoil" the soldier, and all of her or his special foods and cakes are prepared. These preparations are most elaborate for sons who are in prestige and combat units. The Army encourages parents to visit soldiers at their boot camps (bringing food and goodies) when they are not released for the Sabbath, often arranging transportation for families without cars.

Caring for elderly and chronically ill parents is another area of family work which falls fundamentally within the woman's domain (Cibulski, 1981). The woman not only cares for her own parents, in all sectors of Israeli society, she also cares for her husband's parents. With the aging of the population, with health care policy geared to reducing hospital budgets, and with services for the elderly as inadequate as they are, women's work for the family continues to expand. When the grandmothers are healthy, they often serve as babysitters for their grandchildren. Thus, it is not unusual to find a professional woman who has reached the peak of her career, balancing her job and her own home responsibilities, making time to care for her parent and arranging to take care of her daughter's children. For better or for worse, the Israeli woman's work for the family is never done.

REFERENCES

Abu-Baker, Khawla (1985) "The Impact of Cross-Cultural Contact on the Status of Arab Women in Israel." In Safir, M., Mednick, M., Izraeli, D. and Bernard, J. (eds.). *Women's Worlds: From the New Scholarship.* New York: Praeger Publishers.

Butler-Por, Navah (1983) "Giftedness Across Cultures: A Study of Educational Values." In Shore, B., Gagne, S., Tarievee, T. R. and Tumbey, R. (eds.). *Face to Face with Giftedness*. New York: Nillian Books.

Central Bureau of Statistics (C.B.S.)(1988) *Statistical Abstracts*. Jerusalem.

Cibulski, Ora (1981) *Social Support Networks of the Elderly*. Unpublished Doctoral Dissertation, Ramat Aviv: University of Tel Aviv.

Davis, Leo (1983). "What's Happening in the Israeli Family: Recent Demographic Trends. *Israel Social Science Research* 1(1):34–41.

Katz, Ruth and Peres, Yohanan (1986) "The Sociology of the Family in Israel: An Outline of its Development from the 1950s to the 1980s." *European Sociological Review* 2:148–159.

Peres, Yohanan and Katz, Ruth (1984) "Is the Israeli Family Losing its Character? A Reply to Leo Davids." *Israel Social Science Research* 2(1):138–143.

Shahar, Rina (1977) Sex Role Expectations among Israeli Youth. Unpublished Masters Thesis, Tel Aviv University (Hebrew).

Simon, Rita James (1978) *Community and Change: A Study of Two Ethnic Communities in Israel*. Cambridge: Cambridge University Press.

Growing Up Female
and Palestinian in Israel

Manar Hassan
(Translated by Sharon Ne'eman)

Even before she first sees the light of day, the female Palestinian infant is enveloped in a dense network of webs, whose purpose is to reproduce the patriarchal social system. This network will be woven and expanded into a tangle of bonds and chains, which will condition and shape her spirit, supervise her education and rearing, and transform her into one of the mainstays of the patriarchy.

Each birth is anxiously awaited by the parents. The women in the family pray for the birth of a male offspring. The mother-to-be receives best wishes for the birth of a son, wishes which contain an implicit condemnation of the other, *unwanted* possibility, the birth of a daughter. The father's "sensitivity" increases as the date of birth draws near. Will his wife bless him with a son, thus improving his status and even changing his name to reflect his paternity; or will she disappoint him with a daughter, detracting from his worth as a man and leaving him with his childhood name?

During the Jahilah, or pre-Islamic period, there were tribes that buried their newborn daughters alive. While Islam forbade this custom, it did not, however, change the basic value of women. It did not proscribe the physical or mental castration of women, nor did it modify their status as inferior beings who, under certain circumstances, could even be murdered in defense of that monster known as "family honor." From the moment of her birth, the patriarchal society, through the agent of the nuclear and extended family, operates a system of conditioning designed to transform the child into the epitome of possible female development—a wife—that is, a handmaid and receptacle for male lusts and desire—and a mother.

The success of a Palestinian girl is determined by her ability to measure up to the social expectations transmitted to her through the family. The faster she succeeds in renouncing her own needs as a child, detaching herself from them, and internalizing as many stereotyped female characteristics as possible, the more favorably she will be looked upon by her environment, including the deity, her father. Strive as she may, however, she will never receive the appreciation displayed toward a son. Even after reaching physical maturity,

66

she will forever remain a second-class human being; any man, even her retarded younger brother, *is superior to her by virtue of his masculinity alone.* The Arabic term which best defines the status of the Palestinian woman is "qasar," meaning "handicapped" or "minor," that is, irresponsible, undeveloped, immature, irrespective of her age, education, or social status.

From childhood, I remember a girl who was always held up to us as an example of a "good" girl. She was a relative who, from the age of three, utterly renounced her own needs as a child and assumed the role of a highly valued assistant servant within the female ranks of her family. The family spoke admiringly of her enthusiastic participation in women's housework: hanging laundry, washing dishes, and performing spontaneous services for male relatives. The greatest token of their appreciation was a gift presented her at the age of three: a wooden bench placed beside the kitchen sink, to make it easier for the devoted little girl to wash the dishes. In our village, this girl served as a positive role model to which every other girl of roughly the same age was compared. The purpose was to instill a feeling of constant guilt in those girls who did not, could not, or would not attain such a "high" standard of "proper" behavior. Many of the scoldings, punishments, beatings, and humiliations I received as a child were accompanied by unfavorable comparisons to the shining example of that girl.

However, service to men, performance of female tasks, and *formal* acceptance of female values are not enough. The girl must provide her family with a guarantee of her intentions—a "loyalty oath," as it were, which promises good behavior and provides continuous proof of proper conduct—including not only what she actually does, but also what she feels about her actions. She must fulfill her obligations while completely internalizing the expectations of society, and *must feel within herself* that these are indeed the rules of suitable behavior. In other words, it is not enough for her to be a handmaid; she must view this role *as if it were her greatest wish and desire.* She must love these functions in the "I-love-my-Master" manner of a lowly slave, who considers her slavery the epitome of human existence. Failure to comply with these terms leads to severe punishment—not only for actions, but also for incomplete acceptance or latent criticism. Incomplete internalization of female traits is viewed as incipient rebellion, as a threat to the very foundations of the patriarchal family. Such phenomena are duly punished, with Islamic religion and tradition—which justify the "natural" inferiority of the woman and her possibility of becoming no more than a successful servant to a man—providing criteria for compliance with expectations and constituting a constant, omnipresent system of evaluation. This reality is in stark contradiction to all humanistic principles of individual freedom, and the right of a human being to develop her own talents and capabilities.

The division of characteristics into "masculine" and "feminine," observed in many societies, is even stronger and more rigid among Palestinian society.

While curiosity is admired in boys, in girls it is considered in bad taste and evidence of preoccupation with trivialities. Initiative, a welcome trait in boys, is viewed as shameless boldness in girls and punished accordingly. The desire to leave home in order to study is rewarded in boys with sympathy, admiration, and even financial support; in girls, on the other hand, it is seen as laziness, shirking of responsibility, and parasitism. Girls who try to imitate boys, even at a very early age, are punished and censured in a thousand ways—as brash, foolish, lazy and even dishonorable creatures whose low morals bring shame to their families.

These contradictions become even more pronounced in adolescence. Teenage Palestinian women receive no sex education whatsoever—not from the family, the community, nor the school system. An adolescent trained to the role of wife and mother awaits her womanhood eagerly, assuming that her maturity will finally satisfy her patriarchal environment and compensate her for her oppressed childhood. She is swept into the emotional whirlpool characteristic of adolescence, but the joy she feels in the physical changes in her body and in the intensification of her emotions, is shocking to her family. Condemning glances become even sterner. Every bodily change imbues her with feelings of guilt and sin much stronger than those that accompanied her childhood. The adolescent soon realizes that she is constantly on trial, that the judges are not only her family but the whole society, and that she is doomed to *the solitary confinement of her feelings*. Thus, along with the loss of her rights as a child (games, fun, and even laughter) she is branded as a criminal, a danger to family and society: a walking explosive charge whose every movement is observed and criticized or even condemned. In order to survive in this suffocating environment, the adolescent begins to censor herself: Not only her feelings, but her movements, her bearing, and her outward glance; she becomes a marionette, hanging from the strings of censure and oppression.

The attitude toward menstruation illustrates this process. Palestinian girls receive no sex education, due to the belief that ignorance and innocence are synonymous. Thus, the menarche appears as a bolt from the sky or as a mysterious illness. When the women of her family discover her state, the feeling of illness is exacerbated by a sense of guilt and sin. The subject is discussed in whispers, far from the ears of men. The teenager is given no scientific explanation of the physiological phenomenon; yet the menses themselves become a monthly proof of her sinful state.

The instructions received by the young woman are practical and explicit, but do not include any comprehensive explanation capable of reassuring her or increasing her understanding. On the contrary: these instructions carry additional concealed messages. The menstrual flow is to be absorbed with cotton wool—which, of course, must be hidden before use and burnt clandestinely afterwards. Even used toilet paper, which may be thrown into the bathroom wastebasket, as is the practice in many Palestinian households, has a lower negative impact. Thus a completely normal physical process becomes a focus of guilt and conveys a feeling of perpetual pollution.

As stated above, the "instruction" of the adolescent female takes place in whispers and in secret. This, at first glance, might create the impression that the women of the family constitute a protective and supportive phalanx within the mechanism of patriarchal oppression. However, this is not the case: the mother, as a trained agent of the patriarchal system, must report to the father that his daughter has become a walking time bomb, liable to sully the so-called "family honor." Thus, while exerting pressure on her daughter to conceal any fact related to her development, she herself, of course, reports to the Supreme Commander. This becomes immediately apparent: supervision is increased, and the father's disapproving and fearful glances make it clear that the terrible sin is known to him. The feeling of guilt becomes a permanent element in the life of the adolescent female.

The most important training undergone by the Palestinian woman during adolescence is preparation for her intended role as merchandise to be sold on the marriage market. She prepares her dowry, perfects her knowledge of handiwork in embroidery, sewing, and knitting circles which abound in nearly all Arab towns and villages. The patriarchal family views its females as goods which must be preserved so that they can be offered for sale in the best possible state; accordingly, there is no need for serious investment in their education. In high school, the number of young women enrolled is far smaller than that of young men; the disproportion increases in institutions of higher learning. One-third of Palestinian college students (within the Green Line) are females, and only one-fifth of Palestinian college graduates are females. If one considers schooling in terms of the investment required from family resources, one finds that, as the need for investment increases, the number of Palestinian women students declines. Thus, for example, the number of Palestinian women doctors educated within the state of Israel can be counted on the fingers of one hand, due to the large investment required. It should also be noted that the higher a woman's level of education and personal independence, the lower her value on the marriage market. Even educated Arab men prefer to marry wives whose level of education is less than, not equal to, their own. The main reason for reluctance to invest in daughters' education is rooted in the tradition according to which sons bring their wives into the family, whereas daughters abandon their family for another; in other words, any investment in a daughter will benefit not the investor, but the family of his son-in-law.

The status of Palestinian women within the state of Israel is basically no different from that of Arab women in other countries. Despite the avowedly democratic nature of Israel, Israeli Palestinian women rarely marry out of free choice. Even more rare is intermarriage between members of different Arabic-

speaking communities, Druze, Christians, and Moslems, despite their belonging to a single nation. This does not derive solely from the "divide-and-conquer"
policy of the Israeli authorities, but also from the structure of the Palestinian
family. The privileges accorded to Israeli Jewish women are not granted to
Palestinians. First of all, the family of the Palestinian woman decides whom
she will marry. For example, it is common to find exchange marriages, in
which a family gives its daughter in marriage to the son of another family,
so that the son of the first family may marry the bride he has chosen, or in
order to rid itself of the burden of an older, unmarried daughter. Second, marriage and divorce are entirely in the hands of the *qadi,* or religious judge and
registrar of marriages; the Israeli Palestinian women cannot appeal to the district court, as can her Jewish sister.

One of the claims frequently made concerning the status of Palestinian
women within the Green Line is that it is much higher than that of her sisters
in the Arab countries, due to the fact of her residence in a democratic country. This claim has no basis in reality.

The special status of the Palestinian population within the Green Line, that
is, its subjection to national, political, social, and cultural oppression, led to
the development of defense mechanisms based on a return to patriarchal tradition and the zealous preservation of the values implied by that tradition.
Enlightenment and its attendant humanistic values are forced to recede before the threshold of the patriarchy. The *hamula* (extended family) and its
values become sacrosanct as a distorted response to the cultural oppression
of the Israeli regime. The primary victim is the Palestinian woman, the last
remaining property of the dispossessed Palestinian male. It is a common er-
ror to view the national and cultural repression on the part of the Israeli government as a foreign or alien force exerting equal pressure on all components
of Palestinian society. Not all classes and sectors of the oppressed people suffer
equally, nor do they share an equal interest in liberation. The traditional leadership and the upwardly mobile have some interest in freeing themselves from
discrimination and oppression. But the lower classes of laborers and peasants
suffer far more, as they are also exploited within the Palestinian social framework itself. At the bottom are the women, especially the women of the lower
classes, since some of their oppression is a result of the patriarchal framework itself. This means that for women, national and social liberation are
closely interrelated.

The *hamula* and its values are viewed favorably and encouraged by the
Israeli authorities. Covert cooperation obtains between the traditional Palestinian leadership and the state of Israel, which may be seen in the attitude
toward such phenomena as the murder of women "in defense of family honor,"
on one hand, and the attitude toward Palestinian women political prisoners
from the occupied territories, on the other.

The Palestinian tradition of "family honor" means that the honor of the Palestinian man resides within the body of his wife, daughter, or sister. Wherever the woman goes, the man's honor goes with her; if anything happens to her, it is deemed not to have affected her personally, as she is no more than a receptacle for the honor of her family. This is especially striking in cases of rape. In every rape of a Palestinian woman, the responsibility devolves on her. By "responsibility," I mean that it is she who will eventually suffer all the consequences of the dreadful crime committed on her person. I became personally acquainted with the cast, as it were, of one such drama which took place in an Arab village in the Galilee. A "respectable" married man raped a young woman in her twenties from a family considered less respectable than his own. The woman's family tried to pressure the man into marrying her. He refused, but, fearing revenge, approached an official of the Israeli administration and confessed to him, promising that, if no charges were pressed against him, he would serve as a collaborator for Israeli authorities. The man was given a gun, which he carried openly and proudly; the entire village was aware that he was under the protection of the government. The young woman was fortunately not murdered, as a 75-year-old man from a remote village agreed to marry her; a short time later, she became a widow. This incident illustrates the relationship between the Israeli authorities, the Palestinian notables, and the traditional leadership in general, and the deals concluded among those parties at the expense of the Palestinian woman.

In a symposium on "family honor" murders held in Beer Sheba in 1983, the Israel Government Advisor for Arab Affairs, Nissim Kazaz, proposed that a rape victim be married to the rapist. None of the participants appeared shocked, and no negative reactions were expressed. This phenomenon is familiar in Palestinian society; it often happens that the rape survivor's father begs the rapist to marry his daughter; otherwise, the father will be forced to kill her. Middle Eastern Studies expert Gideon Karsel, who investigated the phenomenon of murder "in defense of family honor," stated that between 20 and 40 corpses of women are discovered each year, of which only a small fraction are reported as those of murder victims.

The cooperation between the government and the patriarchal leadership is strikingly reflected in the behavior of the police toward young Palestinian women who run away from home. The police generally return them to their families or villages, in exchange for an empty promise by the father or other notable that the young woman will be "looked after," yet all the parties involved are aware that blood may be spilled. Indeed, in many such cases, before twenty-four hours have elapsed, the young woman's body is found in a well or distant field. The police classify these murders as suicides or accidents, despite the fact that they have evidence that the deceased was in real danger in her own home. Murderers "in defense of family honor" have developed a wide range of methods for ensuring an alibi, and the police are content to simply accept these and close the case. Journalist Matti Regev stated that "I know of several cases in which the police delivered the victim into the hands of the murderers" (*Monitin* 1988). The courts are also "considerate" toward thes*e* murderers, exhibiting a patronizing sort of "understanding." The prison system shows them an especially lenient attitude; some are pardoned or have their sentences reduced.

The return of a persecuted young woman to her family via a *qadi, sheikh,* or other notable not only reflects the cynicism of the law-enforcement apparatus which uses the victim as a commodity in order to improve its own relations with the notables and the traditional leadership. Essentially, it amounts to recognition on the part of the Israeli authorities of the right of patriarchal tradition to determine the punishment to be meted to rebellious daughters. In other words, the state, which is responsible for the security and welfare of all its citizens, is prepared to renounce its sovereignty in this sector in order to reinforce the traditional leadership, at a very low cost: the body of one more Palestinian female.

Family-honor killings are generally viewed by the Israel public and press in a "folkloristic" manner, which actually belies a deep-rooted racism. This approach enables Israelis to look down on Palestinian society as "primitive," and to draw implications for Palestinian national ambitions and the struggle against oppression. Even the leftist parties are not beyond reproach in this respect. The Progressive Peace List, for example, expunged all reference to women's liberation from its Arabic language platform; Uzi Borenstein, spokesman of the New Communist list, explicitly referred to the phenomenon of murder for family honor as folklore, comparing it to the kidnapping of wives by Georgian Jews. Most of the Israeli Left hesitate to deal with the subject: On one hand, they are part of a racist Israeli society; on the other, they are afraid they will be accused of racism.

The Palestinian uprising, which began in December 1987, swept many Palestinian women in the occupied territories into its wake. Many have since been arrested and have been subjected to sexual abuse during their detainment.

Analysis of the situation of Palestinian women political prisoners and of the attitudes toward them exposes the social mechanisms blocking the Palestinian woman's way, as well as the crude and cynical exploitation of the values of traditional patriarchal society by the Israeli administration. The Jerusalem group "Women for Women Political Prisoners" has assembled dozens of testimonies regarding the extraction of confessions from female prisoners by means of sexual abuse and threats of rape. Additional testimony indicates the attitude shown toward the women by their own families, both in prison and after their release. In a number of cases, parents prevented their daughters from returning to school after their release; in one case, a young woman was beaten by her father for having been exposed to sexual abuse by Israel Security Services investigators. And in Gaza, a young woman was murdered by her family, because of a rumor that she had been raped while detained by the military administration. On 14 March 1989, the Palestinian newspaper *al-Nahar* published a full-page interview with Israeli Jewish members of "Women for Women Political Prisoners." Although the interviewees were quoted with meticulous accuracy, the entire passage dealing with sexual abuse was omitted from the interview. These incidents reflect the fact that a woman exposed to bodily harm or sexual abuse is held responsible for her own abuse.

In Palestinian society, nationalist ideologies often limit the struggle of women to the area of national liberation. These ideologies are propagated by persons who consider themselves radicals and even Marxists. An obvious example is Gazi al-Khalili, a self-styled revolutionary who published a book entitled *The Palestinian Woman and the Revolution* (1981). This book includes many passages that reveal a profound masculine anxiety regarding any possibility of a real Palestinian feminist struggle and warns against separate, independent organization on the part of women (al-Khalili, 1981: 57). For example, in a passage comparing the Palestinian woman to the soil of Palestine, that is, using the word "rape" to reflect the conquest of the land by Zionism, he claims that the Palestinian woman has no choice but to renounce some of her own demands, in order to preserve national unity. This claim, made under the guise of "understanding" the situation of doubly oppressed Palestinian women, projects the message that the Palestinian woman should renounce her own specific demands (al-Khalili, 1981: 112). Further in the book, the author states that there is a "dialectic connection" and tension between the term "women's liberation" and the national question, and proposes slogans advocating woman's role as mother, sister, and helpmate in the Palestinian rearguard, not as leader, but as agitator, spurring the men to combat (al-Khalili, 1981: 113). Yet the main thrust of his argument is revealed when, dividing the struggle into stages, he claims that in the stage of national liberation, women must actually renounce their aspiration for gender liberation, and concentrate on national liberation. According to al-Khalili, the national struggle has no place for women's liberation, which belongs to the later stage of socialism (al-Khalili, 1981: 140). This is a classical reformist approach, which defers missions of immediate urgency into the rosy future, in order to avoid them in the present.

Al-Khalili refuses to consider women's liberation as a vital democratic mission. His hysterical hatred of the women's movement leads him to claim that the entire enterprise is bourgeois and reactionary (al-Khalili, 1981: 45). He pretends to understand the educated woman, forced to suffer the limitations imposed on her by society, and he blames the woman herself. He argues that the educated woman must understand the society in which she lives; she has no right to an individual perspective which could lead to revolt against her society's values. He accuses the "rebellious" woman of displaying bourgeois values and a lack of national responsibility (al-Khalili, 1981: 56, 57, 123).

Al-Khalili's hypocritical howls against Palestinian women "infected" by the "women's liberation movement," as well as his opposition to all-female organizations, indicate his affinity to the petty bourgeois radical faction, which desires national liberation, but no real social change; defending a social order characterized, among other things, by the low status of women. His arguments also indicate a profound masculine anxiety, which uses ideology to perpetuate the oppression of woman. Despite their radical camouflage, Al-Khalili and his like are, in reality, frightened creatures who spread a poison more virulent than the chains of the patriarchal family structure itself.

REFERENCES

al-Khalili, Gazi (1981) *The Palestinian Women and the Revolution*. Acre: al-Aswar Press (Arabic).
Regev, Matti (1988) "The Sacrifice of Fatma." *Monitin*, January (Hebrew).

Teaching Girls to Be Women
in Israeli Jewish Schools

Shoshana BenTsvi-Mayer

The Jewish public school system in Israel includes both state secular and state religious schools, as well as independent schools for the ultra-Orthodox and a few experimental schools. [Jewish and Arab students attend schools belonging to separate systems—Ed.] Although Israeli education is essentially centralized, there are signs of a new, pluralistic trend both within and outside the state system. Moreover, schools are now actively encouraged to develop autonomy in curriculum planning, evaluation, and other important aspects of education. In fact, teachers may actually have more options than they choose to utilize.

Since the vast majority of sex role research in Israel has been done in Jewish schools, this chapter will be restricted to these findings. The figures in Table 1 show the breakdown of Jewish schools (Statistical Yearbook, 1988).

Education is compulsory from age five to sixteen (kindergarten–10th grade). The great majority of pupils start schooling before and continue beyond the compulsory age. Schools are articulated into $8+4$ or into $6+3+3$ grade-structures, preceded by at least one year of preschool.

In Israel there are virtually no equivalents of the secular, single-sex schools found in Europe; sex-segregation seems to be exclusively a matter of religion, and it is characteristic of the religiously orthodox. The more traditional-religious the school, the more likely that sex-segregation will be the rule.

State secular school classrooms are and have always been mixed, while state religious schools increasingly segregate the sexes from the age of 13 or earlier (in the past they were often mixed). Frequently parents are the ones who demand segregation in order to strengthen their sons' program of Judaic-Talmudic studies, subjects in which the curriculum for girls is markedly different. The political youth movement "B'nei Akiva," associated with the state religious schools, is presently undergoing change from mixed to single-sex groups. The rationale given for this change may be applicable to the issue within the schools as well: "When we were small and weak, we had to attract as many young people as possible, even at the cost of sacrificing the principle of sex-division. Now that our ranks are strong, we are free once again

75

Table 1. Distribution of Jewish Schools According to Type

Type of School	State Secular %	State Religious %	Independent %
Elementary	72.2	21	6.8
Intermediate	82.7	16.7	0.6
Secondary (high)	75.5	18.9	5.6

to apply this all-important maxim" (television discussion, 1986). The third largest sector, ultra-Orthodox independent education, has always practiced complete segregation of the sexes.

The possible advantages of single-sex schooling for girls, which in other societies has been proposed as a remedy to the androcentric nature of mixed classrooms, are not among the considerations of the Israeli religious single-sex groupings. Rather, segregation is rooted in strong convictions of the different worlds, natures, and indeed divine roles for the two sexes. Thus, sex groupings in Israeli Jewish religious schools can be viewed as direct, overt and fully intentional sex-role socialization.

Secular state schools have identical overt curricula for both sexes, except for some time-honored segregated programs, like physical education in the upper grades, and crafts (sewing, metalwork). The latter is, not without staff reluctance, in the process of opening up to accommodate both sexes. Sex grouping in the crafts can be seen as residues of separate schooling for boys and girls. However, like any systematic sex-segregation, it may serve as a reinforcing agency for sex-typing. Many school principals simply have never heard of a rationale for mixed craft-classes, but would probably not oppose the idea. The history of mixed or segregated crafts groupings is uneven, perhaps indicative of the many ambiguities of Israeli sex-equity issues. At the beginning of state education (1953), schools were encouraged, "wherever possible and desirable," to teach all crafts, including domestic crafts, to boys as well as girls. But directives given to schools during the educational reform and reorganization of schools, some fifteen years later, stated that postelementary craft programs such as housekeeping and weaving were to be offered for girls, while agriculture and maritime studies should be considered for boys. These guidelines were specified once again in 1971 (Ben Tsvi-Mayer, 1976). Yet they were never meant to be followed blindly. School principals have always had considerable leeway to counteract them—as many, but not all, actually did, especially in the secular sector. Recently new curricula and new guidelines have been published for the crafts, applying to both sexes, at least in intention. The decision, again, lies with the school, and secular schools often opt for mixed programs.

Over the last two decades, an abundance of findings have reported under-representation of females as well as unrealistic and stereotypic depiction of both sexes in virtually every area of writing for young people of all age groups (e.g., in the United States: *Women on Words and Images,* 1972; Schnell and Sweeney, 1975; Jay and Schminke, 1975; in England: Lobban, 1976; Byrne 1978; in Germany: Karsten, 1977; in Hungary: Sas, 1984). In her study of Hebrew text and illustrations of readers for grades 1-3 in Israel (1974), Malka Maon found three or more male characters for every female. She also found that when both a male and female were mentioned in a story, the males almost invariably came first. Maon identified 140 male occupations in the reading material, compared to 13 female ones, even when "wife," "sister" and "grandmother" were counted among the occupations. She also found that men and boys were assigned many more positive traits than women and girls. While young male characters seemed to plan their future with much ado, the female characters acted like "little mothers," and not much remained for them to aspire to in the future. Old men were generally regarded as wise elders, old women as feeble, silly or mean. Boys never ventured into the feminine sphere. Maon discovered that the children themselves did not necessarily harbor images as stereotypical as those in the books; thus these readers (still in use) may be viewed as designed to steer children toward conventional attitudes. Later a study was made of readers for grades 4 to 6, and similar findings were reported (Scher, Norman and Hershkowitz, 1981). Shlomith Kaufmann (1976) explored early childhood literature and concluded that their stereotypical sex-role divisions did not correspond to the real situation of males and females in Israeli society: for example, a much greater proportion of women worked outside the home than was depicted in children's books. Amir Ben David (1986) analyzed hundreds of juvenile magazine features and found that male main characters outnumbered female main characters by a ratio of 9:4; male-centered occupations outnumbered female-centered occupations by a ratio of 4:1. He also found that males were shown as embodying many more positive traits than females. BenTsvi-Mayer (1979) researched math word problems in textbooks for grades, 3, 5, 7 and 9, as well as pupils' choices in assigning male or female characters to math problems, and found many more problems with only males than with only females. This tendency increased in junior high: in seventh and nine grade textbooks, the ratio of male-centered to female-centered problems was 15:1. Moreover, males were assigned 36 roles and occupations: Females were assigned only nine, and these consisted of either family roles or low-prestige, stereotypical female jobs. Again, the higher the age of the learner, the more stereotypical the texts. Pupils were also found to associate mathematical problems with male rather than female characters.

There is a wealth of studies on gender-related verbal interaction patterns in the classroom (Jackson & Lahederne, 1967; Leinhardt & Seewald, 1979;

Sadker, 1984; Wilkinson & Marrett, 1985; Enders-Dragaesser & Fuchs, 1987), many of which report a tendency for boys to receive the majority of opportunities for expression. This issue has not yet aroused much research interest in Israel, but the little evidence there is points to similar tendencies. In a pilot study (BenTsvi-Mayer et al., 1987) that observed interactions in the first and second grades, the teachers were found to initiate more contacts with boys than with girls. In a study of gifted eleventh grade science students (Sabar & Levin, 1987) boys turned out to be "teacher's pets." They were allowed 75 percent of all interventions, both by their female teacher and their female peers. When interviewed, girls admitted to displaying similarly modest behavior during other school lessons. Nonetheless, the girls' final grades in this class of gifted children were no lower than those of the boys, thereby raising the question of whether verbal participation should be considered indicative of academic achievement. What is of special concern in this case is the girls' tendency to play down their own capabilities. The authors concluded: "It seems that the expected social norms are so strong that even in a high status project with high achievements, social norms set the tone." They recommended systematic assertiveness training for the girls. However, the teacher, who represents the educational system, did not believe that the girls' passivity was any cause for concern. Nor did she use any of her expertise in leading classroom discussions to increase the girls' participation.

In a different type of classroom interaction study (Romm, 1984), high school teachers were observed for their reactions to blatantly sexist student talk. It was found that the main strategies of the female teachers were ignoring the issue and making indulgent jokes, thereby often joining the students in their ridicule of women, and appearing to condone sexist remarks of both sexes.

Numerous studies on intellectual gender differences (Maccoby and Jacklin, 1974) indicate that whenever differences are found, they tend to occur at puberty, with males gaining an advantage in mathematics and spatial ability, and females in verbal ability tests. In Israel, the findings are markedly different. Girls were found to function as well as or even better than boys at age six, but boys began to surpass girls in verbal tests (!) by the age of nine, an advantage that became statistically significant at age 11. Boys continued to excel in virtually all subtests, and at 16 years of age they scored an average of 12 points higher than girls on the Total I.Q. (Lieblich, 1985). A study of gifted seventh through ninth graders produced even more extreme results (Safir, 1986). Lieblich concluded that the reasons for this gap should be sought in the family, the school, and the culture. Other researchers (Nevo, Safir & Ramraz, 1981) agree that intellectual gender differences found in Israel are greater and more extensive than those found in Europe and the United States. Nava Butler-Por (1983) discovered that parents expressed greater concern over schools providing intellectual development opportunities for their sons than for their daughters. Drora Kfir (1982) speculated that girls were often rewarded for neatness and conformity rather than for realistic objective achievements.

Researchers often find differential attitudes of teachers to and expectations for the two sexes (Hartley, 1978; Kedar-Voivodas, 1983). In a recent Israeli study (BenTsvi-Mayer et al., 1989) teachers of grades K to 6 recalled significantly more boys than girls as their prominent students. In general, boys were perceived as the best overall students and the best math students, as having the highest potential, as occupying the teacher's mind the most, and as presenting the most discipline problems. Girls were perceived as excelling in social skills and language-arts. Thus, the directions of most sex-differences were stereotypical. The authors concluded that such perceptions, unsupported as they are by objective psychometric evidence in the early grades, may impede sex-equity and deprive girls of opportunities for full development in the classroom.

Following the International Women's Year of 1975, the Prime Minister appointed a Committee on the Status of Women to examine many aspects of women's life in Israel, including education. The committee submitted its findings and recommendations in 1978. It was the first attempt on the national level to attract public attention to the issue of sex-equity in schooling: 38 recommendations were made concerning textbooks, feminization of staff, sexist curricula, stereotypical vocational options, and other educational issues (Report of Subcommittees, 1978). To date, only 12 of these have been implemented, half of them only partially.

Specific material counteracting sexism for young people is still scarce. One program (Felstein, 1984) has been published by the National Family and Sex Education Office of the Ministry of Education and Culture. A more comprehensive project, "To be a Boy, to be a Girl — Does it Really Matter?" (BenTsvi-Mayer, Ben Zeev, with Abrahami 1985) suggests a variety of individual and group activities aimed at increasing knowledge and raising consciousness about gender issues. It is being increasingly employed in schools and teacher training colleges and courses.

Teacher awareness is often emphasized as the most important anti-sexist intervention. Yet, Israeli teachers' colleges do not, as a rule, devote slots in their curricula to the issue of sex-role socialization. This is probably the place for feminist educators to concentrate their efforts.

REFERENCES

Ben David, Amir (1986) Seminar paper, University of Haifa. Cited in La-Isha, June 23 (Hebrew).

BenTsvi-Mayer, Shoshana (1976) "The attitude of Israeli teachers and students toward the two sexes and their sexually stereotyped behaviors." Doctoral Dissertation, The University of Connecticut.

BenTsvi-Mayer, Shoshana (1979). "Male and Female in Mathematics Word-problems." Ha-Hinukh, a-b, 73-79 (Hebrew).

BenTsvi-Mayer, Shoshana; Hertz-Lazarowitz, Rachel; Safir, Marilyn P. (1987) "Teacher-student interaction in the Israeli elementary school." Unpublished pilot study.

BenTsvi-Mayer, Shoshana; Hertz-Lazarowitz, Rachel; Safir, Marilyn P. (1989) "Teachers' Selections of Boys and Girls as Prominent Pupils," *Sex Roles* 21 (3/4): 231-245.

Butler-Por, Nava (1983) "Giftedness Across Cultures: A Study of Educational Values." In Shore, B., Gagne, S., Tarievee, S., Tali, R., Tumbrey, S. (ed.). *Face to Face with Giftedness*. New York: Nilian Books.

Byrne, Eileen M. (1978) *Women and Education*. London: Tavistock Publications.

Enders-Dragaesser, Uta and Fuchs, Claudia (1987) "Feminist School Research: Gender and Interaction." Third International Disciplinary Congress on Women, Dublin, 1987.

Felstein, Meira (1984) *Masculinity, Femininity, The Unit for Family and Sex Education*. Jerusalem: Ministry of Education and Culture (Hebrew).

Hartley, David (1978) "Teachers' Definitions of Boys and Girls: Some Consequences." *Research in Education*, 20, 23-35.

Jackson, Phillip W. and Lahederne, Henriette M. (1967) "Inequalities of Teacher-Pupil Contacts." *Psychology in the Schools* 4: 204-208.

Jay, Winifred T., and Schminke, Clarence W. (1975) "Sex Bias in Elementary School Mathematics Texts." *The Arithmetic Teacher*, March.

Karsten, Gaby (1977) *Mariechen's Weg Ins Glueck?* Berlin: Frauenselbstverlag.

Kaufmann, Shlomith (1976) "Sex Role Stereotypes in Early Childhood Text Books and Story Books." Master's Thesis, Tel Aviv University (Hebrew).

Kedar-Voivodas, Gita (1983) "The Impact of Elementary Children's School Roles and Sex Roles on Teacher Attitudes: An interactional Analysis." *Review of Educational Research* 53: 3, 415- 437.

Kfir, Drora (1982) "Home Environment and Social Composition of Schools, and their Influence on the Course of Study and Aspirations of Israeli Girls from Asian-African Origin." Doctoral Dissertation, University of Tel Aviv (Hebrew).

Leinhardt, Gaea; Seewald, Andrea M.; Engel, Mary (1979) "Learning What's Taught: Sex Differences in Instruction." *Journal of Educational Psychology* 71: 432-439.

Lieblich, Amia (1985) "Sex Differences in Intelligence Test Performances of Jewish and Arab School Children in Israel." In Safir, M. P., Mednick, M. S., Izraeli, D., and Bernard J., (eds.). *Women's Worlds: The New Scholarship*. New York: Praeger Publications.

Lobban, Glenys (1976) "Sex-roles in Reading Schemes." In *Sexism in Children's Books: Facts, Figures and Guidelines*. London: Writers and Readers Publishing Cooperative.

Maccoby, Eleanor E., and Jacklin, Carol N. (1974) *The Psychology of Sex Differences*. Stanford, CA: Stanford University Press.

Maon, Malka (1974) "Socialization for Sex Roles in the State School." Master's Thesis, Hebrew University, Jerusalem (Hebrew).

Nevo, Baruch; Safir, Marilyn P.; and Ramraz, Rachel (1981) "Sex differences in Intelligence— Test performance of University Applicants in Israel." Paper presented at the International Interdisciplinary Congress on Women: Women's Worlds, Haifa, Israel.

Reports of the Subcommittees on the Status of Women (1978) Office of the Prime Minister (Hebrew).

Romm, T. (1984). "Sexual Stereotypes in the Israeli Classroom: Theoretical Conceptualization and Observations." *Israel Social Science Research* 2 (2): 42-54.

Sabar, Na'ama and Levin, Tamar (1989) "Still Waters Run Deep: Sex Differences in Science Classroom Discussions." *Journal of Research in Science Teaching* 26 (8).

Sadker, David; Sadker, Myra; Baucher, Joyce (1984) "Teacher Reactions to Classroom Responses of Male and Female Students." Paper presented at the American Educational Research Association Annual Meeting, New Orleans.

Safir, Marilyn P. (1986) "The Effects of Nature or of Nurture on Sex Differences in Intellectual Functioning: Israeli Findings." *Sex Roles* 14 (11/12): 581-590.

Sas, H., Judit (1984) *Noies Nok Es Ferfias Ferfiak*. Budapest: Akademiai Kaido.

Scher, Dena; Norman, Gabi; Hershkowitz, Ruth (1981) "Sex Roles in Israeli Elementary School Readers." *The Journal of Social Psychology* 114: 291-292.

Schnell, Thomas R. and Sweeney, Judith (1975) "Sex Role Bias in Basal Readers." *Elementary English*, May.

Statistical Yearbook of Israel 1988. Jerusalem: Central Bureau of Statistics.

To Be a Boy, to Be a Girl—Does it Really Matter? (1985) Haifa University and The School of Education of the Kibbutz Movement, Oranim.
   1. Ben Tsvi-Mayer, Shoshanna; Ben-Zeev, Avinoam; Abrahami, Judith E. *Trapped in Pink and Blue—Girls and Boys in Society* (Hebrew).
   2. Fox, Thilde; Drori, Irit; Ur, Penny *Fair Play for Boys and Girls: Towards Equal Opportunity*.
   3. Ariel, Mira. *Women and Man in the Hands of Language* (Hebrew).

Wilkinson, Louise C. and Marrett, Cora B. (eds.) (1985) *Gender Influences in Classroom Interactions*. Orlando: Academic Press.

Women of Words and Images (1972) *Dick and Jane as Victims: Sex Stereotyping in Children's Readers*. New Jersey: Princeton University Press.

Change and Mate Selection Among Palestinian Women in Israel

Fatina Shaloufeh Khazan
(Translated by Sharon Ne'eman)

In any study attempting to analyze the status and position of "the Arab woman in Israel," it is important first to consider the complexity of that term. In addition to the specific cultural aspects stemming from the Arab woman's existence in the state of Israel, one must also take into account the cultural religious background deriving from her identification with the Arab-Islamic world in general, and with Palestinian culture in particular.

The direct or indirect interaction of Arab society with Western cultural values, as well as the ambition to achieve an equal footing with the dominant Western culture, have brought the status of Arab women to the foreground—as has the revolutionary ethos that spread because of the desire for social change and development. The Arab woman has thus become the symbol of societal transformation; her status has been enhanced by her new role as the mainstay of cultural and religious values. This position is conspicuous in the claims of certain nationalist and socialist organizations and also in regimes which emerged after the 1950s (Kazi, 1987), and in the positions taken by some Islamic religious leaders and philosophers. The latter claim that the survival of Islamic society is contingent upon the religious fervor of its women; that is, religious Moslem women are held responsible for reinforcing religious norms among their men (Haddad, 1984).

In a context specifically relevant to Palestinian women, Hamida Kazi (1987) has stated that, in addition to the two severe problems with which the Palestinian woman has had to contend—the nationalist struggle and the struggle against social oppression—a third problem has been the dispersal of Palestinian society following the 1948 war, and the concomitant lack of a permanent state or "home base" for Palestinian Arabs. The resultant feeling of instability caused the Palestinian family structure to assume increased importance, with the Palestinian woman held responsible for maintaining the continuity of Palestinian cultural values, whether she resides in the homeland or outside of it.

Analyses of these positions, according to the theory of Hans Kreitler and

82

Shulamith Kreitler (1978), reveal that the Palestinian woman has been assigned conflicting tasks. On one hand, there is a belief system that is consistent with a positive image: that of the Arab woman as central, active and responsible for the preservation of cultural, religious, and national continuity. On the other, she is asked to accept and internalize a contradictory belief system that includes her own inferiority: a considerable portion of the cultural values which the Palestinian woman has been responsible for upholding constitutes, in fact, the same values which have discriminated against her and deprived her of status for many generations.

A similar situation prevails on the religious dimension. Despite Islam's claim to have improved the status of women believers relative to that of other religions, true equality has not been achieved. Under the contemporary vision of Moslem traditionalists and revolutionaries, the Arab woman's role is perceived as determined by the biological functions of her gender. Not only was she created to conceive and bear children, all of her roles are defined by her relations to the men in her life. Only rarely is she depicted as an independent person in her own right.

Notwithstanding all of the above limitations, the Arab woman is asked to believe in herself as a central, redeeming and responsible entity! It should also be noted that throughout the entire process of ascription of roles, central or secondary tasks, the Arab woman has never been a party to the process, but rather, has been compelled simply to accept them, and in so doing, to believe at one and the same time in both her superiority and her inferiority. The obvious questions that arise are how these contradictory beliefs affect women, and what conflicts they engender.

Three different approaches have been employed by Arab society to deal with the woman problem, each with its own continuum.

The first is the liberal-secular approach, whose continuum measures the degree to which women are offered the chance to adopt "modern, secular" ideas, taking into consideration the "positive" values of the past, so as not to jeopardize women's sense of security in their Arab identity. The status of the Arab woman as defined by the proponents of this approach has been one of subjugation and dependence. Her identity does not depend on herself but is defined in relation to a particular man, be it a father, brother, husband, or son.

Among those belonging to this approach are such well-known authors as Butrus al-Bustani and Qasim Amin. The latter, an Egyptian, wrote several books on the subject (1899). Nevertheless, it is important to note that his starting point was male interests, that is, he supported the education of women so that they might serve as more understanding wives and mothers. Though basically opposed to polygamy, he nevertheless countenanced it under certain circumstances.

Since Amin, many scholars have contributed to this field, among them women writers who have dealt with it in a far more sophisticated manner, although their focus has not been the liberation of woman but the liberation of Arab society as a whole. Even Arab feminist leaders have expressed opposition to any attempt to provoke a confrontation between women and men or women and religion. Prominent women writers of this school include Leila Ba'albeki, Gada al-Saman, Fatima Mernissi, and Nawal el Saadawi. The latter, an Egyptian physician and writer, has called for the establishment of a feminist movement which would take up the struggle against nationalist, societal, and sexist oppression. According to el Saadawi, only through such a movement can the Arab woman divest herself of her political alienation and assume an active role in social and cultural change (el Saadawi, 1982). Also pointed out by el Saadawi are the extreme hypocrisy and discrimination in the approach of contemporary Arab culture to the socialization and education of boys and girls. Writing in a critical, even sarcastic vein, she notes the relationship between men's social status and mental health (as defined by society and culture) on the one hand, and women's chastity and the cult of virginity, on the other (el Saadawi, 1977).

Another researcher, Halim Barakat (1985), has attempted to explain the inferior status of the Arab woman as the result of the interaction of two sets of variables: the socioeconomic system, division of labor, and relations of production (independent variables); and culture, religion, tradition, tribal norms, and psychological tendencies like sadism or masochism (intervening variables). The dependent variable in the study, of course, was the low status of the Arab woman. However, Barakat has not presented empirical evidence to support his theory.

In another article, on the socialization of the Arab woman, Abdalla M. Soliman (1987) claims that the main factor affecting Arab women is the religious tenets of Islam and their interpretation. For instance, Islamic law allows a woman to inherit only one-half of what a man may inherit, and in court the testimony of two women is equal to that of one man. The religious tenets are unequivocal regarding women's principal roles as mothers and wives. In addition, the religious prohibition of extramarital sexual relations leads to the adoption of extremely stringent familial, cultural, and societal sanctions regarding daughters, in comparison with the highly permissive approach adopted toward sons. The behavior of the Arab woman is viewed as a matter of honor, al-sharaf, by her entire family. Women have less freedom, less power, and less authority. As a result, Arab women tend to hold negative belief systems concerning themselves.

In general, the contribution of this approach may be summarized as having greatly increased the sensitivity of Arab society to the need for change in the status of women, as a prerequisite for a more progressive, more highly developed society. It has raised the Arab woman's consciousness of her female identity and extended further opportunities for women's education and integration into political, social and economic processes as decision-makers rather than as mere performers. Moreover, it has led to demands for the redefinition of the present concept of "work," which recognizes only employment outside the home as productive. This definition discriminates against a very wide sector of Arab women who work within family farms or businesses. In turn, such discrimination results in women being excluded from official development plans (el Saadawi, 1982; Fernea, 1986).

The second approach is the traditional-religious one, which is basically defensive in nature. In every debate on the status of women, adherents of this approach adopt the traditional definition and position delineated in the Scriptures of Islam. The continuum of this approach concerns the degree to which the Arab woman accepts and internalizes the doctrine that dictates that her life is to be determined by biological functions; women have no right to enter public life, and work outside the home is degeneration, while housekeeping and raising children are sublime missions. This approach views women's liberation as an anti-Moslem, missionary plot aimed at undermining Arab Islamic society. In contrast, Islamic revolutionary religious philosophy considers the role of women to be more active than does traditional philosophy; women are viewed as responsible for the maintenance of Islamic values in the face of attacks by Western values (Haddad, 1984).

The third approach deals with content rather than explanatory processes. Its main premise is that women can attain equal rights by active participation in national struggles for liberation, or through active support of the establishment and strengthening of a particular regime. Many scholars in the field have expressed doubt as to the validity of this claim. Examples have been cited from the experience of women throughout the world in general and the Arab world in particular, in an effort to show the weaknesses of the approach. For instance, in the Algerian War of Independence, women played an active role in the struggle for liberation; however, once the new state had become firmly established, the women were asked to return to their traditional cultural role, and did not succeed in maintaining the longed-for equality.

Suad Joseph (1986) claims that women often do not choose the moment or the context for their political involvement. Their participation in politics may be evoked by the state, the rulers, the politicians, or others in authority. Women become subjects of mobilization, targets of political action and programs. As they are mobilized, they may begin to assume—on their own behalf or that of others—public identities separate from the private ones of kin and community. On the other hand, Judith Tucker (1986) argues that women's political activism has not brought about any structural change in Arab women's lives. Although Julie Peteet (1986) finds a potential for feminist consciousness in the Palestinian Liberation movement, she does not view the movement as providing any opportunity for feminist action, as Palestinian women are found only in secondary and supportive positions, not in leadership ones. It is worthwhile pointing out that while the first approach supports the active involvement of Arab women in the political arena and in national struggles,

it also stresses their conflicts in other fields, with the aim of turning these conflicts into bases for women's political activism.

The questions remain thus: How far have the abovementioned approaches
succeeded? And if they have succeeded, on what level and in what areas?
Furthermore, have such changes remained on the level of acquiring clusters
of new beliefs supporting a positive female self-concept orientation, without
reaching behavioral levels and programs in the areas of social and emotional
relations, as well as politics? If this is the case, wouldn't these unrealized beliefs lead to conflict and tension?

Gazi Khalili (1977) claims that in Palestinian society, young women may
be more tense and hesitant than their male counterparts. He adds that the
more the Palestinian woman is aware of her female identity and her oppression, the more hesitant and tense she becomes. Khalili's conclusions, based
on research on the attitudes and status of Palestinian women in Lebanon, show
that Palestinian women tend to be traditional, or almost traditional, in their
attitudes towards family and emotional relationships (with parents, children,
relatives), but less so in other areas, like the right to work, choice of career,
education and culture. The question is whether this claim is still as valid today as it was in 1977. What about Palestinian women in Israel, who have
to cope with additional social values and political outlooks, as a result of their
contact with Jewish society? There are many points that require further study
and elucidation: For example, whether the Israeli Arab woman is more traditional than the Israeli Jewish woman in various areas of life.

A recent research project revealed the attitude of Palestinian women living in Israel towards marriage and family. The study was conducted by David
Buss and some of his colleagues (1989) as part of a comparative project carried out in 37 countries. I participated in research on 120 female and male
(Christians and Moslems) Palestinian Arabs in Israel, between the ages of 18
and 40. Most of the participants had at least a secondary education, limiting
the generality of our conclusions to a certain extent. In addition, there are
some doubts as to whether the Arab woman is really free to choose her mate.
It must be borne in mind that in Arab society, marriage is considered a social
action and not merely an individual one; therefore the choice of mate takes
into consideration the attitude of the woman's family, on the one hand, and
the personal traits and qualities of the potential husband, as well as his family background, on the other. (However, this study deals only with preferences of *potential* mates.)

In general, little is known about what characteristics people value in potential mates, how these values vary across cultures and sexes, and whether there
exist typical choices that transcend gender and culture (Buss et al., 1989).
The findings of the present research project can be summarized as follows:

1. The most pervasive difference between cultures appears to be a tradi-
    tional versus a modern orientation towards mate selection, with the

former placing great value on chastity, home and children, domestic skills and resource provisioning, and the latter devaluing these traditional attributes in favor of ambition and industriousness, similar education, intelligence, a pleasing disposition, and an exciting personality.

2. Gender has consistent effects for the valuation of a few mate preferences, such as appearance and resource potential, but its overall effects on other mate choice differences are small when viewed across all samples. Thus, cultural effects are generally stronger than gender effects.

3. There are strong similarities across cultures and between sexes on the preference ordering of mate characteristics. This implies a degree of psychological species unity that transcends geographical, racial, political, ethnic, and sexual diversity.

4. As far as the Israeli Palestinian sample is concerned, the findings show that the greatest departure from international norms is the high value placed on similar political backgrounds. Also highly valued is a mate who desires home and children and who is chaste and religious. Further, Israeli Palestinians deviated from the norm in that they assigned lower value to dependability and financial prospects.

We were interested in comparing Arab females with both Arab males and Jewish females. The findings demonstrate that, as in all the societies that Buss studied, physical attraction, love, maturity and emotional stability, a pleasing disposition, and kindness were important. The factors that were significant for Arab males and females in choosing a spouse were: chastity, similar political background, sociability, good health, good looks, emotional stability, good cook and housekeeper, ambition and industriousness, and refinement and neatness. The qualities preferred more by Arab women than Arab men were: similar religious background, favorable social status or rating, pleasing disposition, emotional stability, dependable character, similar political background, education and intelligence, similar education, ambition and industriousness, good financial prospects, and sociability. It can be seen that six out of the 11 qualities chosen by Israeli Arab women exemplify modern societies; only three reflect traditional tendencies: similar religious background, dependable character and good financial prospects.

Arab men stated that the following qualities were important to them in their choice of a wife: desire for home and children, good cook and housekeeper, chastity, good health, refinement and neatness, good looks, and similar political background. Unlike Israeli Arab women's choices, those of Israeli Arab males reveal a strong traditional orientation: six out of the seven qualities are traditional.

Comparing Israeli Arab women with Israeli Jewish women, we find that both groups show the same preference for the following qualities: education and intelligence, favorable social status, a pleasing disposition, mutual attraction, and a dependable character. However, Israeli Arab women found good financial prospects and similar education less important than Israeli Jewish women, and similar religious background, ambition and industriousness, and emotional stability more important.

From the foregoing, it can be concluded that Israeli Arab women are more modern in orientation than their male counterparts when it comes to the choice of a potential spouse. This supports the idea that changes in Israeli Arab society in the direction of modernization affect women more than men.

The differences in the belief systems of women and men as reflected in their choices of qualities in potential spouses may constitute the basis for potential conflict in marriage. Women's expectations from marriage appear to be different from those of men: For example, men show higher preference for home and children, good cook and housekeeper, and good looks, whereas women seek emotional stability, education and intelligence, ambition and industriousness. This supports Khalili's findings (1977) that 50 percent of the Palestinian women in Lebanon sought emotional stability in marriage, and only 3 percent motherhood. The explanation, according to Khalili, is not to be found in the negation of motherhood per se, but rather in the women's aspiration for self-realization in other areas. Arab girls, who are deprived of liberty and self expression, have expectations of finding these in marriage.

Significant cultural differences are reflected in the preference of certain qualities by Arab women and men, especially the desire for similar political background and the value of chastity for Arab males, while Jewish females and males give much higher preference to good financial prospects and similar education. Because of the Palestinian problem as a whole and the crisis engendered thereof, among Palestinians in Israel in particular, politicization and political consciousness are very important, endowing political affiliations with a new value and a special meaning, even in mate selection.

While there was no significant difference between Arab and Jewish women in the choice of "modern" traits in potential spouses, as both stand to gain from these, there was a significant difference between the "modernity" of the choices of Arab and Jewish men. Only 15 percent of the Arab men's choices were for "modern" traits, compared with over 40 percent of the Jewish men's. Arab men remain traditional in their approach to family and emotional life, however modern and educated they may be.

REFERENCES

Amin, Qasim (1899) *The Emancipation of Women.* Cairo (Arabic).

Barakat, Halim (1985) "The Arab Family and the Challenge in Social Transformation." In Fernea, E. (ed.). *Women and the Family in the Middle East: New Voices of Change.* Austin: Texas University Press.

Buss, David et al. (1989) *International Preferences in Selecting Mates: A Study of 37 cultures.* Journal of Cross-Cultural Psychology 21: 5–47.

el Saadawi, Nawal (1977) *Women and Psychological Conflict.* Beirut: Dar al-Nashr al-Arabi (Arabic).

el Saadawi, Nawal (1982). *Women and Their Role in the Arab Unity Movement*. Beirut: Dar al-Nashr al-Arabi (Arabic).

Fernea, Elizabeth, (1986) "Women and the Family in Development Plans in the Arab East." *Journal of Asian and African Studies* XXI (1-2): 81–88.

Haddad, Yvonne (1984) "Islam Women and Revolutions in Twentieth Century Arab Thought." In *The Muslim World* 54, July–October.

Joseph, Suad (1986) "Women and Politics in the Middle East." In *Middle East Report*, No. 138, January/February.

Kazi, Hamida (1987) "Palestinian Women and the National Liberation Movement: A Social Perspective." In *Khamsin: Women in the Middle East*. London: Zed Press.

Khalili, Gazi (1977) *The Palestinian Woman and the Revolution: An Empirical Study*. Beirut Research Center (Arabic).

Kreitler, Hans and Kreitler, Shulamith (1978) *Cognitive Orientation and Behavior*. New York: Springer.

Peteet, Julie (1986) "No Going Back? Women and the Palestinian Movement." In *Middle East Report*, No. 1 138, January/February.

Soliman, Abdalla M. (1985) "The Socialization of the Arab Women." In *Arab Journal of Social Sciences*, 2(2): 235–255.

Tucker, Judith (1986) *Women in Nineteenth Century Egypt*. Cairo: American University Press.

Comparison of Israeli and American Successful Career Women at Midlife

Amia Lieblich

The following is an in-depth study of a small sample of Israeli and American women at mid-life: women who have had an uninterrupted career in their respective professions, and have attained some objective measure of success. Successful career women appear to combine both feminine and masculine traits (Lieblich, 1986), and have, therefore, become the models for the "new woman." Moreover, a retrospective study of women at midlife allows for the understanding of longer developmental processes. Psychologists consider midlife a period characterized by the tendency to become introspective and review one's life and successes (Brandes, 1985; Levinson, 1978; Neugarten, 1964, 1968), which facilitates direct data collection from this age group.

In-depth interviews were conducted with samples of women in the United States and in Israel. The study was carried out in two stages: interviews were collected from American and, then, Israeli women of similar backgrounds. The women were at about midlife (average age of the American sample, 42, and of the Israeli sample, 41), had had uninterrupted careers (defined as having had the maximum of a three-month interruption at a time), and were considered by peers as successful in their fields. The American women were from a Midwestern university town in the United States, and the Israeli women from Jerusalem. The sample was obtained through personal contacts and informants in the communities, and an attempt was made to represent a wide spectrum of careers.

To the American sample, the project was presented as a cross-cultural study about career women conducted by a foreign psychologist (myself). Twenty-nine women were contacted by phone, and 25 consented to participate. Later, it was found that one woman had had a longer career interruption than acceptable; therefore the final American sample consisted of 24 women. The following year in Jerusalem, 25 women were asked to participate, and 24 cooperated. The following report is based on these two groups of twenty-four women each.

From Lieblich, 1987. Adapted with permission.

Each participant was interviewed in-depth and all interviews were non-structured; they were between 1 and 2 hours long. Good rapport was established with most of the women. The introspective tendencies of this age, noted by Neugarten (1964) seemed to facilitate communication, and the women did not have difficulty discussing thoughts, feelings and concerns with the investigator.

The interviews covered work history, including a detailed description of present occupation, family status and history, coordination of private life and career, conflicts between the two, factors affecting development (i.e., role models, norms and expectations, association with the women's movement), experience of discrimination, and feelings concerning midlife. For the Israeli sample, an additional theme for the interview was changes in adulthood—a subject which had emerged spontaneously in the American sample.

All the material was taped and transcribed. The transcribed interviews were content-analyzed into 17 categories, which were developed by myself and an independent reviewer after a long process of discussion to identify the most important themes. Following are the categories for which quotations were collected: history of the career and family situation, motivation for career and family situation, coordination of work and family, relationships outside family, career and family situation of siblings, husband's career, husband's attitude towards wife's employment, role division in the family, past and present role models, becoming a role model for others, self-evaluation as feminine-masculine, major conflicts, experience of discrimination, attitudes towards the women's movement and feminist organizations, mid-life crisis, and major transitions in adulthood. Some of the categories, such as motivations or conflicts, were evaluated according to intensity as well as content. Due to the qualitative nature of the data and the small number of cases in each group, no statistical analyses were carried out. The comparative results are based on the cumulative impressions of the investigator and her assistant. The results should be regarded as preliminary, or rather, as hypotheses for future empirical study. Not only was the sample small, but the fact that I myself interviewed the women, analyzed the data and drew the conclusions puts certain limitations on the generalizability of the results.

The results presented below pertain to the categories in which systematic and interesting differences were noted between Israeli and American career women, according to their self reports.

ATTITUDES TOWARDS WORK

All women were asked about their career history and their motivation for working. It was immediately evident that more of the American women saw their occupation as a "career." When commitment to careers was explored, most women provided more than one motive for working. A total of seven motives were mentioned by the participants. In the Israeli sample, the most frequently presented motives were satisfaction and interest in life, and economic need of the family. In the American group, satisfaction and interest was accompanied by "ambition" or the motive for "social reform" (e.g., they work and strive to achieve in order to prove that women can hold such positions, or in order to change a specific work place—such as a construction firm—by introducing women into an all-male team of workers). These two motives were almost entirely lacking in the Israeli women's reports. On the other hand, economic need of the family was less often mentioned by American career women, whose life styles generally indicated that they were quite well off. The need to escape from the feminine roles of housekeeping and childcare was presented by about one-half of the married women in both cultures. Two other motives which were mentioned but much less frequently in both samples were to continue parents' choices and to win husband's respect.

Our general impression was that American women were highly motivated to succeed in their fields, and that they viewed their work as a source of pride or frustration. They were driven by a need for excellence and achievement in competition with others. Moreover, American women often used the term "struggle." They seemed to be struggling by the mere fact of leading an active life in the world of work. They struggled against the prevalent attitude that women should not be so serious about their work, should not compete with men; they struggled against men who discriminated against them, parents and husbands who did not support their career choices, and against the system in general. Even those who were not feminists, according to their own definitions of the term, saw themselves as leaders or role models in a social movement aimed at drawing women into more active participation in the various spheres of life. They therefore saw their decision to be career women as fairly unusual and expressed pride both in their choice and in their achievements.

For Israeli women, however, the choice seemed self-evident, based on the need for more income for the family. The Israeli participants—notwithstanding their high objective achievements—were not at all "heroic" in their attitude towards their work life. They did not impress us with having had to struggle against prejudice or discrimination. All in all, in comparison with the American group, Israeli career women seemed passive in their attitudes toward both their work and their success. Often they presented their success as incidental, attributing it to all kinds of external circumstances or luck, rather than to their own efforts, skills or "struggle." They did not take direct credit for their achievement, and tended to be very modest about the position they had attained. The opposite seemed true for the Americans, who noted all their achievements, even minor ones, and described themselves as interested in promoting themselves and in achieving higher aims in their careers.

Several of the Israeli career women were next in line for the position of director or manager of their department, office or firm. When asked about future plans, all of them firmly declared that they were not interested in being promoted to the top, because this would only make them more responsible and visible, and would actually diminish the inherent interest of the work. On the other hand, several of the American participants reported without hesitation that they aimed at becoming state governor, university president or the best economist in the world.

ATTITUDES TOWARDS FAMILY LIFE

A larger proportion of the Israelis were married at the time of the interviews and, had, on the average, larger families. (Of the American women, 14 out of 24, and of the Israeli women 19 out of 24 were married at the time of the interview.) This familistic orientation appeared also in the verbal reports. Israeli women generally stated that they had a family because "everybody does." They were unaware of having made any choice and felt that they had simply followed the path paved for them by society. Some of them talked about the *number* of children as a matter of choice, and mentioned that they had wanted a large family to provide security and warmth. A few spoke about the need to "produce" children for a larger Jewish nation. In general, it seemed that the Israeli career women were pleased with their families, especially their children. They spoke warmly and proudly of them. The Israeli single women presented their situation as the result of external circumstances, of not yet having met the right partner. It was not their choice to remain unmarried, just as it was not the choice of any of the Israelis to be childless.

The situation was quite different in the American sample, which included a larger proportion of presently unmarried women. Those women who lived in the traditional frame, namely as wives and mothers, were similar to the Israelis in presenting their life-course as not resulting from any conscious choice. Marriage and motherhood were the norms when they were young, according to their report, and they had had no inclination to deviate from the norm. However, several of the American women reported regretting it and spoke about educating young women to see marriage and motherhood as possible options in life. Generally, they were not as expressive of positive emotions towards their children as the Israelis. One of the American women may represent a more modern trend: Having the first, and only, child at 35, when she was sure that this could be handled in combination with her career.

In contrast, unmarried or divorced American career women always presented their marital situation as a matter of choice. Several mentioned a preference for remaining single, or divorcing their husbands. They talked about their need for independence, their unwillingness to compromise, and their conviction that successful women were threatening to men. Most of them objected to marriage on ideological grounds and expressed satisfaction with their present life style. Two of them reported that they objected to parenthood, either because there were too many unfed children on earth, or because the future of humanity was tenuous. None of these arguments and thoughts appeared in the Israeli data.

FAMILY–CAREER ROLE CONFLICT

All of the women were asked about the amount of role conflict they experienced in their lives. This question was, of course, more relevant to married women, or those who were divorced with children. The following summary will therefore deal with career women who share a household with either husbands or both children and husbands.

In general, women from both groups reported experiencing conflict between their roles as workers and as wives and mothers. In both cultures, the conflicts had much in common. The focus was on mothering, manifested in complaints that dedication to a career could hardly be reconciled with the role of a good mother. Self criticism, worry, anger and guilt were expressed by the majority of the participants. However, when the proportion of women who experienced role conflict in the two groups was compared, American women seemed to suffer more seriously from this condition. There were more American than Israeli career women in the categories of moderate and severe conflict. Americans often presented such moving descriptions as the following: "I was holding her with one arm (the baby) and reading Whitehead (which I was holding with the other), the tears streaming down my face in— as I realize now—frustration. I was really in conflict about wanting to do both of these things. It was just terrible, not knowing how to work that out." Or: "I find being a career woman and a mother extremely difficult. I feel inadequate every day, it never ends." Or: "Although it was years ago, I realize I still feel guilty about leaving them (her young children) to go to work."

Following the description of this internal state of affairs, the American women went on to describe their technical arrangements, and dismay, regarding the daily management of childcare. Many employed various combinations of private sitters and public services and, in general, expressed dissatisfaction with all of them.

The situation of Israeli career women in terms of childcare arrangements is similar to that of the Americans in content but is relatively moderate in intensity. More Israeli women described a situation where their responsibility for home and children occupied them throughout their work day. They called home frequently and made various arrangements for the family from their offices. However, in terms of technical arrangements for children, Israeli mothers seemed to be less worried and more content, and the emotional conflict in the daily event of leaving one's children in the care of others seemed less acute. (Government-supervised daycare is more readily available for working women in Israel.)

Looking into the details and nuances of the interview materials on this subject, it appears that the situation of the American woman was not really more difficult, as she had fewer children to be concerned with. (But less daycare!) However, Israeli women felt more in line with general social norms, which accept and value working mothers, and thus more supported in their double role. For example, they were not under the threat of losing their positions because of occasional problems they had to take care of at home or school. (They are entitled by law to take off 6 days a year to tend to children's needs.) In addition, since Israeli women appear to be less ambitious than their American cohorts, they are able to avoid some of the persistent stress, conflict and guilt feelings. Generally, one could say that although statistics show that the percentage of educated Israeli and American women participating in the labor force is about equal, the attitudes towards women in the double role of mother and wife and worker are quite different.

SOURCES OF SUPPORT

Sources of possible support for the woman in her double role could be located inside or outside of the family. In particular, I was interested in the support and help gained from the husband and growing children, parents and role models, and women's networks or political organizations.

While Israeli women reported that their husbands were in favor of their careers, the terms used to describe their attitudes were much less enthusiastic. A frequent response was: "Both of us have to work in order to support the family and provide what we feel are essential opportunities for the children. So of course my husband supports my working outside the home." Since the prevalent attitude towards work is that this is the natural life course for adult women, additional support from the husband seems unnecessary. From the women's reports, it appears that Israeli husbands or fathers were less involved in sharing the responsibility for housework than their American counterparts. Israeli career women more often hired help at home. Their older children also shared some of the responsibility by babysitting for younger siblings or helping out with household chores. Furthermore, due to the tendency of Israeli women to work shorter hours (work is spread over a six-day week), and the more flexible time schedule in their jobs, women often came home earlier and were able to take care of most of the daily housework and childcare. The fact that the women came home earlier than their husbands and did most of the housework (with help from older children) reinforced their husbands' nonperformance. However, there was almost no resentment in the Israeli sample concerning this division of labor in the household.

A clear difference between the Americans and Israelis emerged in regard to parents of the career woman. Most of the American women experienced criticism from their mothers for choosing a career. Moreover, they had very few role models. If any encouragement was given, it usually originated from the woman's father. In comparison, Israeli women often had working mothers. They reported that parents were supportive of their careers and took pride in their success. Frequently, retired grandmothers and even grandfathers were quite helpful in raising grandchildren.

THE WOMEN'S MOVEMENT

Finally, affiliation with the women's movement as a possible source of support was explored. Most of the Israeli women did not report either the need for political or group support or the experience of receiving it. When asked directly, they responded that they did not identify with the feminist movement, although they accepted part of its egalitarian ideology. About a third of the participants claimed that they rejected feminism altogether. (My impression is that this rejection was often based on misconceptions.) At the time of the interviews, none of the Israelis belonged to a politically active women's group. Only one had participated in a consciousness raising group. This may be a result of the lack of a broad base for the women's movement in Israel, which is far from popular, even among the more educated career women. Most Israeli women found my questions about discrimination at work irrelevant to their own history. As mentioned above, working was considered the outcome of economic need, or the motive for self actualization, but never as part of a political struggle.

Identification with the women's movement was not unequivocally expressed by all American women interviewed. Some objected to or reported disappointment with feminism, but even for those it seemed to be part of their life history. In other words, all of the American women had devoted time and thought to testing the feminist ideology. About half reported that they had been active in women's groups or networks. The same proportion reported that they had experienced some kind of discrimination in the work sphere, and that this reinforced their affiliation with the women's movement. Again, these results demonstrate the visibility of women's political struggle in the United States, a phenomenon entirely absent from the Israeli scene.

The profiles of the Israeli and American career woman at midlife are, of course, overgeneralized and simplified, but they may shed some light on the cultural differences under consideration. Our impression is that the Israeli woman tends to combine career and family life. She is more likely to work in public administration than in business, and often reaches the position of second in command. She is not consciously ambitious about her career and does not view her success with any special pride. She works for personal satisfaction and to provide for her family. She has a family, in conformity to the norm, and she takes pride in her children. She is the main caregiver in her household, yet she has moderate role conflict and is quite satisfied with her combination of work and family life. She gets support from her husband and parents, not from formal women's groups or organizations.

In comparison, the American career woman of the same age appears to struggle with her commitments and choices, and to feel more intensely about her achievements or conflicts. She may be either married or single. If she is single, it is out of choice. If she is married, she seems less enchanted by her family and complains about serious role conflicts. Her career is just as likely to be in business as in administration, and she is motivated by interest as well as by the desire to compete and prove a point to men and society. Support for her choices comes from her husband, if she is married, as well as from women's networks or feminist ideology. A reason for divorce is the husband's lack of support for her behavior.

It should be noted that the conversational style of the women in the two samples is very different. American women tended to be more emotionally expressive in describing their struggles, conflicts, misgivings and achievements. Israeli women were generally more subdued or controlled. This difference in intensity of responses was clearly apparent to the two investigators. How can this difference be interpreted? It may reflect discrepant socialization practices in the two cultures: Where Americans learn to be more open to their feelings, Israelis limit their expression in accordance with the "myth of the hero," to cope all by oneself. The differences in emotional tone may reflect differences in reality, or "just" in the manner of speaking to the interviewer. A third interpretation is also possible, namely that higher awareness of feminist ideology makes the American reports more affectively intense. However, an exception to the generalization about the lower emotional tone of the Israelis has to be made with regard to references to their children. This, therefore, is not a purely stylistic matter, but has to do with content as well.

In comparison with American middle class culture, Israeli society is more family oriented (Peres and Katz, 1980). This basic attitude is shared by Israeli career women. On the other hand, American culture stresses competition and individual achievement, and this orientation permeates the lives of career women. For Israeli women, self-esteem results, among other things, from having a healthy, happy family. In the United States, at the beginning of the feminist movement (Friedan, 1981), self-esteem from that source was devalued, and for women under the influence of this era self-esteem depended on individual achievement in the sphere of work rather than on family life.

As a result of the familistic orientation of Israeli society, and the fact that security concerns promote inequality between men and women (Safir, 1986;

Bar Yosef and Lieblich, 1983; Hazelton, 1977), feminism has never reached the popularity it has in the United States (Izraeli and Tabory, 1986). Israeli women do not view themselves as being discriminated against, and they are not bitter about the lack of their husbands' participation in housework or childcare. The gender struggle that has altered the American scene over the last two decades is muted in Israel by other concerns. Work and career are just normal dimensions of adult lives, not outstanding individual achievements. Personal ambition is not a central motivation, certainly not one to be openly and perhaps not even consciously admitted. Moreover, it is especially unbecoming of women, whose complex image in the culture also includes that of the tender mother and wife, providing aid and comfort to men, struggling for economic well-being and national security. The cumulative effect of these values and processes is to reduce role conflict for career women in Israel as compared to their American sisters.

REFERENCES

Bar Yosef, Rivka and Lieblich, Amia (1983) "Comments on Brandow's 'Ideology, Myth and Reality: Sex Equality in Israel'." *Sex Roles* 9:419–426.

Brandes, Stanley (1985) *Forty: The Age and the Symbol.* Knoxville: University of Tennessee Press.

Friedan, Betty (1981) *The Second Stage.* New York: Summit Books.

Gutmann, David L. (1985) "The Parental Imperative Revisited: Towards a Developmental Psychology of Adulthood and Later Life." *Contributions to Human Development* 14: 31–60.

Hazelton, Leslie (1977) *Israeli Women: The Reality Behind the Myths.* New York: Simon and Schuster.

Izraeli, Dafna N., and Tabory, Ephraim (1986) "The Perception of Women's Status in Israel as a Social Problem." *Sex Roles* 14:663–677.

Levinson, Daniel (1978) *The Seasons of a Man's Life.* New York: Ballantine.

Lieblich, Amia (1983) "Between Strength and Toughness." In Breznitz, S. (ed.). *Stress in Israel.* New York: Van Nostrand Reinhold.

Lieblich, Amia (1986) "Successful Career Women at Midlife: Crises and Transitions." *International Journal of Aging and Human Development* 23:301–312.

Lieblich, Amia (1987). "A Preliminary Comparison of Israeli and American Successful Career Women in Mid-Life." *Israel Social Science Journal,* 5(1&2), 164–177. Beer-Sheva, Israel: Hubert H. Humphrey Institute for Social Ecology, Ben-Gurion University of the Negev.

Lieblich, Amia and Friedman, Gitza (1985) "Attitudes Towards Male and Female Homosexuality and Sex Role Stereotypes in Israeli and American Students." *Sex Roles* 12:561–570.

Mead, Margaret (1935) *Sex and Temperament in Three Primitive Societies.* New York: William Morrow.

Neugarten, Bernice L. (ed.) (1964) *Personality in Middle and Late Life.* New York: Atherton Press.

Neugarten, Bernice L. (1968) *Middle Age and Aging: A Reader in Social Psychology.* Chicago: University of Chicago Press.

Peres, Yohanan and Katz, Ruth (1980) "Stability and Centrality: The Nuclear Family in Modern Israel." *Megamot* 23:37–55 (Hebrew).

Safir, Marilyn P. (1986) "The Effects of Nature or Nuture on Sex Differences in Intellectual Functioning: Israeli Findings." *Sex Roles* 14:581–590.

MUSINGS OF AN ISRAELI SUPERWOMAN
Avirama Golan
(Translated by Barbara Swirski)

At 12:30, I parked the car and hopped into the bank. Upon return, I found my car blocked by a double-parked truck. I waited for a few minutes. Fateful matters raced through my mind: I have to pick up my daughter at preschool, let's see, what can I make her for lunch. What's taking him so long. Of course, he's got all the time in the world. He doesn't have to count the minutes and he's not expected to accomplish in five hours of work what any normal person does in eight, all the while keeping in mind all the minute details connected with the lives of one or two short, small creatures called children, whose needs are urgent 24 hours a day.

I hated him. It never occurred to me that the driver could have been a woman; it was easier for me to hate a man. Everything was against me that day: earlier an income tax official had asked me why I was getting so upset about losing a couple of shekels, after all, my income was supplementary, as I had a husband to support me. Then I interviewed the prospective baby-sitter, a large, elderly woman who assured me that she would be sure to feed my daughter liver at least twice a week. "Don't call me, I'll call you," I told her.

Where the devil is the driver, I muttered, as I began to honk, somewhat hesitantly. Maybe he's already on his way out, I thought. Why greet him with loud honking; after all, it's only been a few minutes. A few minutes! Time is flying. I honked once again, and a passerby nodded his head in sympathy.

Exasperated, I got into the car and tried to maneuver my way between the three cars around me. Maybe if I honk while I'm doing this, I'll save time. No go – Two or three kind souls (male, of course) came up to me and tried to give me advice on how to get out: "back up a little," "give a little less gas, you're killing the engine," "don't even bother, he'll be back in a minute," and "just a little more and you'll be clear."

I began to think about the women of my generation. A generation caught in its own contradictions: No longer full-time housewives and worrisome, harried mothers, but not yet ready to demand equal rights for themselves and to play according to the rules of a man's world. For the time being, they mainly complain, mostly to each other, that's what gets me.

Israeli women have another problem. They don't come from a world in which women were trained to be little and cute and obedient and to be satisfied with fine dishes and other material goods, like Nora in *A Doll's House*. No, we were raised differently.

Adapted from an article that appeared in the Hebrew daily, *Davar,* November 28, 1986.

We were raised on a different bluff, seduced to believe that women in Israel have equality. Take Golda, for example, and my aunts who worked at road paving, and the women in the Palmach. Just like men, they were. But when you make an enlargement of that pretty picture, you find that's not exactly the way it was.

The deception is compounded, because no one bothered to tell those tough women about motherhood, and in our society, sex equality comes into question the moment children enter the picture. When you're pregnant and then give birth and find yourself waiting your turn in the well-baby clinic, you find out that you're not equipped to deal with these female situations. You suddenly find yourself alone with all those women you once looked down upon. Suddenly you have something in common with them, because you, too, have a communication problem with the man you thought was an understanding partner.

No one ever told you that everyone around you, including yourself (what a trap) would take it for granted that you would be the one to drop out of the race in order to take care of the children. Even if you make the concession willingly, you can't escape the feeling that you've been deceived. Where is that famous Israeli equality if the kindergartens and schools are over at noon, and you need everything you earn to pay for babysitters and housekeepers, as though you yourself were a luxury item in the family. And if by some chance you're a real careerist, come home late, and spend a lot of time and energy on the job, don't expect anyone to forgive you for it.

I have a friend who can fill a book with the comments she receives from colleagues at work and kind-hearted friends about her over-ambitiousness and how she neglects her husband and children. The trick, of course, is to live with the situation without becoming bitter towards your partner. But it's almost impossible not to be infected by the ugly, destructive man-hating that characterizes many feminists. I swear, the men are no more to blame than the women. It seems like we all cooperate in the system of deception, because it's convenient for all parties except those women who try to fight for their own identity and play all the parts at one and the same time.

For the sake of all those around me, I constantly fight to suppress the bitter demon that whispers in my ear: "Look at 'A' go to his rented room every morning, leaving the world behind. His wife keeps the hearth fires burning, and he knows he can depend on her. Look," says the jealous, evil demon, "look at how the children tiptoe around when he works at home and how no one complains that he's working instead of telling his children a story or changing a diaper. Look how steadfast of purpose he is, how family and friends are devoted to his creative activities, how charming a hostess his wife is for all his colleagues and students.

"A room of one's own and money of one's own are not enough, Virginia," says the demon. The whole system has got to change. As long as the family is at the center of society, as long as people need children, love, a friend for life, a family nest, and as long as the family is perceived as a home built around the woman, there is no chance of reversing the roles. I know a lot of women who would be willing to change places with "A's" wife, because of the compensations: it's called being *the wife of.* The wife of "A" is immortalized in his paintings or poems and is known to all as "the beautiful" or "the charming" or "the wise and strong wife of "A." I don't know one man who would be happy with the compensation called being *the husband of.* Not because there's anything wrong with men or because they're not willing to give or any other such nonsense. They, too, are the victims of their upbringing. They were told: get ahead, get ahead, otherwise you're not worth a cent.

When I'd given up and was about to lock the car and get a cab so that my poor child wouldn't be left abandoned in the preschool, the driver suddenly appeared, walking with the serenity of someone whose time is his own. He moved slowly, a pita stuffed with salad and fried eggplant and hot sauce in one hand, a belly to match, and a smile of satisfaction on his face. Exhausted and dying of hunger, I showered him with all the gripes I had against the entire world.

What gets me is not the obstacles and not the inequality. That's how it is. What gets me is the deception: Israeli society is still not ready for equality and women's liberation, because all of us are still chained to our traditional roles. Right now we operate under the pressures of religion and state and serious budgetary limitations (a long school day and good day care are expensive), so let them stop trying to sell young girls the beautiful myth of the liberated Israeli woman; it's worth no more than the photograph of the woman soldier on the magazine cover. Let them stop saying that every woman can, because the real test comes much later, when the woman is no longer a soldier, but a mother running hither and thither to get everything done, or a career woman who never stops hearing questions about when she is going to get married or have children, or a divorcee who paid a heavy price for her identity and will continue to pay for many years to come because Israeli society doesn't think much of divorcees. The cost is high, whatever the case may be, and the one who pays is always the woman.

I got to the preschool in time. All the way home, I couldn't forgive myself for jumping down the throat of the driver, who almost choked on his food. When he recovered from the shock, he turned to me with a kind expression on his face and said: "What's the matter, baby. Why you so riled up?"

You mean it shows?

Anything for a Baby: Reproductive Technology in Israel

Alison Solomon

Reproductive technology is widely employed in Israel. For its population of 4 million, Israel has 16 *In-Vitro* Fertilization (IVF) – "test tube baby" – clinics. Fourteen of them are public, giving Israel more publicly-funded clinics per capita than any other country in the world. For example, Australia, one of the leaders in reproductive technology, has 17 clinics for a population of 15 million. Treatment in Israeli public clinics is free, and there are no waiting lists. Israeli doctors are among the foremost in the field, and the technologies used are the most up to date available; Israel was the first country to enable a woman without fallopian tubes to become pregnant and give birth.

The Israeli image of reproductive technology is a positive one: hundreds of happy mothers, Jews and Arabs, rich and poor, coupled with happy doctors, proud of their, and Israel's wonderful achievements. Every now and then a cloud appears on the horizon: Aliza Eisenberg's death during IVF treatment in 1985 and Rivi Ben Ari's death following Pergonal treatment in 1987. But new pictures – the mother of IVF quints, a 45 year old IVF mother, frozen embryo "twins" born a year apart – are soon superimposed, and reproductive technology forges ahead.

Very little public debate has accompanied the development or use of reproductive technology in Israel. It has been assumed that this is a a scientific or medical issue with no societal implications. The technology has been viewed as a positive development – what could be wrong with giving women opportunities to have babies?

There is, however, a growing belief in the international women's communities, as well as in the World Health Organization, that reproductive technology is being misused. The Feminist International Network Resisting Reproductive and Genetic Engineering (Finrrage), claims that reproductive technology is not a cure to infertility, but a new industry that exploits women's bodies for raw material: that reproductive technology is misogynous and based on male profiteering; and that reproductive technology brings about a new division between women, those worth of being mothers and those who are unworthy.

In the following pages we will examine whether the claim is relevant to Israel. First it should be noted that in Israel those industries concerned with giving and taking life: energy, irrigation, arms, and reproductive technology are among the most advanced in the world. Second, reproduction has always been a national issue; controlling it is seen as one solution to the so-called "demographic problem" – the "danger" of an Arab majority in Israel, as the Arab birthrate is higher than the Jewish one. There are those who believe that the answer to this problem lies in encouraging Jewish women to bear more children, and in limiting abortion rights. Thus, in 1967 David Ben-Gurion stated that "increasing the Jewish birth-rate is vital for the survival of Israel" (Hazelton, 1977: 63). In 1977, the liberalized abortion law was changed to the detriment of women in order to honor coalition agreements with the religious parties. In 1987, a foundation worth hundreds of millions of dollars was created to encourage Jews to have more children (*Jerusalem Post*, 10.23, 1987). Lest it be doubted that IVF is relevant to this sort of politics, we have only to note statements such as that of Motta Gur, Member of Knesset (MK) and former Israeli Defense Force (IDF) Chief-of-Staff, who stated that although IVF was expensive, it was still cheaper than the cost of bringing in new immigrants (Levy, 1987).

While political attitudes are geared to a pronatal atmosphere both for Jews and Moslems, they are backed by social and religious attitudes. In 1986, at the Sixth National Conference of the Family Planning Association, the theme of which was infertility, MK Yitzhak Artzi opened by saying that "this conference is about those who are unable to fulfill the supreme command given to humanity." (The supreme command given to (male) Jews is "to be fruitful and multiply," Genesis 1:28.) Jewish law entitles a man to take a second wife if his first wife is infertile – there have been cases in Israel where the Rabbinate has indeed permitted bigamy, or recommended divorce, if the first wife was unable to become pregnant or to bear male children. Jewish religious life revolves around the family, and a woman without a child may find herself a social outcast. In traditional Moslem homes, a childless woman faces the threat of bigamy and is devoid of social status.

Secular women feel the stress of being childless no less than their religious counterparts, whether in the town, the village or the kibbutz. In kibbutzim there is a "family hour" from four to seven every afternoon, during which children are to visit with their parents. No social activities take place during these hours, and the childless woman feels just as left out as her sisters in ultra-Orthodox Jerusalem or Arab villages in the Galilee.

Sociopolitical conditions thus support a pronatal outlook. They also support industrialization of female functions: Prostitution, pornography and pornographic forms of advertising flourish in Israel. While the most blatant manifestation of the reproductive industry, surrogacy, is banned, there are other more subtle forms of abuse. For example, a three-day workshop for infertile couples conducted by Dr. Iris Reizes-Kelerman and Shula Elsheich reported that all the women felt that they were "physiological prostitutes." They described how each treatment involved endlessly opening their legs and having their intimate parts displayed, poked, prodded and invaded by a succession of (male) doctors (Shilon, 1988).

If conditions are ripe in Israel for the industrialization of female reproduction, what basis is there for a belief that in Israel reproductive technology follows the misogynous patterns of those in other countries? Below are some indications; the list is by no means exhaustive:

- Ministry of Health regulations state that single women may only receive artificial insemination (AI) and IVF following a psychiatric opinion and a report from a senior social worker.
- Despite the fact that these regulations make no specific mention of lesbians, the director of the Gynecology Department of the Hadassah Ein Kerem Hospital in Jerusalem has publicly stated that he would not allow lesbians to be treated in his clinic.
- Following the death of Rivi Ben Ari from ovary hyperstimulation caused by Pergonal, a journalist interviewed Professor Lonnensfeld, the discoverer of Pergonal and a colleague of Dr. Elsner, the doctor treating Rivi Ben Ari at the time of her death:
  Interviewer: "What are the side effects of Pergonal?"
  Lonnensfeld: "There are no side effects."
  Interviewer: "None?"
  Lonnensfeld: "No. None. The stuff itself has none."
  Interviewer: "That is, any connection between Pergonal and ovary-hyperstimulation is coincidental?"
  Lonnensfeld: "No. If you take too high a dosage, hyperstimulation can occur, it's true. But this is not a direct side effect of the drug, but rather a reaction of the ovary" (Levy, 1988).
  The above is illustrative of doctors' belief that the medicine and the technology are perfectly safe and always work. It is the women's bodies that are at fault.
- At least three women have died in infertility treatment in Israel, and none of the physicians treating them has been indicted in any way (indeed one of them has since been promoted to professor).
- In a 1986 survey of IVF clinics, nearly every clinic viewed male infertility as an indication for IVF (Solomon, 1986). Three years later, the only form of research on male infertility was on sperm. This means that instead of men undergoing invasive or uncomfortable treatment for their infertility, they merely produce the sperm by masturbating, after which it is treated

and perfectly healthy women are expected to undergo dangerous, invasive and damaging hormone treatments, followed by surgery in order to have the sperm introduced into their bodies (from an interview with Professor Shenkar, Jan. 31, 1989).

* New Ministry of Health regulations state that AI may *only* be done by physicians in authorized hospitals. AI is the only "user-friendly" low-tech reproductive technology, and in recent years it has been successfully used by single women and lesbians, who were treated by doctors in private practice (charging high prices). It remains to be seen whether doctors will continue to dispense privately.

Besides the specific examples given above, it should be clear that science and scientists do not develop in a vacuum. They are part of society and share the dominant values. Thus in a society where the most common media portrayal of women is reductionist—treating women not as whole beings, but only as parts—it is not surprising that doctors treat their patients in a similar way. This reductionism is reflected in the fact that the majority of women undergoing IVF do not receive counseling, despite the fact that for most women this is an extremely traumatic experience. Indeed, the only form of counseling given is usually to encourage women not to stop treatment.

This field of obstetrics and gynecology is highly competitive, and in order to obtain both prestige and funding, new innovations and "firsts" must be constantly achieved. The first woman to have frozen embryo "twins" a year apart stated on TV that the idea of having the second baby when she did, was neither hers nor her husband's. Her *doctor* called her up and suggested that she have a second child. She was quite aware that she had frozen embryos in storage (couples may pay for storage for up to five years). This "gentle reminder" was clearly to make sure that the doctor in question would be the first to set a new record. Indeed, according to Professor Shenkar, a leading IVF specialist, there are far too many IVF clinics in Israel. This leaves the road open to exploitation of women, because in order to justify the existence of the clinics, women must be treated, and some of them will be treated unnecessarily.

Whereas IVF used to be offered only to women with problems with fallopian tubes, almost any type of infertility is now an excuse for IVF. Part of the reason for this evidently lies with the need for human genetic material. Despite the fact that the Helsinki committee forbids many forms of genetic research, it is no secret that hospitals and microbiology labs work in close contact and that individual doctors have agreements to transfer human "material," (i.e., eggs), to university laboratories (Solomon, 1989). The women in these clinics have never been asked to donate or for permission to use their eggs for research.

While it is clear that the elements which lead to industrialization of female reproduction exist in Israel, what is less clear is what safeguards may be taken against possible abuses. Israel is already beyond the stage of a public ethics committee, such as the Warnock Committee in Britain, and has firm laws controlling the use of IVF. However, the above examples of misogyny occurred under these laws. In the two investigations conducted after the deaths of Aliza Eisenberg and Rivi Ben Ari, all medical personnel were exonerated of all blame. Thus the usual safeguards, laws and public investigations, are no guarantee against abuse.

It will be argued that the idea of comparing the industrialization of female reproduction with other industries exploiting women is not legitimate, that it is the women who want reproductive technology, that women participate of their own accord and that if it were really humiliating or destructive, women would not participate.

We have heard these arguments many times before to justify exploitative situations of women. Battered women, it is claimed, would leave if their lives were so terrible; models would refuse to model if it were so degrading; prostitutes choose freely to sell their bodies for easy money. However, we know that if we ask why women choose to undergo one form of degradation or another, the answers are not hard to find: battered women are often economically dependent on their husbands; many prostitutes were sexually abused as children, and have low self-esteem, or no other way of earning a living. Why do women undergo humiliating and dangerous reproductive technology treatments? Is it because of low self-esteem? Is it because of guilt over a past abortion (which may be the cause of the infertility)? Is it because they believe a woman who is unable to conceive or produce children has no worth?

It is for all these reasons and more. Certainly women in Israel have little worth if they are not mothers. Certainly many women have abortions (often in place of contraception, as sex education is almost nonexistent). Certainly women's low status means that they are accustomed to being in degrading situations. But there are other reasons—reasons that have to do with the technology itself.

The first is that women are not told the truth about treatment success rates. A 1986 survey showed that clinics use pregnancy per laparoscopy as their usual measure of success. For example, one clinic had 350 patients, 54 pregnancies and six babies (including two sets of twins). It gave its success rate as 26 percent (Solomon, 1989). Even "take-home baby" rates are misleading. A recently quoted figure is one in twelve (Yona Barak, public lecture, June 22, 1989). What the clinics do not tell women is that each of these one in twelve women will have undergone an average of five IVF treatments, so that the actual success rate is one in 60 treatments (V. Levy, 1987). Professor Shenkar believes that the real figure is about six percent, which means that 94 out of 100 women go home without a baby. Compare this to a newspaper article which stated that "IVF success rates range between 20-25 percent . . . while natural fertility rates for each menstrual period give a 25-30 percent chance of pregnancy" (Levy, 1987: 6). It is clear that most women believe their chances of success are much higher than they really are.

Once women begin treatment they do not give up easily, because each treatment makes them feel that much nearer to becoming pregnant, makes them that much more committed to the technology. A recent innovation is that of showing couples the embryo through ultrasound just after it has been implanted in the woman's uterus. This makes women feel they are actually pregnant and that next time they will certainly succeed in keeping the pregnancy. In addition, many women have made having a child the central and only goal in their lives, sometimes giving up careers, and using up savings. If they stop treatment without a child, they will end up with less than they started with.

Third, since women believe that the technology is successful, when they do not conceive, they see themselves rather than the technology, as the failures. This sense of failure is often so overwhelming that the only way to overcome it, is to sign up for another try.

Women do not necessarily want the technology. What they want is a baby, and if the technology will bring them one, or if they think it will, they will undergo whatever danger or humiliations are necessary. The time has come for us to question such situations as acceptable and to recognize the misogyny inherent in such acceptance.

REFERENCES

Hazelton, Leslie (1977). *Israeli Women: The Reality Behind the Myths*. New York: Simon and Schuster.

Levy, Hanita (1987). "Heshbon Ubar Veshav." *Olam Haisha,* January 1987 (Hebrew).

Levy, Vered (1988). "The Life and Death of Rivi Ben-Ari." *Al- Hamishmar,* July 29, 1988 (Hebrew).

Shilon, Noga (1988). "Warning, Fragile." *Halr,* November 4, 1988 (Hebrew).

Solomon, Alison (1986). "Survey of IVF Clinics in Israel." Unpublished manuscript.

Solomon, Alison (1989). Personal communication received from a candidate for doctoral placement at a laboratory in the Weizmann Institute, Rehovot, Israel. In the course of the interview, the candidate asked Prof. X where he obtained his material for egg research and was told that he had an agreement with one of the IVF clinics in Tel Aviv.

The Pressure to Be Heterosexual

Jo Oppenheimer

Assumptions that the Israeli lesbian confronts the same issues as her counterpart in the United States are generally without basis, as little research has taken place in Israel on lesbian issues. Although there are many similarities between the two societies, the Jewish Israeli lesbian faces additional difficulties evolving from the modern history of Israel and the Jewish tradition, both of which form part of an Israeli culture. (This chapter can only deal with Jewish lesbians as there is no information about Israeli Palestinian lesbians available to the author at this time.)

Two of the most profound influences on this culture are the necessity for survival of the Jewish people and the effect of certain aspects of the Jewish religion. Many Israelis are Holocaust survivors and Israelis have participated in a series of wars during their 42-year history that have resulted in the deaths of many males. The Jewish religion, with its patriarchal attitudes towards gender roles, sees marriage and procreation as the highest ambitions to which a woman can aspire and the family, consisting of father, mother and 2.8 children, as central to the society. These factors combine to produce a society in which approximately 98 percent of the women are or have been married. Thus the pressure on the remaining two percent to marry, to be part of the "norm," is monumental.

Orthodox Judaism rejects homosexuality as an "abomination." Lesbianism is a threat to the family as the duty of women is to marry and to produce children. Marriage, family, and children are central to Israeli society and societal pressure on women forces them to find their identity, security, and social role in marriage (Nugent, 1983), which also represents respectability and, above all, protection. As research in the United States has shown, women often enter heterosexual marriage and later become aware and accepting of their same-sex orientation; 35 percent of U.S. lesbians have been married

The author wishes to thank several Israeli lesbians whose input was invaluable. As none of these women are out publicly, they cannot be thanked by name. It is part of the invisibility within Israel that must be maintained for survival.

previously (Ross, 1972). Whether women marry because of nonrecognition of a lesbian side of the self, or because once married, they will have "proved" their heterosexuality and will then be free to pursue a lesbian lifestyle, is not clear. In Israel, the lesbian population consists of both unmarried and married or divorced women. We do not know what the statistics might be in Israel for married lesbians, as there has been no research on this question. However, the author organized a support group for married lesbians in 1987, during which the problem of living in both words was a main focus. It was apparent then that married lesbians tend to have their own subcommunity, relating only to one another.

The choice of some lesbians to become single mothers is an additional threat to the traditional Israeli family. Artificial insemination has been accepted as a method of inducing pregnancy for women in Israel who are married, heterosexual. A regulation instituted in 1989 states that artificial insemination can only be carried out in recognized clinics and that single women will be allowed to participate in the program only after approval by a psychiatrist and a supervising social worker. Moreover, Professor Shenkar, director of the clinic at Hadassah Hospital, Ein Karem, Jerusalem stated in an interview for a local Jerusalem newspaper, that lesbians who declare their lesbianism will not be allowed to participate in the Hadassah program because "all single women must pass a psychiatric and social worker examination on their fitness to be mothers." A declared lesbian "will not fulfill the hospital's criteria" (Jerusalem, 1989: 1). None of the other seven clinics involved in the program have made such an open declaration. Lesbian women will have to look for gynecologists willing to go not only against the prejudicial attitudes of their colleagues but also against the new regulation.

In a society such as Israel that treasures "tradition" and "family," homophobia is another factor which creates pressure on women to be heterosexual. Although homophobia is not confined to Israeli society, it must be examined briefly as a factor that affects Israeli lesbians.

Homophobia, an irrational fear or intolerance of homosexuals, is a product of sexism. Externalized homophobia is a belief system that supports "negative myths and stereotypes about homosexuals; (e.g., all lesbians look like men, or all lesbians hate men). It is the use of language offensive to lesbians. . . . It is a system that does not value homosexual lifestyles equally with heterosexual lifestyles and assumes that women are 'innately sexually oriented' towards men" (Oppenheimer, 1988: 1–2). Lesbianism challenges the traditional definition of gender role expectations by challenging the necessity for a male counterpart. It also challenges the traditional patriarchal assumptions of male supremacy (Gatrell, 1981: 506; Rich, 1980; Rule, 1975), as lesbians are unwilling to be dependent on men for emotional or financial support.

The more conservative the society, the more conservative the sexual attitudes and gender role limitations (Minnigerode, 1976), contributing to an externalized homophobia. As lesbianism is in direct conflict with the traditional patriarchal role expectations of Israeli society as a whole, and with parental and peer expectations, it is viewed with extreme prejudice:

> Lesbian is about the worst name the sexist forces can hurl at a woman. It means someone who has stepped outside of the role that defines female. It implies something unspeakably evil, something immoral, sick and ugly. It is a name used to keep women in line (Dempsey and Fawley, 1988: 5).

Israeli lesbians, having few role models and few support systems, often "pass" as heterosexual in order to diffuse externalized pressures. "Passing" means appearing to be who you are not, being invisible to those who would disapprove. It imposes a tremendous psychological burden on the individual (Dykewomon, 1988: 3). Passing is a constant way of life. In Israel, it begins with the assumption that all unmarried women are heterosexual. The Israeli lesbian passes to survive. As her acceptance into the mainstream is based on a lie, there is always the fear of discovery. She has to choose her words carefully, so as never to reveal her identity, especially using the pronoun "we" when referring to her lover in order not to give away her lover's gender. It also means not challenging antilesbian or homosexual comments. She may be constantly pressured by her family to marry or bear children. The lesbian who does not wish to date men will have to refuse to date without an explanation. Being heterosexual incorporates privileges supported by the laws and traditions of the land. There are no laws that protect lesbians.

Passing has its dire consequences. "We are so busy being whom we are not, we forget who we are. Our sense of self becomes tenuous. Our self-hatred deepens as we betray ourselves and incorporate society's hatred of who we are" (Dykewomon, 1988: 4). Society's rejection of her life style causes the added factors of guilt, shame, and self-hatred, which contribute to internalized homophobia. As a result, many lesbians tend to withdraw from society, frequently leading a lonely life in which isolation and depression become a "natural" consequence.

Even more than in the United States, in Israel young females are taught that they must always think of others first. Their goal in life is the nurturing of others; through this role they expect to find "happiness" and "fulfillment." As a female matures, she is socialized to ignore her own needs. Anger, self-aggrandizement, strength and ambition do not fit the role of the normal heterosexual Israeli woman. She is prepared to have little or no power within the society, and there are very few exceptions. Subordination decreases the possibility for self-esteem. Therefore, women are impeded in their striving for equality both by the internalized pressures to be selfless and the external pressure of outside expectations.

The Hebrew language, with its use of masculine and feminine endings, denoting both the speaker's gender and the gender of those to whom one is speaking, contributes to the displacement of women, both in the larger society and within the lesbian community. For example, in a room with 50 Israeli women and one man, masculine endings must be used. Heterosexual women often use masculine endings even when dealing with other women, indicating the sexism inherent in Hebrew. In a consciousness raising group for lesbian feminists facilitated by the author, some lesbians used masculine endings under certain circumstances. "When I want to be spoiled, babied," or "when I am sad, tired" was the explanation. This was regarded as a way of getting attention, of getting what the individual needed. The women themselves linked this usage to boys receiving more attention. Paradoxically, concepts like "sad" and "babied" are more feminine than masculine, for few men are allowed to be "sad."

In addition to having to be heterosexual, survival in Israel depends on group orientation. Not individualism but rather "group think" is encouraged. This is not to say that individuals do not exist or do not think differently from one another, but that by working in groups, be it the Army or peer relationships, grouping is encouraged.

Because of its size, living in Israel is like living in a small town where everyone knows everyone else; privacy is difficult to maintain. Social life depends upon the good will of one's neighbors. A woman who is lesbian is often closeted to "protect" her family, which may include an extended family as well as close relatives, from finding out about her lesbianism. If she risks telling her family, she is often met with bitter resentment based on the assumption that she made a conscious decision to be lesbian. Parents are unaware of her inner struggle. In order to remain part of the accepted social fabric, and to retain the feeling of belonging to a family, the Israeli lesbian must remain invisible.

Invisibility is one of the factors that results in so few lesbians being involved in the lesbian community. Being active in the community, (and only a small percentage of the total lesbian population is involved actively in the Community) but not "out" publicly requires a duplicity of roles that is stressful. Activists sometimes use pseudonyms in order to protect both themselves and their families. For example, at a recent International Jewish Feminist Conference (December, 1988), an Israeli lesbian spoke to the participants about being lesbian in Israel. In order to protect herself and her family, she used a pseudonym, "Lilith." It was an act of courage to allow her face to be seen.

The bonding together of lesbians and the lesbian movement began in 1976 at the First National Feminist Conference. The conference dealt with many feminist issues but not lesbianism. One lesbian stood up and demanded to be recognized both as a lesbian and a feminist. Her act of publicly coming out encouraged other lesbians present to stand with her. In a moment of camaraderie, the entire audience stood, recognizing a concept of "sisterhood."

Lesbians were involved in the formation of *Kol Ha'isha* (The Voice of Women), feminist cultural centers in Haifa and in Jerusalem. These organizations served as resource centers with libraries of feminist books and articles from the United States, including material on lesbians. They were also places for foreign feminists, some of them lesbian, to meet Israelis. As the lesbian community became stronger, their involvement in Jerusalem's *Kol Ha'isha* became greater, until heterosexual women became the minority.

Three years later, the first publicly advertised consciousness raising support group for lesbians was formed. A twelve week seminar was devoted to issues of coming out, the first acknowledgement and "coming out" of lesbians. A second group followed. These groups were decidedly political but there was a social aspect to them as well; parties, hikes, and camping trips were held.

With the closing of *Kol Ha'isha* in 1984, lesbians continued to meet every three weeks. Discussion topics were chosen which directly related to lesbians and lesbianism. Involvement in each other's lives was now on a more personal basis; a support system was established and lesbians worked together, helping one another to move from one flat to another, caring for sick women on a rotation basis, "and always the parties."

About the time of the 1976 feminist conference, another organization was established in Tel Aviv, The Society for Protection of Personal Rights, known as the *Aguda*, for both gays and lesbians. Its purpose was both educational and political. A hotline was established for gays and lesbians, which is still in existence—*Kav HaLavan* (The White Line). Working within the political arena, the *Aguda* supported the decriminalization of homosexuality, finally achieved in 1988, after a 15 year battle.

In 1987, a political force within the *Aguda* was born, *Otzma* (Power), whose aim is to raise the consciousness of heterosexuals and homosexuals to the existence of gay and lesbian power. It has been working on rights for single sex couples, and rights for gays and lesbians in the army and the workforce, and is now involved in the fight to allow lesbians the use of artificial insemination.

In 1978, *Alef* (Organization of Lesbian Feminists), was formed. Its members were made up of many of the lesbians involved in the *Aguda,* who felt the necessity of forming their own group separate from gay men. The membership ranged from radical lesbian feminists to nonfeminist lesbians. Because of differences between the two groups of women, *Alef* disbanded.

In 1979, a feminist cultural center was opened in Tel Aviv which gave space to lesbians. Many lesbians joined the movement. It was not until 1986, however, that lesbians established a coffee house and a bimonthly schedule of meetings for lectures, poetry readings and group activities. The informal group became formalized in 1986(-87), with the establishment of the Community of Lesbian Feminists, known as *Klaf*. Lesbians also meet under the aegis of *Isha L'Isha,* the Haifa feminist center.

Klaf organizers perceived the need for an Israeli lesbian organization that included its own unique culture rather than importing the lesbian culture of the United States, which had been the main source of books, music and philosophy prior to this time. In coalition with the *Aguda* and *Otzma*, *Klaf* has continued its support of Israeli lesbian culture through encouragement of writers, composers, and poets. *Klaf* publishes a newsletter with free distribution to about 250 lesbians. Discussions sponsored by *Klaf* have been written up in pamphlet form and distributed to the Israeli feminist centers and the Tel Aviv University library.

Prior to 1988, therapy for lesbians was largely ignored by the mainstream therapeutic community. These needs are now being met by a newly formed feminist therapy collective, The Counseling Center for Women, with centers in both Jerusalem and Tel Aviv.

Education is a prime tool for introducing information about lesbian issues. The author has lectured on the subject of lesbians at Haifa University's School of Social Work and Women's Studies program. With three other members of the *Aguda*, a presentation was made to psychiatric residents at the Beer Sheba Medical School in order to familiarize them with patients they might see in the future. Battered women's shelters are just beginning to be educated about the unique problems of battered lesbians, an issue that is gaining recognition within the Israeli lesbian community. But these are the exceptions and not the norm.

Until Israeli society can accept the differences that exist within its society, and view lesbians as a viable part of what it is and what is good, lesbians shall mostly remain invisible in order to survive. Job and apartments will be maintained and children will not be lost through custody suits. Until organizations such as the *Aguda*, *Otzma*, and *Klaf* can reach larger numbers of lesbians, so that the Israeli society is aware of their existence, the majority of Israeli lesbians must remain invisible.

REFERENCES

Dempsey, R. and Fawley, S. I. (1988) "The Oppressive Power of the Lesbian Label." *National NOW Times*, December/January.

Dykewomon, Elana (1988) "Passing." *Sinister Wisdom* 35 (Summer/Fall): 3–6.

Gatrell, Nanette (1981) "The Lesbian as "Single" Woman." *American Journal of Psychotherapy* 25 (4): 502–509.

Minnigerode, Frederick A. (1976) "Attitudes Toward Homosexuality: Feminist Attitudes and Sexual Conservatism." *Sex Roles* 2(4): 347–352.

Nugent, Robert (1983) "Married Homosexuals." *The Journal of Pastoral Care* 37 (4): 243–251.

Oppenheimer, Jo (1991) "The Influence of Homophobia on Lesbian Identity Formation in the Therapeutic Setting: The Consequences and Rewards for the Acceptance and Non-acceptance of the Self." In Pheterson, Gail; Essed, Philomena; Richardson, Diane, et al., *Between Selfhelp and Professionalism*, Vol. 3. Amsterdam: Stichting de Maan—The Moon Foundation.

Shenkar, Joseph (1989) "Declared Lesbians Will Not Be Entitled to Artificial Insemination." *Jerusalem* June 2, 1.
Rich, Adrienne (1980) "Compulsory Heterosexuality and Lesbian Existence." *Signs* 5 (4): 630–660.
Ross, H. Laurence (1972) "Odd Couples: Homosexuals in Heterosexual Marriages." *Sexual Behaviour,* 42–49.
Rule, June (1975) *Lesbian Images.* New York: Doubleday.

Section Three

Society Under Siege—
The Spectre of War

Living in a State of Siege

Regine Waintrater
(Translated from the French by Sharon Ne'eman.)

Being in a war zone, Israelis live with a double rhythm. One rhythm, the private, is that of their personal, civilian life, with its work, social interaction, friendships and romantic attachments. Permanently superimposed on that rhythm is the other, public rhythm, composed of periods of reserve duty or mobilization, military exercises or false alerts. Any woman with an adult Israeli male in her life will see him leave for the army at regular, scheduled intervals, for reserve duty or for war with no advance notice. Let us recall that every [Jewish, Druze, Bedouin, Circassion — Ed] male citizen of Israel between the ages of 18 and 55 may be mobilized and is called up for reserve duty for one to three months a year according to circumstances.

This separation strongly resembles a bad grade-B movie. Each plays his or her own role, but cannot really be him or herself. The man must be brave and must not show his fear; the woman, too, must be brave, letting him go without making the parting difficult. In this, as in all extreme situations, there is little room for subtlety of feeling. War, an extreme situation par excellence, reduces feelings to the most basic. Does this mean that Israelis have only the most basic emotions? What seems probable is that in extreme situations (this term is borrowed from Bruno Bettelheim, and was brilliantly developed by him with regard to other experiences in 1943), mechanisms such as denial and repression appear indispensable to the mental and emotional survival of persons confronted with such situations.

In time of danger or stress, individual reactions are more or less guided by defense mechanisms. When the man leaves, the woman remains behind, charged with maintaining the home and with the very clear assignment of "acting as if," that is, acting as if life were continuing normally, as if nothing had happened. This constant attempt to normalize the abnormal leaves a definite mark on Israeli society. Here, an entire society reacts, and by its reactions, dictates the behavior of each individual. Women are affected as strongly as men, although in a different way.

When their men are in service, Israeli women must deal with all of the everyday problems of existence—in Israel there are many—by themselves, and this may well be for the best; they channel their anxiety into the things they do best, at times, to the point of absurdity. For example, during and after the Yom Kippur War, when men were mobilized for six months and women found themselves very lonely and powerless, a flour shortage occurred: The women were baking too many cakes, and continued to do so even when the shortage was made public!

Yet baking cakes, even in large quantities, does not keep a person from thinking, and even less from feeling. Israeli women, waiting for their men to return, cannot help but feel anxious, and at times, even angry. Against whom can they direct their anger? Against their parents, no less anxious for having sent a son or a son-in-law off to the front, and just as much in need of reassurance? Against their colleagues at work, most of whom are in the same situation and engrossed in the same effort to continue functioning? Against the injustice of fate and society, which force them to undergo this trial? Or against their husbands, who have abandoned them to go to a war which men were not wise enough to prevent?

The greatest difficulty does not always come where it is expected. The abovementioned denial and repression combine to form an absolute prohibition against certain emotions coming to the surface. Feelings such as ambivalence have no place in wartime; in Israel, they have for many years had no place at all. Ambivalence tends to immobilize, and any woman abandoning herself to it could lose the strength which she so desperately needs.

A woman who has had to confront all the problems of life in the rear without men is liable to fall prey to mixed feelings, which disturb and perplex her. For example, her soldier comes home on leave; she has prepared all his favorite dishes, the house is spotless, she has invited her in-laws, and so forth, but her mood is often not in tune with his. She has been waiting for a long time, afraid that he will not arrive; she has been hoping that the children will get to see their father, and has even promised that they will, sometimes lying outright, just to reassure them. Yet she, too, would like to be fussed over; she would like him to assume responsibility, once the first moments of reunion are over. As for him, he often has nothing to say, or he may speak of things which seem foreign to her, or show no interest in what has transpired on the home front, and she is disappointed; after all, she waited so long for this moment. He is tired; he sleeps a great deal; she understands him—he has not slept in a real bed since he left for the war. She begins to reproach herself for not being up to the task, for not being able to bear her share of the burden.

War, then, imposes something close to self-censorship on women; they do not feel they have the right to complain, or they do so with a great deal of guilt. The nationwide taboo leaves its mark even on the way they behave among themselves. Women compete for courage and adulation. Systems of ranking soon emerge, often based on Draconian criteria. For, as we have seen, war leaves little room for subtlety of feeling.

Some women, naturally enough, would also like to escape into reserve duty. But there is no reserve duty for married women or single women [over the age of 24 – Trans.], no legitimate way to walk away from everything: worries, family, work, social obligations. True, it is not always easy for men to leave, and in recent years, with the *Intifada*, reserve duty has become unbearable for many. But in better times men were allowed to complain, to look forward to reserve duty as an escape from daily responsibility, while women, who often felt abandoned, were not. Women had no comradeship as strong as the masculine comradeship of the reserve unit, with its slang, its customs, and its exclusion of females. In certain cases, "they" even cook for themselves; yet, at home, a wife may have to put her foot down before her husband agrees to make a salad or fry an egg!

Of course, things are not always so dramatic. Women may, and often do, take advantage of their husbands' reserve duty to visit their women friends and to have evenings "out with the girls." In this connection, it is interesting to note that many women – usually young women, childless or with infants – go back to live with their mothers while their husbands are in the army. In effect, they are volunteering to return to wardship, as if their self-concept were one of an eternal minor. When asked about the reasons for this behavior, the young women make various excuses (convenience, fear of sleeping alone); in fact, no one really knows what drives them to it.

What complicates relationships between women and men are the intermittent periods of intensity which interrupt the everyday routine of family life. Obviously, it is impossible to live in a state of intensity all the time. High levels of feelings are limited in duration, and the alternation of periods of danger with calmer, more or less safe periods generates attrition in individuals called upon to switch back and forth, with no interval of transition, between two emotional registers. Many long for routine, or even boredom. For others, the return to the everyday becomes unbearable; day-to-day life seems narrow and stultified after such exhilaration.

Another visible effect concerns the primacy of family. Like holidays, wars are a family affair, and those who have no families may often feel left out. Single women with no men in their lives are forced to experience the country's times of emergency by proxy, through their relatives. Certain women are in a particularly false position: the mistress, who has no official existence, and who, when her loved one leaves for the war, may well remain uninformed. Reserve duty has sometimes been exploited in bourgeois dramas, where adultery is facilitated under cover of military orders. One cannot refrain from citing the case of the adulterous couple who, on the pretext of reserve duty, set out on a little trip abroad and unexpectedly ended up in Entebbe, as hostages of the hijacked Airbus. History does not record what happened when the hostages were freed.

What we have referred to as the public rhythm of women's lives involves other phenomena as well: numerous social scientists, as well as journalists, have commented on the high level of violence in Israeli society. This includes verbal as well as physical violence, and one encounters it in the streets, the home, and even in the Knesset. It may well be that the level of violence, evident particularly on the roads (and finding tangible expression in the high accident rate) is at least partially attributable to the stress caused by living in a constant state of siege. The presence and availability of firearms—conscripts and reservists take their guns home with them—may also be a factor contributing to the high level of violence.

The state of siege has resulted in the development of a large defense industry, run exclusively by men, since in Israel, as everywhere else, war is considered men's business. Managerial positions for women are further limited by the fact that a great number of career officers, most of whom are men, retire at the age of 40 to begin a second career in administrative positions in the public and private sectors. Retired military men are almost invariably preferred over female candidates.

Yet another effect of the state of siege is that defense matters continue to receive first priority, and only men are perceived as qualified to make decisions concerning them; this situation helps to perpetuate women's lack of political power.

The public sphere constantly threatens the private: Every married woman risks becoming a war widow, who is, by definition, a national institution. The government is officially responsible for war widows and orphans, as well as bereaved parents. When a man dies in the army—besides wars, there are training mishaps and a great many road accidents—his widow immediately comes under the financial and moral protection of the Defense Ministry, which assigns her to a social worker charged with following her case until she remarries or dies.

Notification of a soldier's death is given at home, by at least two representatives of the deceased's unit: an officer and a military doctor, who is always on hand to "drug" her so she can "cope" with her bereavement because she must be "brave." The funeral is organized and paid for by the Ministry of Defense; the soldier who falls in the line of duty is buried in a military cemetery. The widow has no control over the ceremony.

Jewish tradition dictates the *shiva* (a compulsory seven-day period of mourning) during which the mourner is relieved of all outside obligations. If all goes well, the religious code is then replaced by a social code. "All goes well," in this context, means that the widow does not have the additional misfortune of falling into one of two categories made problematic by Jewish law,

which governs all matters of personal status. If the husband dies without issue, his widow is automatically subject to levirate marriage; that is, she is
required to marry her dead husband's brother, if there is one who is not already married. She can only escape this fate by undergoing the rather un-
pleasant ceremony of *halitza*, in which the widow must take off her
brother-in-law's shoe in the presence of a Rabbinic court, a gesture symboliz-
ing her supposed anger at the brother-in-law's refusal to assure her of progeny
and carry on his late brother's line. Fortunate are those who receive release
by means of this rather outmoded ceremony; some women become objects
of blackmail on the part of their late husbands' families, who, with religious
law to back them, do not hesitate to inflict additional pain on the unfortunate
widow for financial gain.

The second threat is even more terrible, being without remedy. A woman
whose husband is declared missing—the wife of a soldier whose death cannot be confirmed—cannot remarry. Too many women come under this category. The fate of Druze widows is more dreadful still: no Druze widow may
ever marry again.

The war widow not belonging to either of these two categories must
nonetheless undertake an extremely constricted lifestyle, intended to lead her,
in obligatory stages, to "rehabilitation" (a term also employed in Israel for the
ill and socially handicapped). In this area, explicit and implicit codes of behavior are subtly interwoven. The widow must obey unwritten rules; she is
entangled in a net of solicitude and social expectations, which she has no
choice but to accept. War widows, in a sense, are the property of society.
It is for society that they have sacrificed their husbands; it is society which,
feeling responsible, takes them into its wardship without leaving them a choice
in the matter.

From that point, it is not hard for women to begin to feel like memorial
monuments. Women often have expressed precisely this feeling. On the one
hand, they describe the care and attention given them; on the other, they complain of the administrative muddles through which they must wade alone.
The Ministry of Defense is a bureaucracy like any other in Israel, with its in-
efficiencies and its foul-ups, and war widows often feel quite dependent on
it. Their status may inspire jealousy within the community for their financial
status may improve as a result of their pensions and the exemptions they receive from certain taxes, including the very heavy tax on automobiles. The
envy cannot but make them feel bitter.

The status of war widow also entails obligations. A "good widow" must
conform to certain social exigencies. First among these is the duty of com-
memoration, in all its forms. In Israel, remembrance of the past and commemo-
ration of the dead are universal public duties. The country is young, and its
memories emotionally laden. Victims of Israel's wars are especially recalled

on the eve of Independence Day, as a debt owed by the country to its fallen. On that day, Israel looks different, to a great extent, because of the omnipresence of ritual. Widows and their grief are officially honored. However, some find that their sorrow has become too much a national affair, yet another invasion of the public into the private.

A "good widow" is also one who welcomes visits by comrades and officers from her dead husband's unit, who, for a long time afterward, will come to see her once a year on the anniversary of her husband's death. The situation is at times difficult, or embarrassing, but no one would dream of setting a limit to these ritual visits.

Finally, if they have the means, a "good widow" or bereaved parents feel obliged to establish a foundation or find another tangible way of commemorating their husband's or son's memory. They may plant trees in his name, or donate his library to an institution, or set up a scholarship in his memory, thus denoting their willingness, as it were "to join the collective" of war widows and bereaved parents. They may also publish a booklet in memory of the deceased, with testimonies written by friends or relatives, and they may take charge of organizing commemorative evenings, in the purest Jewish tradition.

Last but not least, the wife must remarry, or at least find an official life-partner. For a "good widow" is also one who, after a decent interval, agrees to resume her life, thus enabling society to put aside its guilt. A good rehabilitation reassures everyone. The situation of the bereaved parents is often more difficult. The Ministry of Defense also takes responsibility for providing financial aid for these parents. However, when the widow remarries, the parents-in-law may see this as disloyalty to their son's memory, and this may create tension that increases progressively with the number of "bereaved" grandchildren. Every community has bereaved parents that devote the remainder of their lives to perpetuating the memory of their fallen sons.

In Israel, war has had extremely important indirect effects on Israeli women's status and self-perception. On the social level, war has contributed to widening the gap between a female intelligentsia accustomed to introspection, and the masses of women, difficult to mobilize, entangled in the net of social expectations, with few means of cutting themselves free. Furthermore, any efforts that were made in this direction were set at nought by each new war, which, by indisputably reestablishing the stereotypes, returned the situation back to its original state. [The new feminist movement had its beginnings in 1970. Between 1972 and October 1973, women joined in ever increasing numbers. However, many women who were active in the Feminist Movement, dropped out during the Yom Kippur war (October 1973) and the ceasefire that followed, some never to return—Ed.]

In a society where en brera (no choice) has long been the national philosophy, it has been especially difficult for women to struggle for a better status.

Often they did not feel they had even the right to initiate such a fight. As long as there is a national consensus, minorities have difficulty making themselves heard: often, in a pattern of self-censorship, they forego the effort.

REFERENCES

Bettelheim, Bruno (1943) "Individual and Mass Behavior in Extreme Situations." *Journal of Abnormal and Social Psychology* 38 (4): 417–452.

Jewish and Druze
War Widows

Ruth Katz

There are about 172,000 widows in Israel, triple the number of divorcees in the country. Many of them are war widows. They are generally young, and most of them have children. Widows constitute 29 percent of the single-parent mothers in Israel, compared with 9 percent of the single-parent mothers in the United States (Norton and Glick, 1986; Keren-Ya'ar and Souery, 1983).

The laws dealing with widow's rights distinguish between three categories of widows, according to the cause of death of the husband: (1) widows whose husbands' deaths were caused while serving in the military or as a result of hostile acts; (2) widows whose husbands' deaths were caused by work accidents; and (3) widows whose husbands' deaths were caused by any other reason. War widows, whose husbands are perceived as having sacrificed their lives for the country, are regarded as entitled to lead "respectable" lives. The government is legally responsible for providing them and their children with financial, vocational, and social support (Shamgar-Handelman, 1981; 1983; 1986). Some widows find that their economic status has substantially improved following their husband's death. Therefore many of these young widows chose not to remarry so as to retain their government pensions. In 1976, a law was passed to remedy this situation: the widow who had remarried was allowed to regain her widow's pension if she was divorced within five years of the second marriage if she was childless, and within seven years of the remarriage if she had children. Out of concern for the fact that some widows were still avoiding remarriage for fear of loss of economic status and security, the law was amended once again in 1989 to increase the above time periods to ten and fourteen years, respectively.

Widows whose husbands' deaths were caused by work accidents are eligible for social security benefits and other privileges which may enable them to maintain a semblance of the lifestyle they enjoyed before their husbands' deaths. Women in the third category of widows are entitled to only a minimal standard of living. This "hierarchy" reflects Israeli values.

Studies show that all three types of widows exhibit lower psychological well-being than married women. Despite the fact that war widows receive comprehensive support and many of their needs are taken care of, often at a higher level than they were accustomed to prior to their husbands' deaths, they do not differ significantly from other widows on a depression scale (Katz, forthcoming). This may be attributed to the fact that Israel is a family-oriented society (Katz and Pesach, 1985). Examining the changes that occur in a war widow's life, one finds both "costs" and "benefits." She feels that her social life is less satisfactory and that the double burden of being a working woman and a single parent is quite heavy. At the same time, she perceives an improvement in her relations with her children and in her development at work, as well as an increase in self-assurance.

Most of the widows report a feeling of loneliness. At the beginning they are surrounded by family, friends and neighbours who try their best to support them emotionally and help them in practical ways. But as time goes on, they find themselves trapped in a double-bind. Those who continue to receive intensive family support are expected to adjust to a restricted role, that of the widow. This involves a network of support for them and their children, but also constricts on their developing new social and intimate relationships (Amir and Sharon, 1979). Those who try to carry on with the same social activities as before, find themselves outsiders in a society based on couples, one that has been described as "a society with the rules of Noah's ark."

War widows have another problem. The general reverance for those who have died in battle makes war widows feel ambivalent about their own social lives. At least in the beginning, they tend to neglect their former contacts and avoid developing new ones. The inner conflict, as well as the tension between the widows and those around them, cause them to reduce social contacts. Renewing them after a prolonged period of time is a difficult and sometimes impossible task (Shamgar-Handelman, 1986: 112–144).

In contrast, young war widows perceive improvements in the parental and occupational domains as a result of their widowhood. Widows who were employed before being widowed, as well as those who begin their working careers only afterwards, express a sense of increased self-confidence, particularly in regard to occupational success. They invest more time and energy in their work outside the home, and they derive more satisfaction from it. Even though they feel overburdened, being a single parent and holding down a job, they sense a great deal of personal enrichment being able to accomplish both of these tasks. Shamgar-Handelman found that war widows sometimes attempted to take over their husbands' businesses. In cases of partnership, the arrangement did not work out, mainly because the partners refused to cooperate with a woman (1986: 157). In general, the psychological well being of the employed widows was better than that of their counterparts who were homemakers. A study of working mothers in Israel which examines the balance between strain and enrichment in their lives found that for women with high levels of resources such as schooling, occupational prestige and income there was reciprocal contribution to the parenting and employment roles. Although the study involves working mothers of intact families, its conclusions can be applied to working widows (Katz, 1989).

The widow's own salary brings her higher social status and contributes to her positive self-image. The conjugal power relationship during the marriage also has an impact on the widow's well-being. The more equal her participation in family decision-making, the better her situation as a widow. The ability to take an active part in the financial management of the family contributes to her independence and equips her with essential skills for her new role as the head of a family. Resources at the disposal of the widow, like education and earning power, also appear to be of critical importance to the widow's ability to cope.

DRUZE WAR WIDOWS

The following statement was made by a 30-year-old Druze widow with four children: "It's hard to describe my situation after the disaster. Every day I die a thousand deaths. I can hardly bear getting up in the morning and not finding him beside me. I feel I'm going mad. I fear the future and I don't know how I'll get through tomorrow. I live only for the children. My husband loved them so much and dreamed of seeing them grown-up and successful" (Medzini, 1987).

The Druze in Israel constitute about 1.7 percent of the population; they live in villages in the northern part of the country, mainly in mountainous regions. In contrast to other minorities, Druze males serve in the Israeli armed forces. Druze society is patrilocal, patriarchal and patrilineal. The median marriage age is relatively low: 23.4 years of age for men and 18.8 years of age for women (Central Bureau of Statistics [C.B.S.] 1988) and the total fertility is 4.17 (C.B.S., 1988).

In spite of the compulsory education laws, less than half of Druze women complete elementary school. Very few are high school graduates or graduates of teacher training colleges. The reason for the high dropout rate is that parents object to their daughters attending a mixed school; they claim that the girls are needed to help out at home (Layish, 1982). As a result, the labor market participation of Druze women is also very low.

As blood relations are considered stronger than relations through marriage, a Druze woman is never an integral part of her husband's family, and at the death of her husband, she is not considered the natural guardian of her children. If after being widowed she is awarded guardianship, it is not as a right but as a favor, usually when no "natural" guardian (from her husband's family) is available (Layish, 1982).

The Druze war widow is entitled to the same state benefits and privileges as her Jewish counterpart. However, the combination of a traditional community, which prevents her from developing personal resources like education and a job, and a formal-modern agency of support, the Israeli government, is hazardous to her well-being. Although the Druze war widow knows what her opportunities are (for example, continuing education, vocational training, psychological counseling, or a new car), the values and norms of her environment prevent her from taking advantage of most of these benefits. Women are expected to remain at home, not to study or work outside, and it is not usual for them to drive. As a result, her morale is very low. In comparison with five other groups of married and widowed women, she was found to scan the top of a depression scale, her mental condition resembling clinically diagnosed depression. Moreover, in a comparative study of reactions to the sudden death of a relative, significant differences were found between Jews, Moslems and Druze. All the Druze respondents perceived the death of a husband as the most difficult, painful and traumatic event, while 75% of the Moslems and only 37% of the Jews shared this perception (Watad, 1989). The situation of the Druze war widow is, most probably, a result of her lack of personal resources and the uncertainty of her parental authority as well as a support system which does not provide for the special needs of war widows.

REFERENCES

Amir, Judah and Sharon, Irit (1979) "Factors in the Adjustment of Widows of the Israeli Defense Forces." *Megamot* 25:120–130 (Hebrew).

Central Bureau of Statistics (1988) *Monthly Bulletin of Statistics,* Supplement, 39(3), Jerusalem.

Katz, Ruth (1989) "Strain and Enrichment in the Role of Employed Mothers in Israel." *Marriage and Family Review,* 14(1/2) 195–216.

Katz, Ruth (1990) "Marital Status and Well-being: A Comparison Between Widowed, Divorced and Married Mothers in Israel." *Journal of Divorce* 14(1).

Katz, Ruth and Pesach, Nurit (1985) "Adjustment to Divorce in Israel: A Comparison Between Divorced Men and Women." *Journal of Marriage and the Family* 47(3): 765–773.

Keren-Ya'ar, Hanna and Sourey, Miriam (1983) *Families With Children in Israel 1970–1983.* Jerusalem: The National Insurance Institute (Hebrew).

Layish, Aharon (1982). *Marriage, Divorce and Succession in the Druze Family.* Leiden: E.J. Brill.

Medzini, Bina (1987) Support Systems and Personal Well-being in a Traditional Society: The Case of the Israeli War Widows of the Druze Community. M.A. Thesis, School of Social Work, University of Haifa.

Norton, Arthur J. and Glick, Paul C. (1986) "One-parent Families: A Social and Economic Profile." *Family Relations* 31(1): 9–17.

Shamgar-Handelman, Lea (1981) "Administering to War Widows in Israel: The Birth of a Social Category." *Social Analysis* 9: 24–47.

Shamgar-Handelman, Lea (1983) "The Social Status of War Widows" *International Journal of Mass Emergencies and Disasters* 1(1): 153–169.

Shamgar-Handelman, Lea (1986) *Israeli War Widows: Beyond the Glory of Heroism.* Massachusetts: Bergin and Garvey Publishers, Inc.

Watad, Saladin (1987) A Comparison Between the Scoring of Jews, Muslims, Christians, and Druze: The Traumatic Level in the Death of a Spouse, a Parent and a Son. M.A. Thesis, School of Social Work, Tel Aviv University.

Women in the Defense Forces

Anne R. Bloom

Israel's army was established on May 26, 1948, by decree, shortly after the Declaration of Independence of the new state. Its roots, however, date back to the first decade of the twentieth century, and women have played a significant role throughout its development. The debate over the extent and nature of women's participation in the Israeli security forces is not a recent development, but was carried on among the various groups within the Jewish community in Palestine and has continued uninterrupted since the establishment of the state. More impressive than the changes has been the remarkable consistency in the arguments presented for and against women's integration into the defense apparatus.

The first prestate defense organization, *Hashomer,* was created in 1909. Consisting at first of only a few dozen people, it took the warrior Bedouin as its model, transforming it into the ideal prototype of a courageous Jewish watchman, a figure on horseback ready to protect any settlement in need. At least two women were founding members, Manya Shochat and Esther Becker (Becker, 1936). As *Hashomer* membership grew and demand for watchmen increased, woman's role in guarding was heatedly debated. Many men supported women in their demands for equal participation, while others questioned and even ridiculed the idea.

Like their sisters in the collective agricultural settlements, the women in *Hashomer* were role innovators. "They had no one after whom to model themselves . . . no way of knowing which was better and which way worse, what work they should do and what work they should not do" (Izraeli, 1981). They sought active participation in defense activities and equal responsibility, and constantly argued for their rights, but they were not always successful. In effect, there were two distinct types of roles for the women associated with the *Hashomer.* The first was represented by Manya Shochat and Rachel Yanait who, along with some of the other women, became full-fledged members.

This is an abridged and updated version of (1982) "Israel: The Longest War." In Goldmann (ed.) *Female Soldiers—Combatants or Non-Combatants,* West Port, CO: Greenwood.

These women were active participants at meetings in which the purchase and concealment of arms and organizational and operational matters were discussed. The second group were the "wives of" *Hashomer* members, clearly relegated to second-class status and not allowed to attend those meetings. At annual *Hashomer* conferences, the debate about combat training and the use of weapons by female members persisted. Although all the women wished to take an active part, no clearly favorable resolution was agreed upon. The women of *Hashomer* infused the concept of role equality into the national psyche, but they also showed the men that they would settle for less than they asked for.

The Arab attacks of 1920 on Tel Hai and Kfar Giladi and in 1921 on Jerusalem and Jaffa made it clear that *Hashomer* was inadequate to the increasing security demands. Political and strategy debates ensued. The prevailing opinion was to include all able-bodied Jews, male and female alike, in a new, secret defense organization called *Haganah* (literally, "defense"). The *Haganah* had three objectives: to acquire arms, to provide military training to members of agricultural settlements, and to set up self-defense organizations in towns and cities. But even after the *Haganah* established a national command, its authority remained limited and ineffective (Schiff, 1974). The members were not professionals but volunteers. Training, which usually took place in the evenings and on weekends, depended on local leadership. Given so loose a structure, women's roles depended largely on the local situation.

Primarily because the *Haganah* was a secret organization whose decisions, plans, and strategy were determined on an ad-hoc basis, there are few precise records of those early years, and we are dependent on diaries, depositions, and interviews for information about the role of women. The reported pattern was as follows: A young woman joined the *Haganah* at approximately 17 years of age. She was usually recruited either through membership in a youth movement or by recommendation of two people vouching for her as an individual who was reliable, responsible, strong enough to handle assignments and keep secrets, and dedicated to the cause (Esther Herlitz, 1979, personal interview). She was introduced to discipline and organization and then taught to handle weapons. More often than not, she was trained in communications and first aid. Women learned and then taught all the techniques of transmitting information, from the personal (and often dangerous) carrying of messages, through training carrier pigeons, operating transmitters, to stringing wires for telephone connections. They were also responsible for medical assistance when the need arose and for the organization of medical facilities. During those years they were always few in numbers.

The National Service Act was passed in England in December 1941 conscripting unmarried women between the ages of 20 and 30 into the Auxiliary Territorial Services (ATS). Because the British were reluctant to send their own women to the Middle East, they recruited Palestinian women to serve in their armed forces. Recruitment began the first week in 1942. Women from the ages of 18 to 50 were eligible for service. Many women volunteered, enlisting either directly through British offices or through Jewish authorities. Four thousand women were recruited, about nine hundred of whom were WAAFs (Women's Auxiliary Air Force). Following the original British pattern, a cadre of women was to be selected and trained who in turn would become officers and NCOs (noncommissioned officers) and would train those who followed. Of the first group to volunteer, 66 were selected for the officer cadre, including three Christian Arabs and three Armenians. Among the 60 Jewish recruits, one-half were *Haganah* members, while the others had been recommended by the various women's organizations.

A deliberate attempt to include kibbutz women in this leadership group was met with resistance. The kibbutz arguments against recruitment came primarily from men, who felt that women should serve locally in the *Haganah* or, alternatively, serve only as nurses and doctors, not as drivers for officers (Gelber, 1977). Despite the fact that most of the kibbutz women did not agree with these arguments, they accepted the decision of the kibbutz authorities. Some kibbutz women revolted: "I was ashamed, remembering all our discussions about the question of women's recruitment. Our friends regarded this as a matter of the 'women question': should women be defended; should a protective arm be placed around them? They do not regard this as the expression of the independent Jewish woman who knows her destiny" (Rabinowitch, 1942).

On a personal level, the women recruits faced many obstacles. All the women interviewed reported having heard accusations that Auxiliary Territorial Services (ATS) recruits were "loose" women. If not labeled outright as prostitutes, they were called adventure-seekers, husband hunters, or escapees from unhappy marriages. Many women reported that their families were ostracized. They said that without strong family support, particularly from their fathers, it would have been impossible for most of them to join.

On May 19, 1941, the *Palmach* (Jewish assault companies) were created to carry out special and dangerous duties assigned by the *Haganah* High Command. In the spring of 1942, the British, threatened by Rommel in Africa, offered the *Palmach* assistance for training. With this aid, *Palmach* membership doubled. The *Palmach* was now based in kibbutzim, where members worked part-time (to help pay for their support) and trained. In effect, this arrangement allowed the *Palmach* to become a standing force stationed in training bases, living under military regimen (Bauer, 1973).

When the question first arose regarding the recruitment of women to the *Palmach*, the *Haganah* chief of staff issued explicit instructions against it. During the winter of 1941–1942, Israel Livartovsky, the commander of the Jerusalem company, disobeyed the order and assembled a small group of Jerusalem women, the first female formation in the *Palmach*. Later the national command agreed to include women (limiting the number to ten percent of the total group), but it did not say what the function of the female recruits would be. One of them, Sarah Braverman, writes:

> "Each one of us saw ourselves as a guinea pig. We were more or less one unit in each company. In training we were dispersed as individuals, one in a squad, two in a platoon. The prevailing notion was that the female member could participate in the same activities as the male member, so we were trained in all the professions, using the rifle, pistol, grenades, stens and were given physical training. We shared all the combat experiences and our effort was unbelievable" (Braverman, 1955: 67–69).

In September 1943, the first convention of *Palmach* women was held to evaluate the past and plan for the future. These innovators were fully aware that the failure of one woman would cast doubt on the entire group, and that the failure of ten percent could end women's role in the military. They presented the organization with recommendations geared toward improving the method of absorbing women into the military framework.

At the end of 1943, the *Palmach* had 1,113 members, far short of its goal of 5,000 (Bauer, 1973). Financial support from the British was no longer forthcoming. In early 1944, the *Palmach* changed its system of membership. The decision was made to call up the youth movement groups preparing for settlement in kibbutzim. While the kibbutzim would assist in financing their training, members of the groups would work part-time to pay their way. Primarily young men and women from urban middle-class or well-established working-class families, these young people all shared socialist ideas of collective living and dedication to public service.

One half of each *garin* (core group) was female. An agreement signed in 1944 by the *Palmach* and the youth movements guaranteed the enlistment of all the girls and the autonomy of each group. While the youth movements organized only a small percentage of the members of their age groups, these volunteers were the trend setters.

In March 1944, Britain issued the White Paper, the purpose of which was to limit Jewish immigration to Palestine. As a result, the Jews mobilized for armed struggle against the British. The major military organizations were the *Haganah* and the *Irgun*. The latter was a dissident group that regarded the British rather than the Arabs as the main enemy of the Jewish settlement in Palestine.

During the height of the struggle, the *Irgun* had a membership of two thousand, 20 percent of them women (E. Lankin, 1978 interview). These women were distributed among propaganda, information, education, medical and combat units. Their jobs consisted of putting up anti-British posters, running ammunition, and maintaining contact between members who had gone underground. The assignments were often dangerous; the first woman caught with a bomb was an *Irgun* member, Rachel Ohevet Ami, who was sentenced to 15 years imprisonment. Some women served in the combat units, although there was a great reluctance among the men to involve them in direct combat action.

The United Nations resolution to partition Palestine into a Jewish and an Arab state with Jerusalem an international zone, triggered a war between the Jews and the surrounding Arab countries that lasted sixteen months, from December 1, 1947 to March 10, 1949. It was in the *Palmach,* the most active branch of the forces of the Jewish community, that women participated in the largest numbers. Elsewhere, the story was different. By February 1948, the *Palmach* had grown to 4,035, including twenty percent women who were classified at the highest level of physical capability, and ten percent men and women with a low profile" (Pa'il, 1979). By June 1948, there were 6,000 mobilized *Palmach* members, including 1,200 women. During the first six months of the war, the *Palmach* served as the defensive screen behind which the rest of the Army could mobilize.

Palmach women served as combat soldiers or commanders; as saboteurs, wireless operators, and medics; as drivers and instructors of soldiers from abroad. They handled all cultural programs at the outposts. Back at the bases, they functioned as instructors, cooks, secretaries and administrators.

Women played leadership roles in both combat and training. Five women officers commanded combat units, remaining in service until the end of the war. At a central training camp where most of the recruiting was done, the commander, Major Dvora Spector, was described as a "real professional." One of women soldiers' most important assignments was in communication. Meir Pa'il, a Knesset member and colonel in the reserves, reported: "Women were excellent—there was not a single incident of a female soldier not behaving correctly under fire" (Pa'il, 1979).

In the Battle of the Roads, women made up one-third of the convoy escorts. They hid ammunition, operated the wireless, administered first aid, and fought when attacked. The job was arduous and hazardous. One veteran reported that she was on a convoy every day for four and a half months. As a wireless operator, she rode in the first armored car. During an ambush, when the commanding officer froze in shock, she became the link between Jerusalem and the others in her convoy. In effect, she was in command.

While the *Palmach* women remained in action until the end of the war, women serving in the *Haganah* did not. Esther Herlitz tells of her experiences in the spring of 1948, when she and another former ATS officer were asked to form a women's battalion in Jerusalem.

"One of the things we had to do was to take the *Haganah* girls out of the front line. It was a decision about which there is controversy till this day. In Jerusalem one woman was killed in Sheik Jarrah and another taken prisoner in the old city—both were soldiers. Of course it is difficult to say where the "front" is and what is "nonfront." But the decision was to take women out of the fighting units. Ben-Gurion's explanation was that for everyone in the front line, you need so many in the rear. Since boys would be better fighters, that was the arrangement. The *Haganah* girls didn't like it, especially the radar girls. It kept them from getting good jobs in the army, in lower ranks, and out of decision making posts. They resented it" (Esther Herlitz, 1979 interview).

Soon after he proclaimed the birth of the state of Israel, David Ben-Gurion moved to unify the Jewish fighting forces. His goal was to create a professional and depoliticized army based on the British model, while retaining and strengthening the pioneering spirit within the new state. Controversy arose immediately regarding women in this new army. The first issue was whether they should be included at all, and second, what their role would be.

The question of inclusion arose primarily from the religious bloc. During the debate in the first Knesset, Rabbi Levin called female military service "an absolute contradiction to the spirit of Israel" (Ben-Gurion, 1972). However, there are no religious laws that prohibit women from bearing arms. The underlying reasons for opposition had to do with the definition of "women's place." Although Ben-Gurion was a secularist, he believed that the Bible occupied a central place in the life of the Jewish people and was, therefore, willing for the Jewish state to come to terms with its religious minority. He laid down the principles of women's participation in the Israeli Defense Force (IDF):

"We are told that women are not drafted into any other army in the world. We, too, have no intention of putting women into combat units, though no one can be sure that, should we be attacked and have to fight for our lives, we would not call on the services of every man and woman. But the law in question deals with a peacetime situation, and we want to give women only the most basic training" (Ben-Gurion, 1972).

The Defense Service Law of 1949, enacted by the Knesset and amended several times, stipulated (1959) that:

1. Women who reach the age of 18 are eligible for conscription to serve for a period of 24 months (for men, 36 months).
2. Married women and mothers of children are exempt, as well as women for whom religious convictions preclude their serving (this amounts to 25 percent of the age group as opposed to 2 percent for men).
3. Deferment of service is available to women studying in institutions which the army recognizes. Upon graduation, they are required to serve the full period of military service, regardless of their marital status (this is true for men as well).
4. Reserve service is obligatory. After the term of national service, a woman is obliged to serve in the reserves until the age of 34 (in actuality, women perform such service only until 24 years of age) or until the birth of the first child (men serve in the reserves until the age of 55).

5. Unmarried physicians, dentists, surgical nurses, physiotherapists and occupational therapists serve until the age of 34 (IDF Spokesman, February 27, 1980).

Within these broad outlines, policy for recruitment and utilization of women
evolved as the army developed. Two lines of thought were in conflict from
the outset. The first was to duplicate the British pattern, with the women's
corps entirely separate. Under this plan, female soldiers would be sent to serve
in men's units, but the rest of their military life would remain under the jurisdiction of the Women's Corps (CHEN). This included separate storehouses,
technical schools, and training and judicial responsibilities. The second proposal, offered by the *Palmach,* was for total integration of female soldiers into
those units in which they served, minimizing separateness. Organizationally,
these two plans were merged during the first two years, making the Women's
Corps the authority responsible for training and judicial matters, while all work
assignments became general army manpower decisions.

Within CHEN itself, there were conflicts between the two approaches regarding style, attitudes towards military life, and relations between officer and
recruit. Probably the most crucial issue of all was the extent of military training. The Auxiliary Territorial Services women were inclined to emphasize the
auxiliary aspect of women's participation in the war, while at the same time
setting high standards for achievement in all undertakings. Although they accepted not serving in combat, they felt women could perform a wide variety
of tasks. One woman commander told how she attended the first officer training course, was given a ribbon, appointed a camp commander and sent to
help form an army base in Mt. Carmel, Haifa. "We reproduced everything
from the British army in exact duplicate, from the "Order of the Day" to the
payroll, saluting, and insisting that the uniform be worn a certain way. This
is what we knew" (Retired Colonel Stella Levy, 1980 interview).

For the *Palmach* women, on the other hand, standing at attention and all
other military conventions were an anathema. A commander who organized
a camp in Tel Aviv tells of her debate with a *Palmach* officer:

> "The first day they came in, she wanted to teach the girls shooting and throwing
> bombs. I said to her, let me first organize things so they know where to go,
> teach them what the army is and what it expects from them. At the very begin-
> ning we only had the girls for a few days, but I had to give in, and find a day
> for rifle training" (interview with former Women's Corps officer, July 1978).

The argument revolved around just how far the "self defense" concept would
be translated into active military participation and how seriously "military behavior" was to be taken in the newly formed army. The change from underground to regular army was difficult and painful. During the first year, many
Palmach women returned to their kibbutzim or went on to university and
other studies. The Women's Corps leadership was left primarily in the hands

of the former ATS women; until 1970, the commanding officer of the women's corps was always a former ATS officer.

The Women's Corps is not a corps in the true sense of the term, but rather an administrative cadre governing training assignments and military careers of women in the IDF (IDF Spokesman, 1980). Until 1988, the highest-ranking officer was a colonel. In 1988, due to agitation from feminists and women's groups, the incumbent, Amira Dotan, was promoted to the rank of Brigadier General. The commander of the Women's Corps serves as a member of the General Staff, under the manpower division. She advises the Chief of Staff on problems of training, vacations and leaves, housing and hygiene, and other general conditions of service pertaining to women in all branches of the IDF— land, sea, air, military settlements, and youth battalions (Rolbant, 1970). Each of these units has a chief officer from the Women's Corps who advises the male commanding officer regarding the women in the unit. Manpower decisions are made in each separate branch of the service. Therefore, whether or not women are utilized in various professions are decisions made outside of the Women's Corps by men. The women's corps only advises in this area.

Regarding this arrangement, the Commission on the Status of Women pointed out that:

"When the IDF was first established, the state recognized the right of the women to serve in all jobs on a voluntary basis. As time elapsed equality has disappeared. The only considerations are army efficiency and economic ones. Jobs are opened and closed to women on this basis. As a result, the IDF lags behind other armies which are more resourceful in absorbing women" (1978).

The Commission found that in 1976 women filled only 210 out of 709 jobs (29.6%). Following their recommendations, 296 out of 796 jobs were available to women in 1980 (an increase of 8.6%). These occupations included secretarial, administrative and clerical jobs, held by approximately 65 percent of women soldiers; technical and mechanical jobs; and operational tasks. By the end of 1985, women were eligible to serve in 60 percent of the available jobs in the IDF. In fact, the number of jobs open to women doubled between 1976 and 1985.

According to Brigadier General Hedva Almog, the current (1991) commander of the Women's Corps, in 1988 women were actually serving in 234 out of the 500 jobs open to them. She explained that she did not encourage women to go into some jobs, like chauffeur or truck driver, but did encourage women to go into new technological jobs. However, many of the latter demand additional, advanced training. In order to be eligible for training, the soldier must sign up for at least one additional year of service. General Almog reported that most female recruits were still unwilling to enlist for the additional period. At the same time, she reported that during her three years as Women's Corps commander, the number of women who have attained the rank of colonel has increased by 33 percent (Almog, personal, written com-munication, 1989).

In addition to filling the needs of the IDF, two factors enter into a recruit's placement: her own choice and her total profile, which includes her medical profile, IQ scores, knowledge of Hebrew, and educational level. The scores range from 41–47 through 48–51 to 52–56, attained mainly by high school graduates. Individuals who rank 52–56 are considered potential officers. In 1978, 20 percent of the female recruits scored at this level, while only 10 percent of the male recruits did so (Commission on the Status of Women, 1978). In 1988, 50 percent of both female and male recruits scored in this range (Almog, 1989).

Two areas of responsibility belong to the Women's Corps alone. One is to provide basic training for all recruits and officer training. The other is to serve as the sole judicial authority for all women soldiers, regardless of where they serve. The recruit is directly responsible to the commander under whom she works, a person who is most often a male. That commander cannot, how-ever, punish or pass judgment on her without consulting and receiving the consent of an officer from the Women's Corps. This brake on a commander's ultimate authority regarding female soldiers causes him difficulties he does not encounter in dealing with male recruits. "It makes him mad—and at the very least it's a great inconvenience," one senior officer stated in a personal interview (June 1980).

The ambivalence of male commanders towards female soldiers is clear. On the one hand, women are seen as excellent workers, conscientious, dedi-cated and able, often far superior to their male counterparts. On the other hand, their special privileges create difficulties not encountered with male recruits. They credit women with creating a "humanitarian" atmosphere within the units, but also regard them as curbing the clubby atmosphere of the man's world. Just how far these organizational and interpersonal aspects restrict the utilization of women on a larger scale still needs to be analyzed.

Whereas female participation in combat and front-line combat support had been debated in the prestate period, the IDF put an end to this debate. All jobs involving combat, jobs that had to be carried out under harsh condi-tions, and jobs whose physical demands were regarded as too great for fe-males were closed to them (Commission on the Status of Women, 1978). The implications of this decision extended beyond the issue of actual fighting. It is important to note the meaning of combat in the IDF.

"The officer, whatever his actual job, is thus defined (as an image, if not a descrip-tion of reality) as a combat leader. It goes without saying that combat activities also have the highest prestige, as they are given the highest priority. If a civil-ian, employed by the IDF, in his professional capacity (say, as a psychologist) is also an officer in the reserves, he will typically be sent to his combat unit during his call up. Economically, it would probably be more efficient for the IDF to keep him in his profession at the reservist's low pay, rather than conceding his professional services for the 45 days during which he is a platoon leader. But the norm of priority to combat is the dominant one" (Schild, 1973).

While it has been pointed out that at the very most, only 15 percent of the army goes into battle, the image is a powerful one. Women only participate in that image by freeing a man for combat, and this is repeated to her as liturgy. However, some advances have been made. The situation of female tank instructors is a case in point. Following the recommendations of the Commission on the Status of Women in 1978, women became eligible to become tank instructors. They could teach how the motor works, how to drive the tank, how to repair it, how to use all the equipment in the tank. The teaching took place in a classroom and then in the tank. There was general agreement that the female instructors, like their male counterparts, knew everything there was to know about the tank. However, while the male instructor was allowed to go out into the field, the female instructor was confined to the classroom. He had first-hand experience, and she did not. There was general agreement that the female instructor would be a better classroom teacher if she taught in the field as well, but because the field was considered combat training, she was prohibited from doing so (interviews with two Armored Corps instructors, July 1980). Following a review of this situation, the rules were revamped and the female instructor in the tank corp, now goes out into the field with her trainees.

The prevailing explanation for the IDF's decision to keep women out of actual combat is fear of their being taken prisoner and of possible mistreatment and torture in the hands of the enemy. Yet documentation regarding such incidents is difficult to find. Dr. Meir Pa'il, a former commander, wrote in the *Jerusalem Post:*

> "I feel obliged to respond to comments about the "horrible fate of the few girls who did fall into Arab hands alive." To the best of my knowledge those few Jewish girls, soldiers and civilians, who happened to fall alive in Arab armies' hands were treated in a respectable manner. The most important case concerning the question occurred some time before the Six Day War, when a bus carrying about 30 women soldiers happened to cross the Lebanese border by mistake, was captured by the Lebanese armed forces and brought back after a few days to Rosh Hanikra. According to the girls' report, the Lebanese treated them honorably." (Pa'il, *Jerusalem Post,* June 22, 1978).

Reinforced by protective legislation, the woman soldier's life remains sufficiently circumscribed to allow her both to do national service and to return to society understanding her role as a woman. The message is a double one, and she cannot help but be affected by it. Binken and Boch (1977) contend that "The character and composition of a nation's military system mirror the society that it is established to protect and defend" (p. 1). The Women's Corps has truly reproduced what is present in Israeli society, and indeed, is its mirror image.

REFERENCES

Bauer, Yehuda (1973) *From Diplomacy to Resistance.* New York: Atheneum: 16–67.

Becker, Esther (1936) "The History of the Watchman's Family." In Meged, M. (ed.). *The Book of Watchman.* Tel Aviv: Dvir Co. Ltd. (Hebrew).

Ben-Gurion, David (1972) *Israel, a Personal History.* Tel Aviv: American Israeli Publishing Co.; 54.

Binken, Marlin and Boch, Shirley (1977) *Women and the Military.* Washington D.C.: The Brookings Institute.

Braverman, Sarah (1955) *The Army and War in Israel and the Nations.* Tel Aviv: Sifriat Poalim; 767–769. (Hebrew)

Commission on the Status of Women, Report on the Status of Women (1978) Prime Minister Office Jerusalem; 101.

Gelber, Yoav (1977) *Volunteerism in the Yishuv.* Ph.D. Dissertation, Hebrew University, Jerusalem.

Izraeli, Dafna (1981) "The Zionist Women's Movement in Palestine, 1911–1927." *Signs,* 6.

Pa'il, Meir (1979) *The Emergence of Zahal (Zmora).* Tel Aviv: Bitan, Modan; 241. (Hebrew)

Rabinowitch, Rivka (1942) "On the Women's Recruitment," Givan Haim Diary, March 27. Reported in Gelber, Yoav (1977) *Volunteerism in the Yishuv.* Ph.D. Dissertation, Hebrew University, Jerusalem. (Hebrew)

Rolbant, Samuel (1970) *The Israeli Soldier.* New York: T. Yosaloff.

Schiff, Zeev (1974) *A History of the Israeli Army, 1870–1974.* San Francisco: Straight Arrow Books; 12.

Schild, E. Ozer (1973) "On the Meaning of Military Service in Israel." In Curtis, M. and Chefkoff, M. (eds.). *Israel: Social Structure and Change.* New Brunswick, New Jersey: Transaction Books; 428.

AMIRA DOTAN: ISRAEL'S FIRST
FEMALE GENERAL

Brigadier-general Amira Dotan plans to lead her female troops against the challenge posed by the image that young women have of themselves. Promoted from colonel this month, the head of Israel's Women's Corps is intent on moving a significant percentage of female soldiers out of conventional clerical jobs where most pass their two years of obligatory military service to tasks at the cutting edge of new technologies hitherto occupied almost exclusively by male soldiers. For this, the women will have to undergo intensive training in a wide range of vocations, from electro-optics to computers, and sign on for additional military service ranging from four months to four years to make that training worthwhile to the armed services.

"This involves working against everything that young women think about themselves," said the 39-year old general. "They don't see themselves doing this kind of work. They don't see themselves maintaining their femininity if they practice these kinds of skills. Neither does the *yiddishe mama,* who thinks her daughter should study literature and history and not math and electronics. It's not going to be an easy task."

It is a task, however, well under way. In the four years since Dotan became commander of the Woman's Corps, the number of female soldiers occupying technological posts in the military has increased from a few dozen to several hundred, and the upward trend will continue. Dotan regards her promotion to general — the first time the head of the Women's Corps has held that rank — as a recognition by the armed services of the increasing importance of women in the country's technological military machine.

The appointment of a female general was greeted with not inconsiderable muttering by senior male officers, who wondered why in a period of sharp military cutbacks the Women's Corps was being upgraded. "I know there are men and women too, who object to the whole idea of a new role for women," says General Dotan. "The old notions seem much more comfortable."

The role of women in the country's military has taken several turns — although not full circle — since the days of the *Palmach,* when small numbers of highly motivated women trained and fought alongside their male comrades in the War of Independence. When it was decided in 1948 to establish the Women's Corps and to make military service mandatory for women, they were initially not integrated into regular units. This came about only the following year. Serving

---

Adapted from Abraham Rabinovich, "My Mother the General," *The Jerusalem Post,* Oct. 24, 1988.

for one year, and later for two, female soldiers did useful work in fields such as communications, intelligence and teaching. A large percentage, however, found themselves saddled with boring clerical duties.

In the far-ranging reorganization of the armed forces following the Yom Kippur War, when the need became apparent for maximalizing use of manpower and womanpower, women began serving as instructors to male soldiers in combat courses ranging from tank driving to artillery spotting. The increasing emphasis on technology is the latest and perhaps most meaningful shift for women soldiers since the War of Independence; it gives them operational equality in numerous important areas requiring a high level of skills important to the military.

General Dotan does not wish to see modern women soldiers emulating the female *Palmach* fighters, even though she believes that physically and psychologically they are capable of being combat soldiers. For one thing, she notes, the *Palmach* women volunteered for their combat role and were not sent to the battlefield by higher authority. Beyond that, Dotan believes that sending women into battle would violate something basic in the Jewish heritage: "We cannot ignore our heritage. There is a special role for the Jewish woman as a mother and the center of the family. I fight for equal opportunities for male and female soldiers, but we must recognize that there are certain differences."

To narrow those differences in noncombat areas, Dotan regards it as essential to provide women with role models who combine success in "male" jobs like electronics with femininity. She plans to step up the practice of sending successful female soldiers holding such jobs to visit high schools in order to encourage girls to take vocational courses that will prepare them for interesting jobs in the army — jobs that could also serve them well in civilian life afterwards.

Born in Tel Aviv, Dotan is married to a businessman and has three children: two girls, ages 16 and 9; and a boy, 14. She holds a degree from Ben-Gurion University where she studied psychology. "I had worked very hard but it was only when I was 33 or 34 and had three children that I realized that I was a career woman — I recognized it and admitted it loudly to myself and to society."

A game is played in every woman's officer course in which a hypothetical figure is presented to the class — a very successful surgeon named Rachel — and the women are asked to sketch in her personality as they imagine it. "These are 19-year-old girls who are the highest quality we have, wonderful girls" says General Dotan. "Inevitably, they will portray Rachel as a woman with talons and elbows, someone who is very aggressive. She goes to a psychiatrist at least once a week and her children, if she has any, have psychological problems. And of course she is divorced. Always. No man can live with a woman like that. This is the picture these wonderful young women have of women who succeed at a career."

General Dotan sees one of the major tasks of the Women's Corps to help change that deeply implanted image. Probably no other country in the world has an institution so well positioned to make the effort. Sixty-five percent of Israeli girls serve in the army – 25 percent opt out on religious grounds, the remainder are exempted for physical, mental or marital reasons – and they serve at a critical point in life, during the passage from adolescence to young womanhood. "These two years between 18 and 20 are really a school for life," says Commander Dotan.

What she is attempting to do during military service, and in the high school briefings that precede it, is to coax the girls out of their inclination to follow safe "traditional" paths for women that avoid grappling with the complexities and promises of modern technologies. In a society where women wish to share equal rights, she says, they must also share this new challenge. "Female soldiers have to recognize this even if they have to pay a price in the additional time they would be required to serve, in learning new skills, in changing their attitude towards technical areas they never thought about before or in working harder."

In its early years, the primary role of the Women's Corps was a motherly one, protecting its young charges during their national service. In recent years, says General Dotan, "we are looking at them more as grownups and giving them the tools to cope with life." Asked whether she regards the female soldiers as girls or women, she says, "In between."

Women Against War: "Parents Against Silence"

Nurit Gillath

(Translated by Aviva Hemi Hoffman and Barbara Swirski)

Forty years of frequent wars and reserve duty, in which Israeli men are called upon to protect the borders of the state and its citizens, together with factors such as memory of the Holocaust, seem to have resulted in a conservative, familial society, one in which women are to play the role of devoted housewives whose major tasks are to rear the children and cultivate a private oasis for soldiers returning from the battlefield. In such a context, it is no simple matter for women to organize politically against war or other security issues, perceived as exclusively male domains.

Israeli women have rarely organized around political issues; the exceptions serve to prove the rule. One such effort was initiated by a group of women affiliated with RAFI—a splinter political party no longer in existence. These women, nicknamed "the merry wives of Windsor," came together and fell apart on the same day (June 2, 1967). They called for the appointment of Moshe Dayan as Minister of Defense on the eve of the Six Day war. A less well known organizational effort was that of the women of "the first circle," led by journalist Ora Shem-Or. In 1975, this group made a public demand not to withdraw from the occupied territories. The feminist movement dealt with military and defense matters in the platform of a women's party created (and disbanded) in 1977. And since the beginning of the *Intifada* (December 1987), there has been intensive feminist activity against the occupation.

Against this background, women's political activity during the Lebanon war, designed to end the war and bring home the soldiers, is outstanding, from the point of view of women's perceptions of their position both vis-a-vis the "masculine" political leadership and conservative Israeli society.

About a year after the outbreak of the Lebanon war (1983), a letter written by a woman named Shoshana Shmueli appeared in *Ha'aretz*, a daily newspaper. A teacher, married and the mother of two, the woman wrote ". . . with

142

each news broadcast bringing horrible news, I ask myself again and again: Where are the mothers, where are the fathers? Why do we grit our teeth, dry our tears and keep silent? Why do we let depression and despair paralyze us? . . . a week ago my son got up in the morning, put on his uniform, packed a backpack . . . and got on the bus that took him—for the third time—to a cursed war in a foreign, hostile and threatening country. I have but one course left—to refuse to keep silent . . . . I feel it's my duty to turn to all the other parents who are apprehensive about their sons' lives . . . to cease to be silent, to protest against those who bear the responsibility for this cursed war . . . and not to relinquish the struggle until our sons come home."

Shoshana Shmueli's call fell on ready ears. Her phone started ringing at 6 a.m. and kept on ringing, and she called the first meeting of "Parents Against Silence" the following week, in the hope that parents of both sexes would join. The media called the new organization "Mothers Against Silence" because most of its activists were women.

Who were these women? What induced them to become involved in political protest against the war, what brought them out into the streets, what gave them the strength to organize assemblies, conferences and rallies, and to confront a hostile public, in a machoistic society in which military service and rank gave a person higher status and the moral right to talk about policy and defense matters? Member of Knesset (MK) Nechamkin (Labor) expressed the general attitude towards these persistent women: "It is not women, but mothers we are speaking of. Their feelings are understandable, but State decisions cannot be guided by them." The newspaper Hadashot published a bitter open letter from a group of reserve duty officers (April 21, 1985) against "Mothers Against Silence": "They are partly responsible for each victim who has died in the past month and a half (in Lebanon) because of the pressures they are putting on the military system." MK Cohen-Avidov (Likud) called them "Dizengoff cows" and stated: "I don't have any respect for them. Why doesn't one see women from Kiryat Shmona, Kiryat Gat and the development towns among them? Because those women are busy with their housekeeping and not with gossip." That is to say, there are women who know their place, and the protest activities of others is termed—in a belittling manner—"gossip," because women's place is not in politics. But MK Avidov was right about one thing, the social representation of the women in "Parents Against Silence." These women were of Ashkenazi origin, secular, educated, middle or upper class, employed outside the home in "feminine" professions (teachers, nurses, social workers, librarians), had served in the army, and were doves in their political outlook. The active women had the same characteristics as persons who are politically active in all democratic, liberal, Western countries (Milgrath and Goel, 1977), whether in institutionalized or protest activity.

The activists of "Parents Against Silence" numbered between 40 and 50 women (and a few men who gave support primarily behind the scenes). The main mailing list had 600 names on it. The organization was active for two years, during which it maintained a high level of activity. It published 82 proclamations, issued 12 press releases, distributed stickers and explanatory material at supermarkets, beaches, demonstrations, and special stands set up to collect signatures on petitions.

The women organized their own demonstrations, as well as participating in demonstrations initiated by other groups. They themselves initiated some 28 demonstrations and protest rallies, some of which continued from 10:00 a.m. to 11:00 p.m., for an entire week, and one was held every day between 2:00 and 5:00 p.m. for three weeks. The demonstrations were held all over the country, from the northern border to the south. Protest rallies were held near the Prime Minister's office in Jerusalem, in one of Tel Aviv's main squares and near the Ministry of Defense in Tel Aviv.

In addition, the group organized 10 national conferences and sent 16 telegrams and numerous letters to Members of Knesset and ministers. A good part of this material was passed on to the media, and some of it was printed and distributed in the form of newsletters during demonstrations. Some 250 articles about "Parents Against Silence" appeared in the Hebrew press, accompanied by 47 photographs of meetings, demonstrations and activists. Only seven percent of the news articles were unsympathetic to the movement. Whoever has not been involved in organizing this type of activity, cannot appreciate the enormity of the efforts of the women of "Parents Against Silence," and the success they achieved during the two years they were active—until the Israeli Defense Forces partially withdrew from Lebanon.

One of the activists, Rachel Ardinenst, told a woman reporter from La Isha magazine (May 30, 1984) "It was a woman's organization. We knew we were taking on a difficult struggle, and we didn't think fathers would join. We wanted to prove to our sons that we could do more than just complain; we also showed courage, we became 'tigers' protecting their young." And in the daily Ha'aretz, another mother stated (June 6, 1984): "The activity entails a great deal of traveling, hours of standing on your feet to distribute information, writing press releases, and 'nagging' the media. For all of us, this is in addition to working outside the home, and the usual business of keeping house." A kibbutz member said, "We have been accused of making trouble for Israel, and some of us have begun to doubt whether we are doing the right thing." The media paid a great deal of attention to the activities and tribulations of the women active in "Parents Against Silence." Articles were generally sympathetic, especially those written by women reporters, who tried to create a motherly, concerned image of the activists. The women themselves did their best to appear calm, composed, restrained and respectable, rather than emotional or hysterical. For example, this is what Tamar Avidar wrote (Ma'ariv, May 27 and June 13, 1983): "Cry out, mothers, shout. In the U.S.A. shouting influenced the withdrawal from Vietnam . . . . I ask myself if the parents of the

Palmach generation were also so worried about their children . . . perhaps one sees in the mothers of the soldiers in Lebanon a sort of 'fatigue,' not only because of the Lebanon war, but for all the recent wars . . . who if not the mothers will protest their sons having to stay at the frontier during the present Shouf (mountains in Lebanon) war?" Yehudit Oriyan of *Yediot Aharonot* wrote (June 24, 1983): ". . . never have the mothers interfered, nor is motherhood politics. Mothers, as opposed to politicians, have license to be naggers, worried and frightened rather than courageous. They are always justified because they are mothers . . . I wouldn't be surprised if those mothers, the worrisome, hysterical, crazy, 'yiddishe mammas' didn't just lie down on the road in front of their sons' high army boots one day . . . ." But they did not do that, though some of them, the extremists, had wanted to. The majority favored balanced, not extreme activity, presenting themselves as parents and citizens (they always made sure to have a man present when meeting with government officials and the media). Their strategy was to appear respectable, and to make their demands assertively and with determination and self-respect. Their activity was not violent. They never broke the rules of the game, but they were definitely an anomaly on the Israeli political scene. The movement received legitimization from the establishment, because its class basis was very much like that of the establishment (that is, Ashkenazi, educated, secular, and upper middle class).

Further reasons for the legitimization of the movement were: the demonstrators were mothers who were perceived to be worried and anxious about the fate of their sons fighting in Lebanon, in a war that—for them—was not justified, and not backed by a wide consensus within the cabinet or outside of it. (One must remember that in addition to "Parents Against Silence" there were other protest movements against the Lebanon war.) The women were not demonstrating against war in principle, but against one particular war. They went out into the streets on a one-time basis, and because of their background and style, they received support from broad sectors of the public, from the media and from a substantial part of the political establishment.

"Parents Against Silence" was not a peace movement or a universal antiwar movement. It was an isolated instance in which private interest, mothers' concern for their sons in a war of choice, and the public interest, of all the parents and citizens of the state to bring the soldiers back from Lebanon, converged.

The movement disbanded by a resolution voted for by the majority of members a short time after the partial withdrawal of the I.D.F. from Lebanon. Very few, if any of the activists have been involved in protest activities connected with the *Intifada,* despite the fact that they are doves (Gillath, 1987). The conclusion to be drawn from the case of "Parents Against Silence" is that mainstream Israeli women may well organize against future wars, for which there is no broad national consensus. There is also the possibility of their creating a peace movement. This possibility exists only on the condition that women come to realize that they have the right and obligation to opinions on all issues, including foreign affairs and defense. In fact, a recent survey (*Ma'ariv,* August 1988) revealed that Israeli women are more concerned than Israeli men about issues of defense and security and perceive the connection between solving the problem of the occupied territories and the attainment of peace and security more than men.

In conclusion, the activists of "Parents Against Silence" had no awareness of the fact that noninvolvement in political action affects their status as citizens. Their one-time activity, even though it was prolonged, had neither a specific nor a general effect on their awareness as political women. While the women developed leadership and other skills and resources, they lacked a willingness to use them for other activities, and as a result retired from public and political action as soon as their object had been attained. The vast majority of these women have not become involved with feminist or any other political organizations. Mainstream women have potential for changing the political climate in Israel. Why they don't use that potential is a good question for research.

About a year after the outbreak of the *Intifada,* a short letter was published in the newspaper *Ha'aretz* calling on parents with children serving in the occupied territories to join in an appeal to the government to find a solution to the unbearable burden the soldiers face: "Stop the *Intifada* and begin negotiations." A woman signed the letter. The same short letter appeared several months later. It seems this call was effective, and on March 11, 1989 a large advertisement appeared in *Ha'aretz* bearing 580 names (men and women in equal numbers). Nine of them were former members of the "Parents Against Silence" group. The new organization calls itself "Parents Against Erosion" (in Hebrew the names of both groups sound the same), and its tactics and strategies seem to replicate those of "Parents Against Silence." Their goals, too, are similar. While the women seem to realize their power, they are still employing it for very limited goals.

REFERENCES

Gillath, Nurit (1987) *Parents Against Silence.* Unpublished Masters Thesis, University of Haifa, (Hebrew).

Milgrath, L. W. and Goel, M. L. (1977) *Political Participation.* Chicago: Rand McNally College Pub. Co.

Palestinian Women in Israel Respond to the *Intifada*

Nabila Espanioly

On Friday, October 10, 1989, a group of Israeli Jewish and Palestinian women from different parts of Haifa gathered for the weekly demonstration of "Women in Black" to silently protest Israel's occupation of the territories. There were 50 women present, in contrast to the usual 15 to 20, as the previous week the group had been harassed by members of "Tehiya" and "Kach," two parties from the extreme right which demand the transfer of Palestinian Arabs from Eretz Israel/Palestine to Arab countries.

On Saturday, October 11, 1989, a group of Palestinian women from different parts of Nazareth, the largest Arab city in Israel, gathered at Mary's Well Square for the demonstration of "Women in Black" to silently protest Israel's occupation of the territories. The reactions on the Nazareth street were entirely different. "God bless you," "God give you the strength to carry on."

The two cities are only 30 kilometers apart, but they seem to be in two different worlds. The two accounts of "Women in Black" represent two entirely different circles. As a participant in both demonstrations, I couldn't help but be aware of both the differences and the similarities. Both women's groups desired to act for peace, but they are looking for answers to different questions.

In Haifa, we "Women in Black" wrestle with the questions of how to make a bigger impact, how to recruit more women, how to change the hostile attitudes toward our activity on the Jewish street, how to make Jews in Israel aware of the effect of the occupation, how to make them see the connections between the occupation and unemployment and other social ills.

In Nazareth, we "Women in Black" (all Israeli Palestinians) ask ourselves the same questions, but also others: how to find new ways of expressing our solidarity with the struggle of Palestinians in the occupied territories, how to persuade the government of Israel to negotiate with the Palestinian Liberation Organization (PLO), how to help our brothers and sisters in the occupied territories, how to involve more women in our activities, and how to develop actions in keeping with our culture that would have an impact on the Arab street.

"Women in Black" began to hold protests in Jerusalem, Tel Aviv, and Haifa two months after the outbreak of the *Intifada*. By September 1989, the protest had spread to 25 locations, from Eilat in the South to kibbutzim in the far north. The women who participate come from cities, villages and kibbutzim: they include Jews and some Israeli Palestinians and they hold a wide variety of political views.

The kinds of hostility that "Women in Black" encounter in different parts of the country have a common denominator. Besides pelting us with eggs and tomatoes and spitting at us, passers-by feel obliged to remind us that we are women living in a chauvinist society. They tell us that our place is in the kitchen, or they say they'd rather see us on the beach. The more sexist and vulgar among them call us "Arab fuckers" or "Arab lays." A few restrict themselves to political epithets, like "traitors."

"Women in Black" is one of several women's peace groups that organized in the wake of the *Intifada*, as women were the first to respond. The various groups, especially "Women in Black" and the "Peace Cloth," tried to mobilize a wide coalition of women for peace, and that is why their demands were very general: "End the occupation," or "talk with the PLO." Not because women lack specific proposals on how to make peace, but because we felt that if we specified our demands, we would only cause splintering; some of us want two states for two peoples, others prefer one state, and still others find it very important to stress their Zionist image.

Women, then, have been very active in the Israeli peace movement. Sometimes Arab and Jewish women work together, for example, in "Women in Black" in Haifa and Acre, which are mixed cities, or in the framework of the Democratic (Communist) Women's Movement, in the north of Israel. In addition, Arab and Jewish women jointly organized a peace conference held in December 1988, the theme of which was "A Feminist Response to the *Intifada*," and the Peace Tent and peace march that formed part of International Women's Day activities in March 1989. We can observe a continuous growth in women's peace activities. For example, in 21 months of activity, "Women in Black" grew from 3 to 25 groups.

Arab and Jewish women usually work separately, however, for we move in two different circles. Very few Palestinian women in Israel know that there are so many groups of Jewish women demonstrating as "Women in Black." And very few Jewish women know about the activities of their Palestinian sisters in Nazareth, Acre and Kufir Yassif, only 30 kilometers away from Haifa. This can be partly explained by the fact that the Israeli media rarely report the weekly demonstrations of "Women in Black" or the daily activities carried out by female peace activists all over Israel. This is especially true when the activity occurs in an Arab village, because the Israeli media have no interest in portraying Palestinians as peace seekers. The media cooperate with the government in maintaining the stereotype of the Palestinian as an enemy against whom Jews must defend themselves.

Is there any truth to this contention? What do Palestinians living in Israel really want? This is a question which very few Israeli Jews can answer, for we move in two different, closed circles. We may live in the same town, shop in the same supermarket, go to the same film or listen to the same television program, but we rarely emerge from our closed circles.

To answer this question, we have to step back into Israeli and Palestinian history. Until 1948, Palestinian society in Palestine/Eretz Israel was mainly agriculturally based, with the institutions and values typical for such a society. During the 1948 war, thousands of Palestinian Arabs moved or were forced to move from their homes, becoming refugees in other Arab countries and in other parts of the world. More than 380 villages were totally destroyed. The 150,000 Palestinian Arabs who remained in Israel after 1948 were left with a shattered economy, society and institutional infrastructure. The effects of the war, coupled with the Israeli government's policy of massive land expropriation, made it impossible to reclaim agriculture as the mainstay of Palestinian Arab life. Many Arabs were forced to search for work outside their villages. Women, who normally worked in the family field, were also forced to seek employment in the wider economy. The land confiscation and transfer of ownership from Arab to Jewish hands made the Arabs in Israel totally dependent on a Jewish dominated economy.

While the Israeli government granted citizenship to Palestinian Arabs, it did not recognize them as a national group. This was clearly reflected in its calling them "minorities," "Israeli Arabs," "non-Jews"—anything but Palestinians. Between 1948 and 1967, the question of identity was largely neglected by the majority of Palestinian Arabs. It was only after the 1967 war, when Israeli Arabs met with their brothers and sisters in the occupied West Bank and Gaza, that they began to feel the need to emphasize their identity as Palestinians. For the first time, Arabs living in Israel felt they were members of a larger collective.

The meeting between Palestinians in Israel and the occupied territories marked the beginning of a process of redefining our identity, a process that is still going on. After 1967, we began to identify as Palestinians, as a national minority struggling for its own rights within Israel. Another factor which contributed to the process of redefinition was Israel's victory over the Arab world in the Six Day War. This victory came as a terrible shock. For years, many Palestinians had lived under the illusion that the Arab countries would liberate them. The 1967 war destroyed this illusion, as well as that of a united Arab front bound charismatically by Jamal Abdul Nasser.

The 1967 war made Palestinians living inside Israel realize that help would not be forthcoming from the outside; they would have to find it within themselves. It was then that they began to create their own institutions and formulate their own political program. The major institution founded was the Council of the Arab Heads of Local Councils (1975), which includes almost all mayors of Arab towns and villages. Other bodies include the Committee of Arab Representatives, composed of the former and the Arab members of Knesset, as well as various national committees, including a Land Defense Committee, a Social Services Committee, a Health Committee, a Housing Committee, and an Education Committee. In fact, these committees have been engaged in the rebuilding of the infrastructure of Palestinian society inside Israel, as part of the larger Israeli society. This is the *Intifada* of the Israeli Palestinians—a fight against discrimination and for equality within the state of Israel.

The Palestinians in Israel are still second-class citizens. According to my feminist arithmetic, Israeli Palestinian women rank eighth in Israel society, after (1) Ashkenazi men, (2) Ashkenazi women, (3) Oriental men, (4) Oriental women, (5) Ethiopian men, (6) Ethiopian women, and (7) Palestinian men. That is, Israeli Palestinian women suffer from discrimination not only because of their gender, but also because of their national identity.

The Israeli Palestinian women who engage in peace activities are motivated primarily by national considerations rather than gender ones. When a Palestinian woman in Israel sees a Palestinian woman in the territories facing a soldier, she identifies with her; she also feels proud of Palestinian men facing the same situation. Of course she will say that this woman is "just like the men." It appears that to be aware of your role as a woman and the oppression you suffer at the hands of your own man and your own society is much more difficult than to be aware of the oppression suffered by your people (and yourself as part of them) at the hands of "the enemy."

It is more difficult, first of all because as a national minority you learn that you have to stick together, and in such a situation it is easier to see the external enemy than the internal one. Second, it appears that there is a direct connection between identity, consciousness and struggle. Our national identity has actually been nurtured by discrimination. In Israeli Palestinian society, women's identity is formed, that is, misformed, by stereotypes, so that it is difficult to determine what we really are. Are we really incapable of working as the director of a department, or has society prevented us from becoming directors?

Very few Palestinian women in Israel see the contradictions of the "revolutionary" man who speaks day and night about equality, but as soon as he goes home to his wife, mother or sister, begins to act like a "sheik" who needs to be waited on and made to feel that he is the boss. These few women are struggling not only for peace, but also for their own equality in Israeli Palestinian society, while the majority of Israeli Palestinian women are motivated only by national feelings.

I often am asked how, as a feminist, I can continue to struggle for the national rights of Palestinians. Haven't I learned anything from the struggle of the Algerian women? I would reply that emancipation is a long process. When a woman feels she is able to struggle against the occupation, it is the first step in the direction of her struggle for her own rights as a woman. Women who join the struggle today as Palestinians will learn about themselves, their abilities and their power. They will become conscious of themselves and their sisters, and they will experience solidarity.

Aside from demonstrating as members of "Women in Black," Palestinian women in Israel have been working to collect food, clothing, blood and medicine for Palestinians living under curfew in the occupied territories. Women in Nazareth, Shfaram, Tamra, and Um el-Fahem have been active in committees organized by political parties like the Communist Party and the Progressive List to collect financial aid for the occupied territories. They have been going from house to house asking women and families to contribute to the Palestinian cause. Israeli Palestinian women also staged large demonstrations in the cities of Nazareth and Um el-Fahem and the villages of Kufir Yassif, Kufir Kassem, and Kufir Kara.

There have been other activities as well. In a campaign called "A Sweatshirt for Every Palestinian Prisoner," (originally initiated by women in the occupied territories), the Democratic Women's Movement organized several workshops in a number of Palestinian towns and villages in Israel to sew sweatshirts, and 350 were completed on the first day of the campaign. This activity enabled a large number of Israeli Palestinian women to participate in solidarity activities, including village women whom traditional norms prevent from taking part in street demonstrations. The campaign was successful, and all 4,500 Palestinian prisoners from the occupied territories received a sweatshirt from their sisters in the occupied territories and in Israel. "*Intifada* bazaars" were organized to give Palestinian women from the territories an opportunity to sell handicrafts, traditional Palestinian dishes, and other wares as a way of lending indirect financial support. The Democratic Women's Movement of Nazareth set up a workshop to mend used clothing which they collected, to be sent to families in refugee camps in the occupied territories.

These activities are some of those carried out by Palestinian women in Israel, women who are struggling for the self-determination of the Palestinian people as well as for equal rights for themselves as Israeli citizens. There is a connection between the two struggles. If Israeli Jewish women perceive the connection between Israeli Palestinian women's struggles for peace and equality and their own efforts, the two circles will come closer together.

Israeli Women and
Peace Activism

Naomi Chazan

The Palestinian uprising (*Intifada*) has been accompanied by the proliferation of Israeli peace and protest groups in which women play a prominent role. This article examines the frameworks, motives, composition, organization, activities and impact of women's peace action since December 1987 and analyzes some of their political consequences based on data compiled through field work, participant observation and interviews with Israeli women peace activists.

The study reveals several distinctive styles of Israeli women's peace efforts, a plurality which suggests a continuing tension between women's quest for equality within the existing political system and their search for a more fundamental change within the basic structures of Israeli politics (see, i.e., MacDonald, Holden, and Ardener, 1987). Women's peace action within Israel illustrates ongoing processes of political reorientation occurring in the Israeli polity as a whole (visible on the right of the political spectrum as well as on the left), and offers a commentary on the complex relationship between women and war (Caldicott, 1984; Elshtain, 1987).

The presence of women has become increasingly apparent in the four major types of organizations which comprise the rapidly growing peace camp in Israel (numbering close to 170 different groups by the end of 1989). The first category consists of formal political parties advocating negotiations with Palestinians and the exchange of territories for peace (segments of the Labor party and especially its dovish "Mashov" circle, the Citizens' Rights Movement, Mapam, Shinui, the Progressive List for Peace, and Rakah, the Communist Party). Female representation in party institutions appears to be a function of the party's commitment to these principles and their concern with issues of equality: Whereas in the parties on the right of the political spectrum

The research was conducted within the framework of a project conducted by the author and Galia Golan on "The Attitudes and Behavior of Israeli Women on War, Peace and Conflict Resolution," funded by the MacArthur Foundation and the Harry Frank Guggenheim Foundation.

and in the religious parties women constitute less than five percent of the membership in central party organs (although Geula Cohen heads the far-right Tehiya party), in the Labor party 17 percent of the central committee are women, in Shinui 20 percent, and in the Citizens' Rights Movement (also headed by a woman, Shulamit Aloni), over 35 percent. Five of the seven female members of Knesset are drawn from these parties, which received more votes from women than from men in the 1988 elections (Burkett, 1989: 141). However, women activists in these peace-oriented parties have not confined themselves to work within the party; they have also been heavily involved in protest activities conducted in less formal settings.

Extra-parliamentary movements form the second, and largest, framework for peace activities. At least 110 groups fall within this rubric, which includes older extra-parliamentary organizations (such as Peace Now, the major coalition advocating a negotiated settlement of the Arab-Israeli conflict, and Oz Ve'Shalom, its religious counterpart); newly formed grassroots movements (Year 21, for example, a group that advocates a two-state solution and civil disobedience tactics, and Israelis by Choice, an organization of immigrants opposing the occupation); associations based on professional affiliation (Professors and Lecturers Against Occupation, Concerned Students in Israel, Lawyers Against the Occupation, Mental Health Workers Against the Occupation); human rights groups (Betzelem, a new research organization monitoring the status of human rights in the occupied territories or the Association of Civil Rights in Israel, the veteran Israeli group concerned with the protection of personal freedoms in Israel); organizations formed around a single issue or incident (The Israeli Committee for Beita, a Palestinian village harassed in the wake of an incident in the spring of 1988, or The Committee for Mubarak Awad, the head of a Palestinian center for nonviolence recently deported from Israel); and finally, educational, dialogue and coexistence groups (like Neve Shalom, an Arab-Jewish settlement involved in peace education, and the International Center for Peace in the Middle East, which has organized numerous research projects and symposia in Israel and abroad to promote a peace momentum).

With the exception of a few organizations of soldiers and reservists who refuse to serve beyond the Green Line (such as Yesh Gvul: There is a Limit), these extra-parliamentary groupings include both men and women, with women comprising at least 50 percent of participants in decision-making forums, demonstrations, vigils, and grassroots activities. In the newer grassroots organizations women play a dominant role. Several, although ostensibly gender-mixed, are in fact totally female in composition (Witnesses of the Occupation, a branch of Year 21 which organizes solidarity visits to the territories and documents Israeli human rights violations, stands out in this regard). Indeed, if in the past 57 percent of politically-involved women were active in informal frameworks (Wolfsfeld, 1987), field observations indicate that this proportion has risen substantially since the beginning of the Palestinian uprising.

At the same time, women have carved out a third, exclusively female, type of peace organization. Some existing women's political groups have, in the past two years, reoriented their activities towards conflict-related issues: Ha'Gesher (The Bridge: Israeli Peace Movement of Jewish and Arab Women), a Haifa-based dialogue group devoted to education and promoting peace, and The Movement of Democratic Women in Israel, formed in 1948 by Jewish and Arab women identified with the Communist Party. Several new women's groups were established around specific types of activities: The Peace Cloth (Mapat Hashalom) founded in January 1988 as an ongoing project devoted to preparing a symbolic covering for the negotiating table (over 200 meters of peace messages made by thousands of Israeli Jewish and Palestinian women have already been stitched together); a slide show on the Intifada organized in early 1988 by the feminist journal Noga; the Peace Tent constructed during International Women's Day in 1989, and numerous petition initiatives dealing with specific problems related to women and the occupation. Another type of women's action consists of Israeli-Palestinian women's dialogue groups, usually established at the local level (most notably in Beer Sheba, Kochav Yair, and in the Tel-Aviv area by the newly formed Women's Movement for Coexistence).

Three women's peace organizations have emerged at the forefront of women's peace action. The first, the Women's Organization for Political Prisoners, is a single issue group concerned with monitoring the detention of Palestinian women activists, providing legal and medical assistance to women prisoners, and disseminating information on their treatment by Israeli authorities. The second, Shani—Israeli Women Against the Occupation—has concentrated on education and political mobilization, hosting a variety of meetings, symposia and forums, and organizing encounters between Israeli and Palestinian women both within the Green Line and in the occupied territories. The third, Women in Black, is by far the best known. Once a week, on Friday afternoons, the Women in Black hold a silent vigil to protest Israeli policy on the West Bank and in Gaza and to demand an end to occupation. Launched in Jerusalem in January 1988, this persistent symbolic initiative has spread to twenty-five locations throughout the country and to several major cities within Europe and North America (Svirsky, 1989). In early 1989 an umbrella organization: Women and Peace: Women's Peace Movement, was formed to coordinate the activities of these various organizations.

Women's peace activities have begun to take place within a fourth major framework: established women's associations. Leaders of major women's organizations and movements in Israel such as the vastly different Na'amat, the Israel Women's Network (a lobby organization composed mostly of professional women) and the Israel Feminist Movement (a Tel Aviv based feminist group), reluctant in the past to take positions on security and foreign affairs issues, began in 1989 to speak out—on an individual basis—on these topics, and have exhibited an increasing willingness to meet with their Palestinian counterparts. During 1989 prominent figures in mainstream women's associations visited Palestinian women in the West Bank and Gaza and hosted public meetings with Palestinian women in Jerusalem and Tel-Aviv (although some groups such as The Women's International Zionist Organization [WIZO] and The Association of National Religious Women [Emunah], have not participated in these programs).

Women peace activists took further steps towards creating a broad women's peace coalition with the founding of the Israel Women's Peace Net (*Reshet*) in the aftermath of the Israeli-Palestinian Women's Conference held in Brussels in May, 1989. The women participating in this effort include representatives of all the four major categories in the peace movement as well as prominent women unaffiliated with any particular group. They have coalesced around the seven-point Brussels declaration which recognizes the right to self-determination and security of all the peoples in the region, calls for an end to the occupation and advocates a negotiated settlement of all aspects of the Arab-Israeli conflict. Women's peace action thus covers a wider organizational range and is more diversified ideologically than that of men.

The reasons for growing female involvement in peace work in general, beyond the explanations common to both men and women, are diverse and at times even contradictory. First, the limited opportunities open to women in the formal political process have played a role (Randall, 1987). Since women have been unable to find appropriate channels for articulating their positions in institutionalized settings, they have tended to operate in informal contexts or to create their own frameworks, especially during periods of heightened political mobilization. Second, immediate situational circumstances, and specifically the nature of the uprising itself, have had a significant impact on women. Unlike previous Arab-Israeli confrontations, the current Palestinian resistance does not conform to the terms of conventional military warfare. Essentially an intercommunal struggle, the *Intifada* has involved face-to-face confrontations between Israelis and Palestinians. Israeli women, previously distanced from the field of combat and embodying the idea of the homefront (Bar-Yosef and Paden-Eisenstark, 1977/8), have found themselves more directly affected by the new course of the conflict, further blurring the already ill-defined lines between the private and the public in Israel (Sapiro, 1987). Moreover, repression, harassment, humiliation, beating, brutalization and stone-throwing have had a differential gender effect, mobilizing women to political action (Fornari, 1974).

Third, some women have become involved in peace activities because of a heightened identification as Israelis and Zionists. Women's peace activism during periods of conflict, like women's ultranationalist militancy, is frequently motivated by an increased sense of the collectivity and the crystallization of definite views on what is needed for its maintenance (Kellet, 1985). Fourth, in a somewhat different vein, the substantive issues in the current phase of the Arab-Israeli conflict have a particular resonance for women attuned to feminist themes: oppression, self-determination, human dignity, mutual security, justice and equality. On the attitudinal level this female sensitivity has been exhibited in a greater willingness to trade territories for peace and in a greater openness to negotiations with the Palestinian Liberation Organization (PLO) than that shown by men (Arian and Ventura, 1989: 23). Fifth, growing recognition of gender inequalities in Israeli society and intensified action aimed at improving the status of women have highlighted the close connection between the situation of women, the ongoing conflict, and the gradual militarization of Israeli society (Chazan, 1989; Eshkol et al., 1987; Matras and Noam, 1987; Reardon, 1985). Awareness of these relationships has prompted some women to participate more directly in activities related to matters of peace and security (other proclaimed feminists have studiously shunned such an involvement). Finally, the symbols of motherhood have been used to explain women's peace action (most notably by those involved in Parents Against Erosion) as well as to account for female right-wing extremism (Steinson, 1980).

Clearly no single explanation suffices to account for the heterogeneity of women coalescing around peace action. Some women are drawn into peace work because they are mothers and wives, while others reject these stereotypes. Activists include women frustrated by their incapacity to affect decision-making in other frameworks, and those who have shifted their attention to women's actions on tactical grounds, viewing the women's constituency as fluid and hence more malleable and receptive to politically significant mobilization. Finally some women have joined women's peace movements because they feel a need to do something and are more comfortable in the nonhierarchical and less threatening setting of all-women's groups.

The background of women peace activists is as variegated as their motives. During the first year of the *Intifada* the bulk of female participants were either born in Israel of Ashkenazi parents or had themselves come to Israel from Europe or North America. They ranged in age from teenagers to octogenarians. The majority of the first activists were college graduates, some were university faculty, and a large proportion were school teachers, psychologists, social workers, editors or artists, that is, members of the urban middle class. Socially, however, because of their radical or feminist background, they were often perceived as elitist (Azoulay, 1989) and, in the case of some women's group activists, also as outside the mainstream of Israeli society. This image was reinforced by the fact that the initial core of participants was relatively small and active in several organizations simultaneously. With overlapping membership commonplace, they were able to generate a great deal of activity without significantly expanding their constituency.

The second year of the uprising has witnessed some shifts in these patterns. The incorporation of women in political parties and established women's organizations into the activist ranks has somewhat diversified the composition of the women's peace camp as more kibbutz and Sephardi women, whose educational and occupational background is more varied, have joined in peace activities. This new crop of activists also includes Orthodox women, previously absent in women's peace circles, as well as some heretofore inactive Palestinian-Israelis. The mobilization of new members has taken place both on an individual basis and in groups, with the extent of social contacts among activists varying accordingly. Lower income women and residents of development towns and the poorer neighborhoods of the major cities are distinctly under-represented, indicating a close link between personal background and peace activism, especially in an immigrant society such as Israel.

The shifting composition of female peace activism has yielded two somewhat contradictory results. First, as the social and political parameters of peace activism have been extended, internal friction between more radical and more moderate women has increased; and second, women's peace activism has begun to attain a modicum of social acceptability, with some of the most innovative elements of peace work associated with the activities of women not clearly identified in the past with these efforts.

Politically, peace circles represent the opinions of approximately one-third of the Jewish population of the country, with the more focused protest movements backed by roughly twenty-five percent of this increasingly distinct constituency (Arian and Ventura, 1989). Women's peace action encompasses these sectors as well as broader women's groups, but to date constitutes a minority (albeit a salient one) of the female population of the country. Most women in Israel remain politically inactive, and a small group is involved in organized right-wing politics (especially in the newly formed Gush Emunim-affiliated Mothers in Support of Israel, and Women in White, a small group which has demonstrated periodically against Women in Black).

The mark of the first year of women's action was spontaneity. A basic distinction can be made between older and more established mixed groups, such as Peace Now, where a sexual division of labor has evolved (women are more active on the logistical side and behind the scenes in decision-making circles, whereas men are more visible as spokespeople) and newly formed grassroots organizations, where gender divisions have been less apparent. The newer organizations, at least in their initial stages, generally lacked central institutions, clear membership criteria, any degree of organizational continuity, independent resources, or defined leadership positions. Intriguingly, even in grassroots organizations dominated by women, during periods of peak activity the media attention given to male activists has been much greater than that accorded to female participants.

The lack of coherent organization has been especially visible in all-women's groups. For example, Women in Black (particularly during its first year) had no leadership structure, and there were relatively few contacts among women demonstrators in different locations. No internal hierarchy was established in any of these organizations, which were loosely run by a collective leadership, usually on a rotating basis (Miller, 1976). In almost all instances, operating funds were lacking, and little effort was put into creating an organizational basis for future action (in the case of the Women's Organization for Political Prisoners, membership was closed). Fragmentation, apparent in the peace camp as a whole, was especially prevalent among women.

The continuation of the uprising has been accompanied by some changes in the organization of the peace camp. First, all movements, including all-women groups, have exhibited a greater sensitivity to fundraising (both in Israel and abroad). Second, they have consolidated lists of activists and improved intramovement communication. Third, in a few instances they have hired office staff. Fourth, they have put a premium on improved coordination. These processes have been especially noticeable among women, who have participated in several joint conferences and attempted, despite serious differences, to forge a broad working coalition. Consequently, some duplication has been averted and the scale of activities has expanded.

The growth of women's peace activism has been accompanied by a diversification of tactics and activities (Carrol, 1989). At first both mixed and all-women's groups concentrated on three types of initiatives: consistent and continuous symbolic action against official Israeli government policy (the Peace Cloth, Women in Black), concrete and direct action aimed at dealing with immediate human problems in the field (petitions to reopen educational institutions, visits to hospitals, supply of food to areas under curfew, legal aid) and educational and dialogue activities directed at political consciousness raising and promoting intercommunal understanding and tolerance. These activities palpably lacked a clear political focus or a specific women's political agenda.

The inclusion of more women with different interests and concerns in the peace network during the course of 1989 resulted in much more effort being devoted to the Israeli side of the equation. Women peace activists increasingly addressed themselves to Israeli as well as Palestinian audiences, organizing a series of public and private meetings among previously unmobilized women with divergent political orientations. Techniques of persuasion were used more widely, in addition to the prior emphasis on protest, defiance and civil disobedience. The theme of coexistence was countered by a growing emphasis on communal separation, sometimes involving Palestinian self-determination but often side-stepping this issue (Gilligan, 1982). Women began to apply more direct pressure on the Israeli government (while continuing their efforts to alter public opinion) through lobbying, cooptation of influential women politicians and leaders, and formal and informal conversations with decision-makers. Finally, in tandem, some women's political action moved from a preoccupation with specific problems of an immediate sort to political concerns of a longer-term nature. For example, in somewhat different ways, both Shani and the Israel Women's Peace Net began to formulate a political program and to define specific actions to achieve their declared goals.

How effective has women's peace work been? On the level of policy, it is doubtful whether women (or men) involved in peace action have been able to directly influence Israeli government decisions or political initiatives. On the level of ideology, however, women have been at the forefront of reassessments taking place within the Israeli body politic. On the level of social activism, women's efforts have focused on the human dimensions of the conflict and helped to sustain the symbolic dimension of peace efforts in the country. Above all, perhaps, women's peace activities have been marked by a high degree of persistence, patience and commitment.

Women's engagement in Israeli peace activities has important conceptual, comparative and practical ramifications, as it has supported multiple styles, orientations and patterns of behavior. Attempts to draw an inevitable connection between feminism, political radicalism and peace activism (Hartsock, 1982, 1983) bear little relationship to the evidence available on Israeli peace activists, let alone to the even more diverse approaches to conflict apparent among the female population of Israel.

The role of women in the quest for peace appears to be influenced, primarily, by the immediacy of conflict. Women living in areas not directly affected by war or civil strife may be more predisposed to adopting antimilitaristic positions than women in combat regions who experience political violence on a daily basis (Lipman 1988). Women who experienced the ravages of war may relate to such situations differently than those who have no such memories. The duration of conflicts may be important. The responses of women in protracted conflict situations may differ from the reactions of those who have been exposed to a single eruption limited in time and place. The particular nature of conflicts may also play a part: defensive wars may elicit different female responses than offensive ones, and reactions to interstate wars may diverge from those provoked by domestic confrontations. In turn, intercommunal struggles may fuel forms of behavior different from those generated by ideological or policy-related conflagrations. The historical phase of conflict may be central. National liberation struggles have sometimes been accompanied by demands for gender equality, as in the contemporary Palestinian case (Giacaman, 1988; Giacaman and Johnson, 1988). In other instances, especially when nation-building has involved a military struggle, the status of women may have been adversely affected (Bowes, 1986; Elshtain, 1987). Postindependence situations offer a different range of possibilities for women's peace, protest or feminist action. In many significant respects, the existence of a link between women and peace may be an outgrowth not only of the extent of female access to state institutions but also of the divergent forms and nature of the state itself (Charlton et al., 1989).

This analysis suggests that women's political action cannot be usefully divorced from the political context in which it operates and from the political processes of which it is a part. Women's peace activities in Israel are reflective of the polarization and uncertainty inherent in Israeli politics in general. The contribution of the Israeli women's peace camp to the negotiating process may lie precisely in its divergence of styles and its ability to encompass an increasingly broad range of people and concerns. Herein lies the challenge and the potential of Israeli women and women's peace action.

REFERENCES

Arian, Asher and Ventura, Raphael (1989) "Public Opinion in Israel and the *Intifada:* Changes in Security Attitudes 1987–1988." Tel-Aviv University: Jaffee Center for Strategic Studies, JCCS Memorandum No. 28.

Azoulay, Katya Gibel (1989) "Elitism in the Women's Peace Camp." *Jerusalem Post,* July 2.

Bar-Yosef, Rivka and Paden-Eisenstark, Dorit (1977/8) "Role System Under Stress: Sex Roles in War." *Social Problems* 25: 135–145.

Bowes, Alison (1986) "Kibbutz Women: Conflict in Utopia." In Ridd, R. and Callaway, H. (eds.). *Caught Up in Conflict: Women's Responses to Political Strife.* London: Macmillan; 138–162.

Burkett, Elinor (1989) "Knesset Comedown." *Ms.,* January/February: 141.

Caldicott, Helen (1984) *Missile Envy: The Arms Race and Nuclear War.* New York: William Morrow.

Carroll, Bernice A. (1989) "Women Take Action: Women's Direct Action and Social Change." *Women's Studies International Forum* 12 (1): 181–185.

Charlton, Sue E.; Everett, Jana; Staudt, Kathleen (eds.) (1989) *Women, the State and Development.* Albany: State University of New York Press.

Chazan, Naomi (1989) "Gender Equality? Not in a War Zone!" *Israeli Democracy* 3 (2): 4–7.

Elshtain, Jean Bethke (1987) *Women and War.* New York: Basic Books.

Eshkol, Eva; Lieblich, Amia; Bar-Yosef, Rivka; Wisemen, Hadas (1987) "Some Correlates of Adjustment of Israeli Women-Soldiers to their Military Roles." *Israel Social Science Research* 5 (1/2): 17–28.

Fornari, Franco (1974) *The Psychoanalysis of War.* New York: Anchor/Doubleday.

Giacaman, Rita (1988) "Palestinian Women in the Uprising: From Followers to Leaders?" Birzeit University: Draft manuscript, September.

Giacaman, Rita and Johnson, Penny (1988) "Building Barricades and Breaking Barriers: Palestinian Women in Politics in the Occupied Territories." Birzeit University: Draft manuscript, December.

Gilligan, Carol (1982) *In a Different Voice.* Cambridge, MA: Harvard University Press.

Hartsock, Nancy (1982) "The Barracks Community in Western Political Thought: Prolegomena to a Feminist Critique of War and Politics." *Women's Studies International Forum* 5 (3/4): 283–286.

Hartsock, Nancy (1983) *Money, Sex and Power: Toward a Feminist Historical Materialism.* New York and Boston: Longmans and Northeastern University Press.

Kellet, Anthony (1982) *Combat Motivation: The Behavior of Soldiers in Combat.* Boston: Kluwer Nijhoff.

Lipman, Beata (1988) *Israel: The Embattled Land (Jewish and Palestinian Women Talk About Their Lives).* London: Pandora.

Macdonald, Sharon; Holden, Pat; Ardener, Shirley (eds.) (1987) *Images of Women in Peace and War: Cross-Cultural and Historical Perspectives.* London: Macmillan.

Matras, Judah and Noam, Gila (1987) "Schooling and Military Service: Their Effects on Israeli Women's Attainments and Social Participation in Early Adulthood." *Israel Social Science Research* 5 (1/2): 29–43.

Miller, Jean Baker (1976) *Toward a New Psychology of Women.* Boston: Beacon Press.

Randall, Vicky (1987) *Women and Politics: An International Perspective* (2nd edition). London: Macmillan.

Reardon, Betty (1985) *Sexism and the War System.* New York: Teacher's College Press.

Sapiro, Virginia (1987) "Changing Gender Roles and Changes in Political Socialization." Paper Presented to the International Workshop on Political Socialization and Citizenship Education in Democracy, Tel Aviv University, March 1–7.

Steinson, Barbara (1980) "The Mother Half of Humanity: American Women in the Peace and Preparedness Movements in World War I." In Berkin, C. R. and Lovett, C. M. (eds.). *Women, War and Revolution.* New York: Holmes and Meier; 259–284.

Svirsky, Gila (1989) "Women in Black." *Present Tense* 16 (4): 52–53.

Wolfsfeld, Gadi (1988) *The Politics of Provocation: Participation and Protest in Israel.* Albany: State University of New York Press.

Section Four
The Work Women Do

Women and Work: From Collective to Career

Dafna N. Izraeli

IN THE BEGINNING

On the eve of World War I, even before women's right to vote had become a public issue, women pioneers within the Labor Zionist movement organized to fight for the opportunity to do "men's jobs" such as building houses and paving roads. Women's demand for a share of the scarce jobs was legitimated in terms of their right to contribute to the creation of the new society. The rhetoric of motives was couched in collective not individualistic terms: It was an ideology not of personal entitlements but one of social obligations, not of equal opportunity for individual advancement, but of commitment to a collective shaped by the ideal of social equality. In fact "career" was a pejorative term implying that the individual put his or her personal success above the needs of the collective. After statehood (1948), this collectivistic ideology translated into public policy. On the one hand, it was pronatalist, encouraging women "to be fruitful and multiply" in order to replenish the Jewish people, but it also enabled women to combine having a family with employment. It was a family-based policy that did not involve a commitment to provide women with equal opportunity for better paying jobs and advancement.

FOLLOWING THE CREATION OF THE STATE (1948–1968)

While there are no figures available, the proportion of women in paid work prior to 1948 was probably greater than in the years following. The major (although not only) reason for the decline was the mass immigration of Jews from countries of the Middle East and North Africa. Between 1948 and 1955, over 400,000 new immigrants came to Israel, increasing the population by approximately one-third. For the immigrant women, the combination of a patriarchal family structure which traditionally sheltered women from public life, early age of marriage, a high birth rate and a high rate of illiteracy, were not conducive to employment. Furthermore, the economy could not absorb such a large number of immigrants into the labor force. Government employment policy was directed at creating jobs primarily for men, not women. With a view to modernizing the economy, labor-intensive industries with simple technologies, such as textiles and food processing, were introduced to the new development towns, opening employment opportunities for women. Although women's employment was not a priority, the absorbing society regarded the entry of immigrant women into the labor force "as a first sign of successful adaptation to Israeli society" (Honig and Shamai, 1978: 405).

During the 1950s and even into the 1960s, attitudes towards women's employment correlated strongly with ethnic origin. Jews from Europe and the English-speaking countries were more favorably disposed and less burdened with children (Hartman, 1978) than those from the Moslem countries. The latter, as well as the Arab population, tended to confine women's roles to the family. A number of laws, such as universal compulsory education, a minimum marriage age of 17 and monogamy, undermined both the traditional structure of the community as well as traditional cultural norms.

AFTER THE SIX DAY WAR (1967): NEW OPPORTUNITIES

A number of developments during the 1970s led to the accelerated entry of women into the labor force. There was a growth in demand for workers to fill the jobs created by the expansion of financial, insurance, community and other services. Many of the new jobs were in occupations in which women were already represented. Between 1973 and 1980, the net increase in the civilian labor force was 161,000 persons, and the public and community services alone had a net growth of 98,000.

By the mid 1960s, the immigrant population had been absorbed into the labor force. The creation of new military units to service the territories conquered in the Six Day War, the extension of army service for men from two to three years (and for women from a year and a half to two years), as well as the growth of the universities, combined to reduce the available supply of men in the civilian labor force. Between 1964 and 1969, the proportion of men in the civilian labor force dropped from 77 percent to 70 percent. The shortage of qualified men made employers more predisposed to hire women for the types of jobs previously filled by men (Izraeli, 1983).

At the same time, a number of factors combined to increase the supply of women who could be drawn into the labor force. These included an increased level of education among women, the drop in the birth rate among Jewish women from Moslem countries and "the coming of age" of the baby boom generation. Furthermore, attitudes among the more traditional sectors of the population became less resistant to the idea of women's employment. Among the Arab population, the association of "modernity" with Jewishness and thus with a loss of Arab identity, which had intensified the resistance to change in women's status, was weakened by the encounter with Palestinians in the occupied territories, which led to the realization that women's inequality was not a Jewish-induced problem, "but rather an issue of indigenous concern to Palestinians" (Mar'i and Mar'i, 1985: 255). The new job opportunities, especially for more educated women, provided an incentive to work outside the home. In addition, the growing economic value for the family of providing education for women was an incentive to keep girls in school.

Public policy facilitated combining work and family life. A body of legislation and collective agreements provided working mothers with mandatory 12 weeks maternity leave with nearly full pay; the right to take up to a year's leave without pay, protection from dismissal due to pregnancy; shorter working hours in the year following childbirth, and in the public sector, also for those with young children. In the 1970s, the Ministry of Labor and Social Welfare subsidized the building of day-care centers, creating tens of thousands of places for children of prekindergarten age. In the 1970s, when government policy was to encourage women to enter the labor force, particularly the factories in the development towns, fees were graded to the mother's income, rarely amounting to more than a quarter of her gross earnings. While the policy reenforced the view that childcare is the wife's responsibility, the low rates provided an economic incentive for women to go to work. In the 1980s, when unemployment was on the rise, fees were linked to the per capita income of the total family. This more egalitarian policy did not affect women's participation in the urban areas but made employment less feasible for the low earning women in the development towns.

The school day, only four to five hours long through most of elementary school, was not lengthened. In fact, under the pressure of budget cuts in the 1980s, teacher hours were reduced and the school day made shorter still. As we shall see, this meant that while married women could take a job, they were constrained from pursuing a career.

Changes in the tax regulations during the 1970s substantially increased the incentives for women to participate in the labor force (Honig and Shamai, 1978). The 1975 tax reform introduced a credit system for working women to compensate for the extra costs of housekeeping and child care. However, reductions were based on the number of children and not on actual costs incurred as the result of women's going to work. The reforms were an incentive only for women with higher earnings. For the majority, earnings were below the taxable minimum, so that the credits were not relevant to them.

SOME FACTS AND FIGURES ON WOMEN'S LABOR FORCE PARTICIPATION

The following data summarize some of the key trends in women's labor force participation. (Unless otherwise indicated, all statistical data are taken from the publications of the Central Bureau of Statistics: Statistical Yearbook of Israel and Labor Force Survey for the relevant year. Except in tables and specific exceptions, all numbers were rounded to the closest digit.)

Participation Rates

Between 1954 and 1989, the proportion of women aged 15 + in the civilian labor force grew from 21 percent to 40 percent. Women constitute 38 percent of the total civilian labor force in Israel. The growth in women's participation came at a time of declining participation for men, so that over 60 percent of the new workers in the past two decades have been women.

Age

Since the 1960s there has been a continuous decline in participation rates among younger women aged 15 to 24, due largely to the prolongation of education and partly to the deepening of military recruitment. In 1970, peak participation was by the 18 to 24 age group; in 1975, it was the 25 to 34 age group; and by 1984, it had shifted to women 35 to 44. This upward drift reflects the growing tendency for younger women to remain in the labor force as well as for older women to enter it. The proportion of married women going to work grew from 26 percent in 1968 to 46 percent in 1988. Among Jewish women, it reached 51.7 percent. The presence of small children has become less of a deterrent to women's employment in recent years. In 1987, almost 60 percent of all ever-married Jewish women whose youngest children were between two and four years old were in the labor force. The level of participation is significantly lower for Arab and Druze women. The pattern of their age distribution is similar to that of Jewish women in 1970—with participation peaking at 18 to 24 and then declining with marriage or the birth of the first child.

Ethnicity

Labor force participation varies among the ethnic and religious groups. It is higher among Israeli born than among foreign born. Among the former, it is highest among women whose fathers came from Europe or America (61%), and lowest among women whose fathers came from North Africa or Asia (46%). These differences may be attributed primarily to differences in educational attainment: Women of families from Europe or America are on the average more educated. The participation for Christian women is 22.3 percent, for Druze women 11.6 percent, and for Moslems 8.5 percent.

Education

Education is the best single predictor of women's labor force participation. The more educated a woman is, the more likely she is to be in the labor force. This applies to Arab women as well as for Jewish women, although the effect of education for the former is not as powerful as it is for the latter. The lower participation rates of first and second generation women from Asia or Africa become negligible when we compare women with the same levels of education. Furthermore, among women with 16 years or more of education, participation rates are the same as for men (approximately 77 percent).

It is likely that the upward trend in female labor force activity will continue as women get more formal education. Even the rise in the rate of unemployment that occurred in the second half of the 1980s did not lead to a decline in the rate of women's entry into the labor force. On the contrary, unemployment brought new recruits, as housewives never before employed were spurred by economic need to seek paid work. As a consequence, however, unemployment rates among women increased at a faster rate than for men, and the gap in unemployment rates between men and women, which until recently was consistently around two percent (lower for men), widened.

TEACHER, SECRETARY, NURSE: GENDER AND THE STRUCTURE OF OCCUPATIONS

In Israel, as elsewhere, the occupational distribution of women is very different from that of men (Table 1). As in almost all industrialized countries, women are concentrated in a small number of large, female dominated occupations. In 1983, 73 percent of the women were concentrated in three of the ten aggregated occupational categories: semi-professional and technical workers, clerical workers and service workers. Every second woman was employed in one of the following eight occupations (out of a list of 90): teachers and principals, social workers and probation officers, nurses and paramedical workers, bookkeepers, secretaries, typists and key punch operators, general office workers, and sales workers. In other words, women are concentrated in the middle status occupations with a smaller proportion than men in either the high or the low status occupations.

A large proportion of the female labor force is concentrated in the academic, semi-professional and white collar occupations. However, in all institutional spheres—political, military, economic, educational, religious and cultural—the higher the position, the smaller the proportion of women. For example, in the universities, women constitute 42 percent of the instructors, 31 percent of the lecturers, 17 percent of the senior lecturers, 8 percent of the associate professors, and only 4 percent of the full professors. In Government service they constitute 51 percent of those employed but only about 11 percent of those in the top five ranks of the administrative hierarchy and only 20 percent of those at the top of the professional hierarchy (Toren, 1987).

Two developments which in the U.S. were instrumental in moving women into higher positions, affirmative action legislation and the decision of career-oriented women to delay childbirth, did not occur in Israel. Consequently,

Table 1. Employed Persons by Occupation and Sex: 1972 and 1987.

Percent women in occupation			Percent Distribution			
			1972		1987	
1972	1987	Occupation	Women	Men	Women	Men
		Total	100	100	100	100
33.5	38.9	Scientific and academic workers	5.9	5.5	9.5	9.4
54.6	58.7	Semi-professional and technical	19.3	7.1	23.4	11.2
7.4	13.9	Administrators and managers	(0.7)	4.2	2.4	9.0
52.0	65.5	Clerical and related workers	24.1	11.3	32.7	12.5
26.0	32.1	Sales workers	8.2	8.3	5.0	5.5
54.0	58.4	Service workers	21.5	8.6	17.3	9.9
17.0	16.2	Agricultural workers	6.1	8.5	0.5	2.3
11.2	12.7	Skilled workers	11.2	38.2	7.6	34.8
15.7	18.9	Unskilled workers	3.0	8.1	1.7	5.4

women have usually moved into middle and higher level positions only where the competition with men became less intense, either because men left the occupation, as occurred in education, or because there was a rapid expansion of the occupation, as occurred in personnel management and training, marketing and public relations. Both conditions were evident in the State Attorney's Office. In recent decades, men have left for more lucrative private legal practice, and there has been a growth in the number of positions for attorneys in the Office. In 1984, women constituted approximately 41 percent of the lawyers in Israel and 61 percent (123 of 203) of those in the State Attorney's Office. They also constituted 20 percent (64 of 321) of the judges, compared to 8 percent in 1976. Women responded to the new opportunities by increasing their investments in University training in nontraditional fields. For example, between 1974 and 1988, the proportion of women among all students enrolled in law increased from 32 percent to 41 percent; in business and administration, from 12 percent to 30 percent; and in medicine (including dentistry), from 20 percent to 41 percent.

These shifts in the occupational distribution of women, which changed the gender character of some 67 occupations (Cohen et al., 1987: 104) are characterized by contradictory trends. On the one hand, many of the occupations in the community service and clerical fields that were female dominated a decade earlier, became even more segregated, as their expansion attracted more women and the low level of pay pushed men out or into more senior jobs. On the other hand, a number of high-status professional and traditionally male-dominated occupations, such as law, medicine, accounting, pharmacy, and specializations within management such as marketing and personnel became less segregated as their expansion created a demand for workers and the insufficient supply of qualified men forced employers to accept women. This was especially true in the less financially lucrative public sector, which in Israel employs approximately 40 percent of the labor force.

DISCRIMINATION AND THE
EARNINGS GAP

The law requiring equal pay for equal work for men and women was introduced in 1965 and amended in 1973 to include work that is essentially equal. Nonetheless, women continue to earn less than men. The most comprehensive study of gender differences in earnings to date (Efroni, 1980), conducted among civil servants, found that women earned 78 percent of what men with similar characteristics earned, and furthermore, if women were compensated for their education, training and experience at the same rate as men, their income would indeed be two percent greater than that of men. Though the seniority gap between men and women in the civil service has decreased in the last decade, the earnings gap has deepened. In 1978, women's hourly earnings were approximately 78 percent those of men; by 1988, they had decreased to 71 percent those of men (Efroni, 1988).

Efroni explains the gender difference in earnings primarily by the lower rate of return that women receive compared to men for their human capital resources. Employers discriminate between men and women in essentially similar jobs by means of differential allocation of fringe benefits such as overtime payments, telephone and car allowances (which can account for 40 percent of the take-home pay), and in the assignment of different job titles for what is essentially the same work. Furthermore, as elsewhere women are discriminated against in promotions to more lucrative jobs (Shenhav and Haberfeld, 1988).

Women are less able to take advantage of career opportunities than men. Although over 90 percent of the families in which the woman is employed depend on her income to maintain their standard of living, neither the division of labor within the family nor the social institutions which service the family are well adapted to the needs of a dual earner family with children. Social norms regarding women's responsibilities for care of the home and children, as well as for many of the tasks which link the family to services in the wider society, operate to encourage women to forego potentially higher income jobs for those with shorter and more convenient working hours and locations close to home. For their part, employers assume, not always incorrectly, women's reluctance to take on added responsibilities, and often overlook those who, with some encouragement, would be ready to do so. Unfortunately, the growing number of aspiring women prepared to make the necessary sacrifices become the victims of employer discrimination.

BALANCING WORK AND FAMILY

Working mothers are constrained to develop special strategies to balance work and family obligations. They gravitate to part-time jobs, jobs close to home and those which are synchronized with the children's school schedule, such as teaching, or that have flexible working hours, such as nursing. Studies of work values among the adult population (e.g. Gafni, 1981) find that "working hours" or "working close to home" are more important job characteristics for women than for men. A study of sources of job satisfaction among 137 physician couples (Izraeli, 1988a) found that for women (but not for men), overall satisfaction with work was correlated with satisfaction with the opportunity afforded by the job to integrate home and work. Whether or not men are satisfied with how well they integrate work and family, it does not affect their overall satisfaction with their jobs.

Part-time Employment

The most prevalent strategy is part-time employment. With the increase of married women in the labor market, the percent of women working part-time (less than 35 hours a week, including preparation) increased from 30 percent in 1970 to 42 percent in 1987, and among scientific, academic and semiprofessional workers, the proportion is closer to 48 percent. Seventy percent of part time workers are women. The average working week is 29 hours a week for women and 40 hours for men. Part-time work is often more a matter of having to balance family and work than an indication of lack of commitment to work. For example, a study of a comparable sample of some 900 men and women managers (Izraeli, 1988b) found that the higher men rated on a measure of work involvement, the more hours a day they actually worked. Among women, the level of work involvement did not affect the number of hours a day they worked. The assumption was that the latter was more influenced by situational constraints.

While the availability of part-time employment, especially for educated women, contributed to their entry into the labor market, it is also a reason why women are more apt to find themselves in jobs in which opportunities for promotion or power and authority are limited. Gender differences in prestige and power in turn affect women's ability to negotiate a more equitable rate of exchange for their labor.

Female Niche

A second strategy, used also by professional women, is to select occupational niches which permit them to control their hours of work. Convenient and congenial working hours are among the major attractions of the Civil Service, where 53 percent of those employed are women (Civil Service, 1987).

Women constitute 71 percent of the pharmacists and 57 percent of the law-yers employed in the public sector (Civil Service, 1987:177) compared to 46 percent, and 41 percent respectively, of those employed in the general labor force. A study of the occupational specialization of physicians found that, with the exception of pediatrics, 83 percent of the women but only 38 percent of the men specialized in fields which independent judges rated as high on time control.

Opportunities Foregone

Constrained by the demands of the family, women have tended to juggle family and work by foregoing job opportunities or avoiding demanding oc-cupations or occupational roles. Management, for example, has none of the characteristics which facilitate the juggling of multiple roles (Izraeli, 1988). It is resistant to part-time work. Only 27 percent of female administrators and managers work part-time, compared to 48 percent of female academic work-ers and 51 percent of other professional and technical workers. While managers generally have more discretion to determine their work schedules than lower level participants, their workload is also less predictable and more likely to expand beyond official working hours. In addition, working over-time has important symbolic value as an expression of one's commitment to the organization. In this sense, the managerial role intrudes more sharply into the domestic time sphere than other occupational roles, causing resentment on the part of spouses and offspring and guilt in the women. This may in part explain why only 50 percent of ever-married women administrators and managers have children at home under age 14, compared to 67 percent of academic and professional workers and 74 percent of other professional and technical workers. (Since one is generally promoted into a managerial posi-tion, managers are, in addition, generally older than those employed in most other occupations.) Given the heavy demands of both the women's domestic roles and of managerial jobs, until recently the latter had less appeal to mar-ried women with children than alternative professional routes.

Late Upbeat

Another coping strategy is for a woman to keep her work simmering "on a low fire" while the children are small and to increase her investments in the workplace as they grow more independent. It is interesting to note that between 1979 and 1984, the only age group where there was an increase in the proportion of full-time workers was the 35 to 44 one. In a study of over 900 Israeli managers, 48 percent of the women and 35 percent of the men indicated that they had on some occasion refused an opportunity for promotion or held back their career advancement. The reasons for doing so, however, differed by gender: 77 percent of the women and only 21 percent of the men cited "fear of causing harm to children" while "lack of interest in the job offered" was mentioned by 47 percent of the men and only 19 percent of the women (Izraeli, 1988b). "The low fire" strategy would be a feasible solution were it not for the fact that career timetables, built as they are on the male experience, expect people to reach the height of their careers by their mid-forties, not to begin building them at that age.

THE COSTS

In the short run, women are not penalized for taking part-time jobs. In Israel, in contrast to many other countries, part-time workers enjoy the same rights as full-time workers in terms of security of tenure, social security and worker benefits. Furthermore, as Noah Lewin-Epstein and Haya Stier (1988) point out, Israeli women benefit from the unique occupational structure of the public sector, where more than 50 percent of the female labor force is employed. Comparing the public sector with the core and periphery segments of the labor market, they found that "workers in the public sector—both men and women—enjoy the most advantageous arrangements; they earn the highest income on the average despite the fact that they work fewer hours per week than other workers" and have greater job stability. In contrast to the situation in other western countries, women in Israel are under-represented in the less advantageous peripheral sector.

It is the long term consequences of women's career strategies which seriously damage their competitive position. An example of such a strategy and the lack of symmetry between men and women in this respect is demonstrated in a study (Doenias, 1988) of the decision of university academics to take sabbatical leave. Doenias found that in the process of deciding whether to go on sabbatical, the men gave more weight to factors related to their own careers than to those related to the careers of their wives. Women, on the other hand, gave greater weight to considerations related to their spouse's careers and less to factors related to their own. Women were more likely than men to spend their sabbatical in Israel rather than go abroad. Of those who went abroad, women were more likely to go for a shorter period of time. If we consider that the sabbatical offers a unique opportunity for the academic to establish and strengthen informal network ties, critical in a myriad of ways for career advancement, Doenias's findings contribute another dimension to our understanding of why the proportion of women narrows so radically as we move up the academic ladder.

It is difficult to assess the long term cost to women for compromising their labor market investments. For example, the readiness to travel longer distances to work increases the range of job opportunities. A recent study by Moshe Semyonov and Noah Lewin-Epstein (1988) shows that women who worked outside their community of residence had higher earnings and higher occupational status than women who worked in their community of residence. Furthermore, 57 percent of the earnings gap between commuters and noncommuters among women was due to the advantageous market conditions associated with commuting. Semyonov and Lewin-Epstein found that 46 percent of the working men in Israel were employed outside their community, compared to only 32 percent of the women. The percent of married women among noncommuters was higher than among commuters. Moreover, noncommuting women had more children on the average than commuting women. This suggests that mothers forego opportunities associated with spatial mobility in order to work close to home.

Clearly many women accept and express satisfaction with secondary work roles in order to devote themselves to culturally valued family roles. However, for those women who out of economic need or a desire for career advancement seek more extensive involvement in the labor force, the pressures emanating from social norms and the barriers posed by family responsibilities are severe. For example, in her study of a representative national sample of 28 year old married mothers, Amy Avgar (1985) found that 45 percent of those working part time indicated that they would prefer to work full-time, but that full-time workers were considerably less satisfied with their ability to integrate family and work than were part-timers. In the same study, Avgar examined the level of women's satisfaction with different characteristics of their jobs and found that both full-time and part-time women workers ranked "satisfaction with opportunity for advancement" the lowest or near the lowest out of 15 job characteristics.

INTO THE 1980S AND BEYOND: FROM PROTECTION TO EQUAL OPPORTUNITY

The 1980s brought a growing concern among women's groups for issues related to equal opportunity. A reevaluation of the policy of protective legislation and special benefits for working mothers, once considered a great achievement, led to the conclusion that the costs in opportunities lost were greater than the benefits. Consequently pressure was brought to bear by women's organizations and the Prime Minister's advisor on the status of women. As a result, the legal prohibition on women's night work was abolished and the pension age for women (previously 60 years) was made equal to that of men (65). In both cases, women retained the legal prerogative to refuse to work the night shift and to retire at 60—indicating the ambivalence about foregoing privileges when opportunities are in fact not yet equal. Maternal leave rights for childcare became parental rights, but the change did not apply to collective labor agreements, which provide mothers, but not fathers of young children, the right to work fewer hours. Two equal opportunity laws came into effect in 1981 and 1988, the second more encompassing than the first, but both with ineffective enforcement mechanisms. Their value is now being tested in the courts. In most major departments of the public sector, including the Civil Service, government owned enterprises, the Jewish Agency and all the universities, a woman has been appointed to be "in charge of the status of women," a position lacking in authority and resources. Frequently the position is offered (by a male superior) to a woman without consideration of her attitudes toward feminism or her qualifications for the assignment, which is an addition to her regular job without additional compensation.

The growing importance of employment for women and women's increasing self-confidence on the job have led to rising expectations for greater rewards. Collective values have weakened in Israeli society, and women are being affected by a more individual sense of entitlement. To be "assertive" is a phrase that has entered the Hebrew lexicon as a model for women's behavior, and thousands of women have been exposed to assertiveness training. Looking to the 1990s, it appears that when the *Intifada* ends and the economy begins to revitalize (and the two are related), the issue of women's entitlement to more equal rewards for their investments in human capital and for their potential contributions to economic life will have greater probability of moving closer to center stage.

REFERENCES

Avgar, Amy (1985) *The Integration of Work and Family Roles Among a Cohort of Young Israeli Women.* Report presented to the U.S.-Israel Binational Fund, Jerusalem.

Civil Service (1987) *Annual Report No. 37.* Jerusalem: Ministry of Finance.

Cohen, Yinon; Bechar, Shlomit; Reijman, Rebecca (1987) "Occupational Sex Segregation in Israel, 1972–1983." *Israel Social Science Research* 5(1/2): 97–106.

Doenias, Iris (1988) *The Decision to Go on Sabbatical in Academia Among Dual Career Couples.* Unpublished M.Sc. Thesis, Tel Aviv University, Faculty of Management (Hebrew).

Efroni, Linda (1980) *Promotion and Wages in the Public Sector: Are Women Discriminated Against?* Research Report. Jerusalem: Work & Welfare Research Institute, Hebrew University (Hebrew).

Efroni, Linda (1988) *Women in Government Service: A Comparison 1979–1988,* Research Report. Jerusalem: The Civil Service Training and Education Service, (Hebrew).

Gafni, Yael (1981) *The Readiness of Women and Men in Israel to Accept Top Management Positions.* M.A. Thesis, Bar Ilan University, Dept. of Political Science, Israel (Hebrew).

Hartman, Moshe (1978) *Roles in the Economy and in the Family of Jewish Married Women in Israel,* Research Report, Tel Aviv University.

Honig, M. and Shamai, N. (1978) "Israel." In Kamerman, S. B. and Kahn, A. S. (eds.). *Family Policy, Government and Families in Fourteen Countries.* New York: Columbia University Press; 400–427.

Izraeli, Dafna N. (1983) "Israeli Women in Work Force: A Current Appraisal." *Jerusalem Quarterly* 27: 59–80.

Izraeli, Dafna N. (1988) "Burning Out in Medicine: A Comparison of Husbands and Wives in Dual Career Couples." *Journal of Social Behavior and Personality.*

Izraeli, Dafna N. (1988a) "Family-Work Conflict Among Dual Career Physician Couples in Israel." Paper presented at the Annual Meeting of the Academy of Management, Women in Management Division, August, Washington D.C.

Izraeli, Dafna N. (1988b) "Women's Movement Into Management." In Adler, N. and Izraeli, D. N. (eds.). *Women in Management Worldwide*. New York: M. E. Sharpe.

Lewin-Epstein, Noah and Haya Stier (1988) "Labor Market Structure, Gender and Socioeconomic Inequality in Israel." *Israel Social Science Research: A Multidisciplinary Journal*.

Mar'i, Mariam M. and Mar'i, Sami Kh. (1985) "The Role of Women as Change Agents in Arab Society in Israel." In Safir, M., Mednick, M. T., Izraeli, D. N. and Bernard, J. (eds.). *Women's Worlds: From the New Scholarship*. New York: Praeger. (Reprinted in this volume).

Semyonov, Moshe and Lewin-Epstein, Noah (1988) "Local Labor Markets, Commuting and Gender Inequality." Paper presented at the Conference of the Israeli Sociological Association Section on Stratification, Haifa University, April (Hebrew).

Shenhav, Yehuda A. and Haberfeld, Yitzchak (1988) "Scientists in Organizations: Discrimination Processes in an Internal Labor Market." *The Sociological Quarterly* 29:451–462.

Toren, Nina (1987) "The Status of Women in Academia." *Israel Social Science Research* 5 (1/2): 138–146.

Women, Work and the Law

Frances Raday

Labor law provisions relating to women were initially founded on a combination of the socialist philosophy that everyone should be engaged in productive labor and the social commitment to development of family, in which women were perceived as playing the role of homemaker. A strong legal infrastructure was thus created to ensure that women would be able to integrate work and homemaking. The result of this infrastructure was, on one hand, facilitation of the integration of work and family and, on the other, perpetuation of the stereotyping of women as primary homemaker and secondary employee. The need to guarantee equal opportunity for women in the labor market was ignored, except for the introduction of an equal pay law in 1964, which protected women against wage exploitation. The labor courts first expressly recognized equal opportunity in the early 1970s, but it wasn't until 1987 that legislation made this a major concern of the legal system.

The employment sector is the only sphere of private sector activity in which the legislature has intervened not only to regulate women's issues but also to guarantee equality of opportunity between the sexes. The historical development of this legislative regulation falls into two phases. The first phase, from 1954 to 1964, involved the establishment of a legislative infrastructure to provide women employees with protective guarantees in the labor market; this phase was characterized by the Knesset's prompt adoption of all the protections for women workers recommended by the International Labor Organization during those years. The second phase, from 1973 to date, has involved the development of a legal right to equal employment opportunity between the sexes; this phase has been marked by interaction between the labor courts and the Knesset. The labour courts introduced the concept of equal employment opportunity in 1973, but after changes in the composition of the National Labor Court, failed to implement it. Since 1987, the Knesset has intervened to establish, or reestablish, rights to equal employment opportunity, and to remove sex role stereotyping. In 1990, the High Court of Justice reconfirmed that there is a basic right of equal employment.

INTEGRATION OF WORK
AND FAMILY — FROM
MOTHERHOOD TO PARENTHOOD

In the first phase, the main thrust of the legislative effort was provision of protection to working mothers. In 1954, working women were given the right to three months maternity leave — the employer was prohibited from employing the woman during that period, or from dismissing her, and she was given the right to payment in lieu of salary from the National Insurance Institute (Women's Employment Law, 1954, secs. 6, 8, 9; National Insurance Law, Chapter on Maternity Benefits). After her maternity leave, the mother was given the right to take up to a year's leave without pay, or to resign with entitlement to severance pay (Women's Employment Law, 1954, sec. 7[d]; Severance Pay Law, 1963, sec. 7).

The labor relations infrastructure also took measures to encourage "working mothers." Collective agreements provided that women could use part of their own sick leave to care for children and would work one hour less a day if they had two children or more under the age of twelve. Na'amat and other women's organizations, Women's International Zionist Organization (WIZO) and Emunah, created an impressive infrastructure of child care centers.

All these protective measures were of great practical value in facilitating the integration of motherhood with participation in the labor market. However, they were also responsible for the perpetuation of stereotypes, for they were based on a female role image as primarily caretaker of home and children (Raday, 1983). In 1988, an important move was made to remove this stereotyping. The Knesset passed legislation which converted maternal rights to parental rights. The right to sick leave to care for sick children (The Equal Employment Opportunity Law, 1988, sec. 4), the right to resign with severance pay in order to care for a baby (sec. 22), and the right to unpaid leave after the termination of the three month mandatory maternity leave (sec. 23) were all converted to parental rights. The formula was that rights not exploited by the mother passed to the father.

There is controversy, both legal and sociopolitical, as to the continuing validity of the remaining maternal rights not converted to parental rights. The legal controversy centers on the question of whether maternal rights not mandated by legislation, such as the right to a shorter working day for mothers, can survive the scrutiny of the antidiscrimination provisions of the Equal Employment Opportunity Law (Raday, 1989). The sociopolitical controversy centers on the statutory preservation of a mandatory three month maternity leave and on the prohibition of overtime work after five months of pregnancy. There are those who claim that these prohibitions are paternalistic and restrict women's opportunities, while others assert that they are the minimal protection for women's physical and mental health and that they prevent employers from trying to keep women from enjoying the rights which the legal system grants them.

EQUAL PAY

In 1964, the Equal Pay Law provided that an employer had to pay female employees a wage equal to that of male employees in the same workplace for work essentially equal. The Law did not succeed in achieving a redistribution of wages between the sexes. The Commission on Women's Status in 1978 reported that women's wages were considerably lower than men's wages, both on the average and on the basis of academic qualifications, economic branch, profession and skill. More recent research has shown an increase in the gap between women's and men's wages in both the private and public sector, on the basis of equivalent human capital characteristics (Efroni, 1988; Haberfeld and Shenhav, 1987). The effect of the Law in litigation has been little better than its effect on wage statistics. Although the first suit to be brought under the Law (1978) was successful, it was the only one ever decided. (The facts in the case presented a very clear picture of wage discrimination, since the female employee plaintiff had been receiving a lower wage as replacement for an absent male machinery operator and expert evidence had been presented to the court that she performed essentially the same work: *Elite Chocolate Industries Ltd.* v. *Lederman* ([1977/78] 9 P.D.A. 255). The overall failure of the Law to achieve its purpose led to current attempts to amend it. Proposals include extending the definition of wages to include emoluments and fringe benefits such as car allowances, telephone, travel, overtime and geographical allowances and introducing a legislative requirement of pay equity, or comparable worth.

EQUAL EMPLOYMENT OPPORTUNITY

The second phase of labor law development—the development of a concept of equal opportunity between the sexes in employment—was initiated by the labor courts in a landmark 1973 decision: *El Al Israel Airlines Incorp.* v. *Edna Hazin et al.* ([1972/3] 4 P.D.A. 365). The decision was made in the context of a suit brought by air stewardesses against El Al Airlines to contest their exclusion from the rank of chief steward, the highest rank for cabin crew. Although there was no existing legislative framework prohibiting discrimination in employment conditions, the Regional Court and the National Labor Court both held that the promotion provision in El Al's collective agreement was discriminatory and that the Court had the power to declare such discrimination void as contrary to public policy (Raday, 1983).

The potential impact of the *Hazin* judgment was considerable. It appeared to open the way for extensive litigation against discrimination in employment.

However, the potential of the case was never realized in the courts. During the ten years following the judgment, the only litigatory activity which it generated was a single action brought in the Haifa regional labor court in 1980. This was a suit to invalidate a decision by the Prime Minister's Office not to employ the plaintiff, Hana Kinar, as a field assistant for Arab affairs because the job was considered dangerous for a female employee. The action was settled out of court. The reasons for this dearth of litigation are complex and have been discussed elsewhere (Raday, 1983). Amongst other causes, are the inadequacies of the legal remedies available under *Hazin*. A 1981 Law did not effectively add to the remedies available under *Hazin* (Equal Opportunities in Employment Law, 1981). The Law introduced criminal prohibition of discrimination in the acceptance of job applicants into employment, since under the ruling in *Hazin,* the right not to be discriminated against, was limited to the employment conditions of persons already employed. (The public policy power to invalidate discriminatory contract provisions under that ruling could not be applied to a situation in which a contract had not yet been concluded.) The 1981 Law added an important dimension to the theoretical scope of the protection against discrimination. It did nothing, however, to improve the potential for implementation of this right through civil litigation and the criminal liability which it introduced remained a dead letter; not a single conviction was made under the law for discrimination in acceptance of job applicants (Raday, 1983).

Against this background of nonlitigation, a series of suits were brought in the early 1980s to contest discrimination against women in retirement age. In 1983, two medical professors sought an injunction against the Hadassah Medical Organization to prevent it from forcibly retiring them five years earlier than their male colleagues. The early retirement was in accordance with the provisions of a collective agreement between Hadassah Hospital and the doctors' unions. The case terminated in an out-of-court settlement in which the plaintiffs achieved full equality in retirement age. In 1985, Dr. Naomi Nevo, a senior sociologist in the Jewish Agency, brought a similar action for an injunction against her employer. The labor courts refused to grant her a remedy. In spite of undisputed evidence of injury to the plaintiff's economic and professional standing, the National Labor Court held, in a majority decision given in 1986, that under the *Hazin* ruling, imposition of early retirement age did not constitute unlawful discrimination. The majority held that going out on pension was not a "condition of employment" and hence the *Hazin* ruling was not applicable (*Dr. Naomi Nevo* v. *The Jewish Agency,* [1986/87] 18 P.D. 197,219).

The labor court finding that mandatory early retirement for women was not unlawful discrimination resulted in corrective legislation. In 1987, the Equal Retirement Age for Female and Male Employees Law was passed by the Knesset. The new law provided that retirement age for men and women was to be equal under collective agreements but that where the agreement itself provided for an earlier retirement age for women, women retained the option of retiring at the earlier age.

There were additional aspects of the *Nevo* decision which necessitated further legislative intervention. According to the majority decision, the silence of the legislature with regard to discrimination in any specific aspect of employment (and in the present case as regards discrimination in retirement age) showed that its intention was not to prohibit such discrimination. The Court held that the policy of the legislature had been to specifically prohibit discrimination in acceptance to employment (the 1981 Law), and in payment of wages (the 1964 Law). Hence the Court concluded: "where the legislature wished to prevent discrimination (or create absolute equality) it did so specifically; as regards a subject not regulated by an express provision of a statute — the presumption is that the legislature reached the conclusion that the time is not yet ripe for it" (at. 220).

In 1988, the Knesset passed the Equal Employment Opportunities Law. This law introduced a wide ranging prohibition on discrimination in employment, citing specifically each and every aspect of employment covered: acceptance to employment, conditions of employment, promotion, training and professional study, dismissal and severance pay (sec. 2). The wide specification indicates the desire of the legislature to cover the whole range of employment discrimination.

The 1988 Law also included specific prohibition of sexual harassment. Section 7 provides that an employer must not injure the employee's interests in acceptance to employment, conditions of employment, promotion, training and professional study, dismissal and severance pay, "on grounds of the employee's refusal to accept any offer or of his or her rejection of an act which is of a sexual nature and was done by the employer or by the employee's direct or indirect supervisor." This provision prohibits sexual harassment related to an economic threat but does not expressly include a sexually harassing environment. It may, nevertheless, be possible to contest a sexually harassing environment under the Law's general prohibition of discrimination in employment conditions. (For a full discussion of this alternative and an analysis of the U.S. and Canadian Supreme Court decisions, see Raday, 1989.)

The 1988 Law provides some of those remedies which were lacking under the *Hazin* ruling. It provides both civil and criminal rights of action against employment discrimination. It provides that the posing of irrelevant conditions may constitute discrimination, thus allowing an action for indirect discrimination or discriminatory impact (sec. 2[6]). It places the burden of proof on the employer in civil actions based on the Law (sec. 9). It bestows on the labor courts the power to give enforcement orders, in spite of the general rule of contract law that there is no specific enforcement of contracts for personal services, and to award damages even if there is no proof of economic injury (sec. 10). The formulation of the remedy of enforcement in sec. 10 is problematic—the labor courts are directed to give this remedy "if the award of damages alone is not enough" and the court "must take into consideration the effect of the enforcement order on labor relations in the workplace and the possibility that another employee will be injured."

The 1988 Law has already produced a number of employment discrimination suits. The first suit to be brought was by ground stewardesses against El Al Airlines. The suit revives memories of the 1973 precedent-setting case of the air stewardesses. The ground stewardesses claim that their promotion is integrated with that of traffic officers—they participate in joint courses and are promoted together to the level of traffic controller—but that they are excluded from the station managers' course. This level is the next stage of promotion and the key to all senior management jobs in ground operations. El Al claims, variously, that as women the ground stewardesses cannot work in maintenance, the work performed by traffic officers at the commencement of their career, and that therefore they do not qualify for the station managers' course; that the ground stewardesses' maintenance experience as replacements for the traffic officers in times of war does not qualify them; and that the job of station manager is by its very nature unsuitable for women. Another suit has been brought against the Hilton Hotels for discrimination against waitresses in promotion and wages. Yet another has been brought against the Red Carpet Company for discrimination in acceptance to employment on the grounds that at the job interview, the applicant was told that as a mother of a young child she couldn't meet the job requirement of work-hour flexibility. At this writing, these suits are pending hearing in the regional labor court.

While the Knesset has shown willingness to inculcate the principle of equality in employment and has indeed intervened to correct the conservative policy and the inactivism of the labor courts on this issue, it has not been prepared to pay a fiscal price for its policies. The 1988 Law does not provide a budget for any enforcement agency. The promotion of civil litigation under the Law depends on the victims of discrimination themselves, with all the psychological and financial burdens this entails. The civil suits brought to date have been supported by voluntary groups, Na'amat, the Israel Women's Network and the Civil Rights Association, but the problem of financing litigation arises anew with every case. Both the 1981 and 1988 Law give powers of investigation and criminal prosecution to the Ministry of Labor, and this has contributed to enforcement of their provisions as regards discriminatory job advertising. However the problems of proof in criminal trials make this an unsatisfactory option for more factually complex discrimination cases, such as discrimination in acceptance to employment, promotion, or dismissal.

Finally, the Law does not incorporate the concept of affirmative action on the model of the 1980 United Nations Convention for the Elimination of all Forms of Discrimination against Women or of the Canadian Charter of 1982. Such models endorse affirmative action programs intended to close the existing gap between men and women. However, the Israeli legislature employs the dated concept of preservation of "privileges" for women (sec. 7) rather than the socially dynamic concept of equality implicit in the endorsement of affirmative action programs (Raday, 1988).

IMPLEMENTATION OF EMPLOYMENT OPPORTUNITY GUARANTEES— JUDGES AND STEREOTYPES

Implementation of the statutory rights to equal employment opportunity is, of course, through the courts. The 1988 legislative guarantees have not yet been tested. It is therefore a question for speculation how the labor courts will respond to the challenge. Some sign of what may be expected appears in the past record of judicial attitudes to stereotyping of women's societal role.

To what extent have Israeli judges accepted the stereotyping of women's role and how will this affect the outcome of the issues to be decided by them? Since there has as yet been no systematic research into this question, reporting on the issue can at present be only anecdotal. Since this writing, however, the Supreme Court has issued a clear directive to the lower courts to examine differential treatment with heightened scrutiny to ascertain that it isn't based "on stereotypic generalizations which derive only from prejudice" (Bagatz 104/87, *Nevo v. The National Labour Court et. al.,* 22.10.90.

In 1951, Justice Zusman roundly endorsed prevailing stereotypes regarding the role of the married woman as homemaker. (*Steinberg v. Attorney General,* [1951] 5 P.D. 1062). Upholding the differential treatment of men and women for purposes of army service—the granting of far wider exemption from service on grounds of religious conscience for women than for men—he held that the purpose of the guarantee of equality under the Women's Equal Rights Law was to protect women, not men (at 1067). Commenting with approval on the exemption of married women from army service, he remarked: "The man is discriminated against, but the discrimination is justified because the special role of a married woman in her home justifies her exclusion from the sphere of application of the Defense Service Law."

In a different context, stereotyping of male and female roles in the family was rejected by the Tel Aviv District Court in 1987. In this case a moshav (cooperative settlement) refused to grant women rights as worker-members, on the grounds that the right to be a worker-member was restricted to the "head of the family." Women could not, according to the cooperative, fulfill this requirement—even if they had no spouse! District Court Judge Aloni had no hesitation in dissenting with this stereotype of women's role in the family. He held that this constituted discrimination between men and women and that it was "unimaginable" that such discrimination should be found in a labor cooperative (*Glasman v. Beit Herut,* Tel Aviv District Court 5.6.88, following *Beit Hanita v. Friedman,* [1964] 18[3] P.D. 20).

In 1989, the National Labor Court, repeating a request from Bedouin women for multiple payments of minimum income from the National Insurance Institute for polygamous families, held that the technique of divorcing one wife before marrying another wife did not preclude regarding such families as one family units where there was evidence of a continued domestic connection with the husband. Jude Adler commented that, although he was aware of the economic hardship of these women, the Court could not condone any interpretation which would in practice give recognition to polygamous arrangements, that are against the law and injurious to women's status (*Fatmah Dib Abulban* v. *National Insurance Institute* 20 P.D.A. 334, 339).

The protective stereotype of women which was expressed in the Supreme Court in 1951 has not, however, wholly disappeared. In a recent case, refusing to accept the State's request for extension of the arrest of the respondent, a mother of five children, Justice Elon expressed the opinion that "although it is a basic principle that all are equal before the law, both in rights and in duties, . . . for all that, there are certain situations in which a woman's sensitivity and vulnerability are greater than those of a man—arrest and imprisonment are amongst them." Justice Elon did not regard this as a question of proven fact in the specific case before the Supreme Court but rather as a general principle established in the writings of the Talmud and of Maimonides (*State of Israel* v. *Evoksis,* [1978] 32[2] P.D. 247,251).

If women are the weaker sex, it of course goes without saying that they are the fairer sex! Thus in examining the evidence in interim proceedings for an injunction, Tel Aviv Regional Labor Court Judge Flitman remarked in his interim judgment that since the interviewing employer had, according to his evidence, found the job applicant unsuitable because of her "appearance," the latter had failed to make a prima facie case that she was qualified for the job. The job was that of assistant to the manager of the Red Carpet Company, which provides a reception service for V.I.P. travellers. The plaintiff had complained that during her job interview, most of the questioning centered on her ability to work at unconventional and unplanned times—in view of the fact that she was the mother of a six-year-old child—and that this constituted discrimination on grounds of parenthood, prohibited under the 1988 Law. Judge Flitman did not seem to even consider the possibility that the employer might have been discriminating on grounds of a beauty requirement for women (*Plonsker* v. *Red Carpet Co.,* Tel Aviv Regional Labor Court).

On more than one occasion, judges have expressed the idea that the status quo cannot be immediately changed even if its continuation is inegalitarian for women. Thus Judge Gabrielli commented, in the Regional Court judgment in the *Nevo Case* that even if the early retirement of women was no longer in women's interests, the courts were not the place to carry out the revolutionary change required (*Dr. Naomi Nevo* v. *The Jewish Agency,* Tel Aviv Regional Court 27.11.85 para. 15[6]). Judge Nachtomi put the same proposition into Biblical aphorism in an interim judgment in the *El Al Ground Hostesses Case:* while on the one hand he called for a new leaf in the policy of El Al, on the other, he commented that the ground hostesses' refusal to accept a "well intentioned offer" from El Al was due to the fact that "they were not prepared to regard themselves as 'a generation of the desert,' in whose footsteps others would follow . . . to 'the promised land' " (*Peled et. al.* v. *El Al Airlines Incorp.*, Tel Aviv Regional Court 3.4.89). The 1990 *Nevo* judgment in the High Court of Justice laid down clear directives for the courts to seek actively to uncover stereotypes which adversely affect women, even where there is no proof of discriminatory intent.

CONCLUSION

The legal framework for women and work in Israel guarantees a comparatively high level of protection for the integration of work and family. Maternity leave, paid by the National Insurance Institute, is mandatory and the woman is protected against dismissal during both pregnancy and maternity leave. There have been recent legislative measures to remove the maternal role stereotypes which were implicit in the early legislation, leave for purpose of early childrearing and care of sick children has been converted from maternal to parental leave.

The inclusion of a goal of equal employment opportunity is recent and incomplete. Equal pay guarantees remain narrowly defined. Effective equal employment opportunity legislation was not introduced until 1988: even then, the legislation did not include affirmative action in its definition of equality nor did it provide for enforcement agencies to implement its principles of equality through the courts. The tendency of the courts in general and the labor courts in particular has been, with few exceptions, to accept protective stereotypes of women's role, even where these limit her ability to compete equally in the labor market, or to regard the move to equality as a social revolution which should be promulgated outside the courts. The 1988 Equal Employment Opportunities Law changed the equation in that, for the first time, it clearly designated the labor courts' jurisdiction to intervene and provide remedies for a wide range of discriminatory practices in employment. It is to be hoped that the labor courts will meet the challenge.

REFERENCES

Efroni, Linda (1988) "Promotion and Wages in the Public Service—Comparative Analysis 1978 and 1988." *Women in the World of Work: The Status of Women*, No. 21. Jerusalem: Office of the Advisor to the Prime Minister on the Status of Women (Hebrew).

Haberfeld, Yitzchak and Shenhav, Yehuda (1987) "Beyond a Smoking Gun Type Discrimination: A Firm Level Analysis of Rewards and Opportunities." Tel Aviv: Pinhas Sapir Center for Development, Tel Aviv University.

Raday, Frances (1983) "Equality of Women Under Israeli Law." *Jerusalem Quarterly* 27: 81,84.

Raday, Frances (1989) "Labour Law and Relations—Trends and Directions 1988." *Israel Labour Law Journal*, 1 (Hebrew).

Arab Women in the Israeli Labor Market

Saniya Abu Rakba
(Translated by Hazel Arieli)

Arab society in Israel is still eddying in a whirlpool of conflicting currents, striving to find its way in a complex reality; external pressure is accompanied by internal reshuffling, and nationalist aspirations are coming to the surface against the background of generational struggle. Israeli Arabs find themselves torn between their people and their state. They are engaged in a struggle to define their identity, and at the same time, they are being swept into a clash between traditional leaders and a new sense of self, created by external forces (Shtendal, 1975).

Among the many changes occurring in the Arab sector is the shift of economic focus from the village to the town, with an increase in the number of people working outside the village and a decrease in the importance of agriculture in the local economy. The accelerated economic development following the Six Day War intensified this process. Arab laborers sought jobs in the towns and were "snapped up," especially in the construction, light manufacturing and service industries. The demand for workers caused wage rates to rise considerably, thus increasing the general level of income in Arab families. As a result of the entrance of workers from the territories into the Israeli labor market, Arab construction workers from villages in Israel became foremen and sub-contractors or opened their own construction firms (Shtendal, 1975).

Many changes have occurred in the socioeconomic structure of Arab society since the establishment of the state of Israel as the result of the disintegration of traditional Arab society. A slow but powerful process of modernization has begun. The clan framework is breaking down, and the young person who has acquired secondary or higher education is replacing the head of the clan. With regard to women, several laws have been passed, which form the basis of equality for Arab women, the most important of which is the Law of Compulsory Education; this law has increased the rate of school attendance by both boys and girls (Yisraeli, 1980). In addition, increasing contact with

187

western values is gradually opening new options for Arab women. This is reflected on several levels:

1. Education for girls has expanded. Girls attend secondary schools in greater numbers, and Arab women now study at universities (Shtendal, 1975). Women constitute 21.6 percent of all Arabs who have earned a first degree, and 22.5 percent of all Arab academics (Al-Haj, 1988). Female education has economic value, as well as being a source of status for the women and their families. The presence of female pupils provided legitimization for women to become teachers, and this, in turn, gave further legitimization for girls' education (Mar'i and Mar'i, 1985).
2. On the political level, the Arab woman's voice is still not audible. Granting her the right to vote, against the background of her still inferior status, in fact has strengthened the traditional framework, doubling the political power of the clan (Shtendal, 1975).
3. More women are working outside of their homes. The economic recession in the years 1965 through 1967, when there was a high rate of unemployment among Arab men, along with the rise in the standard of living, created economic pressure which spurred Arab women to join the secondary, unskilled work force, particularly in low-level occupations (Mar'i and Mar'i, 1985).
4. Arab women have begun to learn about their rights, and to dare to demand them (Shtendal, 1975).

The distribution of occupations in Israeli society varies according to ethnic origin (Tyree, 1981), and the most outstanding difference is between Jews and Arabs, to the extent that the two groups form two almost entirely separate labor markets. The sexual structure of an occupation also influences both income level and educational requirements. However, the differences between Jews and Arabs in Israel are greater than the differences between the sexes, and the hierarchy of occupations among Arabs in Israel is somewhat different from that of Jews. The two groups are much more separate than are blacks and whites in the United States for example. Moreover, for security reasons, professions such as electronics and aviation are closed to Israeli Arabs, as are Civil Service posts at medium and upper echelons (Algazi, 1971).

The main employment problem for Arab women is the scarcity of suitable work places, particularly for the university educated (similar to the problems of university educated men). Qualified engineers work as teachers and so do computer programmers. Since there is no industry in the Arab villages, the only possibility for productive work is in textiles and garment workshops. There is still a lack of support for working mothers, which makes it more difficult to leave home. There is a total absence of vocational counselling and planning services, and this, too, is a serious deficiency that needs urgently to be rectified (Eran and Milson, 1987).

The overall percentage of women in the Israeli civilian work force in 1985 was 37 percent, and there was a huge gap between the rate of participation of Arab and Jewish women: the participation of Jewish women was 39 percent, whereas the participation among Arab women was only 11 percent.

Arab women in the Israeli work force fall into two general categories, women working in services and industry and women working in white collar jobs.

WOMEN WORKING IN SERVICES AND INDUSTRY

Between 1965 and 1984, the percentage of Arab women in industry increased fivefold, from 5.3 percent to 28 percent. The absolute number of Arab women in industry was 6.3 thousand in 1984, a fifteen-fold increase over their numbers in 1965, 0.4 thousand. Service jobs, mostly in cleaning, and jobs in textile factories or garment shops are characterized by low wages, no overtime pay, no social benefits, and few or no vacations or sick leave. They carry no job security or opportunities for advancement. Most of the workers are young, unmarried women. The work is usually arranged through contractors, who are generally relatives of the workers. The textile plants where the women work are generally in their own villages or towns or nearby, because it is still considered undesirable for women to work far away from home, unless they have a male relative working in the plant. The Arab women also receive the lowest wages (Nimer, 1971). In addition, some women work in their homes, as dressmakers and nursemaids for children whose mothers go out to work. Others work as cleaners, but only in institutions or homes outside their neighborhoods.

WOMEN WORKING IN WHITE COLLAR JOBS

In 1984, almost half of the Israeli Arab women in the work force were in social and public services: 46.1 percent; twice as many as worked within these sectors in 1965. Teaching, nursing and social work were the first professions to gain social legitimization in Arab society in Israel and other parts of the Middle East, perhaps because of their resemblance to woman's traditional roles. Teaching has become a feminine profession in Israeli Arab schools, just as it has in western societies. In 1972, one out of every three teachers in Arab schools was a woman (Mar'i and Mar'i, 1985). Teaching was the first profession entered by women when they broke with tradition and went out to work. While most women working in industry leave their jobs after getting married, teachers generally continue working after marriage. However, the Ministry of Education requires only a limited number of secondary school graduates each year, and many turn to clerical work in lawyers' offices or other businesses. Educated women also work as social workers or nurses, or in public offices, and recently also in private offices: as doctors, lawyers and pharmacists. Some women have set up independent businesses, such as boutiques and insurance companies.

Women receive academic training mainly in teachers' training colleges and universities. There is a growing tendency to live away from home during the period of their studies, a custom unheard of in the past. However, it is still difficult for Arab women to get into universities, because the standard of secondary education in the Arab sector is lower than that in the Jewish one.

In the 1986–1987 academic year, women constituted approximately 43 percent of all the Arab students studying at Haifa University. In 1982, Arab women academics formed 21.6 percent of all Arab academics with a first degree, and 22.5 percent of those with a second or third degree (Al-Haj, 1988). Interestingly, female high school students study mathematics and science in higher percentages than their Jewish peers.

The percentage of female academics working away from their places of residence is higher than that of men. Women who have managed to acquire higher education have had to overcome many social obstacles, although recently there have been signs of greater openness in Arab society to outside work for women, especially in white collar occupations (Al-Haj, 1988).

Studies show that attitudes concerning women working outside the home have changed and are still undergoing change. In a study of sex role perceptions among Arab students and teachers in Israel, Mariam Mar'i found that only 22.3 percent of the men, and 85.3 percent of the women believed that a woman's personal fulfillment was more important than her family obligation (Mar'i, 1983).

Still, the Arab woman is doubly disadvantaged. First, like the Jewish woman, her primary role is defined as connected with the home; she is considered a secondary wage earner, while the man is the breadwinner. It is easier to fire a woman, and her salary is lower than that of a man. Second, she is a minority within a minority. The Arabs in Israel have limited educational opportunities and face ethnic bias. Many professions are closed to them on security grounds.

REFERENCES

Algazi, Joseph (1971) "Upbringing and Education Among Arabs in Israel." *Values* 3 (15): 49–56 (Hebrew).

Al-Haj, Majid (ed.) (1988) "Problems of Employment for Arab Academics in Israel." *Middle East Studies,* No. 8, The Jewish-Arab Center, University of Haifa.

Bureau of Statistics, *1986 Yearbook.*

Eran, M., and Milson, A. (1987) "Women in the Israeli Work Force." Man and Work 1 (1): 36–39 (Hebrew).

Mar'i, Mariam (1983) "Sex-Role Perceptions of Palestinian Males and Females in Israel." Ph.D. Dissertation, East Lansing Michigan State University.

Mar'i, Mariam and Mar'i, Sami Kh. (1985) "The Role of Women as Change in Arab Society in Israel." In Safir, M., Mednick, M.T., Izraeli, D.N. and Bernard, J. (eds.). *Women's Worlds: From the New Scholarship.* New York: Praeger (Hebrew).

Nimer, Odette (1971) "The Arab Woman in Israel." *Values,* 3 (15): 44–47 (Hebrew).

Shtendal, Uri (1975) "The Status of the Arab Woman in Israel Towards the Year 1976." *Social Security* 9–10: 137–143 (Hebrew).

Tyree, Andrea (1981) "Socio-Economic Occupational Status in Israeli Society." *Megamot* 27: 7–21 (Hebrew).

Yisraeli, Eitan (1980) "Adult Education in the Arab and Druze Sector." *Studies in Education* 25: 139–154 (Hebrew).

Oriental and Ashkenazi Jewish Women in the Labor Market

Deborah S. Bernstein

The Israeli labor market is highly segregated; most women and most men enter different sectors and pursue different occupations. Most women find themselves primarily among women, while most men find few women in their midst (Izraeli, 1979). This segregation appears to remain relatively stable. While there has been a gradual and consistent increase in women's participation in, and share of, the labor market, this has not had much effect on the division within the labor market. An important change that did take place was feminization of occupations that had previously been predominantly masculine or mixed gender, primarily teaching and clerical work (Bernstein, 1983). Feminization followed rapid growth of the occupation, new options for men who previously "manned" the field, and a shortage of new men to fill the new needs, developments that occurred in Israel in the 1950s and early 1960s.

Limited as they are to the "female labor market," do women experience additional divides, ones that distinguish between one woman and the other? Ethnic affiliation, whether one is Ashkenazi or Oriental, is a central, class-related factor determining dominance and subordination in Israeli society. The structure of dominance was shaped primarily in the 1950s during the period of mass immigration (Bernstein and Swirski, 1982), and has been reproduced in the second generation, born and educated in Israel (Nahon, 1984). The central question in this discussion will be the significance of ethnic affiliation of women within the labor market; what does it mean to be an Oriental or an Ashkenazi woman when it comes to work related characteristics and behavior? The second generation, born and bred in Israel, will be of special interest, the question being how do young Oriental women compare with both their mothers and their peers, Israeli-born women of European or American origin?

The level of education is a critical factor for determining a woman's working life: the higher the level of education, the higher the labor force participation (Central Bureau of Statistics [C.B.S.], 1988). Also, the level of education determines a woman's occupation, within the limits of a gender segregated labor market.

Comparing Oriental and Ashkenazi women, we find that in 1982 the Oriental immigrant women had the lowest level of education: just over one quarter had no formal schooling at all, a situation almost nonexistent in other groups. Somewhat over half (58.4 percent) had no more than eight years of schooling, which restricted them to unskilled or possibly semiskilled jobs. While a fair proportion of European and American immigrant women also had eight or fewer years of education, this amounted to 32.9 percent rather than 58.4. At the other end of the educational scale, the relative disadvantage of Oriental immigrant women is once again clearly apparent. Only 8.8 percent of them received postsecondary schooling, and only 5.6 percent matriculation certificates. Among European and American immigrant women, 26.9 percent attained this level of education and 18 percent obtained certificates at the postsecondary and academic levels. It is these levels of education which open the way to the more prestigious occupations *within* the female labor market and to the possibility of entering the more advantageous desegregated and male dominated positions.

The educational picture among the young, Israeli born generation is very different. By 1982 they had obtained much higher levels of education than the immigrant generation, but at the same time, the disparity between the Oriental and Ashkenazi among them was more than reproduced. Oriental women, born in Israel, had almost all attained at least elementary education. The largest concentration was at the level of full, or almost full secondary education. However, few went beyond that. Indeed 11.2 percent had some postsecondary education (13–15 years), and 5.7 percent possessed a certificate at the postsecondary level, but the comparable levels among their peers, the second generation of Ashkenazi women, was much higher – 30 percent had some postsecondary education, with 17 percent obtaining certificates at this level. Even more striking is the disparity at the highest level of academic education (16 + years) – only 3 percent among Oriental second generation as compared to 18.2 among the Ashkenazi young women. Academic certificates, an important prerequisite for more prestigious positions in the labor market, provide a final indicator, with 15.6 percent of Ashkenazi second generation women having obtained an academic certificate, as compared to only 2.1 percent of their Oriental peers (C.B.S., 1986).

Labor force participation is, as noted above, related to levels of education. At the same time, this is not the only factor determining the extent to which women join the labor force. By 1987 Ashkenazi and Oriental immigrant women exhibited very similar levels of participation: 36.6 and 35.4 percent, respectively, despite the striking differences in their levels of schooling. In 1972, 15 years earlier, the corresponding figures were 34.4 and 25.6 percent. The situation is different for the second generation; here the disparity in levels of participation increased over the years. Even though second generation Oriental women participated to a greater extent than the immigrant generation (43.7 percent compared to 35.4 percent), or second generation Oriental women fifteen years earlier (43.7 percent compared to 37.5 percent), the young Israeli women of European parentage surpassed them: 58.3 compared to 43.7 percent. The labor force participation of second generation Ashkenazi women (58.3%) exceeded that of the first generation (36.6%) by 21.7 percent, while second generation Oriental women (43.7%) surpassed the first generation (35.4%) by 8.3 percent. As a result the gap between the two increased. In 1972 the labor force participation of Ashkenazi women (second generation) exceeded that of their Oriental peers by 8 percent, while in 1987 they surpassed them by 14.6 percent, reaching the level of 58.3 percent participation in the labor force (C.B.S., 1974; 1988).

Participation in the labor force involves, as noted above, entering a highly segregated labor market. What happens to the different groups of women once they enter this segregated arena? How do the differences of education affect the location of the different women within the female labor market?

The distribution of women among the various occupational categories indicates, once again, an interplay between ethnicity and generation within the overall parameters of gender segregation. Even though their labor force participation was equal to that of the Ashkenazi immigrant women in 1987, Oriental immigrant women were still characterized by concentration within the services—38.1 percent (compared to 12.1 percent among their immigrant peers). The two other major occupations for Oriental immigrant women are the two main components of the female labor market in general, clerical work and semiprofessional occupations (i.e. teaching, nursing etc.) These occupational categories together accounted for another 37.6 percent, with production (skilled and nonskilled) accounting for another 9.3 percent. Thus, even in 1987, almost half of all Oriental women born abroad worked in unskilled or semiskilled (and some skilled) blue collar jobs, a situation which did not characterize any other group of women.

The second generation of Oriental women showed significant change. Their largest contingent was no longer in the services but rather in clerical work: 40.3 percent. The second largest concentration, almost 20 percent, was still in the services, with the "female professions" close behind. The pattern of concentration in clerical work was already set in 1972 and seems to be on the increase. It can be attributed to the structure of education of the young Oriental women, on the one hand, and of the female labor market, on the other. As noted above, approximately half of all young Oriental women have 11 to 12 years of schooling, no less, but also no more. This level of education enables one to move out of the unskilled or semiskilled occupations, but does not open the way beyond the office, particularly filing, typing, and routine office work. It does not make much difference whether the young women have academic or vocational high school training, if they stop at 12 years of schooling. Just over half of the girls in vocational schools are trained in clerical work; both tracks lead primarily to the same type of occupation.

While this is the course followed by women of Oriental parentage, the second generation of European women have moved into other parts of the female labor market. A full 31.4 percent of them have entered the female semiprofessions (as compared with 18 percent of their Oriental peers) while another 14.2 percent are scientific and academic workers. The latter can be seen as having made somewhat of a breakthrough out of the female occupational ghetto. The general category of scientific and academic workers is desegregated, and while some occupations within it have been female dominated for some time (such as psychologists), others have witnessed a relatively large entrance of women over the last decade and a half. This changed their gender composition, desegregating some male occupations (such as lawyers and architects), making other desegregated occupations female dominated (such as pharmacologists and sociologists), and increasing the proportion of women in still other occupations dominated by males (such as headmasters of secondary schools) (Cohen et al., 1987). If scientific and academic work is the most accessible route out of the constraints of the female labor market, it necessitates a high level of education, which at present is demonstrated primarily by the Ashkenazi women. The latter, 18.2 percent of whom have 16+ years of schooling and 15.6 percent of whom possess an academic degree, have far greater occupational opportunities than the Oriental second generation, only 2.9 percent of whom have 16+ years of schooling and only 2.1 of whom have an academic degree (C.B.S., 1974, 1988).

To conclude, all women are, to a major extent, well within the female labor market. But two major patterns emerge in examining the differences between Jewish ethnic groups. First, there are significant differences in the concentration of the different groups: the "bottom" of the female labor market, service and production jobs, are typical of Oriental immigrant women; at the "center," is clerical work, typical of second generation Oriental women, and at the "top," is semiprofessional and scientific work, typical of second generation Ashkenazi women and, to a lesser extent, first generation as well. Second, the ability to break out of the confines of the female labor market seems to be conditioned primarily on educational achievement, and here the second generation of Ashkenazi women are way ahead. Young Oriental women still have a long way to go if they are to move out of not only service work, but also the female labor market.

REFERENCES

Bernstein, Deborah (1983) "Economic Growth and Female Labour: The Case of Israel." *The Sociological Review* 31 (2): 264–292.

Bernstein, Deborah and Swirski, Shlomo (1982) "The Rapid Economic Development of Israel and the Emergence of the Ethnic Division of Labor." *British Journal of Sociology* 33 (1): 64–85.

Cohen, Yinon; Bechar, S.; Reijman, R. (1987) "Occupational Sex Segregation in Israel." *Israel Social Science Research* 5 (1/2): 97–107.

Central Bureau of Statistics (C.B.S.) (1974) *Labor Force Survey—1972,* No. 451, Jerusalem.

Central Bureau of Statistics (C.B.S.) (1986) *Publications of the Census of Population and Housing—1983,* No. 10, Jerusalem.

Central Bureau of Statistics (C.B.S.) (1988) *Statistical Yearbook of Israel—1988,* Jerusalem.

Izraeli, Dafna (1979) "Sex Structure of Occupations: The Israeli Experience." *Sociology of Work and Occupations* 6: 404–429.

Nahon, Ya'acob (1984) *Trends in the Occupational Status—The Ethnic Dimension.* The Jerusalem Institute for Israel Studies, No. 10, Jerusalem (Hebrew).

IT'S LIKE GOING TO A MOVIE:
FEMALE ASSEMBLY LINE WORKERS
(Translation by Barbara Swirski)

When Koby Siter, head of the Human Resources Department at the Elcint Company (electronics) was asked why women are employed on the assembly line, he replied: "The work requires low-level skills. . . . It can't be denied that because of the low level of skill, we pay relatively low salaries. The logical result is that men, who have to support a family and who demand higher pay, don't go into work of that kind. Women, who look for work in order to supplement the family income, will go for this kind of thing . . . . Over the years a label gets attached to the job—this job is for women and not for men."

The answer of the Human Resources Department head of another Israeli electronics firm to the same question was: "Women have more patience. A man wants a career—he's looking for action, for interest . . . it's hard to expect a man to sit from 7:30 in the morning till 4:45 in the afternoon doing those things with his hands. Not every woman can do it either. It's been proven that for a certain type of woman, at a certain level of education, of a particular intelligence—it's not a bad job. . . . [The work also requires] a compliant personality. We have a department with an evening shift, from 5:10 to 11:00 p.m. There are women who work it just to get out of the house to get some fresh air . . . for them it's really like going out—some of them even dress up. They get supper, they have unlimited access to hot drinks, there's background music . . . they have transportation, they have meals, they get all kinds of treats; we're talking about the sort of women who have no other employment possibilities. They have no training and no experience."

Swirski, Barbara (1987) "Israeli Women on the Assembly Line," special chapter of the Hebrew version of Annette Fuentes and Barbara Ehrenreich, *Women in the Global Factory*. Reprinted with permission.

A JEWISH FACTORY WORKER
TALKS ABOUT OPPORTUNITIES
FOR PROMOTION
(Translation by Barbara Swirski)

Yael: It really used to get me mad. They'd say to me, "Look, you're a girl, and you'll soon get married. Then you'll start missing work, and, who knows, you may just quit." So I told them, "Why should I quit work? On the one hand, you need laborers badly, they tend to quit on you, and on the other hand, you're actually putting the heat on me to resign. . . . You keep trying to give me the feeling that I'm about to quit, but I'm not. . . ." I remember the time we got a raise. The foreman got 8 shekels more per day; I was called the assistant or the group head. The main thing was that I couldn't be promoted—and all I got was 2 shekels more per day. . . . I did all the hardest jobs. I often lifted and moved (heavy objects) myself. They talk about equal wages, but they don't pay equal wages; their excuse is that a man can lift a certain object or weight and a girl can't (but) I lifted heavy objects, and the (female) production workers did the same. Women in charge—there were only two of us—also did lifting. And when there were cutbacks, the first to be cut back were the women. I asked once, "Why do you always start with the women? Why do you discriminate?" And they answered, "Why do you always have the feeling that you're being discriminated against?" I said, "It isn't a feeling. It's a fact!" I remember how it was at the beginning of the Yom Kippur War. I hadn't been called up yet, and all the men were in the Army and there was no one to keep things going. I remember how I took over and kept things going. Suddenly I was OK and capable of everything, but when the men came back—"Opps! Step aside! You're not capable!" So make up your minds!

Later the foreman said to me, "You know what? I'm going to give you an opportunity to prove yourself. If you do well, I'll promote you. I want you to experiment for me, to try to improve the production method. I did it, proved it could be done. Because I was familiar with the work, I was able to prove that the method was a time-saver. Then they promised to promote me to quality control. By that time I was pregnant. It was supposed to be a matter of two or three days, before I got promoted, but I never got the promotion, because suddenly—oops! There was no one to replace me: suddenly I was indispensable! It was then that I realized I would never make it. I wanted the promotion so badly. I loved the work, and I wanted to continue there. But it didn't work out, and I decided to leave.

Interviewer: Did you turn to anyone for help? The Histadrut has Na'amat (women's division), doesn't it? Did you try to get information about what could be done?

Yael: Yes. First I went to the secretary general of the union in charge of the plant. After that I went to a Histadrut official who was responsible for working women. I told her the whole thing and said, "Look, let's talk woman to woman. I'm sure you understand the matter no less than I do; I'm sure that you, too, are passed over when it comes to promotions, though you're capable of more." Well, at first she made a good impression, but later I saw she wasn't that interested in the matter. More than once I asked her to come to the plant and report on what she saw. I had to literally drag her there. One time we had a visit from the Central Committee of the Histadrut, and a different woman came in her stead. I said to her, "On the one hand, women are encouraged to go out and work; on the other – to be blunt – they are screwed!" Their answer was, "A woman gets married and is absent a lot. When she has children, she has to miss work to take them to the doctor." I replied that men are absent from work twice as often as women, because they're called up to Reserve duty, so what difference does it make? He does his duty – and the woman does hers. She raises the children, which is certainly a duty; she's not out having a good time. And their answer was, "Yes, you're right." . . . It's not enough to be right. Nothing's been done about the situation . . . .

I wasn't invited to Workplace Committee meetings. Once, I just happened to go into the lunch room, where I saw them – I knew meetings were taking place without me. When do you think they called on me to participate? When there was supposed to be a vote, when there was some disagreement, and they needed my vote to tip the scales. So one day I stood up and said, "I'm not going to support anyone! I insist on taking part in meetings. I don't know anything about the matter, how do you expect me to support it? How am I supposed to know what you're talking about?!" "No, listen . . . " they started to stutter. . . . So one day I caught them in the act, as they say. They were meeting with the secretary general of the union. I went up to them and said, "I believe I am also a member of the Committee. . . ." They started to stutter again. "Why are you stuttering? Talk fair, what's the problem?" And they said, "You know what. Your foreman isn't willing to let you off!" "Why didn't you say anything about it before? How come I don't know anything about it? If he doesn't agree, I'll just get up and leave. Of course, I can't leave everything in the middle, but let me know half an hour beforehand, and I'll arrange things so I can get away." One time I went to the foreman – I wanted to keep on good terms with him – and said, "Listen, I'm going to a meeting." "What do you mean? Who gave you permission?" "The whole Committee is meeting, and I'm a member of the Committee." "No, I won't permit it." So I said, "I'm going without permission, and next time we'll bring it up before the management." I really was called in to give an explanation to the management, and they were about to penalize me. "Why? What have I done, sabotage? Have I incited the workers?" . . . The truth is that I did (incite the workers on occasion), but I was quiet about it. I know how to do it. Before I quit I brought the whole department out on strike. The management knew who did it—I was the only one capable. So they came to me and said, "Do something about it!" "What do you want from me? All I want is to return to work!" Then I really made a stink. "I want to take part in those meetings; the plant is not going to close down if I miss two or three hours of work. I have the right to miss a few hours, just like all the other members of the Committee. Otherwise I intend to raise the matter before the central body of the Histadrut. I'll go as far as I have to, because I refuse to be discriminated against—either I was elected to represent the workers or I was elected to act as a puppet. I'm not going to be a puppet; I'd rather resign. But I don't want to resign. I want to fight!" Word got to the manager in no time at all. As soon as he heard about it, he said, "We've got to fire her!"

Swirski, Shlomo (1981) *Orientals and Ashkenazim in Israel: The Ethnic Division of Labor.* Haifa: Mahbarot L'Mehkar U'libikoret (Hebrew). Reprinted with permission.

Section Five

Golda Notwithstanding – Participation and Powerlessness

How Much Political Power
Do Israeli Women Have?

Judith Buber Agassi

Who has not heard that old litany recited by those who claimed that Israeli women were equal, or at least more equal than women in other countries. Therefore Israel had no need of feminism: Golda was proof positive.
The litany also included the Ketuba, that ancient Jewish marriage contract
that put an end to arbitrary divorce; communal childcare in the kibbutz;
women's service in the Israel Defense Forces; and the celebrated Israeli Declaration of Independence.

Golda Meir served in the highest, most powerful political position of the
country, that of Prime Minister; she was helped neither by the influence or
tutelage of a politician father, like Indira Gandhi or Benazir Bhutto, nor by
a politician husband, like Evita Peron, Mrs. Bandaranaike, or Corazon Aq-
uino. Like Margaret Thatcher, Golda rose through years of serving in party,
diplomatic and cabinet posts. But unfortunately, one lone woman in a national leadership position neither signifies the high status of women in that
society, nor guarantees that she will succeed in improving women's position —
or even attempt to do so. Though herself a "strong woman" who had fought
for her own chance to enter politics, Golda certainly was no feminist. She
was a traditionalist concerning gender roles and she did nothing to facilitate
the entry into or the advancement of other women in Israeli politics.

Feminists agree that women's increased participation in public life is important. Some consider an equal share of political power for women synonymous with equal gender status in society. While political power is an essential,
perhaps the most important component of gender status, equality also means
equal access to resources and equal autonomy. These three components are
largely interdependent. As a group, women need access to many more
resources and much more free time and freedom of movement, if they are
to participate in politics, to become candidates, to be elected, and to remain
in politics. On the other hand, more political power is essential for the removal
of some of the major obstacles to women's equal access to resources and an
equal measure of autonomy: Discriminatory and restrictive laws have to be
struck from the books; the legal concept of discrimination against women has

to be broadened, laws prohibiting all forms of such discrimination have to be enacted and the operative means for their enforcement established. Increased political power should also enable women to remove existing legal and other institutional impediments to their reproductive freedom, essential to their autonomy.

Nevertheless it should be borne in mind that political power and legislative and administrative action alone will not suffice to ensure full equality in women's relations with men and to eradicate all male violence against women. It will not suffice to convert overnight the great mass of men into equal partners in family work, childcare and the care of the elderly. Many men will continue to protect their vested interests in women's inferior position in the family and the workplace. Neither will political power alone be able to remove all the psychological and social obstacles to women's free choice of education and training, occupation and career. All this notwithstanding, it would be a serious mistake to consider the struggle for political woman power as unimportant or futile.

The women's movements of the 19th and early 20th centuries fought for the basic prerequisites to women's entry into public life: the right to speak in public, to be regarded as a legal entity, to hold property, to acquire an education, to train for and enter the professions, to pursue an occupation without husbands' permission, and finally, to vote in national elections and to run for political office.

In some countries this process was completed by the end of World War I, in others as late as the end of World War II. Woman suffrage became the hallmark of modernity. It was assumed by many that once they obtained the right to vote, women were equal before the law, indeed, that they had achieved equality.

In many older industrialized societies, important formal legal inequalities remained on the books, especially in family law. Nearly everywhere overt discrimination against women in the labor market remained legal long after they had gained the vote. In the areas of credit, insurance, property transactions, taxation and social insurance, women continued to be treated as men's dependents.

When women first obtained the vote, it was expected that many would be elected to parliaments and to other governing bodies and public offices. In reality, until quite recently, on the average not more than 12 percent of the representatives in national assemblies throughout the industrialized world have been women. In the United States Congress, the number was, and still is, nearer 5 percent. An even smaller percentage of the positions in the most powerful parliamentary committees, in the Cabinet, in the highest echelons of the public and foreign service, and in the highest courts, were occupied by women. For about half a century after women's suffrage, political power remained almost exclusively in the hands of men.

Only with the rise of the New Women's Movement towards the end of the sixties, were concerted efforts made to discover and analyze the obstacles to women's entry into and success in politics and to develop strategies and tactics for overcoming them. These obstacles vary in different countries and under different political systems. Also, different kinds of power have somewhat different weight. Therefore comparisons of women's success in overcoming the obstacles, and of the measure of power that women now hold in different societies, is not easy. Nevertheless, we will attempt to show how Israel measures up.

Elections to the 120-member Knesset have taken place twelve times since the establishment of the state of Israel, with results shown in Table 1. Women's representation in the Knesset did not increase, but rather declined after the first decade of the state. Yet for nearly 30 years, there was no clear trend of additional decline; the number of women Members of Knesset (MKs) alternated between ten, nine and eight. But in the recent 1988 election, it dropped to its lowest point—only seven, less than 6 percent. This decline certainly deserves an explanation.

In the past, there have been situations in which one woman minister or deputy minister served in the Cabinet, the most well-known being Golda Meir, who was Minister of Labor and Minister of Foreign Affairs before becoming the first and only female Prime Minister of Israel. Shulamit Aloni was Minister Without Portfolio for six months. A few other women served, one at a time, in typically female stereotyped ministries: Health, Labor and Social Welfare, or Education and Culture. At present (1989) Israel has a record-size Cabinet of 26 ministers, 5 of them without portfolio, yet not one woman.

Table 1. Female Representation in the Knesset

Year	Number of women elected	Percentage of women elected
1949	11	9.1
1951	11	9.1
1955	11	9.1
1959	9	7.5
1961	10	8.3
1965	9	7.5
1969	8	6.6
1973	8	6.6
1977	8	6.6
1981	9	7.5
1984	10	8.3
1988	7	5.8

Table 2. Female Representation in Municipalities

	1950	1955	1959	1965	1969	1973	1978	1983	1989
Number of local authorities	61	80	98	98	96	98	99	101	104
Number of councillors elected	684	838	1008	1050	1070	1124	1173	1227	1350
Number of women elected	20	34	36	32	39	51	65	93	118
Percentage of women elected	4.2	4.1	3.6	3.1	3.6	4.5	5.5	7.6	8.6
Number of councils with women members	23	25	31	27	31	42	50	56	65
Percentage of councils with women members	38	31	32	27	32	43	5	55	64
Average number of women elected to councils which contain women	1.26	1.36	1.16	1.18	1.26	1.12	1.30	1.66	1.8

Source: Herzog and Berkovich, 1989

In Israel, assignment of women MKs to the Knesset Committees followed the typical pattern. Usually, no woman sat on the two most important and powerful committees, the Foreign Affairs and Security Committee and the Finance Committee. Only in 1984 did one woman succeed in being assigned to the 21-member Foreign Affairs and Security Committee, and another to the Finance Committee. In contrast, there were 4 women assigned to the Labor and Social Welfare Committee. There has never been a woman Speaker of the Knesset.

Whereas women's low representation in national parliaments is very common, in many countries their representation is higher in intermediate state, provincial or regional elected bodies and offices, and even higher in local, municipal government bodies. Israel has no intermediate tier of government between the central and the local. Local or municipal elections have been held every five years on the average. Table 2 shows results for women. Obviously, in spite of the doubling of the percentage of women among local councillors from 4.2 percent in 1950 to 8.6 percent in 1989, their representation is still very small, and more than one third of local councils still are male preserves. It is also not hard to imagine the difficulties of the majority of women councillors in small-town councils, who function in isolation.

In 1975, the local government law was radically reformed to provide for the direct election of all mayors (or chairpersons) by local citizens, simultaneous with the election of local councils. This rendered the position of mayor the only directly elected political position in Israel; apparently the change also raised the prestige of the position and increased men's competition for it. Prior to this reform, between one and three women had generally served as deputy mayors or deputy chairpersons of Jewish local councils; with one exception, all served in small towns of under 10,000 inhabitants. There also was another notable exception: a Christian Arab woman, Violet Khoury, served as mayor of her local authority. Since the reform, women have rarely been backed by a political party as its candidate for a mayoralty. In the local elections that took place in 1989, 29 women competed for mayoralties as heads of independent local lists; only one was elected mayor. (However, 15 of the challengers succeeded in being elected to their councils.)

Parallel to Jewish local councils, there is another type of local body, the religious council, whose function is to look after the ritual needs of the community, including the upkeep of synagogues, cemetery and Mikveh (ritual bath). Formally it was supposed to be an elected body, but in practice it was an all-male appointed body, a sinecure for small-time party functionaries. Recently Israeli women have challenged this anomaly. First, several women councillors offered to serve on the local religious council but were turned down. Then proper elections were held, and a woman lawyer, Rina Shashua-Hason, was elected, despite considerable pressure from Orthodox elements. The Orthodox establishment promptly refused to seat her; Hason continued her struggle in the courts until the 1989 elections, when a male candidate was elected in her stead. In another town, Yeruham, Leah Shakdiel was elected, refused entrance and ultimately seated by court order.

Looking at public service, Israeli women constitute 58 percent of those employed in the Public Service and in the Jewish Agency (a smaller administrative apparatus that administers funds donated by Jews abroad, used mainly for the settlement and absorption of new immigrants). Yet women account for a mere 20 percent of the higher "managerial" echelons. As for the four highest and most powerful grades of the Public Service, women comprise 11 percent of the fourth grade, and 7 percent of the third. There are no women at all in the two highest grades. Among the heads of the main departments in the administration of the three large cities, women are rarely to be found.

The state has a major share in numerous economic enterprises and is a major employer. The top managers of state firms are political appointees. State companies are all headed exclusively by men, usually retired high-ranking military officers. The same holds true for the influential military industries, including the aviation industry. On the other hand, higher financial positions in the Public Service or in the Bank of Israel, the state bank, appear to have opened up for women. In 1982 women occupied the positions of Bank Examiner of the Bank of Israel; Assistant Commissioner of the Income Tax and Property Tax Commission, Ministry of Finance; Assistant-Director of the Economic Planning Authority, Ministry of Finance; and Assistant Controller of Foreign Exchange at the Bank of Israel (Shapiro-Libai, 1982).

The Israeli judiciary poses a curious, contradictory picture (Aloni, 1989): Even during the Mandatory period, Jewish women had never been as excluded from the bench as women were in North America. Whereas previously women judges were appointed mainly to the lower courts, there are now a number of women judges in the district courts and two women judges on the Supreme Court. This process—which is similar to what has happened in the Federal Republic of Germany—may have been aided by the fact that increasing numbers of women have studied law and are practicing it, and there simply may be more qualified women around. (This does not mean that Israeli women lawyers no longer meet obstacles to their careers similar to those encountered by women lawyers everywhere.) Yet, at the same time, women are ineligible to serve in religious courts, which are lower courts.

Although women comprise nearly half of the Histadrut (General Federation of Labor Unions) membership, they are conspicuously absent from the leadership of most individual trade unions, and are poorly represented on the Federation's central bodies: The two top positions of Secretary-General and Deputy Secretary-General have always been occupied by men. In the last Histadrut elections, for the first time a woman was a candidate (unsuccessful) for the office of Secretary-General. The highest Histadrut committee is the Central Committee. In 1987, six out of 42 members were women, that is, 14 percent, and on the next ranking Executive Committee, only 15 out of 196 members were women—less than 8 percent. An example of the harmful effects for women of their relative powerlessness in the Histadrut, was the recent negotiations concerning the introduction of the five day working week in the Public Service. Although the Israel Women's Network had presented a document containing women's reservations and demands concerning this proposed change, the all-male union delegation of the large white-collar union (whose membership is 50 percent female) accepted the employers' suggestions without discussion, despite their disadvantages to women employees with young children.

As in other societies, so also in Israel, women's lesser access to economic resources, their inferior economic power, is both a cause and an effect of their limited political power (Holtzman and Williams, 1989). On the surface, the economic position of women within Israel does not appear to be favorable. During the seventies and eighties, Jewish women's participation rate in the labor market, which had declined during the fifties and sixties, continuously increased to approach that of Western European countries. The average level of education of employed women is higher than that of employed men. Women's share of lower and middle management jobs has increased considerably during the last decade. Yet this impression is misleading. De facto discrimination of women in hiring, pay, fringe and social benefits, training and promotion is so widespread as to make the average income and pension of women, even those who are employed full-time, far inferior to that of men. Recent studies found that women employees in the Public Service earn 30 percent less than their male colleagues in the same grade (Efroni, 1989; Herzog and Berkovich, 1989). On the average, married Jewish employed women do not earn more than a third of their family's income.

What is the significance of this for women's political activity? Very few women control "surplus resources" (Blumberg, 1984). A large part of most mothers' earnings goes into paying for babysitters, daycare, kindergarten, school needs, after-school clubs and lessons, summer day-camps and children's pocket money. Parents also pay adult children's college tuition and purchase apartments for them. Women tend to consider all these items, as well as occasional help with heavy house cleaning, their responsibility. Political party activism costs highly in both time and money. Few women are well established free or salaried professionals or freelancers, tenured academics, top managers or independent businesswomen, and thus few women possess their own "power base," which would allow them to support political parties and election campaigns with technical services, office space, transportation, sizeable donations and contacts with affluent supporters. Israel has a multiparty system, proportional representation, and a choice between party slates of candidates. Having one's own power base is a near prerequisite for becoming a candidate with a secure place on the slate of one of the younger and poorer parties.

On the slates of the older and richer parties and alignments, all the secure places tend to be occupied by the incumbents, professional (male) party politicians; the fights over the ranking of these places between wings of parties and components of alignments—each with its own collective economic assets—used to be settled in proverbial smoke-filled backrooms. In 1988 an attempt to democratize the process of candidate selection in the Labor Alignment was made. Given a modicum of internal party democracy, the newly formed women's caucuses within parties may be more successful in the future.

The question arises: Is Israeli women's relative powerlessness in political institutions and lack of economic resources changing? My conclusion is that women's power is on the increase. However, this growth is not assured, because of the same forces that have in the past prevented Israeli women from gaining more political power.

The relative growth of woman power, as well as the chances for further growth, are due to the organization of an effective women's network, and of the formulation of a women's agenda that is basically feminist. Neither existed 10 years ago. This network is now capable of mobilizing broad, diverse coalitions of women, including party activists, women MKs and women local councillors, some of the official advisors on the status of women, women academics teaching Women's Studies and committed women researchers, members of the establishment women's organizations, together with activists of the various feminist organizations, feminist centres and women's self-help institutions, around campaigns of a clearly feminist character ("Networking for Women," 1989; "Newsletter," "Woman to Woman").

There are still a number of very serious obstacles, some of them shared by other societies, others specific to Israel. Before identifying them it is important to outline the image of gender roles in Israel. There is an extremely traditionalist, Orthodox religious public, which considers sharply divided gender roles and the centrality of males in religious and public life a God-given, integral sector of Jewish values. The influence of these views and values extends far beyond the limits of the Orthodox community. A larger part of the Israeli public supports the—supposedly modern—"super-woman" ideal of the perfect wife and mother (of 3 children at least), who is solely responsible for household and childcare (and is grateful to her husband for "giving her a hand"); at the same time she is also a "secondary breadwinner," and always ready to undertake voluntary work. This ideal is a formidable obstacle in the Israeli woman's struggle for access to power. It is eagerly used by men, the incumbents of economic as well as political power, to dissuade women from seriously competing with them. As late as 1986, Israeli students still considered the discrimination of women in promotion a relatively unimportant social problem (Izraeli and Tabory, 1988; Izraeli, 1989). The super-woman ideal also causes strong guilt feelings in women, and prevents them from entertaining even the possibility of demanding equal division with men of housework and childcare—the work as well as the responsibility. Until quite recently, so-called protective laws remained on the books, and no provisions were made to facilitate equal parenting. In the past the large women's organizations had not pursued the basic feminist goals of abolishing stereotyped social gender roles, and of empowering women for the struggle to erase all forms of discrimination and oppression of women. Most of their membership subscribed, and many still subscribe, to the super-woman ideal.

Recently encouraging signs of a gradual rising of feminist consciousness and increased assertiveness appear both in the older women's organizations and in the political parties. Still, the "super-woman" ideal is far from dead. A serious obstacle to women's empowerment in other countries as well, in Israel it has apparently been strengthened, and its demise postponed, by the unresolved nationalistic tensions and the centrality of the military. Women are socialized to perceive themselves as ignorant concerning the most crucial national interest—that of defense—and thus unqualified to deal with this most important dimension of politics. Men's longer military service and lengthy reserve duties, and especially the physical danger that they face, are used to reinforce the traditional view of women's moral obligation to assume, without complaint, all household and childcare duties as well as other care work.

Another serious obstacle to the empowerment of Israeli women is the weakness of a national democratic civic consciousness. This is due to the nonseparation of nation and religion, and the nonseparation of state and religious institutions. This facilitates the continuation of the unequal, and often very harmful and humiliating treatment of women in the Rabbinic courts. Unfortunately, many women have not yet freed themselves from the claim of the minority Orthodox Establishment that the institution of civil marriage and divorce in Israel would "split the Jewish people." It is interesting and hopeful to note that a wide coalition of women's organizations recently demanded the establishment of a separate, civil court for cases of family violence. It is also a hopeful sign that in a recent study on national awareness of Israeli Jewish high school, technical school and university students, young women expressed significantly more liberal and civic-minded attitudes to national issues than their male colleagues (Berent, Agassi and Buber-Agassi, 1988).

REFERENCES

Aloni, Shulamit (1989) "The Other Estate." *Politics,* July (Hebrew).

Blumberg, Rae L. (1984) "A General Theory of Gender Stratification." In Collins, R. (ed.). *Sociological Theory.* San Francisco: Jossey Bass.

Berent, Moshe; Agassi, Joseph; Buber-Agassi, Judith (1988). "Israeli National Awareness." Tel-Aviv University, Sapir Fund, Working Paper No. 118 (Hebrew).

Efroni, Linda (April, 1989) "Promotion and Pay of Men and Women in the Jewish Agency." Mimeo. (Hebrew).

Herzog, Hannah and Berkovich, Nitza (1989) "A New Generation of Women Politicians? Women Elected to Local Authorities, 1950 to 1983." Mimeo, The Jerusalem Institute for the Study of Israel (Hebrew).

Holtzman, Elizabeth and Williams, Shirley (1989) "Women in the Political World: Observations." In Conway, J. K., Burque, S. C. and Scott, J. W. (eds.). *Learning about Women: Gender, Politics, and Power.* Ann Arbor: The University of Michigan Press.

Izraeli, Dafna (1989) "The Golda Meir Effect." *Politics,* July, 43–47 (Hebrew).

Izraeli, Dafna and Tabory, Ephraim (1988) "The Political Context of Feminist Attitudes in Israel." *Gender and Society* 2 (4): 463–481.

"Networking for Women; A Quarterly Publication of the Israel Women's Network," Vol. 2, No., 4, Spring 1989.

Shapiro-Libai, Nitza (1982) "Women's Participation in Social and Political Life," European Regional Seminar of UNESCO, Bonn, October.

"Women in the World of Work." (1988) *The Status of Women,* Issue No. 21, November, Office of the Prime Minister's Adviser on the Status of Women (Hebrew).

"Woman to Woman." *A Hebrew Newsletter,* The Haifa Feminist Center.

The Role of Women as Change Agents in Arab Society in Israel

Mariam M. Mar'i
Sami Kh. Mar'i

Arab women in Israel and elsewhere (Nath, 1978; Smock and Youssef, 1977; Prothro and Diab, 1974) are becoming divorced from their traditionally passive and marginal roles. Touma (1981) suggests that in Israel, Arab women have become more active participants not only in the sphere of family decision making, but also in all spheres of public life traditionally prohibited to them. While changes in the position of women in Arab society are easily observable (Ginat, 1981), the processes and dynamics underlying these changes are subtle and less evident.

Arab women in Israel, as part of the Palestinian Arab minority, are simultaneously and organically linked to two conflicting forces: the Palestinians on the one hand, and Israel on the other. Like other Arabs in Israel, they are thus vulnerable to the complex sociopolitical dynamics inside Israel as well as in the larger context of the Middle East. Consequently, while trying to understand the role of Arab women in sociocultural change of the last few decades, one must relate the dynamics of change to political developments, especially as these impact on the sense of security of the Arab population in Israel.

One can relate much of men's needs to control women to men's sense of insecurity. John Gulick (1976) suggests that the Arab male develops "ego vulnerability" with regard to aspects of his "significant" female's behaviors. This vulnerability as a rule increases his need to control the female as a potential "stress producer." "Improper" female behavior endangers the male's ability to cope with other sources of cultural integrity in the face of invading cultural forces; and his relationship to the national conflict between his people, the Palestinians, and the state in which he lives, Israel.

Reprinted from Safir et al. (1985) (eds.) Women's Worlds. From the New Scholarship. New York: Praeger.

The Palestinian Arab minority in Israel is manipulated and controlled through a sophisticated system of hegemony devised by Israeli authorities (Lustick, 1980). Until recently men have been the major target of such control. Women were not considered a political or economic threat, since they were rarely politically active, and traditionally were not employed outside the home. Thus, as males attempted to cope with the various stresses in their lives, including stress inherent in their being a target of control and manipulation by the authorities, female behavior became especially significant for their sense of security. This constellation of factors greatly influenced the extent to which Arab women in Israel could play an active part in sociocultural change.

In 1948, when Israel was created, Palestinian Arab society underwent abrupt discontinuity. The internal political institutions and organizations collapsed, the social structure was shaken, vast economic transformations took place, and cultural traditions were challenged. In fact, total communities disintegrated and their members became refugees either on their land inside Israel or dispersed in the neighboring Arab countries. Under such traumatic conditions, cultural traditions, although undermined by the great upheaval, remained the major vehicle through which Arab identity could be nurtured and maintained. Threats to that identity were greatly felt by that segment of Palestinian society that remained on its land and came under the control of Israel after 1948.

1948 TO 1956:
CONTINUOUS STAGNATION

Few observable changes in women's status took place in the first few years following the establishment of Israel. The situation of women in these years was essentially one of continuity with century old traditions. In fact, traditionalism became stronger as a reaction to the overwhelming threat to the identity of those who remained. As both the present and future were uncertain, and as Israeli authorities stepped in to control the lives of the Arabs inside its borders, the heritage of the past became the most salient source from which Arabs drew content and form as they sought to protect and preserve their identity.

The heritage of the past, however, was organically associated with an economic base and a larger system of social relations both of which had been seriously shaken. After much of their cultivable lands had been confiscated by Israel (Jiryis, 1976), the Arab males, for the first time, had to search for external sources of income in the Jewish economic sector. This changed not only the economic base of the community, but also the lifestyle of the family. It meant that men (fathers and brothers) remained outside the family circle all day and in many cases, all week. In addition, Arab men came into contact with a whole new realm of experience in a society and culture different from their own.

Under these conditions, the feelings of insecurity among men were overwhelming. Their continuous absence from home, their subordination to Israeli Jewish institutions and their observation of the behaviors of Jewish Westernized women all intensified the threat to both their identity and their status. While their political and economic subordination symbolized to them that they had been incorporated into Israel, their observation of Jewish women symbolized cultural invasion. Consequently, men in Arab society controlled their women even more intensely, not only as a vehicle of cultural continuity, but also as a response to men's deep sense of insecurity aroused by their new conditions.

However, as Arab men went to work on Jewish farms or in metropolitan areas, their absence created a vacuum. Thus, for the first time in centuries, Arab women were faced with the paradox of having increased discretionary power in areas traditionally defined as male domain. At the same time, they were expected to use that power to pass on traditions and values in which female status was inferior (Mar'i, 1978). This apparent paradox did not seem to have created a conflict at the time. The structural change was not transformed into a subjective consciousness. Women continued not only to be psychologically dependent on men, but also to reproduce the very conditions of their own subordination.

Thus it becomes clear that women had drifted into change rather than having initiated it. The male-dominated Arab society could cope with such a change which was not stress producing. In fact, as women assumed the role of culture preservers, involved in the reproduction of the conditions of their own subordination, stress was greatly reduced. Yet, this change was not without its positive effects for women. They were jolted from their traditional passivity, and became more influential actors in family life. They gained a sense of self-worth as well as of cultural and political relevance.

The introduction of universal compulsory education in the early 1950s was another development that had far reaching consequences. At first, it was met with resistance and was rejected for females. Most parents held traditional stands less favorable to the education of females than to that of males. In addition, they were apprehensive about the school culture and curriculum; it was not a Palestinian school, but rather an Israeli school for Palestinians. Parents who wanted their daughters to have an education enrolled them in all female Christian boarding schools. These schools were not only exclusively for females, but until then, they were untouched by Israeli authorities.

Arab educators, assisted by the compulsory education law, made significant efforts to rehabilitate their educational system. They were instrumental in increasing the number of school children, including females. To them, education was the means through which their society could be rebuilt and their culture reconstructed. In the process, women entered the teaching profession. The presence of female students provided legitimacy for women becoming teachers. The role models provided by female teachers, in turn, heightened the legitimacy of female education. This resulted in the massive enrollment of female students, a breakthrough which was probably the single most salient feature of this period as far as women and change in Arab society are concerned.

1956 TO 1967: RELATIVE OPENNESS

Until 1956, Arabs in Israel viewed themselves as living on what may be characterized as a "provisory" basis. Leaders and the media of Arab countries related to Israel as a rather unfortunate but temporary phenomenon. Arabs in Israel exposed to these messages, therefore, also viewed their existence under Israeli rule as temporary. This attitude heightened resistance to change. Among other things, change meant becoming "modern," and becoming modern was associated with becoming Jewish-like, hence with the loss of identity.

After the 1956 war of Israel, Britain and France against Egypt, Arabs in Israel began to relate to their existence under Israeli rule as a relatively permanent condition, or at least as less temporary than before. Their redefinition of the situation led to a coping strategy of greater openness to change for the benefits it could bring, at least in economic and educational spheres. Change was also associated with social and national development, especially in the eyes of the educated elites, and authentic political movements such as the El-Ard movement and the Israeli Arab Front surfaced in the late 1950s.

Furthermore, after ten years of interaction with Jewish society and institutions, Arabs had acquired a measure of competence and confidence in coping without sacrificing their cultural authenticity. The economic recession (1965–1967), in which unemployment rates for Arab males were especially high, coupled with rising aspirations for a higher standard of living, produced economic pressures which pushed Arab women into the unskilled labor force.

Compulsory education increased the demand for Arab teachers and created opportunity for women. The education of females gained an economic value. It also became a source of status for the females themselves as well as for their families. Access to education, however, was premised on an implicit agreement still in effect, although to a lesser degree, that in return for the opportunity for education and employment, females would continue to conform to the cultural values and traditions. It was understood, for example, that a female student who "misbehaved" or did not conform to traditional norms of behavior could and would be forced to drop out of school.

The period 1956 to 1967 was one in which women's consciousness developed and was reinforced by male and female writers. Tradition was openly criticized as a perpetuator of backwardness and the inferior status of women. Education continued to bloom and in cities of mixed Arab and Jewish populations, the number of female students often exceeded that of males. Education gained popularity as instrumental for accelerating modernity and thus became central in the consciousness of Arabs in Israel. This set in motion the forces that propelled the development of future challenges.

1967: A PERIOD OF CHALLENGE

Israel's military victory in 1967 had far reaching implications for the Arabs in Israel. To begin with, more aggressively than at any time before, they demanded full national and civil rights, as well as recognition as a national minority. They felt that the security claim, which the Jewish establishment had given as the major impediment to equality, could no longer be as easily argued as before the war.

The occupation of the West Bank and Gaza Strip by Israel in the 1967 war created an opportunity for Arabs in Israel to interact with other segments of the Palestinian people. A process of re-Palestinization developed, in which Arabs in Israel emerged with a clear sense of their distinct national identity. Through their interaction with other Palestinians, Arabs in Israel also discovered that women's emancipation was an issue of common concern to the larger Palestinian nation. They became aware that women's equality was not a Jewish induced problem, but rather an issue of indigenous concern to Palestinians. Thus "becoming modern" no longer necessarily meant becoming "Jewish-like." These developments, reinforced by economic recovery from the painful recession, further enhanced the sense of security.

These changes were reflected in the entry of large numbers of women into the labor force, especially in low level occupations, as well as into the universities. The latter movement was especially significant, for example, in three years (1969–1972) the number of female Arab students enrolled in Israeli universities more than doubled (from 141 to 305), while that of the male students increased by only 25 percent (from 450 to 565). For the first time, women became involved in Arab student unions, known for their high levels of political activism. They were elected representatives and executives in these unions. Women's associations and *ad hoc* groups became popular. These developments were the most salient and observable manifestations of women's new awareness in this period of challenge. The greatest transformation was that the role of women had changed from that of culture preserver to that of culture transformer.

Our analysis thus far has focused on macrolevel dynamics of stability and change in the position of Arab women in Israel. We now shift to the microlevel of the Arab community in the mixed city of Acre, through which these macrodynamics and development were observed empirically.

THE CASE OF ACRE'S WOMEN

In 1981, Acre, a town in Galilee in the Northern part of Israel, had a population of nearly 36,000, 31 percent of whom were Arabs. During the 1948 war, the majority of the Arab population of Acre left the town. Immediately after that war, Arab families whose towns elsewhere had been destroyed moved into Acre. Today these families compose most of Acre's Arab population. Lacking leadership, suffering from disrupted social order and organization, and with insufficient education, the Arabs of Acre had to face their new situation in the newly created Jewish state. They were concentrated, by the Israeli authorities, in the ghetto-like Old City and denied the opportunity to move into the new city where more modern housing, advantageous employment opportunities, educational facilities, and interaction with the Jewish population were available (Cohen, 1973).

The abrupt discontinuity with their traditional way of life, coupled with the fact that most families were strangers to each other, reduced social pressures for conformity and permitted change to take place with relatively little resistance. Furthermore, as economic conditions were very difficult, males, including school age children, had to work. Consequently, formal education became and remained until recently, primarily the privilege of females. The availability of Christian schools for girls accelerated the spread of female education. The villagers who migrated to Acre in 1948 escaped the social pressures against female education present in their home village.

The existence of separate educational systems for Arabs and Jews in Acre, coupled with the urgent need for Arab teachers (most of the teachers had fled in 1948) made it easier for Arab women, even though not fully qualified, to penetrate an occupation traditionally filled by men. The benefits to be gained from the opportunity to work within their own cultural community and the status attained by entry into a prestigious position outweighed the potential costs in the form of threats of this development.

The entry of Arab women into the teaching profession, as noted earlier, encouraged the spread of female education. These teachers became role models for other women to follow, not only in their investment in education, but also in their leaving home to enter the labor force. Most teachers initially came from relatively prestigious families traditionally opposed to women's employment out of the home. This break with the traditional pattern made women's employment respectable for women of lower social classes as well.

These developments had two major consequences for Acre's Arab women. One was that many women, regardless of their educational achievement, became economically more independent. The other was that women dominated the educated elite of Acre's Arab community both in number and in level of activity or by what in Arabic is called their "social presence." In 1973, among every ten Arab university students from Acre, seven were women.

Acre's educated Arab women took the lead in the process of re-Palestinization of their community. In fact, the first Arab student on an Israeli campus to have the courage to declare in public that she was Palestinian, was a female. She was a student from Acre studying at the University of Haifa during the early 1970s. It seems that the fact that Acre's Arabs live among Jews magnified their identity needs and made them more urgent. The fact that women dominated the educated elite among Acre's Arabs meant that they took the lead in meeting those needs.

In 1974, the educated elite formed Acre's Arab University Student Association. Initiated and led mainly by female students and graduates, this association had many objectives. The most important objectives were: to improve housing conditions, to upgrade the quality of education, to revive and further develop Palestinian folklore, and to enhance the sociopolitical awareness and commitment of youth. Being Arab, the Association had to cope with Israeli authorities on both local and national levels. Being largely female dominated, it had to struggle against internal forces mainly stemming from the male dominated larger society. However, quite unexpectedly, the local Arab community supported the Association both morally and financially. This paved the way for the Association's success. It seems that the great relevance to the community of the objectives and activities was enough to prevent the expression of whatever objections may have existed.

In the beginning there was no explicit opposition by the Israeli authorities to the existence of the Association. Only when the authorities witnessed the successful activities of the Association and observed the Arab community's growing support for it did they step in. Such opposition was consistent with their policy against independent organization among Arabs in Israel (Lustick, 1980).

The authorities employed two tactics to destroy the Association. First, active measures to deprive members of work opportunities were taken by not permitting qualified teachers to obtain available teaching positions unless they dissociated themselves from the Association. The other tactic seems to have been geared to exploiting a cultural dynamic. As the conflict with the authorities widened, rumors were spread to the effect that authorities were planning a crack-down on members of the Association in order to crush it. The fact that the leaders of the Association were predominantly women, put fathers, brothers, and husbands on the alert as the imprisonment of the "significant" females would be considered a strong violation of their cultural integrity. These two tactics led to the virtual disintegration of the Association in 1976.

However, immediately after the collapse of the Association, a new initiative sprung up. The leading women in the Association reorganized and formed Acre's Arab Women's Association. The formal objectives as well as the activities of the new association were best characterized by the notion that they were depoliticized at least in the immediate sense of political activism. They included: establishing a nursery school, raising women's consciousness, sponsoring cultural activities and training seminars (in preschool education) for women in the surrounding Arab villages, as well as helping women in these villages to organize and become active. These activities, while not directly political, were definitely relevant to society in general and to women in particular, and had important potential political consequences. Under tremendous pressure from the authorities and consequently from their own male dominated society, the women rechanneled their efforts and shifted the focus of their involvement, without, however, relinquishing their self-image as change agents.

In conclusion, our study of Acre's Arab community points to a number of observations that pertain to women as changing agents, which may be summarized as follows:

1. Under conditions of insecurity over cultural identity due to external threats, women were the first to be controlled and guarded from foreign cultural "contamination" (the second group is youth). These conditions changed and women were allowed more freedom and equality in education and employment.
2. Education had great relevance for women as change agents. Indeed, knowledge that enhances awareness is a generator of power. Furthermore, higher education coupled with economic independence had a radicalizing effect on women both socially and politically.
3. Once highly educated and politicized, Arab women ceased to be only preservers of culture. They took charge and became active in the process of culture renewal.
4. Israeli political authorities successfully manipulated Arab society partly through its value system in relation to women, consequently decreasing the level of political activism of the whole community.
5. Finally and paradoxically, the tragedy that befell the Palestinian people in 1948 and which brought dispersion and disintegration of total communities created conditions for the development of women's consciousness, relevance, and relative power in the process of change. The demise of traditional structures and patterns created an opportunity for many women to move out of oppression and to find their way in the process of reconstruction and reestablishment.

REFERENCES

Cohen, Eric (1973) "Integration vs. Separation in the Planning of a Mixed Jewish Arab City in Israel." The Levi Eshkol Institute for Economic, Social and Political Research. Jerusalem: Hebrew University (Hebrew).

Ginat, Joseph (1981) Women in Muslim Rural Society. Rutgers: Transaction Books.

Gulick, John (1976) "The Ethos of Insecurity in Middle Eastern Culture." In DeVos, G. A. (ed.). *Responses to Change.* New York: Van Nostrand Reinhold.

Jiryis, Sabri (1976) "The Arabs in Israel." *Monthly Review,* New York.

Lustick, Ian (1980) *Arabs in the Jewish State.* Austin: Texas University Press.

Mar'i, Sami (1978) *Arab Education in Israel.* Syracuse University Press.

Nath, Kamla (1978) "Education and Employment Among Kuwaiti Women." In Beck, L. and Keddie, L. (eds.). *Women in the Muslim World.* Cambridge: Harvard University Press.

Prothro, Edwin and Diab, Lufy (1974) *Changing Family Patterns in the Arab East.* Beirut: American University Press.

Smock, Audrey C. and Yousef, Nadia H. (1977) "Egypt: From Seclusion to Limited Participation." In Giele, J. C. and Smick, A. C. (eds.). *Women: Roles and Status in Eight Countries.* New York: John Wiley & Sons.

Touma, Emile (1981) "The Issue: Liberation of Arab Women not Sexual Crisis." Haifa, *Al-Jadeed,* No. 12, December (Arabic).

VIOLET KHOURY: MAYOR OF AN
ARAB VILLAGE IN ISRAEL
(Translated by Sharon Ne'eman
and Barbara Swirski)

Violet Khoury came from a family of 14 generations of Greek Orthodox priests. A pioneer in many areas, she was the first Arab woman in Israel to study social work in 1949. She worked in her profession, even during her pregnancy, was active in politics, and was elected mayor of the Local Council—the first woman to serve in such a post in the entire country. She supported peaceful coexistence and abhorred violence, yet fought incessantly for her principles.

Kufir Yassif, Violet Khoury's home village, is a few kilometers east of Acre. The village has some 6,000 residents, most of them Catholics, Greek Orthodox, and Anglicans, with a Moslem minority and a few dozen Druze. Until the middle of the last century, the village population also included Jews. Many residents of Kufir Yassif are university graduates; the proportion of college educated is higher than in any other Israeli Arab settlement. Violet Khoury was proud of this fact, and stated several times that such a high concentration of university graduates was not to be found anywhere else, not even in Jewish settlements. She always stressed the fact that the village women, too, were highly educated.

Violet Khoury was born in 1929, the oldest of three sisters and two brothers. In 1938, when the Arab riots increased in intensity, her father took the family to Acre, where he felt it would be safer. Violet was sent to study at the English High School in Haifa, an institution whose pupils included both Arab and Jewish girls. In 1949, after the establishment of the state of Israel, the residents of Kufir Yassif took part in the elections to the first Knesset. Violet, a nonconformist, refused to vote for Mapai (Israel's Workers Party), as ordered by the military government; she voted for the Communist Party. This symbolic act caused her problems when she applied for admission to a social workers' training course. Nonetheless, she was accepted and became the first Arab woman social worker. Working in her profession, she frequently travelled alone among the Arab villages in the Galilee. She did not marry until the age of 24, relatively late for what was then customary in Arab society; her marriage was arranged, to a man 18 years her senior. In 1983, in a conversation with me concerning the possibility of her leaving Israel, she stated: "It wasn't a marriage of love—and I have no regrets. In a marriage of love, I wouldn't have received the trust and freedom my husband gave me." Fawzy Khoury gave her his total confidence, "even though

Adapted from Yehuda Zur, Violet Khoury: Volcano Extinct. in *Al haMishmar*, January 29; 20–21.

he sometimes complained that his shirts weren't ironed or his dinner was late, and that I was taking care of the whole world, but not my sons."

According to Abdullah, 35, her oldest son, there was at least one argument a week between his parents on such subjects—but the arguments were always good-natured. "My father always complained that my mother took care of everyone except her sons." Khalil, 29, who has just completed an internship in Haifa's Rothschild Hospital, added that Violet taught her sons to manage on their own, and not to come to her with every little problem. "Only after everything else had been tried did she agree to help us, and I believe this was for our own good."

Violet herself stated, 30 years after her marriage: "We were married because society forced me to marry. People feared that I was licentious. Social pressure threatened to block my career. Fawzy was almost 20 years older than I, a handsome gentleman, always elegantly dressed. He understood me and my ambitions."

Fawzy, 76, told us this week: "I married her because she was beautiful, educated, and intelligent; even my father warned me not to miss this opportunity to marry a woman of her stature."

In 1969 Violet succeeded her husband as a member of the Kufir Yassif Local Council; in 1972, she was elected as its mayor. This situation, though not an easy one for the men in the Council, helped advance the status of women. Violet Khoury brought the Local Council its first woman clerk; at present, dozens of women are employed by the Council in clerical positions.

Violet Khoury was one of the greatest fighters for the liberation of the Arab woman. She fought so that women could work outside their homes and be economically independent. The people of her village believe that it was she who paved the way to acceptance of Arab career women.

"It will be easier for them after me. I broke the taboo against women's employment in 'male' professions," noted Violet in the course of numerous conversations in recent years. According to village residents, she was a very good mayor. During her term of office, Kufir Yassif received more government support than under any of her predecessors. Nevertheless, public figures in her village felt she was too independent. After only two years, they collaborated in an attempt to block her reelection; indeed, she was not elected to a second term—due both to their intervention and to the change in election method and institution of personal elections for heads of local authorities.

"Violet Khoury always denied that she was a feminist; yet her example shattered long years of tradition and constituted a breakthrough in the liberation of Arab women throughout Israel," stated Amal Khoury, her niece, a 30-year-old lawyer living in Nazareth. "In Kufir Yassif, the atmosphere is more cultural than in Nazareth. Here, despite all the high-flown talk, most women work as cosmeticians or in fashion, though some work in the free professions. Although no other

Arab woman has yet been elected mayor, Kufir Yassif has a high concentration of women who go on to study and complete their university degrees.

The first and only Arab woman bank branch manager in the country, Jeannette Farah, works in the Barclays Bank in Kufir Yassif. Farah believes that she obtained her post thanks to the example set by Violet Khoury. "She was a wonderful woman. After her, nothing remained the same, and the women of Kufir Yassif gained many new opportunities. I received my post as bank manager because of my professional qualifications. This is exactly the thing that Violet Khoury fought for: equal opportunities and equal rights for women and men in the Arab sector." (Violet Khoury died of cancer at the age of 58 in December 1987.)

Conflict of Interests:
A Case Study of Na'amat

Juliet J. Pope

The political aspect of women's organizations that engage in social, cultural and philanthropic activities is often overlooked. This is particularly true of groups that develop in the context of national liberation struggles. Such organizations can often be regarded as "fighting on two fronts," to promote women's rights and national interests, but reconciling these objectives may be problematic.

Many western feminists have adopted a universalist approach to the issue of women's liberation, and therefore criticize nationalism for fostering divisions between women. Others see the nation-state as a source of women's oppression because of the chauvinistic values it perpetuates. However, women organizing within national movements offer a more integrative analysis which acknowledges the multidimensional nature of their political identities. Their claim is that they can achieve equality as women only as members of an independent national body, and that after independence, they will act to maximize and maintain the political and social gains made in the process of nation-building.

The demands of women's organizations may be legitimized by their participation in a nationalist struggle, but they are also likely to be criticized for promoting internal factionalism and for weakening the collective national efforts. Their agenda will therefore be determined not only by the specific needs of women, but also by the general needs of their society. When different interpretations of nationalism emerge, women's organizations may be further constrained by political loyalties.

Such is the case of Na'amat, the largest women's organization in Israel, which expresses nationalism in the form of labor Zionism. Founded in 1914, as the Council of Women Workers, it emerged as an inseparable but autonomous part of the Histadrut, the federation of Hebrew trade unions. The name of the organization was changed in 1976 to Na'amat (Movement of Working Women and Volunteers), when it began to identify with certain elements of western feminism. Despite this shift in orientation, while composed of factions of women who identify with political parties from the whole spectrum, the majority of Na'amat's members are affiliated with the Labor movement. As a result, Na'amat often supports the Labor party line and party candidates.

Although women in Israel are under-represented in central political institutions, they have not been isolated from political life. This paper will examine the political significance of Na'amat and will highlight some of the difficulties encountered by an organization which attempts to reconcile women's liberation with nationalism.

In order to appreciate the scope of Na'amat's achievements as well as its limitations, it is necessary to examine the context in which it evolved. Guided by their visions of socialist Zionism, the women pioneers of the second and third waves of immigration to Israel aspired to liberation as women through the creation of a more egalitarian social order within a Jewish homeland. As early as 1911, small groups of women pioneers met to discuss their disappointment with the rigid division of labor along gender lines in the Jewish settlement of prestate Palestine; their primary concern became the integration of women into the productive sector of the economy. At the time only men were listed in annual contracts of the Palestine Office of the Zionist Movement, while women were employed by the men. Men engaged in construction and agriculture, and women were usually assigned to the kitchens and to domestic work, a situation which was aggravated by unemployment and lack of training opportunities for women.

Early attempts to train and organize women included *kvutzot,* communes which leased small areas of land to cultivate vegetables, and later, all-female collective farms. Such enterprises created opportunities for women and, at the same time, contributed to the Zionist cause by aiding development of the Jewish national economy in Palestine. While these projects remained small-scale and local, they should be viewed as a precursor to the organization of the Council of Women Workers.

In 1920, the Histadrut, the General Federation of Jewish Labor, was created among Jewish trade unions and workers' organizations in Palestine. It played a crucial role in the development of political, economic and social institutions during the prestate period, but women workers were not represented in its central bodies. Unable to persuade the Histadrut to address the needs of working women, female delegates to the founding convention formed their own organization (Maimon, 1962). To this day, the relationship between the two organizations remains ambivalent. The Council of Women Workers retains the right to determine its own policy; in practice, however, it is structurally and financially tied to the Histadrut.

From the start, the Council of Women Workers was an integral part of the Labor Zionist movement, and it aimed to promote Jewish settlement in Palestine as well as to advance women's economic rights. To this dual purpose, the Council campaigned so that women pioneers would be given immigration certificates in their own right rather than as dependents of their male relatives. Social and educational activities were undertaken to assist the absorption of new immigrants, and an agricultural training school was established to prepare young women for work in the kibbutzim or moshavim. In 1934, the Council launched the publication of its own monthly journal, *Davar Hapoalot,* which was edited for 25 years by labor activist Rachel Katznelson Shazar and therefore expressed the political views of the labor movement.

Today, membership has grown to over 750,000, including 100,000 Arab women living within the pre-1967 borders and in East Jerusalem. Any woman belonging to the Histadrut or whose husband does, automatically becomes a member of Na'amat. Thus it is difficult to calculate how many women are active in the organization; for many, membership may be merely nominal, or at best, passive. However, Na'amat is able to claim that it represents 60 percent of Israeli women.

Elections to a hierarchy of national and local positions within Na'amat are held every four years at the same time as elections to the Histadrut. All candidates are presented according to party lists, but the Labor Alignment has always attained a clear majority. For over four decades, the position of secretary-general was held by Labor activist, Member of Knesset Beba Idelson. Other parties, such as the Likud (which constitute about 25 percent of the membership) and a small Communist faction are represented, but Na'amat is unmistakably associated with the political policies of the Labor party. Unlike the models of western feminist movements, which are based on grassroots organization outside political parties and mainstream institutions, Na'amat is bound to a framework of political and national interests.

Membership dues are paid directly by the unions, and Na'amat receives a substantial part of its budget from the Histadrut. Financial assistance is also sought through Na'amat's sister organization, formerly called Pioneer Women, which grew out of the Poale Zion movement in the United States. Fundraising and publicity for Na'amat are now conducted through Na'amat clubs in twelve different countries. Specific projects may receive the support of governmental agencies or local authorities, but in order to overcome budgetary limitations, Na'amat places a high value on voluntarism. Ironically, it could be argued that the unpaid and part-time nature of Na'amat's work perpetuates the low status of women's activities.

During the first years after independence, the Council of Women Workers served the interests of the state by focusing on the problem of immigrant absorption. Hundreds of female volunteers were encouraged to undertake social work among immigrants, who were temporarily housed in transit camps. In addition to food distribution and relief work, the Council held Hebrew language courses among women and youth, which helped to foster their new Israeli identity. Together with the Histadrut's Agricultural Center, it encouraged auxiliary farming on small plots in immigrant housing developments, and initiated basic vocational training to enable women to join the workforce.

The Council of Women Workers emphasized the important role of mothers in state building. An early activist noted, "Training in Jewish moral values and in citizenship is a basic necessity in Israel today, and it is primarily the mothers who can and must shoulder this task" (Maimon, 1962). Subsequently, the organization has been criticized for reinforcing the traditional assumptions about women's domestic and child-rearing responsibilities.

Volunteers also provided lectures on sanitation, cooking and housework, which were intended to accustom immigrants to their new environment. *Davar Hapoelet* and other publications often portrayed the lifestyles of Yemenite and North African women as primitive, backward, and underdeveloped and stressed the need for women from these communities to "awaken to the twentieth century." In retrospect, some activists recognize that their approach was patronizing and that their attitude to the cultural traditions of immigrants from Arabic-speaking countries undoubtedly reflected a degree of racism.

Similar attitudes may have characterized contacts fostered since the 1950s among the Palestinian Arab minority in Israel. By stressing the advantages offered to Arab women in the Jewish state, such as the right to vote, the ban on polygamy, and free compulsory education, the Council hoped to promote a sense of loyalty and civic identity among Arab women. (There is a certain irony in the fact that while the Council was urging the need to increase the mobility of Arab women outside their homes, it did not tackle the issue of military rule under which the Arab towns and villages were governed until 1966, which limited their movement.) Social activities and sewing instruction were combined with literacy classes in Arabic and Hebrew, and courses in "citizenship." Much publicized gatherings, often attended by (male) Labor party politicians and public figures, were also held to celebrate national holidays such as Israel Independence Day and the anniversary of the Histadrut.

These activities were supervised by Arabic-speaking Jewish women through the Arab Women's Section, until 1978, when Nelly Karkaby, a Christian Arab, was appointed head of the section. Today, adult education programs and vocational training continue in over thirty Arab women's clubs. Contacts between Arab and Jewish women are also arranged through a variety of cultural and educational programs. After the Six Day War, the Women Workers' Council extended its activities to East Jerusalem. The organization does not work with Palestinians in the occupied territories; some services however, are provided to Jewish women in West Bank settlements, the first of which were founded by the Labor government in the mid 1970s.

Na'amat has always subscribed to the view that participation in the productive work force is a crucial means of advancing the status of women; as does the Labor Zionist Movement, it has viewed women's labor as a national resource. This dual commitment requires the organization to reconcile the interests of women with the interests of the state.

Vocational training for women, which began with short courses for immigrants, has gradually expanded into longer programs authorized by the Ministry of Education and closely coordinated with the Ministry of Labor and the Histadrut. The rapid development of the economy after 1967 led the Labor government to set up a special unit to encourage women to enter the workforce; a further impetus was provided after the Yom Kippur War, when special courses were needed to prepare women for jobs traditionally reserved for men. The Women Workers' Council tailored its educational activities to meet these national needs. In recent years, Na'amat has encouraged women to study more technological subjects and enter science-based professions, in accordance with the national emphasis on hightech.

Increasing efforts have been made to train young Arab women to enable them to join the productive labor force. Indeed, many graduates of Council or Na'amat courses have found employment in Histadrut-owned factories in the textiles and electronics industries, where they provide a cheap and often unorganized source of labor. Na'amat acknowledges some of the specific problems facing these women, such as the exploitive practice of hiring women's labor through contractors, but it has been unable to provide any effective opposition, either through the Histadrut or as a pressure group in its own right (Swirski, 1987).

Since the unemployment crisis of 1930, when the Council of Women Workers protested the ban on married women's work, it has upheld the right of married women to employment. It has also advocated the right of married women to hold separate income tax files and the right to equal retirement terms and benefits. It also claims that women running their own households and taking care of their children should be considered workers. The organization therefore advocates the inclusion of housewives in all social insurance schemes and their rights to insurance in case of disability and accidents in the home. In this respect Na'amat could be compared with the "Wages for Housework"campaigners in Britain who aspire to raising the status of women engaged in domestic work at home.

In accordance with its philosophy of encouraging women to join the productive labor force, Na'amat has instituted a broad network of children's daycare facilities, where fees are charged on a sliding scale, based on family income. Recognizing that the social and economic costs of childcare may affect a woman's choice of family size, Na'amat's provision of daycare also reflects the demographic interests of the state.

From 1930, daycare centers were administered through a section of the Council called the Association of Mothers Working in their Homes. The fact that 90 percent of daycare is still provided by women's organizations signifies the failure of Na'amat to persuade the state to support these services. In this respect, Na'amat fulfills a national need, and at the same time, perpetuates the traditional image of childcare as a female concern. Its 1988 campaign to encourage men "to help out" with housework, which adopted the slogan: "Be a Man, Give Her a Hand," does not challenge the notion that women are primarily responsible for domestic work.

The organization has held summer camps for mothers of large families since the mid 1960s, not only to give overworked mothers a rest but also to encourage women to volunteer for community work and to publicize the goals of Na'amat. Such activities also provide an opportunity for Na'amat to spread messages of a more political nature. For example, 5000 Arab and Jewish women participated in a "Fun Day" in Jerusalem in 1987, whose theme was "Mothers Have the Courage to Work for Peace." According to a Na'amat spokesperson, the purpose of the event was to win support for the Labor party peace initiative launched by Foreign Minister Shimon Peres (*Jerusalem Post*, 1987).

Na'amat has lobbied for improved labor legislation, but only limited progress has been made in challenging discrimination against women in the workplace. Even when antidiscrimination laws were passed (1988), no way to monitoring or guaranteeing their implementation were legislated. The problem is both structural and ideological. Despite cooperation between Na'amat and the Working Women's Section of the Histadrut, which encourages women to join workplace committees, women remain poorly represented in mainstream labor institutions. According to a recent report by the Israel Women's Network, women constitute 11.3 percent of the Histadrut Council, 13.2 percent of the Workers Council and 17.2 percent of the Central Committee (Benson and Harverd, 1988). Therefore, despite the efforts of Na'amat and other women's organizations, the demands of women workers are often ignored by trade unions. It has also been suggested that the Histadrut, which employs a significant proportion of the female labor force in its own factories, has an interest in keeping wages low in order to encourage foreign investment and to maximize its own profits and those of the nation (Swirski, 1987).

The way in which Na'amat identifies with national interests can also be seen through its work with women in the armed forces. Before independence, the Women Workers' Council worked closely with the Haganah, the precursor of the Israel Defense Forces (IDS) and during the Second World War it coordinated the recruitment of many Jewish women to the Auxiliary Territorial Services. After 1948, the Council maintained contact with women's units in the Israel Defense Force, providing seminars, visits to Na'amat centers and kibbutzim, and craft courses.

Na'amat recognizes the role of the military in career structuring in Israel. For Jewish males, the IDF can provide training opportunities, work experience, and access to professional contacts which constitute a form of "old boys' network." Stressing the importance of national service, Na'amat has focused on extending these benefits to women, rather than examining how militarism can actually harm the interests of women. Their outlook is reminiscent of "right to fight" feminists who believe that women can only expect equal rights in a society in which they have equal responsibilities.

Thus, Na'amat lobbied against the Military Enlistment Law which allowed more women to exempt themselves from military service on grounds of religious observance and campaigned for women to carry arms in the Civil Guard. Its publicity for rehabilitation programs for women from underprivileged backgrounds emphasizes both the national and personal importance of military service. "Their service in the IDF is not only an expression of social responsibility; in Israel it is also a 'calling card' when work is sought, as it is considered a measure of capabilities." However, in 1987, 40 percent of women conscripts were still engaged in clerical work (*Jerusalem Post*, July 9, 1987).

On her election to the post of Na'amat Secretary-General in 1974, Tamar Eshel declared: "I would like to see our image change from that of a philanthropic and charitable enterprise to that of a fighting movement concerned with the problems of women, as well as with general issues of public importance" (*Jerusalem Post*, August 16, 1974). Thus, in 1976 she arranged the merger of the Women Workers' Council with the Association of Mothers and renamed the organization, Na'amat.

During the United Nations Decade for Women (1975–1985), Na'amat worked closely with the Public Commission on the Status of Women headed by former Council activist, Ora Namir, and beginning in the early 1980s, initiated campaigns identified with the western feminist movement. Assertiveness training for small groups of women were started nationwide and a counselling center for victims of domestic violence was opened.

During this period, Na'amat vigorously opposed the Amendment to the Penal Code (Abortion) of 1977, which deleted the "social clause," thereby tightening the conditions under which an abortion could be obtained. Like the Military Enlistment Law, this amendment was introduced to the Knesset as a result of political bargaining between the newly-elected Likud party and its coalition partner, Agudat Yisrael, a religious party. Na'amat's response to what is termed "religious legislation" was expressed in terms of protecting women's rights, but it also reflected the concerns of the Labor party opposition.

Since 1977, Na'amat has attempted to increase its function as a political lobby through its Department for the Status of Women. Formerly known as the Department for Legislation, Legal Counselling and Social Security, it evolved after the Six Day War, when the Labor-held Ministry of Defense asked the Council to establish an agency to assist bereaved families and war widows.

The department currently provides lectures on legal issues and offers free legal advice on discrimination at the workplace, insurance rights and other matters. One of its main functions is to undertake legal research and to draft legislation. For example, Na'amat's Status of Women month in 1986 publicized problems relating to laws of personal status and the status of women in the Rabbinic courts. Legal experts were commissioned to suggest changes compatible with *halakha* (Jewish religious law) or within a combination of *halakha* and Israeli legal practice.

Na'amat has also conducted media campaigns to broaden public support for women's liberation. In 1988, a Declaration of the Rights of Women (based on the Israel Declaration of Independence) calling for equal representation in all public bodies and for equality in employment and job advancement, was signed by thousands of women nationwide and presented to the Prime Minister. The Declaration also reflected Na'amat's nationalist orientation, in the form of a recommendation that women serve in the armed forces or do some other form of national service, a clause omitted in the Arabic version.

Na'amat has recently shown interest in tackling political issues previously not considered of relevance to women's organizations. At the 1977 convention, where the question of Israel's national borders was first addressed, Na'amat voted in favor of territorial compromise, thus broadening the definition of women's interests, while at the same time mobilizing further support for the Labor party.

Na'amat activists are aware of the organization's potential role as a springboard into the mainstream political institutions. Three former Secretary-Generals, Beba Idelson, Nava Arad and Tamar Eshel, were elected to the Knesset on Labor party lists, while other Labor MKs, such as Shoshana Arbeli-Almoslino and Ora Namir also received their political training in the Women Workers' Council. However, results of the last general elections, in which only 7 of 120 Knesset members chosen were women, prove that the Israeli women's organizations have been largely ineffective in their attempts to increase women's representation.

Na'amat developed as part of the Zionist movement, which was inspired by the need to build a Jewish homeland in Palestine. After independence, it remained part of the Zionist establishment and as a result, Na'amat's objectives in terms of women's liberation have been tempered by national and partisan concerns.

Neither feminist organization, in the western sense of the word, nor trade union, Na'amat does not conform to any model of political organization. However, it undoubtedly represents the political interests of women and of labor Zionists. Yet Na'amat does not wish to be seen as a political organization which caters only to Labor party activists. It phrases its objectives and achievements in terms of broader national interests. According to Secretary-General Masha Lubelsky, "This is a social movement whose decision-making relates to the goals of society and the nation. We do not function on the basis of electoral motivation. We do not want to be a single-interest group" (*Jerusalem Post*, May 27, 1983).

Na'amat's attempts to advance women's rights have been restricted by its members' dependence on party loyalties and institutional ties; these have prevented the creation of a genuine grassroots movement which might constitute an effective women's lobby. At the same time, Na'amat is hindered by its distance from the political core of mainstream institutions; it is possible that the establishment of a separate women's organization has served to marginalize women's issues rather than bring them to the fore within the Histadrut and state institutions.

As it prepares its social and political programs for the 1990s, the question remains: Can Na'amat find a way to resolve these contradictions or has it already fulfilled its potential as a political force?

REFERENCES

Benson, Miriam and Harverd, Dorit (1988) *The Status of Women: The Implementation of the Recommendations of the Israel Government Commission of Investigation.* Jerusalem: Israel Women's Network.

Maimon, Ada (1962) *Women Build A Land.* Tel Aviv: Herzl Press.

Swirski, Barbara (1987) "Israeli Women on the Assembly Line." In Fuentes, A. and Ehrenreich, B. (eds.). *Women in the Global Factor.* Tel Aviv: Breirot Press (Hebrew).

Profile of the Female
Candidate for Local Office

Hannah Herzog

Why should local politics be the logical starting for women interested in moving into politics? If we take the traditional division of labor as a given, local politics should be a good ticket for women to enter politics, since local politics deals mainly with social issues, considered women's domain, such as education, social welfare, art and culture and other community services. Women have a relative advantage in these spheres, as they frequent them both as users and as volunteers. Local politics allows women to remain close to home and continue to function in their roles as wives and mothers. Since Israeli local politics is secondary to national politics, its relatively low status could reduce competition with men. Despite these theoretical advantages, women are under-represented in local politics.

A number of changes have occurred on Israel's local political scene since the late sixties. In order to understand the meaning of these changes, we have to be aware of the fact that Israel is a multiparty system, and that the parties are strong and well organized on both the national and local level (Arian 1986). The first change, one that appeared in the late sixties, is split voting: people vote for different parties on the local level than on the national level. This split indicates that people consider local interests when electing local authorities. The second change is the proliferation of local lists formed to address local needs. The third change is electoral reform. Since 1978, mayors have been elected in direct elections, while municipal councils are constituted on the basis of proportional representation of party lists.

All of these developments point to a growing trend favoring local interests. The question here is whether the predominance of local issues, that is, increasing interest in areas with which women are generally occupied, leads to greater representation for women. If so, can we speak of a new generation of local women politicians?

In the first local elections, held in 1950, women in the Jewish cities gained 4.2 percent of the seats. This low representation decreased even further, reaching its nadir in 1965 (3.2%). Since the late sixties, it increased steadily to 7.6 percent in 1983.

Out of the 292 women elected since 1950, I located 241 women, to whom I sent a questionnaire. The 67 percent rate of response was a high rate for mail questionnaires, which can be attributed to the respondents' awareness as politicians and as women, of the importance of the subject.

No striking changes emerged in the profile of women active in local politics over the years. When first elected, the typical representative is a married woman aged forty-four with three children, the youngest 11 years of age. Her education is above the national average as well as above that of women in her age group. She is also more educated than her male comrade in politics. She works outside the home, in a "feminine" profession, earns above the average Israeli wage. The division of labor within her home follows the traditional division of labor between men and women, very similar to that of the average Israeli family. She divides her time between home, job and political activity. Her entrance into politics was not followed by the family's redefinition of the social roles of women and men. She is more like the typical liberated woman in many western societies—the "superwoman." She also holds the traditional norms regarding politics: That is, she believes that politics is mainly men's business, and she does not have political ambitions. She enters politics as an amateur, does not chair committees, and usually leaves after one term.

The manner in which women enter politics is the only significant change over the years. I asked each woman to write the story of how she entered politics and how her place on the list was determined. In the 1950s, 75 percent of the women received their places on the list through the party machine or nomination committee, whereas in the 1980s, only 43 percent owed their places to the party. Instead, 25 percent were beholden to the head of the party list, the one who ran for the office of mayor on an individual ticket. Among them were fewer party members than in the past. What this means is that party membership is no longer a political resource for women interested in local politics. On the other hand, the more veteran the woman in the party activity, the more roles she holds within the party and within women's organizations, and the lower she is placed on the party list. In the internal power game of the party, women do not succeed in translating their investment in political activity into political bargaining power.

What does this mean? The woman who enters local politics now tries to by-pass obstacles within the party. She uses her local reputation to advance, exploiting the changes that have occurred in local politics. Her human capital, such as high education and experience in community volunteer work, make her attractive to those who run on individual tickets and wish to head an appealing list. The recommendation that may be deduced from this finding is that other women can use this channel of entrance and circumvent discrimination by party machines. Yet, the main shortcoming of this channel is the personal dependence of the woman on her sponsor. The question that remains is does the new channel open new opportunities to women or is it just changing one patron (the party) for a new one (the leader)?

REFERENCES

Arian, Asher (1986) *Politics in Israel*. Chatham, New Jersey: Chatham House.

HOW WOMEN PRESENT
THEMSELVES TO THE ELECTORATE

Naomi Nevo

In a case study, campaign material disseminated by women candidates competing in internal party elections and local government elections for the Labor party (center), Likud party (a right-wing merger of the small Liberal party and the much larger nationalist Herut party), and the Citizens' Rights party (left) was examined for feminist content, that is, for mention of activity promoting equality of opportunity for women, including membership in feminist organizations. A combination of research methods was used, consisting of analyses of written materials, interviews with informants and participant-observation at election meetings.

It was found that women candidates for elected office in Israel do not present themselves unequivocally as advocates of the feminist cause even in its minimalist terms — equality of opportunity. Rather, their self-presentation tends to reinforce the stereotypical woman in Israeli society. There is, however, a certain ambivalence. Women candidates feel that they cannot afford to ignore women's issues, but they present their achievements in these areas cautiously. To quote one candidate: "Someone may look for it."

An examination of the left-right continuum reveals that women on the left stress the feminist cause as part of general human rights issues, while women on the right ignore the subject almost entirely in favor of their nationalist achievements. Women from the center present themselves as feminists but temper this presentation with achievements in immigrant absorption and community building. In short, Israeli women see the wider ideology of nation building, whether in socialist or nationalist terms, as a more attractive asset than feminist principles.

Breaking New Ground
in the Knesset

Marcia Freedman
Member of Knesset (MK) 1973 to 1977

My maiden speech was deliberately noncontroversial. Like everyone else, I read the speech from a prepared text, intent on getting it over with. The Chamber filled to hear the young feminist with the American accent. As I walked the long walk back to my seat, relieved and grateful to my colleagues for listening politely, I barely heard the Chair announce the next speaker, Akiva Nof, a young liberal. Not until I heard my name mentioned did I pay attention to his words, words of welcome for the no-longer virgin Member. As was the custom, Nof said nice things about me. But then he went too far. "I hope," he said, "that in the course of your struggle to liberate women, men will be liberated as well."

The Knesset was scandalized. "Which men do you mean?" someone shouted angrily. "We don't need any liberated men." Those who attacked Nof were not backbenchers. One was the Minister of Transportation. The other was a wealthy industrialist who would become Minister of Commerce under Begin. Nof reddened and tried to extricate himself. "I meant that nation of men who are dominated by women," he said. "What you should have wished for is that this country be liberated from women," shouted someone else who remains anonymous in the Knesset Record.

For several minutes as the Chair futilely tried to bring the Knesset to order, there was pandemonium. I had only one defender for women's liberation, and even he was guarded. Meir Pa'il, a reserve-general and leader of a leftist peace movement called Moked, responded angrily to the antifeminist outburst. "It may well be that this movement has something important to say to us," he said. "Maybe we don't understand and cover it over with typical sabra cynicism. Marcia Freedman is a unique phenomenon in this Knesset."

Based on Marcia Freedman (1990) *Exile in the Promised Land: A Memoir*. Ithaca: Firebrand. Reprinted with permission.

Unique I was. My opinions, my frames of reference, my age, my accent, my size and my sex conspired to differentiate me from everyone else. Above all, I was identified with a movement that seemed to terrify my colleagues. Cooptation was the one thing I never had to worry about.

ABORTION REFORM

Abortion reforms marked the beginning and the end of my political career. It is an explosive issue in a country where everyone is obsessed with the Arab birthrate. The figures are updated as fast as the Bureau of Statistics can gather the data. When survival is the question, it seems, having babies is one of the answers. And since it's in most men's power and not within most women's choice, it remains a masculine form of heroism and a feminine form of service to the state to have large families.

The requirements of survival find a powerful echo in the Biblical commandment, *prohu uvohu,* "be fruitful and multiply." Each pogrom, each expulsion, and finally the Holocaust carved this lesson into the hearts of a nation. Abortion is a divisive issue everywhere, but perhaps more so in Israel. The Woman Question cuts through Israeli society with a finely sharpened blade. The wound bleeds for those who have died and those yet to die. With constant reminders of the Holocaust, the losses of three wars and countless acts of terrorism, life in Israel is a continuous ceremony of mourning. Nevertheless, the right of free choice was well-established among the majority of Israeli women who could afford it. The conflict over abortion was passionate and fierce.

The law in force in 1974 conformed with *halakha,* Jewish law. It prohibited doctors from performing abortion except to save the life of the mother. In practice, the law was not enforced. Israeli gynecologists, almost all of them, operate abortion clinics in their private offices. Of the 60,000 abortions performed in Israel each year, three-quarters are illegal. Legal abortions, performed in hospitals, were all, on paper, performed to save the life of the mother, but in fact were performed for all sorts of other reasons. In extreme cases, poor women who could not afford the high cost of a private abortion, were served publicly. No one ever questioned the high number of ostensibly life-threatening pregnancies terminated in hospitals around the country, just as no one ever questioned the illegal black market in abortion.

The situation was embarrassing for the government and difficult for gynecologists. The women's movement, since 1971, had been demanding abortion reform. Abortion was on the agenda of most of the nations of the west. The Labor government responded by appointing a commission, the Baki Commission, charged with recommending new legislation.

The Commission recommendations, issued in 1974, proposed that abortion was to be restricted to those for whom pregnancy was a misfortune: rape and incest victims, mothers out of wedlock, menopausal women, teenagers, the physically and mentally ill. The Commission recommendations embodied a coincidence of the moderate wings of medical and religious opinion. Religious law permits abortions for *pickuach nefesh,* saving lives. Though two living beings are recognized, moderate Orthodoxy recognizes the precedence of the mother. The gynecologists were interested in preserving their market. The legislation drafted by the Baki Commission respected the wishes of the dominant religious party as well as those of the gynecological establishment by legalizing current practice without altering it.

Drafting the Bill

Several months before the Baki recommendations were made public, I introduced a bill drafted by Nitza Shapiro-Libai, then professor of law at Tel Aviv University, and later appointed Prime Minister's Advisor on the Status of Women. The bill was modeled on the *Roe* v. *Wade* decision as well as the new French and Italian laws. It ended all restrictions on free choice during the first trimester of pregnancy.

Labor's response was the first of many parliamentary anomalies that marked the history of the Knesset on women's issues. The government adopted a rarely used tactic that was surely a sign of extremity: The Labor Alignment released its members from party discipline, allowing each a vote of conscience. The Likud party, equally divided, did the same. Even the National Religious party was divided; some of its members were "unopposed" to choice. It seemed for a while that the field was clear for a rare expression of majority opinion.

Formally, all Labor MKs were free to vote according to their conscience; in fact, there was a small group, all women, who were not. Through them the government managed to control the legislation of abortion reform without ever having to take an official position. They introduced and carried legislation based on the Baki Commission recommendations. Some of these women were prochoice and even publicly supported my bill. Others were antichoice, and there were varying shades between. But they were all equally committed to one proposition—that the survival of the coalition took precedence over the interests of women, whatever they believed them to be. The group coalesced around the Baki recommendations.

I watched, at first with dismay but ultimately with a growing sense of betrayal, as the Labor women secretively met to hammer out an initial amorphous version of the Baki recommendations that every one could live with. Then, like an army of hungry ants, they carried off 15 of the 22 MKs who had cosigned with me. The women refused to meet with Nitza and me and refused any offers of compromise and cooperation. My advocacy of free-choice was part of their strategy. If they could isolate me and define choice as radical, they could legislate conservatively but appear to be moderate.

The abortion issue, the first piece of legislation I introduced into the Knesset and the issue on which I gave my last speech to the Knesset, was my introduction to the nastiness of parliamentary intrigue. I was an innocent, at first outraged and then discouraged by the hypocrisy of the process and, always, furiously at odds with the Labor Alignment women. Their commitment to women had always been tenuous, subordinate to their commitment to their political careers. I was their sacrifice offered up on the altar of political fortunes, the scapegoat branded too radical so that they would not seem too conservative on the one issue about which most Israeli women were in agreement.

But if I was an innocent within the Knesset, outside I was an experienced agitator and organizer. There were a few hundred active feminists around the country and three centers of organized support: Haifa, Tel Aviv and Jerusalem. There were demonstrations, street theater, rallies and petitions. I was able to keep the movement informed of the legislative timetable and to attract the media. The television crews assigned to cover our demonstrations were unusually sympathetic and took pains to make our small demonstrations look good. Women journalists rushed to get in on the story, one of the few that might move them off the women's pages. The women's movement took the lead on an issue that had broad public support. Though they ultimately won the battle in the Knesset, the Labor women's public opinion strategy backfired. By isolating me as the sole proponent of prochoice legislation, a position that was overwhelmingly popular, I became the heroine of abortion reform.

Debate

I dressed slowly the morning of the first vote on the two abortion bills.

My eye caught a red silk blouse and a floor-length denim skirt. Good, I thought, I'll dress for the party, the victory party. I brushed my long dark hair and decided to leave it loose. I dabbed patchouli oil behind my ears and drew lines of kohl around my eyes. "You've never dressed like this for work before," I accused myself in the mirror. "Use whatever weapons you have," the painted image replied. My fingers reached up to undo another button on my blouse. I entered the Knesset that morning entirely focused on winning the vote.

It was the last session of the week, and the abortion bills were among the last items on the agenda. I had to secure the fence sitters, capture some of the indifferent and make sure my supporters remained on the floor for the vote. Long Bedouin earrings chiming gently, I made the rounds of the tables in the MK Dining Room, persuading and cajoling, charming, and where necessary, flirting. I watched the clock, counting and recounting the numbers for and against. When the bell rang signaling the vote, I was ready for my party. The Labor women's bill passed by 43 to 13; prochoice passed too, 26 to 13.

The debate was raucous throughout, but became fevered when I ascended to the rostrum. There was hardly a sentence in my speech that didn't arouse the opponents of abortion, most particularly the ultra-Orthodox MKs.

"Sixty thousand abortions a year are performed in this country, most illegal."—"Tens of millions of Arabs, who are fruitful and multiply, surround our borders."—"There are no unwanted Jewish children."—"Illegal abortion performed routinely in private offices built onto doctor's homes."—"Destroying fetuses, souls, spirits of Israel's children while they're still in their mother's womb." "It is the women's right to choose."—"I want to ask you something? Has Arafat given his consent to this law?"—"Private abortions cost two thousand shekels, the cost of maintaining a family of four for a month."—"The Jewish people are being annihilated."—"Ninety million shekels a year going into the pockets of 600 gynecologists."—"Murderers! To lose a single soul for Israel is to lose the whole world."—"Abortion is the right of the rich, unwanted pregnancies the fact of the poor."—"There is no such thing as an unwanted Jewish child." "There are government documents instructing law enforcement authorities to turn a blind eye on abortions performed by licensed gynecologists."—"In this generation, when Hitler, may his name be blotted out, murdered a third of our people, threw a million of our children into the ovens, how is it possible to permit the murder of Jewish fetuses still inside their mother's womb?"—"The freedom to plan a family is an elementary civil right."—"We've already heard your proposals to legalize prostitution and drugs, but this is the worst yet. Why not permit bigamy as well? Women could have ten husbands, twenty husbands."—"Unwanted children are abused psychologically and even physically."—"There are no unwanted Jewish children."

Gynecological Confrontation

On an intensely sunny June day in 1976, the Israel Association of Obstetricians and Gynecologists held its annual convention at the Hilton Hotel in Tel Aviv. A few weeks earlier, the Association warned in published advertisements that Israel's gynecologists would refuse to cooperate with prochoice abortion legislation on the grounds that it was unsafe.

The doctors were listening to a paper on the latest advances in obstetric surgery when a small group of women carrying placards and shouting slogans entered through a side door of the Hilton that led directly into the main ballroom. The demonstrators marched noisily across the room and onto the podium. They stood facing the audience, shouting slogans. They demanded legal and free abortion. They accused the doctors of getting rich on black-market abortion. The astonished doctors began clapping their hands rhythmically in an attempt to drown out the slogans. Like cheerleaders before a willing crowd, the women chanted in time to the doctors' beat. The Chair called for order, but there was no order.

Later, the press described the action as "unseemly," "scandalous," "shameless" and "hysterical." "Eleven wild-haired, sloppily dressed women" caused a "wild riot." They used "unprintable" language. They were accused of violently attacking the doctors and the hotel security guards.

I could see the four security guards coming towards us out of the corner of my eye. They closed in on our signs and when they could, tore them to shreds. The largest, six feet tall and weighing about two hundred pounds, grabbed the sign I held in my right hand. With the instincts of a childhood spent fighting neighborhood bullies, I reached up for his open shirtcollar and held on tight. We glared at one another. He was afraid to touch me, I knew, but I was afraid his fury and frustration would win out over the restraint he was so obviously fighting to maintain. I watched as his face turned from pink to rose to purple, trying to gauge when my time would be up. When the guard intensified his efforts to wrest the sign from me, I knew that moment had arrived. I released both the sign and the shirtcollar, and with my free hand, gave him a gentle push. Off balance, the giant fell. That must have been what caused the first of the doctors to throw a cast-iron water pitcher at my head. A picture in the next day's newspaper shows the doctor throwing and me blocking. A torrent of water pitchers, flower vases and ashtrays rained down on us. We ducked some, caught others and piled the ammunition up behind us. Disarmed finally, the doctors backed off, stopping only when they reached the far walls, afraid, I suppose, that we would throw the objects back at them. It was a curious sight, eleven women holding six hundred gynecologists at bay.

Left standing in the middle of the room, taking pictures rapidly, were the photographers, one woman and several men. The security guards grabbed cameras and confiscated film. The female photographer stuffed rolls of film inside her bra, signalling us to help her. One of the guards closed in, grabbed her flashgun and hit her over the head with it. A few of us diverted the guard while others surrounded the photographer and led her to the side door she'd opened for us earlier that day.

Israel had never seen anything like it before. Disrespect for Jewish doctors, disruption of a professional meeting, disheveled women carried off in paddy wagons with raised fists, brazen women confronting enraged gynecologists, eleven to six hundred. The "Hilton Affair" made the headlines, as we knew it would. The black market in abortion was exposed. In living rooms and at work, the country talked about abortion and reproductive rights. Opinion polls showed that 75 percent were prochoice.

Spilled blood spread beneath the surface of my skin. I was black and blue, green and yellow. A symbolic sacrifice only, the stigmata disappeared in a few weeks. But their effects lingered on. Our action, though successful in our terms, was deemed inexcusably rude. The country was prochoice but once again anti-feminist.

"Why did you do it, Marcia?" asked Liova Eliav, a former Secretary-General of the Labor Party who had bolted and eventually became my political mentor and father-figure. Liova, who had spent months trying to clean up my act, look exasperated. I began what promised to be a long lecture on the history of feminist civil disobedience when he interrupted impatiently. "Yes, but why did *you* do it?" Liova clearly didn't expect a response, and indeed there was none.

Grassroots activism and electoral politics may share the same causes, but they obey entirely different rules. Politicians, by definition, have to be popular to survive. A politician never willingly creates a scandal. Grassroots organizers do little else.

Going to Committee

Both abortion bills were voted to committee, but three months later, prochoice was defeated by a carefully engineered vote of seven to six. The Committee Chair, Haika Grossman, was a member of Mapam, the Labor Alignment's left wing. With patience and enormous skill, she moved the Committee from a majority in favor of choice to a majority in support of the Baki Commission recommendations with the addition of a "social circumstances" clause. Poor mothers of large families would be exempt from the general prohibition of abortion recommended by the Baki Commission, along with the infirm and the victimized.

Abortion Hearings

Preparing for the hearings as though for a doctoral thesis, I had gathered information, kept my notes scrupulously, and checked the accuracy of my sources. I came to the abortion hearings more expert than any of the expert witnesses. But the facts were hardly central to the committee's deliberations. Sex was on everyone's mind throughout the months and years of committee hearings during which the abortion reform act was negotiated into its final form. The committee room often filled with jokes and lewd remarks, guffaws and snickers. Sexual matters were the focus of most of our discussions: incest, rape, teenage pregnancy, menopause. It made everyone nervous. My neighbor to the right, a dandy of a man with long white hair and flashy clothes, leaned towards me tittering, "Before a woman needs an abortion, there's something else she has to do first." He thought it was so funny he could hardly stop laughing.

These meetings, always loud and excited, always punctuated with suggestive jokes and so dismissive of women, enraged me. I could hardly recognize the abrasive, loud disruptive person I became, for once no different than other MKs.

Two years later, with the Likud in power and the ultra-Orthodox parties within the coalition, the social clause was repealed. The official statistics on abortion reported in 1979 were identical to those reported in 1974, before the "reform." Fifteen thousand legal abortions and at least 45,000 illegal ones were performed yearly. For four years, the Knesset labored mightily, some MKs in genuine struggle with their conscience, to change nothing. Those who could afford it planned their families. Those who could not, continued to contribute more than their share to the country's demographic war with the Arabs.

The Mission is Doomed

It was clear to me that my mission in politics was to put feminist issues on the agenda and try to keep them there. It was a mission that, in political terms, was doomed. Unless I turned my back on the cause that had put me into office, I was bound to fail as a politician. To succeed as a politician, I would have to fail as a feminist. It took years before I understood that, though I could and should have known it on the day of my maiden speech.

Rachel Kagan

When I first heard Rachel Kagan's stories about her years in the Knesset, I had no idea that the information would be so pertinent. Years before I was elected, Kagan taught me what it would be like to be a woman and a feminist in the Knesset. I met her for the first time when she was 85. Kagan had been a Member of the First Knesset (1949–1952), elected by an independent Women's List. The Women's List, representing two prestate feminist organizations, the Union of Hebrew Women for Equal Rights in Eretz Yisrael and the Women's International Zionist Organization (WIZO) or Hadassah, the latter created by Henrietta Szold. Kagan was Szold's protegee and heir to the leadership of Israeli WIZO. Kagan, one of two women who signed Israel's Declaration of Independence in 1948, headed the Women's List in 1949 and was the only one elected.

She was a small, delicate-looking woman with hawkish features. She wore her long white hair pinned back in a loose bun. She walked at least ten miles a day she told me some years later, at 93. I'd just followed her up the four flights of stairs to her apartment, panting and struggling to keep up with her. "Shame on you," she said, as I plopped down on the nearest chair, breathing hard. "I do those stairs four or five times a day and I'm almost sixty years older than you."

Kagan's reminisces about her years as a feminist politician presaged my own. She'd been elected as a feminist, and though there were a few other feminists in the First Knesset, none had been elected because they were feminists. Over the years, Kagan told me how it felt to be a woman and the only committed feminist in the Knesset. How her knees knocked and her legs trembled each time she walked from her seat to the podium. How easily intimidated she felt by the loud, angry, belittling voices of the hecklers. How the female MKs always over-prepared for every speech and every committee hearing, afraid to be found wanting. And finally, how hard it was to remain true to her constituency. They criticized her endlessly for every vote she cast that wasn't on a women's issue. Kagan also told of the dubious cooperation she got from other feminists in the Knesset, whose party loyalty always took precedence over their feminism. One of these women, a Labor MK, once took her aside to give her some advice. Kagan's lips smiled, but her eyes were angry as she spoke. " 'Stop talking about women all the time,' she told me. 'You're becoming a joke.' 'Fine,' I said. 'I'll stop if you start.' " Kagan never did stop talking about women all the time, but could claim only one victory for her four years in office, a victory she herself disclaimed.

Kagan sponsored a bill called the Equal Rights for Women Act. The bill granted married women equality before the law in civil matters—the right to sign contracts, own property and bring suit. Kagan's version included a provision providing for civil marriage and divorce as well. Under the Mandate, jurisdiction over "personal affairs," marriage and divorce, had been given to the religious courts of Palestine, Jewish, Christian and Moslem. With the declaration of statehood, Kagan proposed that jurisdiction over marriage and divorce be given over to civil authorities under laws ensuring the equal rights of both spouses.

On the day of the final vote of her bill, Rachel Kagan received a handwritten note from David Ben-Gurion, then Prime Minister. The note apologized for not supporting her; maintaining religious control over marriage and divorce was one of the conditions for the support of the National Religious Party. Ben-Gurion, a socialist, knew very well that he had sold out women for the support of the religious minority. Kagan's angry eyes filled with tears as she told me that she'd been forced to vote against her own bill to protest the omission of civil marriage and divorce provisions.

The Silence is Broken

Between 1973 and 1977, I thought of Rachel Kagan often. She was a singular point of reference to which I desperately clung to maintain my self-esteem and sanity. I thought of her one last time on the morning of the final vote on abortion and my last speech to the Knesset. I sat alone drinking coffee in the MKs' Dining Room, picturing Kagan, then 90. I caught my reflection in the large window that framed a view of the Jerusalem hills. A small, delicate, greying woman with a sad but belligerent expression, I, too, would vote against the legislation I had invested years in getting passed.

That afternoon, one after another in ritual procession, the women in the Knesset, feminist and nonfeminist alike, rose to the podium to proclaim a great victory for women. In a way it was. Our issue dominated the Eighth Knesset. The bill about to be enacted acknowledged the existence of abortion. The silence had been broken. Nothing had changed, but this was a promising beginning for a struggle yet to be won.

Once again, I stood alone, a feminist opposed to abortion reform. Once again, and for the last time, I spoke to the Knesset about women's right to choose. Four years of speeches made me confident this one last time. I was at home on the podium. The faces that filled the Chamber were familiar. The hecklers no longer intimidated. And I no longer had any illusions.

Section Six

Women of the Dream—
The Kibbutz and the Moshav

Was the Kibbutz
an Experiment in Social
and Sex Equality?

Marilyn P. Safir

The Kibbutz has been presented as a social experiment which succeeded in establishing communal life and property, but yet did not succeed in establishing equality of the sexes because of women's "nature" (Tiger, & Shepher, 1975). The aim of this chapter is to examine how adequately *the experiment* to establish sex equality was designed. In order to achieve this goal, we must examine the social environment in which the *kvutza* ("group" or commune which was the forerunner of the kibbutz) and the kibbutz developed during the early part of this century.

To this end, we examined historical records and found that while social and sex equality were stated goals, formal planning to create the necessary conditions for sex equality did not occur. We did not find evidence of sex equality in the formative period of the kibbutz. What was viewed as sex equality was in fact only the limited movement of women into jobs that were traditionally masculine, along with the rejection by women of a feminine or female appearance. They cut off their flowing locks, threw away their cosmetics and put their dresses, skirts and jewelry away. At the same time, both men and women accepted age-old ideas about their own and each other's biological nature and abilities.

The kibbutz was a dream of Eastern European ghetto youth. They believed that a socialist communal society would free and empower the ghetto Jew. Banding together in Zionist groups that prepared young people to return to their Jewish homeland to create communal utopias, they aspired to establish a new society in the Land of Israel in which there would be social equality devoid of exploitation. In order to achieve these goals in Palestine, production was collectivized and members received goods and services according to their needs rather than according to individual productivity. The welfare of the group took precedent over any individual. Marriage and family were rejected as reactionary, as a cornerstone of traditional economic structure and also as a threat to group solidarity; family ties were also rejected.

251

In the early years, strong prohibitions existed against marriage and child bearing (Talmon-Garber, 1972; Shepher, 1967). When couples did form, they were expected to behave towards each other in public the same way they would to any other group member. The couple never worked together and often did not receive vacations and time off together. They were usually required to share their tent with a third member. These arrangements were made to prevent what was perceived as excessive intimacy which would lead to primary identity as a couple rather than as a group. The group was to replace and to become the family for all of its members, who were expected to place the good of the group before the welfare of any individual. These restrictions were seen as necessary to the maintenance of group solidarity and centrality. As women were outnumbered by at least three to one, they were also seen as a means to prevent jealousies.

Other factors that reinforced antifamilial attitudes were inherent in the original structure of the kibbutz. In addition to being an agricultural settlement, the kibbutz was a military outpost that had to defend the Zionist enterprise as well as its own members. Talmon-Garber describes the situation:

> The kibbutzim overcame almost insurmountable difficulties by channeling most of their manpower and capital into production, and by restricting consumption and services to a bare minimum. The non-familistic division of labor was to a large extent a matter of economic necessity. Centralized communal organizations of the non-productive branches of the economy enabled the kibbutzim to reduce investment in these spheres, and to utilize fully the productive capacity of the members. It also made it possible to reduce the number of women engaged in social services and to draw many of them into active participation in the effort to advance production (1972:5) (emphasis mine).

Why were women outnumbered by more than three to one in the original communes? The answer is that in spite of the economic necessity of women entering traditional male jobs to meet the workpower needs, women settlers not only had to fight prejudice to be allowed to do men's work, they had to fight a quota which allowed them only 10 percent of the membership slots.

An analysis of the Zionist Women's movement in Palestine, from 1911 to 1927, during the period that the communes were being established, revealed some interesting trends and concepts which influenced daily life in Palestine and the early kvutzot or kibbutzim (Izraeli, 1981). Izraeli proposed that while Labor Zionism espoused social and sex equality, in fact, it was not particularly concerned with women's emancipation. Rather, creating an environment conducive to Jewish existence became the overriding goal to which all efforts were directed. Moreover, socialist theory proposed that once exploitative relationships were eliminated, and the traditional patriarchal family destroyed, woman's emancipation would automatically evolve.

During this time period, women never composed more than 30 percent of the immigrants to Palestine, as social constraints prevented all but the most committed from uprooting themselves and travelling alone to face unknown hardships. The majority of these women were activists in their native lands and immigrated to Palestine with the idea of leading productive lives as laborers, rather than remaining in the stultifying roles that bourgeois society prescribed for women. They envisioned themselves (as did their male counterparts) as pioneers and idealized manual labor and a return to the land of the Bible. However, most of these young people did not have agricultural experience and the established Jewish farmers preferred to hire skilled Arab laborers. Those farmers who were willing to make exceptions, were unrelenting in their refusal to hire women as physical laborers. While neither sex had experience in farming, it seemed natural for the farmers and the young men themselves to view men as the farmers of the future. Thus strenuous labor was seen as beyond the women's capabilities. That women were doing this type of work in the Arab villages, made no impression nor raised any challenges regarding women's traditional role in the Jewish settlements.

Women had an additional handicap: Most of them were illiterate in the Hebrew language. The men, on the other hand, had studied Hebrew for 5 or 6 years to prepare for their Bar Mitzvah ceremony. While they might not have been fluent in the spoken language, they could read and write. Upon their arrival, the majority could communicate with Jews already living in Palestine.

The commune was a way of surviving in the face of unemployment. Communes were formed for both construction and agricultural work. While they were established in both urban and rural areas, the ideal became the collective agricultural settlement which "reclaimed the land" for farming. As productive labor was perceived as manual labor, and manual labor as masculine, women were regarded as unproductive. This perception could be carried to extremes. Writing in her diary, a young woman expressed her frustration at not being allowed to work in the fields simply because she was a woman, while at the same time the kvutza allowed a consumptive man to work for one or two hours daily—usually until he collapsed and had to be carried back from the fields (Shazar, 1975).

Women were viewed as naturally suited to domestic labor, and the men were usually only willing to accept women into the kvutza to cook and to do laundry, so as to free themselves for work in the fields. Most of these young women had no real experience in domestic work. B.B. wrote of her experiences upon her arrival (at age 16/17) in Tel Aviv. She went to a workers' club and was offered a job in the kitchen. She refused, as she wanted to join a kvutza "to learn how to work." She was told that a kvutza would not accept a young girl like herself. A second strike against her was that she didn't know Hebrew. For two weeks she received no answer to her request. Then her brother arrived to tell her she had finally been accepted. But her enthusiasm over being accepted into a kvutza dampened when she discovered that she had been accepted in order to replace a woman who had worked in the kitchen and become ill (Shazar, 1975).

These early *kvutzot* consisted of 10 to 30 men and no more than one to three women. Izraeli (1981) reports that in 1909, 165 workers, only 11 of them women, were organized in *kvutzot* in the Galilee, and in 1912, 522 workers, only 30 of whom were women, were organized in Judea. Because they were so few, the women tended to "get stuck" with domestic chores. When there were no women in a *kvutza,* the men would resentfully take turns doing the domestic work.

It should be noted that cooking and laundry were performed under very difficult conditions. Food was cooked in large vats suspended over open fires, and laundry was boiled in vats containing water mixed with lye, conditions not conducive to favorable outcomes and involving frequent injuries to the workers. Not only did nonmarketable service work have low status, but it was hard, tiring and boring. In his history of Kibbutz Degania, Joseph Baratz (1954) wrote that during its initial period as a *kvutza,* Degania had six men but accepted no more than two women because it was believed that women were only capable of cooking and washing. He tells of the men working in the fields from dawn to dusk, of returning home to wash and eat and then of sitting for hours talking with great satisfaction of making the fields arable. He described the men's pride in discussing the growth of their crops, and the women's listening in jealous silence. Finally, they told the men that they, too, had come to Palestine to work in harmony with nature. But instead, they were worse off than their mothers had been in their bourgeois cities. Baratz reports that the men could not understand why the women were unhappy, as their fathers had been the bread winners while their mothers had taken care of the home. He reported that the men were unable to visualize the situation differently. . . . "Should a woman plow? Or should the men cook? What would other people think of us? We would be ashamed before everybody" (p. 52).

What is interesting in this account is that both the men and the women believed there was some validity to the men's argument. While the women insisted that things had to change, the change they envisioned was the establishment of new branches of agriculture designated for them: the purchase of cows and chickens, and a vegetable garden so there would be "real," not just domestic work for women, and so that more women could join the commune. The women of Degania eventually won this battle. The men learned that women could do farm work, . . . "that they can even plow, and they can even fight." Still, Baratz reported that every time a new branch of agriculture was introduced, someone would ask if "a man ought not to be put in charge and the women kept to housework." These personal accounts reveal the lack of consciousness of the prejudicial ideas that men and women held about themselves and about each other. Perhaps, if in those early days, the women of Degania had fought for both men and women to rotate in performing the unwanted domestic chores, the kibbutz might have evolved differently. Certainly the concept of role sharing as we know it today did not exist in this early period.

Among the early pioneers were women with feminist consciousness, and these women founded a Women Workers' Movement (Bernstein, 1987), women's training farms and women's communes. Miriam Schilowitch, an activist in Russia during the revolutionary period in which women occupied important economic and cultural positions, was amazed to find separate, parallel, institutions for women in Palestine. She had believed that . . . "the wall which divided man's work from woman's had fallen forever." She was very disappointed to perceive the insignificant role women played in Palestine and began to doubt women's capability to make contributions equal to those of the men. She decided to work in her profession as a teacher, believing that this creative work would make her contribution equal to that of her male comrades. She relates that a detour to a women's farming commune made her change her mind. There, she saw that women were able to perform as well as men, and she decided to join an agricultural training farm for women where she could work in the fields during the day, and teach the women Hebrew in the evenings (Shazar, 1975).

As the *kvutza* became a stable institution and grew in size, the question of children and childcare became an issue. Early antifamilial policies precluded planning in this area. For example, in 1938, the Welfare authorities removed a child of three from a small settlement in the Galilee that had not made formal arrangements for childcare. The child's mother had returned to work in the fields, and the child was left to its own unsupervised resources (Weiner, 1984). Joseph Baratz describes how difficult the problem was for Degania. " . . . How were the women both to work and look after the children?" It was suggested that women do nothing but look after their own families, but the women were adamant in their unwillingness to give up their communal lifestyle. It was decided that while the children "belong to their parents, the commune would share the responsibility. . . . All the women, whether single or married, should take part in looking after them, then the mothers could do other work as well" (p. 65). In fact, one woman was chosen to look after the children. The decision made at Degania became the model for the other *kvutzot,* without any analysis of the possible ramifications in the future.

With the birth of the first child, a process was set in motion that resulted in the extremes found in the modern kibbutz. At first, no plans were made for communal care of the children; then it was accepted without question that only the mother or some other woman could properly care for an infant. These same young idealists who were so concerned with establishing a new society, unquestioningly accepted the values and beliefs of their parents regarding mother-child relationships. Their equalitarian values were eroded, as more and more women were transferred from production to service work.

Nina Richter described the practices and the philosophies of communal childrearing of the thirties. A great deal of attention was given to the choice of the *woman* who would be the children's caretaker and to the atmosphere in the children's house. It was clear to all that the childcare worker should receive training as an educator. However, an untrained teacher would suffice for the under two's as . . . "her healthy, *natural mother instinct* will help her out . . . " (Shazar, 1975).

The feminization process which later occurred was the outcome of the founding generation's acceptance of women's traditional nurturant role. With the birth of the first children, women returned to childrearing functions. While role-sharing of the masculine jobs was acceptable when the economy demanded it, childrearing was automatically considered an exclusively feminine job. This was due, in part, to the necessity of nursing the infant. Bottle-feeding and sterilized milk are relatively recent innovations in Israel (fresh milk was not pasteurized and bottled until 1966), and sanitary facilities and refrigeration were entirely lacking in the early years.

Richter described the need to institute a rigid system of hygiene, to counteract the danger of infectious diseases that might result from large groups of children living together and from epidemics. She proudly noted that, during period of epidemics, children in communal living arrangements suffered less than children raised in their own families' homes. Official statistics proved not only that infant mortality was lower in the children's houses than among children brought up in individual families; they revealed that their mortality rate compared well with that of the most developed countries in the world (Shazar, 1975).

For at least the first half year after the baby's birth, the mother was bound to work close to the children's house, for too much time would be wasted for her to travel back and forth to the fields between feedings. As more children were born into the kibbutz, the process by which women left production jobs to lower-status service jobs accelerated. (Lower status, from both an ideological and economic point of view.) Very few women returned to production in a reverse process, and prejudicial beliefs about job capability were reestablished. "Men are more successful with heavy work; women are more capable in fine work. Therefore, women are more suitable in the clothing store, doing the mending," was a frequently expressed opinion.

Today, most kibbutz women work in jobs that are analogous to traditional housework. These service jobs have always had lower status than production jobs, despite the fact that they were as hard if not harder than "productive jobs." Although there are no salaries involved, clear differences have been found in the status of various jobs, with production and management jobs most highly rated (Rosner, 1974). Of the service jobs, *metaplot* (childcare workers) and nurses have higher status than persons employed in food preparation or clothing care (Talmon-Garber, 1972). Talmon-Garber said that because jobs like *metaplot* or nurses require long training and specialization, they tend to become permanent assignments. This, in turn, increases competition for such positions, causing permanent devaluation of unspecialized jobs. The unspecialized tasks tend to be "arduous, monotonous or full of tension." If a woman must prepare food for her family, it is relatively easy to plan a menu to the taste of all. However, if she is responsible for preparing meals for 500, she is bound to meet with complaints and dissatisfaction. This, in turn, tends to reduce job satisfaction and increase work tension.

It is relevant at this point to examine the educational aspirations of kibbutz members, as advanced education opens options for jobs requiring high levels of skills (i.e., management and teaching). Rosner et al. (1978) studied second generation kibbutz members and found that the majority of both sexes were interested in continuing their education. Most cited a preference for study courses connected with their current (or possible) future jobs, but two-thirds expressed interest in a general education. Men were more optimistic about their chances of fulfilling their educational aspirations than women were, even though women's academic aspirations were lower than men's to begin with. Women's lack of of optimism proved to be realistic. A follow-up study found that the men's optimism was justified. We may hypothesize that women's disappointment in this area results in a lowering of their aspirations.

Marilyn Safir (1975), Martha S. T. Mednick (1975) and Michael Nathan (1985) have suggested that kibbutz women may turn to traditionally more feminine roles as compensation for their limited and less attractive job choices, or to reduce cognitive dissonance. For example, although kibbutz education encourages women to work in agriculture (Gerson, 1968), most *prefer* to work in education, while in fact *most work* in service areas. Michal Palgi (1976) found that women who worked in agriculture or industry were not particularly satisfied, felt that they were not making the best use of their skills and abilities, and did not hold positions of responsibility. In fact, many of the women's jobs were at the lowest echelons. Thus it was not surprising that research with second-generation kibbutz members revealed that men assigned more importance to work and women, to family. This difference between men and women is greater among those who were born on the kibbutz (second generation) than those who joined the kibbutz (first generation) (Ben-David, Ya'acov 1975; Leviatan, Uri 1976).

We have seen that women's production jobs are generally unskilled, and do not lead to advancement. Service jobs are relatively specific and do not prepare women for leadership roles in the kibbutz structure. This can easily result in lowered aspirations and further channeling of energy into "feminine" pursuits, resulting in a vicious cycle.

In the 1950s and 1960s, Yonina Talmon-Garber found that women were more likely than men to leave the kibbutz, were more likely to be dissatisfied with their jobs, and to experience stress (see Talmon-Garber, 1972). Over a decade later, Tiger and Shepher (1975) found that only 15 percent of women expressed dissatisfaction with their jobs, even though an even higher percent were doing the same type of work they had done ten to fifteen years earlier. We suggest that the increasing movement to nurturant roles resulted in women experiencing cognitive dissonance, and that to justify the time absorbed by childcare tasks, the women themselves began to increase their identification with traditional feminine roles by giving them more positive, attractive images. Contemporary kibbutz women have demanded a return to family sleeping arrangements instead of children sleeping in children's houses. Perhaps kibbutz women are demanding more time with their children in order to give themselves a feeling of increased importance or satisfaction, thereby reducing their cognitive dissonance.

Today, the kibbutz is extremely child centered and motherhood is a high status "profession." Children are seen as an important natural resource of the kibbutz, as practically the only way to increase the kibbutz population. The kibbutz family is composed of 4+ children, while the city family has an average of 2.8 children. The increase in family size has resulted in both a further increase of service related jobs and in children sleeping with their parents rather than in children's houses. Tiger and Shepher (1975) suggested that this latter change resulted from maternal needs. In addition to the hypotheses proposed above, it seems reasonable to assume that it is easier to put four children to sleep in one house than to spend two to three hours putting four children to sleep in four different children's houses. The economic prosperity of the kibbutz is also a factor in the change. A large family needs more living space. In the early days, kibbutzim could not afford to build large apartments. Today, many kibbutzim have four room apartments with small kitchens to accommodate family sleeping arrangements.

Those kibbutz women who are unsuccessful in reducing their dissonance by increasing the value of feminine pursuits should theoretically experience psychological distress. Indeed, Talmon-Garber (1972) found that the dissatisfaction of the wife was a major factor in a family leaving the kibbutz. This was generally accepted as true during the period that Tiger and Shepher (1975) collected their data and true even today. Although exact figures are lacking, we estimate that the wife makes this decision in over 80 percent of the cases in which the family leaves the kibbutz.

The kibbutz experiment was successful in removing traditional economic barriers to equality. However, psychological barriers to equality resulted in polarization of men's and women's work. Both men and women contributed to the institutionalization and stereotyping of what work is suitable for men and for women—without regard to the individual's ability or interest. This resulted in a socialization process that further polarized job choice.

The kibbutz has, however, made a number of contributions to the idea of social equality in the family. Rosner and Palgi (1989) have shown that there is much less role differentiation by sex within the kibbutz family than is typical in Western society. Unlike the traditional patriarchical family, wives are not economically dependent on their husbands, nor are they dependent on them for social status. Each adult is a full and independent member of the kibbutz. Each individual receives the same economic remuneration as all men and women are workers, but children are the economic responsibility of the group. The responsibility for caring for and raising children is also shared by the kibbutz.

The uniqueness of the kibbutz, with its continuing concern for the well-being of all its members, and the continuous self examination through research, discussion and formulation for change, results in a dynamic structure that is in continual flux and development. Rosner et al. (1978) have pointed out that new developments and technological changes have reduced manpower needs in the kibbutz production branches. Polarization by sex may be reduced due to the shifting of men and women to new jobs that have recently been created, or will be created. Sex typing of jobs will also decrease when work that has little intrinsic interest (i.e., laundry, dining hall service, clothing warehouse) is really temporary and all members rotate at them for short periods. Finally, when men and women are psychologically free and able to move into what were once considered "masculine" or "feminine" jobs according to their own interests and not their sex, the goal of sex equality may one day be achieved.

REFERENCES

Baratz, Joseph A. (1954) *A Village by the Jordan: Story of Degania.* London: Hawill (reprinted in 1975); also Tel Aviv: Ihud Habonim (1960).

Ben-David, Ya'acov (1975) *Work and Education on the Kibbutz: Reality and Aspirations.* Rehovot: The Center for Research of Urban and Rural Settlements (Hebrew).

Bernstein, Deborah (1987) *The Struggle for Equality: Urban Women Workers in Prestate Israeli Society.* New York: Praeger.

Gerson, Menachem (1956) "The Attitude of Girls to Work." *Hedim* 10:144.

Izraeli, Dafna (1981) "The Zionist Women's Movement in Palestine, 1911–1927." *Signs,* 6.

Leviatan, Uri (1976) "The Place of Work in the Life of the Kibbutz Female Member." *The Kibbutz* 3–4: 92–109 (Hebrew).

Mednick, Martha S. T. (1975) "Social Change and Sex-Role Inertia: The Case of the Kibbutz." In Mednick, M. T. S., Tangri, S. S., and Hoffman, L. W. (eds.). *Women and Achievement.* New York: John Wiley and Sons.

Nathan, Michael (1985) "Counterrevolution Without Revolution." In Palgi, M., Blasi, J., Rosner, M., and Safir, M. (eds.). *Sexual Equality: The Israeli Kibbutz Tests the Theories.* Kibbutz Studies Book Series, Norwood, PA.: Norwood Editions, Vol. VI; 221–226.

Palgi, Michal (1976) "Sex Differences in the Domain of Work in the Kibbutz." *The Kibbutz* 3–4: 114–129 (Hebrew).

Rosner, Menachem and Palgi, Michal (1989) "Sexual Equality in the Kibbutz: A Retreat or a Change of Significance?" *The Kibbutz* 3–4: 149–185 (Hebrew).

Rosner, Menachem; Ben-David, Ya'acov; Avnat, A.; Cohen, N.; Leviatan, Uri (1978) *The Second Generation in the Kibbutz*. Tel Aviv: Sifriat Poalim; also in English, Cambridge, MA: Harvard University, Project for Kibbutz Studies Monograph.

Safir, Marilyn P. (1975) "Nature or Nurture: The Question of the Kibbutz." Paper presented at the International Council of Psychologists Conference, Paris.

Shazar, Rachel K. (1975) *The Ploughwoman*. New York: Herzl Press (originally published in 1932).

Shepher, Joseph (1967) *The Effect of Sleeping Arrangements of Children in the Kibbutz on Its Social Structure*. Kibbutz Movement (Hebrew).

Talmon-Garber, Yonina (1972) *Family and Community in the Kibbutz*. Cambridge: Harvard University Press.

Tiger, Lionel, and Shepher, Joseph (1975) *Women in the Kibbutz*. New York: Harcourt Brace Jovanovich.

Weiner, Anita (1984) *Away From Home: Child Placement in the Land of Israel During the British Mandate*. Ramat Gan: Kibbutz haMeuehad–Sifriat Poalim (Hebrew).

Motherhood in the Kibbutz

Michal Palgi

The attitudes of kibbutz society towards the family and motherhood have undergone far-reaching changes. In the early years, in order to survive and realize its ideology, the kibbutz developed a number of mechanisms to place the family at its periphery: the "primus" (a small home burner), the name given to additional kibbutz member(s) who shared a couple's tent or room, making intimacy difficult (Basevitch, 1981, 1987); the absence of formal weddings; the rejection of symbols of family or family ties like the appellations "mother" or "father" (Tiger and Shepher, 1975); and the suppression of motherhood and the kibbutz acquisition of parental rights. The attitude towards maternity was not negative but restrictive. Some kibbutzim prohibited women from having children, but the prohibition was regarded as temporary. The decision was a collective one, taken at a time when the majority of kibbutz members were men. The real sanctions were against the seclusion of the family and the formation of a unit that would compete with the collective for the loyalty of its members (Talmon-Garber, 1972).

Once having children was legitimized, an ideology of childcare was developed. The most dominant theme was the expressed distrust of the family as educator. The collective assumed this role; it chose the individuals it believed most suited to educate the children. The children spent most of their waking and sleeping hours with their peers and *metaplot* (childcare workers) in the children's houses and little time with their parents. Parents were allowed to spend a few hours each afternoon with their children, from 5:00 p.m. The children (until they began high school) would come to their parents' apartment, at which time both parents focused all their attention on them, playing, reading, talking or walking together with them. At 7:00 p.m. the children went back to the children's houses, where they were fed, washed and put to bed by the *metapelet*.

During those early days, mothers could visit their babies only if they breastfed them. Otherwise, there was no feasible reason for their visiting during the day. Women who had milk also nursed babies whose mothers had no milk, even if it meant that their own babies received less food. The decision as to who would nurse only her own baby and who would nurse an

261

additional baby (and sometimes two) was made by the babies' nurse (Palgi, 1988). Even in the 1960s it was quite common to meet a new mother and ask her, "Are you a good mother?" meaning, "Do you breastfeed? A good mother breastfeeds." Mothers had to obtain special permission from nurses to visit their babies at irregular times or to take them out of the infants' house (this was permitted only after the infant was six months old). During epidemics or winter colds, only one parent was permitted to visit the child. The babies' nurse was the sole authority on how to raise children (Palgi, 1988). In the late 1950s and early 1960s Melford E. Spiro (1958) and Albert I. Rabin (1965) studied the effects of intermittent mothering on the babies in order to determine if the children suffered from maternal deprivation. They argued that kibbutz children received equal if not more care from the babies' nurse than they would have from the mothers. While they found that kibbutz born children were less emotionally stable during the first year of their life than children born outside the kibbutz, in later years, these differences disappeared. However, none of the researchers addressed the issue of the effect of enforced intermittent mothering on self-esteem, self-assurance and fulfillment of the mothers. It is my belief that this is one of the major factors explaining the familistic behavior and attitudes of kibbutz mothers in later periods. No in-depth research has been conducted on this issue.

The turning point came after the Second World War, when the kibbutzim doubled or tripled in size. Many new immigrants joined, some with different ideologies, and most with an extraordinary devotion to the family, often as a consequence of the Holocaust. The kibbutz was no longer a small, homogeneous community, and kibbutz members began to long for intimacy. Environmental conditions had improved, and there was no longer any danger to children.

In recent years, life in the infants' house has become more flexible. Mothers and fathers can visit whenever they like. Time spent with parents in the afternoon has increased and they have become responsible for preparing evening meals for their children and putting them to bed. This process of change, initiated in the 1950s, began to take a different direction at the beginning of the 1960s. Parents, primarily women, decided that they wanted their children at home with them. It began with the baby sleeping at home for the first 6 weeks, then for 3 to 6 months, a year, and, eventually, in some kibbutzim, until the children were 14 and even 18 years old.

In 1966, the Kibbutz Artzi Movement made a policy change that further legitimized parenting, or, rather, mothering, for from the moment that the kibbutz began to relinquish parental rights and responsibility, there was never any question but that all responsibility revolved around the mother. It called a national conference to discuss issues concerning women. Prior to the conference, studies had shown (Rosner, 1967) that women spent more time than men working in the household, and that women wanted to see their children during the day as well as after work. Concerned that kibbutz women were beginning to resemble their sisters in the West by shouldering a double burden of work inside and outside the home, participants decided to reduce a mother's working day from 8 to 7 hours (not a father's working day). Thus the movement institutionalized kibbutz women's responsibility for childcare and services in the home. Fathers were not regarded as having an equal share of the responsibility; they were urged simply to help out (Kibbutz Artzi, 1966).

A second decision taken at the conference had to do with what came to be known as the "love hour." In response to women's unhappiness at not seeing their children during the day, it was decided to allow each mother with a child under the age of one year to visit her infant for half an hour in the middle of the morning. The importance of the "love hour" increased over the years. It became sacred; indeed, a "good" mother would not miss this hour with her child. The half hour was increased to 1 hour, and the one-year age limit was removed. Mothers began to visit their children in kindergarten and sometimes even in school. Work in the children's houses became organized around the "love hour," because the workers themselves were mothers who wanted to visit their own children.

At the beginning of the 1960s, new mothers had 6 weeks' maternity leave, after which they started working 4 hours a day. The other 4 hours were devoted to looking after the baby (at the morning feed, at lunch, and in the evening). When the baby was six months old, the mother worked 6 hours, and by the time the baby was eight months old, she worked a full day. After the 1966 conference, a demand arose for shorter working hours for mothers of newborns. As a result, today, 25 years later, a new mother works only 4 hours a day until the baby is six months old. In kibbutzim where children sleep collectively, she starts working her full 7 hours when the baby is two and a half; until that time, she receives a half-hour reduction from work for the "love hour." In kibbutzim where the children sleep with their families, the mother usually never returns to work 7 hours a day, but rather works only 6 or 6 and a half hours, according to the norms in her kibbutz. In 1982, an attempt was made by Palgi to introduce a change so that both parents could share in childcare hours, giving women the chance to continue with their careers if they so desired, and giving men the opportunity to experience closer contact with their children from an early age. The proposal was rejected by kibbutz representatives (Silver, 1984).

The birth rate in the kibbutzim has increased rapidly. The first generation had between two and three children per family (average 2.4), the second generation between three and four (average 3.4), though five children was not a unique phenomenon. There are indications that the birth rate of the third and fourth generation is lower, but the change is not significant. The rate of birth in the 16 religious kibbutzim is very high, the average being between five and six children. As the kibbutz birth rate rose, so did the need for workers in education and services (Adar and Lewis, 1988; Palgi et al., 1983).

Special mechanisms were used to ensure women's contributions to these sectors. Each kibbutz found its own formula. The basic principle was that each woman with an infant had to serve her time in education or in services (not the father). It was argued that the good of the baby and the welfare of the kibbutz demanded it. On one kibbutz, for example, the Education Committee proposed that every woman who gave birth be required to work in education for 2 years. The proposal was opposed by women with professions not connected to education or services. They argued that their professional careers would be ruined if they left for 2 years after each birth, especially as they planned to have three or four children. It was also opposed by two women who planned university studies. They claimed that they could visit their one-year old children at 7:00 in the morning and then at 3:00 in the afternoon, when they returned from their studies. The only time they would "miss" being with their children would be the famous "love hour." In reply, one of the initiators of the proposal, who was also an education worker, stated: "My main area of knowledge is education. This is a field in which I am an expert, and I can tell you all that a child will suffer irreversible damage if its mother (not its father!) is not present during the day." The fact that the two women's husbands were willing to come to visit the children during the day did not satisfy the committee. Following a heated discussion, the kibbutz accepted the recommendation of the Education Committee (Palgi, 1988).

Another mechanism to ensure women's contribution to education and services was to invoke in them guilt feelings if they did not attend to their infants during the day. It was impressed upon each of them, in numerous ways, that they did not properly fulfill their roles as mothers. It was not unusual for a mother who came only at the end of the day, to hear that her child had been very unhappy because of her absence. Negative public opinion, in a society based on social rather than material rewards is quite stress-inducing. A third mechanism was to demand that women who did not work in education substitute for sick or absent education workers. This was formalized in many kibbutzim, as a result of which each woman had to devote a day or two a week to education. In addition, they also had to fill in for longer periods of time, two or more weeks a year, when a *metapelet* was absent. "You are a mother and therefore have to help out," was and still is a common exhortation—no such demands are addressed to the father.

A process that has weakened the importance of the "love hour" but has bound mothers even more to the kibbutz premises is the change in children's sleeping arrangements. The discussions for and against familial sleeping arrangements were often fierce. The main argument brought by women for changing the system was that it is only natural for a child to sleep in the same house as her or his mother. It was postulated that a woman's fulfillment as a mother was impaired by this "unnatural" separation from her children during the night (Palgi, 1982). In some kibbutzim, parents simply took their children home, and in others, they threatened to leave the kibbutz if the system was not changed. The consequence was increased childcare for mothers. When children sleep with their parents, the latter cannot obtain outside help to look after them, because the kibbutz is based on self-labor. The father, who usually works in production, leaves home for work at 5:00 in the morning, while the children are still asleep and the children's house is closed. The mothers wake the children and bring them to the children's houses, which open at around 7:00 a.m. If the mother has to start work earlier, or to travel to work, she is in trouble. She might make an arrangement with her husband, who in turn might be criticized for not taking his work seriously enough, or she might have an arrangement with a neighbor or a grandmother. She would also have to be back in time to pick up her young children, as the kibbutz has allotted to her (and not to her husband) shorter working hours.

The importance of the family has increased considerably. This can be seen both in formal structural changes, like the change in sleeping arrangements, and in research findings over the years (Zamir, 1986; Palgi and Rosner, 1983; Palgi, 1976; Talmon-Garber, 1972; Rosner, 1967). One result is that second and third generation women believe that their main aim in life is to look after their families. They do not complain of arrangements that bind them to the family and feel it is only right that the main burden of childraising and housekeeping is on them (Zamir, 1986). In a survey of divorced families in the kibbutz movement, Palgi et al. (1985) found that in kibbutzim with family sleeping, the children sleep mainly in the mothers' houses. This means that she is the one who puts them to bed and who babysits for them, while the father is free from these duties. It also means that she has less privacy, as kibbutz apartments are very small. In kibbutzim with collective sleeping, it was found that there was more equal sharing between the parents in the task of putting the children to bed. Another study (Palgi, 1982) that looked into the differences in the roles of fathers and mothers with different sleeping arrangements found that in kibbutzim where the children sleep with their families, fathers play a more active role than they do in kibbutzim where the children sleep in the children's houses. They are more active within the family and also more punitive. Not many differences were found between the two systems with regard to mothering. One significant difference is that mothers in kibbutzim with family sleeping are more occupied within the family and less interested in being involved in the public life of the kibbutz. In short, the change in sleeping arrangements has not solved the equality problems as some hoped it would (Ben-Rafael and Weitman, 1984). It caused both women and men to be more involved in parenting, but it tied women down to their families and to the kibbutz more than in the past. As a result, they are now less able to study and develop careers. In addition, no evidence has been found that women are more satisfied with their lives or with motherhood in kibbutzim with family sleeping arrangements (Palgi, 1989).

To conclude, the kibbutz attempted to create a new type of motherhood, one that concentrated on the expressive side of the relationship with children and delegated both physical care and education to kibbutz representatives. This was done in order to free women for work and public activities. It did not take into consideration the possibility that while women were freed from housework within the privacy of their households, they would be doing it as part of their public duties. This, of course, was not predetermined but a result of the unwillingness of both men and women to make the effort to involve men in service work and education. A historical analysis of the development of the role of motherhood in the kibbutz shows that the model aspired to was not realized, and that instead, a rigid and enslaving one evolved. This role is similar in many ways to the traditional one. It limits women's opportunities for self-realization and for the optimal utilization of their capabilities.

Women receive positive reinforcement from all members of the kibbutz, men and women alike, for playing the role assigned to them and for keeping the system stable. They are the ones who instigated changes in the direction of increasing the centrality of the family and their focal role in it. They are also the ones who abhorred any suggestions of feminist activity that might alter the situation. This can be explained, at least partially, by the exchange system that developed in the kibbutzim. Women take care of home and children (even if this is organized collectively) and men take care of economics, security, and political affairs. The "goods" each side provides were apparently determined by traditional concepts that guided even the founders of the kibbutzim. The ideological justification for this traditional exchange was made possible by the importance attached to "the equal value of all work" and by the collectivization of housework. It was maintained that all work done in the kibbutz had equal value. There was no "more important" and "less important" work. Any attempt to change the "goods" exchanged would have appeared as a threat to the other side. Therefore there was never any active opposition from either men or women to increasing the role of women as mothers, but there was opposition to attempts to "cross the occupational or parental lines" on the part of both men and women.

REFERENCES

Adar, Gila and Lewis, Chana (1988) *Kibbutz Women*. Yad Tabenkin and the Institute for Social Research of the Kibbutz, Haifa University (Hebrew).

Basevitch, Lilia (1981) *If Only an Echo*. Tel Aviv: Hakkibutz Hameuchad (Hebrew).

Basevitch, Lilia (1987) *In a Race Against Time*. Tel Aviv: Hakkibutz Hameuchad (Hebrew).

Ben-Rafael, Eliezer and Weitman, Sasha (1984) "The Reconstitution of the Family in the Kibbutz." *Archives Europeennes de Sociologie* 25(1): 1–27.

Kibbutz, Artzi (1966) Decisions of the Convention on Women, Tel Aviv.

Palgi, Michal (1976) "The Commitment of Women to Kibbutz Life." M.A. Thesis, Haifa University (Hebrew).

Palgi, Michal (1988) "Interviews with Kibbutz Founders." Unpublished manuscript.

Palgi, Michal (1989) "Kibbutz Survey on Social Indicators." Unpublished manuscript.

Palgi, Michal; Blasi, Joseph R.; Rosner, Menachem; Safir, Marilyn (eds.) (1983) *Sexual Equality; The Israeli Kibbutz Tests the Theories.* Pennsylvania: Norwood Editions.

Palgi, Michal and Rosner, Menachem (1983) "Equality Between the Sexes in the Kibbutz: Regression or Changed Meaning?" In: Palgi, M., Blasi, J. R., Rosner, M. and Safir, M. (eds.). *Sexual Equality: The Israeli Kibbutz Tests the Theories.* Pennsylvania: Norwood Editions; 255–296.

Palgi, Michal; Rosner, Menachem; Shoham, Cheryl; Kaufman, Mordechai (1985) *A Survey of Divorce in the Kibbutz Movement, Institute for the Study and Research of the Kibbutz and the Cooperative Idea.* Haifa University (Hebrew).

Palgi, Yair (1982) "The Effect of Children's Sleeping Arrangements in the Kibbutzim on the Perception of Family Environment." M.A. Thesis, Tel-Aviv University (Hebrew).

Rabin, Albert I. (1965) *Growing Up in the Kibbutz.* New York: Springer.

Rosner, Menachem (1967) *Report on the Woman Member Study in the Kibbutz.* Givat Haviva (Hebrew).

Silver, Vivian (ed.) (1984) *Male and Female Created He Them.* Ramat Efal: Yad Tabenkin (Hebrew).

Spiro, Melford, E. (1958) *Children of the Kibbutz.* Cambridge, MA: Harvard University Press.

Talmon-Garber, Yonina (1972) *Family and Community in the Kibbutz.* Cambridge, MA: Harvard University Press.

Tiger, Lionel and Shepher, Joseph (1975) *Women in the Kibbutz.* New York: Harcourt Brace Jovanovich.

Zamir, Aviva (1986) *Mothers and Daughters: Interviews with Kibbutz Women.* Pennsylvania: Norwood Editions.

MOTHERHOOD: AN EARLY
KIBBUTZ EXPERIENCE

Malka is an 80 year old woman who was among the founders of a *kvutza* (1933) and a kibbutz (1934). She was born in Lithuania in 1908 and immigrated with her family in 1920. She began working on the roads but relinquished this job for work in the children's kitchen. The following narrative is from an interview conducted by Michal Palgi in 1988.

"It was early in 1935 that I was sure that I was pregnant. For the last three months I had feared yet hoped that this was my condition. There was no time to think about it, as we were constantly attacked by surrounding Bedouin tribes, and the burden of work and guarding was too exhausting . . . Also, my friend had a bout of fever. For three weeks, his temperature rose to dangerous heights and then fell again as I stood helpless beside his bedstead trying to make him more comfortable. Every night he mumbled incoherently, calling alternately for his mother and me. This, together with the work in the summer heat and the guard duty, left little time for rest. At first I had attributed my nausea and fainting spells to over-exhaustion—but now I was sure. What was I to do? The Kibbutz had decided that no children were to be born. G. had an abortion, also T., but F. had decided to leave the Kibbutz and have her child.

"Talking the issue over with my friend, we decided to fight the decision. I went to my best friend, Sarah, and talked it over with her. She was horrified. She thought there was no way I could keep the baby and stay in the Kibbutz. I called a meeting of all 23 members—five women and 18 men. How could I make them understand my yearning for this baby? What arguments could I use to convince them? My friend—the father to be—was not as sure as I that it was right to contest the decision. I was almost alone in my fight . . .

"People gathered outside the wooden shack that was our dinning-room. Inside was too hot, outside the mosquitoes bit us mercilessly . . . They were all young people with old faces. . . . I knew the decision we had to make was not easy, and that it would be considered most seriously—but my chances were few, there were too many odds against me . . . . Standing there, my eyes red and puffy, my voice trembling, I explained my yearnings for this unborn child. I was 25, had already miscarried twice and could not bear to lose this baby. On the other hand, I could not bear to leave the Kibbutz. I had been through so many hardships and joys with this group—it was the family I had acquired here. It replaced, in many ways, the family I had left in Galicia. They were not only good friends but also brothers and sisters, fathers and mothers to me. I appealed to their good sense and mercy and tried to convince them that the security, health and economic situation were such that we could afford to bring up children in the Kibbutz.

268

"Many arguments were raised against my request. S. said that the situation had not improved, and he expected it to worsen. As responsible adults, how could we allow a baby to suffer such perils? It would be utterly irresponsible, a surrender to the whims of someone who could not be rational about the issue. P. did not agree with him. He thought that a new baby might bring new hope and happiness to the community. T. could not imagine how we would look after this baby. We had no experience. She suggested I leave the Kibbutz for a few years and come back when the baby was older. S. could not understand how we could dismiss a working member so easily. 'We need you in the cow-sheds,' he said. 'We can't afford to have a baby now. There is no housing for it, no fit food, no clothing. If you have the baby, you won't be able to work and will only be a burden on the community. . . .' The discussion continued into the early hours of the morning. Only when it was clear that I was not going to give up on that baby, a decision was reached. I was to leave the Kibbutz for a year. During that time, arrangements would be made in the Kibbutz for the baby."

Male and Female Created
He Them

Vivian Silver

Life on a kibbutz leaves much to be desired for women. Here is a society firmly divided along gender lines both in work and in management. Many women are dissatisfied with their work and play a limited and often passive role in community life. In the Kibbutz Federations, the umbrella organizations of the two major kibbutz movements, this division is even more acute.

Kibbutz members often refuse to acknowledge that a problem exists. They claim the kibbutz offers equal opportunities to both men and women, according to the principle "from each according to his ability, to each according to his needs." In their view, kibbutz women simply don't take advantage of existing opportunities. This perspective, however, ignores the fact that the starting point for girls is not the same as that for boys. From infancy, kibbutz children are clearly guided (intentionally or unintentionally) in certain directions. They grow up in a gender polarized community and they internalize the messages they receive, believing this to be the natural state of affairs. From an early age, both girls and boys are presented with choices that are gender specified, be it in formal studies, after school interest groups or work places, the range being much more limited for girls than for boys. The problem, then, lies in a society's ability to recognize the latent potential of each individual, without defining this potential according to its own bias. People are often placed in jobs without thought as to where their talents lie, and before they have had a chance to discover them. In a kibbutz, a person's job suitability is judged, by and large, by his or her sex. Girls automatically grow up to be cooks and childcare workers. Boys become farmers, engineers and managers.

There is no need to conduct a sociological study to determine that there is a clear division between men's and women's work in the kibbutz. Eighty percent of women work in education or in services, and this figure has not changed significantly over the past 15 years (Tiger and Shepher, 1975; Adar

---

An earlier version of this chapter originally appeared in Hebrew as the introduction to Male and Female Created He Them. (1984). Ramat Effal: Yad Tabenkin.

and Lewis, 1988). Most second generation men (91%) work in production, as opposed to 15.5 percent of second generation women (Ben David, 1975).

In Amia Lieblich's *Kibbutz Makom* (1981), a record of three kibbutz generations, the limited choice of jobs appears again and again as a major source of distress to women. An explanation for the large number of women working in childcare lies in the high ratio of *metaplot* to children (1:3) that has been the norm on most kibbutzim. Given the unchallenged assumption that the pool of educators is to be drawn from women aged 20 to 45, almost all women in that age group are required to work in education. Within this group, however, are also the women who take a year's leave of absence after the army, go out to study, and bear children. The educational system thus suffers a chronic shortage of workers. In addition, the situation of a labor pool based on gender and not on skill, desire or acquired knowledge, lowers the prestige of education as work on kibbutz. A woman who works with children against her will invariably sees diapers, the floor and dishes to be central to her job. She may well seek excuses to be absent, thereby contributing to the negative image of women on kibbutz. This is not to deny that many people do find education to be a fulfilling profession. The crucial qualitative factor remains choice.

The obvious question, of course, is where do men fit into this picture? Despite the Kibbutz Artzi's 1980 decision that 20 percent of all workers in education and service branches were to be men, in reality this goal is far from being accomplished. Part of the explanation lies in the belief that men cannot be freed from "productive" labor.

Ironically, real hope for change for women lies in the economic crisis the kibbutz movements are currently facing. The kibbutz economy can no longer afford to maintain small groups of children with so many *metaplot;* small groups are merging into larger ones, releasing women from childcare to the general work roster. There is now pressure on women to enter income-producing branches, or, alternatively, to transform traditional service branches into small businesses. Examples abound. On one kibbutz, women opened a daycare business for children from the neighboring city. On other kibbutzim, children's houses are taking in city children for pay. Kibbutz women have turned their sewing rooms into professional ventures by selling clothes to the general public, and kibbutz kitchens have begun catering outside affairs. As successful as these enterprises may be, they alone cannot provide the solution for women and work. There must be a breakthrough for those women who still do not view clothing, food or education as desired professions, even if they are income producing.

Generally because there is a correlation between the job one does and the kind of community positions one fills, women's range of influence on the kibbutz is limited to specific areas. This can be seen in a survey of 170 kibbutzim conducted between 1984 and 1986; it was found that 79 percent of the coordinators of health and education committees were women. Only 12 percent of the economic and management committees were headed by women. Slightly more men than women headed social and cultural committees: 52 percent, as opposed to 48 percent. Secretariats were comprised of two men for every woman (Adar, 1989).

Statistics on central management are no less revealing. While 34.5 percent of kibbutz secretaries-general are women (in itself a significant increase over the past decade), only 5.5 percent of business and finance managers are women (Adar and Lewis, 1988). Within the kibbutz movement, the picture is even gloomier. In 1981, no department of the United Kibbutz Federation was headed by a woman. In 1985, two women were department heads: one directed the Department of Education, and the other the Youth Department. In 1989, following an internal structural reorganization, again no women can be found heading departments, though women do head department sub-divisions.

Although attitudes on the kibbutz further discourage the initiative of women who might consider nonstereotypical jobs kibbutz norms can be dynamic. At a conference on sex equality at Givat Haviva, it was revealed that in kibbutzim that had never had a woman treasurer, the position was considered a man's job. In kibbutzim in which women had served as treasurers, the job was seen as sex neutral (Safir, 1981). Could this development apply to other positions as well? When more women are placed in men's jobs, and more men in women's jobs, new norms may be created.

However, from the time toddlers go for walks with their *metaplot,* they see the role models that will influence their own choices at a later age: Daddy on a tractor or production line in the factory and Mommy in the kitchen, children's houses or laundry. Their books are full of similar stereotypes, and the division of labor at home, though more equal than that in Western society (Rosner and Palgi, 1983), confirms their impression that it is mainly the mother who has responsibility for the house and family, while the father, at best, is willing to help her.

In 1978, Irit Lester studied the socialization of kibbutz children aged three to ten. The children were given a group of pictures to view. In each picture there was an indistinct figure of a person whose sex was not clear. The children were asked to determine the sex of each figure. Three- and four-year-olds, both boys and girls, tended to identify the workers in the dining hall as either men or women. Eight- and ten-year-olds, on the other hand, saw the same figures as women. Furthermore, they identified the sex of figures in pictures of the chicken run, the cowshed, the dining hall, the fields and the children's house according to the existing division of labor between men and women on kibbutz. By the time they were eight years old, these children had already internalized their observations of adult work roles.

The imbalance persists through adolescence. Studies have shown that compared to kibbutz boys, and girls and boys in the city, kibbutz girls fall short in their professional aspirations (Livne, 1982), in their ego development (Birnbaum and Safir, 1981), and in their level of self-confidence, originality and creativity (Edilist, 1980). They are significantly less androgynous than city girls (Ellings, Safir and Lieblich, 1981). Another study (Alon, 1975) revealed that kibbutz high school girls perceived that they were held in low esteem by the group and had a significantly lower self-esteem than boys. Girls were found to be more concerned than boys about avoiding failure and more sensitive to criticism. These findings might explain why at a later age kibbutz women shy away from central leadership roles.

Kibbutz girls tend to delay choosing an occupation, compared with kibbutz boys and city girls and boys, and they have lower aspirations as well. According to Birnbaum & Safir (1981) one of the reasons the kibbutz girl postpones choosing an occupation is because she is aware of a possible conflict between her choice and her remaining on the kibbutz. This delay allows her to avoid confronting her fear that a gap may exist between what she would like to do and what she will be expected to do. Livne found a strong correlation between an individual's choice of occupation and the occupation of his or her parents of corresponding sex. Thus, Livne contends, there is a direct correlation between the daughter's inability to choose a vocation and her mother's lack of identification with her work (1982).

Work is an integral part of the kibbutz educational system. By the end of elementary school, children begin to work part-time, progressing in the later grades to a full day a week or, alternately, two hours each day. For kibbutz girls, this can be a disillusioning experience, as can be seen by the following excerpt from a letter written by twelfth graders on a kibbutz.

> "We began working when we were in the fifth grade. As a matter of course, the girls were assigned to the children's houses and the kitchen, while the boys were sent to the cowshed, the sheep pen and the fields. It all seemed so natural that it never entered our minds that things could be different. But as the years went by, something odd happened. The boys became steady workers in their branches, acquired experience and skills, and even took pride in their work. The girls' situation is different. We wander from the children's house to the infant's house, from the dining hall to the kitchen, according to where we are needed on any particular day. By the time a girl gets used to a place of work—and that is important, especially if she's working with children—she is moved to a new place. We wouldn't complain if the situation were temporary, for a year or two, but six or seven years of impermanence . . . . "

In a 1981 study on the relationship between young people and the kibbutz, boys were found to have stronger ties than girls (Orchen, 1982). The boys were more involved in kibbutz affairs, and more of them intended to live there. When asked about the advantages and disadvantages of living on a kibbutz, more boys than girls pointed out advantages and more girls than boys pointed out disadvantages. Girls more often than boys stressed the importance of creativity and personality development, but they had lower hopes of achieving a creative life than the boys.

The obstacles to overcome in order to achieve gender equality are many. Socialization and formal education, in addition to conventional work assignments for adolescents, pave the way for an adult society with a sexist division of labor. The heavy demands of the kibbutz educational system, coupled with the assumption that education is women's work, create a limited occupational range for women. And this results in few women taking on central leadership roles. The cycle is completed when, for lack of alternative role models, kibbutz children learn to accept the mold as proper and natural.

Of course, there are exceptions. On almost every kibbutz one will find a woman who has either been finance manager, worked in the fields, or even managed a kibbutz industry. A number of women are public personalities. Paradoxically, the exceptions often hamper the possibility for change. These women are viewed as superwomen, making it difficult for the average woman to identify with them as role models. They see the price some pay, be it in terms of social acceptability, strains on their family life, or long working hours.

According to Martha Mednick (1975), another dynamic may be at work: When the average kibbutz woman sees how other women have succeeded, she says to herself, "If I am unable to make of my life what I really want, that proves I am not capable or talented." Such explanations free the kibbutz from all responsibility, and cause the women to seek the cause of their dissatisfaction within themselves. Women do not see themselves as a group who together can make changes. The few women who "have made it," are often unable to understand why all the others are stuck. Besides the "queen bee syndrome," they are unsympathetic to the average woman's fears and lack of self-confidence.

Possible directions for change have been suggested. If the present division of labor is accepted as a given, then it has been proposed by traditionalists to raise the prestige of those branches that employ mostly women. Another argument is that if the reality does not conform to the ideology of equality, then we must change our interpretation of the ideology. In the early 1980s, a small group of feminists in both kibbutz federations organized to found departments for the advancement of sex equality. Department activists have undertaken the ambitious tasks of clarifying the concept of sex equality, of defining related problems and of suggesting a program for change.

Is the Kibbutz Movement strong enough to survive a direct confrontation with the issues and changes that this will inevitably entail? Will the changes be along the lines promoted by the feminists, or will the traditionalists win out? Some members of the Kibbutz Movement admire the energy and spunk of the Department activists, but regret that it is being wasted on such a hopeless cause. Others feel angry and threatened, while there are a few members on each kibbutz, of both sexes, who are hoping they succeed. For them, success will mean less of their energy being wasted in mindless battles, and more of a tremendous potential being harnessed for everyone's benefit.

REFERENCES

Adar, Gila (1989) "Analysis of Female Kibbutz Members' Influence According to Positions They Hold in Kibbutz Management." Paper presented at the Israel Women's Network Conference; Status of Women on the Kibbutz (Hebrew).

Adar, Gila and Lewis, Chana (1988) *Women on Kibbutz, a Survey of Women in Public Life.* Ramat Efal: Yad Tabenkin, and the Institute for Kibbutz Research, Haifa (Hebrew).

Alon, Moni (1975) *Youth on the Kibbutz, in the Eyes of the Educators and the Pupils.* Tel Aviv: Sifriat Poalim (Hebrew).

Ben-David, Ya'acov (1975) *Work and Education on the Kibbutz: Reality and Aspirations.* Rehovot: The Center for Research of Urban and Rural Settlements (Hebrew).

Birnbaum, Sandy and Safir, Marilyn (1981) "A Comparative Study of Ego Development, Occupational Aspirations, and Expectations Among Adolescent Kibbutz and City Girls." Paper presented at the International Interdisciplinary Congress of Women, Haifa, Israel.

Edelist, Miri (1980) "Creativity of Kibbutz Children." Unpublished M.A. Thesis, University of Haifa (Hebrew).

Ellings, Shoshana; Safir, Marilyn; Lieblich, Amia (1981) "Psychological Androgyny in Kibbutz and City Adolescents." Paper presented at the International Interdisciplinary Congress of Women, Haifa, Israel.

Lester, Irit (1978) Term paper, Department of Psychology, University of Haifa (Hebrew).

Lieblich, Amia (1981) *Kibbutz Makom.* New York: Pantheon Books.

Livne, Shoshana (1982) "Vocational Aspirations and Choosing a Vocation—Study of Kibbutz Adolescents." Unpublished M.A. Thesis, University of Haifa, Israel (Hebrew).

Mednick, Martha (1975) "Social Change and Sex-role Inertia: The Case of the Kibbutz." In *Social Psychological Perspectives on Achievement.* New York: Holt, Rinehart & Winston.

Orchan, Eliot (1982) Ties of Kibbutz Children to the Kibbutz and Its Components. *Yediot,* 13. Institute of Research of the Kibbutz, Haifa University and The School of Education in the Kibbutz Movement, Oranim.

Palgi, Michal; Blasi, Joseph; Rosner, Menachem; Safir, Marilyn (1983) *Sexual Equality: The Israeli Kibbutz Tests the Theories.* Norwood, PA: Norwood Editions.

Safir, Marilyn (1981) "Women in the Kibbutz." Talk presented to a conference in Givat Haviva.

Silver, Vivian (1984) *Male and Female Created He Them: The Problem of Sexual Equality on the Kibbutz.* Ramat Efal: Yad Tabenkin (Hebrew).

Tiger, Lionel and Shepher, Joseph (1975) *Women in the Kibbutz.* New York, London: Harcourt Brace Jovanovich.

Ideology and Practice in the Cooperative Farm Village

Naomi Nevo

Israel's rural system is still strongly colored by the ideology of agrarian socialism. The pioneering ethos of the prestate period was presumed to include equality of the sexes. Although still invoked by many, that presumption is now recognized as a myth: Romantic depictions of men and women working side by side in the fields are flawed by equally graphic accounts of women pioneers cooking, cleaning and mending, as well as nursing the (male) pioneers stricken with malaria in the hospital tents. Without doubt, the hardships of both men and women were severe, and the heavier the burdens were, the greater was the prestige accorded to those who bore them, irrespective of gender. While prestige implies neither justice nor power, it is often confused with both. In our context, this confusion engendered the illusion of gender parity over and above hardship and sacrifice.

The kibbutz was organized economically and socially on the basis of equal individual membership in the commune, with collective responsibility for child rearing. In practice however, almost from the dawn of the first such settlement, that particular collective responsibility was carried out exclusively by the women (Bejaoui, 1990)—if not as mothers of families, then as mothers of the community. The cultural inclination to see the biological fact of motherhood as a social constraint expressing further so-called differences as axiomatic to gender did not disappear with the abolition of the family as a social and economic unit (Ben-Rafael, 1988).

If this was so in the self-consciously utopian framework of the kibbutz, how much more glaring was the phenomenon in the moshav, which was deliberately and formally based on the ideology of the family. Although the kibbutz is clearly becoming more family oriented, it has not yet approximated the moshav, where the supremacy of the nuclear family is still the central ideological tenet.

In the moshav, as in the kibbutz, the woman was committed to productive work in a market economy and to participation in the political and public life of the community. But in the moshav, her first commitment was to the family. Although the question of women's status was by no means ignored ("enslavement" of women to home and children was condemned as preventing women from realizing themselves as personalities in their own right, Yaffe, 1919), gender equality and family organization soon proved to be mutually exclusive. Women farmers, who were accepted as members of the first moshav (founded in 1921), irrespective of their marital status or intentions, soon disappeared from the moshav landscape.

The woman's paramount responsibility to her family was institutionalized in the moshav blueprint (Yaffe, 1919), designed several years before the first settlement. The man was to plough the distant fields while the woman was to tend the poultry, sited in the farmyard, so that she could be near the house and children. Although the prevailing ethic placed emphasis on farm work and not on housework, and the founding mothers displayed a socially approved contempt for culinary talents, with time the moshav family began to approximate the bourgeois Jewish family of Eastern Europe that these pioneers thought they were rejecting.

The well-known "double burden" developed in the moshav out of an ideological concept enthusiastically supported by men and women alike. Indeed, the implementation of the second part of the concept—involving women in the political and managerial processes of the cooperative—was correlated with their farming activities. Early protocols of management meetings in veteran moshavim illustrate women's pursuit of economic interests through membership in the moshav's managerial bodies. Although I did not discover one recorded instance of a woman filling elected office in central positions, such as those of Treasurer or Chair of the Management Committee, women were members of other decision-making forums, including specialized agricultural committees. However, my anecdotal material shows that women had difficulties in attending meetings because of domestic and farmyard responsibilities. No attempt was made to restructure roles within the family, and the women soon came to be known as "farmwives," a nomenclature which encapsulates the multiple roles of farmer, mother and housekeeper. In the early years, it was the farmwife syndrome which gradually decreased women's participation in village politics and management; the principle of joint participation in the decision-making process proved to be fragile in the face of a formal social organization based on the traditional nuclear family.

As the cooperative villages began to establish themselves economically, and as their prosperity increased, a further erosion of the pioneering ideology took place: fewer and fewer women were engaged in agriculture. This development is connected with changes in the nature of farmyard operations over the last 25 years. Poultry farming changed from chicken for the domestic market to turkey for export; milch herds increased enormously in size and the branch became fully mechanized; hothouse cultivation developed; specialization increased. In other words, farming became big business, an industry involving government subsidies and complex financial transactions.

I view this change as an intervening variable rather than as a causative factor of women's decreased work in the farmyard. It brought economic prosperity, which resulted in a whole new range of consumer activities and services performed by women: The symptomatic correlate of women's return to the domestic hearth which has been widely researched in industrialized societies (Galbraith, 1975).

Opting out of the farmyard is now normatively legitimized, that is, women who cease to work on their farms are no longer condemned by gossip. Women who do farm are pointed out and highly praised. This hints at the difficulty of distinguishing ideological from economic influences. Often the proliferation of large multifamily farms (intergenerational or sibling partnerships) on a prosperous moshav was accompanied by women's return to domesticity. In numerous conversations with both men and women, I was told that the women had only themselves to blame for this regression. The norm of the female stereotype was brought into play to rationalize women's behavior: mothers-in-law, daughters-in-law, or sisters-in-law were said to cause tension, necessitating their removal from the economic orbit.

Economic inactivity was accompanied by further erosion in political participation, and the economic and agrotechnical committees in the great majority of moshavim are now bereft of women. The more sophisticated these systems are (and they have become part of a labyrinth of technocratic, marketing and financial institutions external to the moshav system), the more "unthinkable" it is to imagine women involved in them.

Female moshav members are no longer expected to be active in the decision-making process. Even a very active and knowledgeable woman is unlikely to be nominated for election. In contrast to past practices, women who speak out at general committee meetings on subjects other than those considered within their purview (e.g., health, education, consumer products, absorption of new members) meet with social disapproval from both sexes. This is so even in those villages in which women come nearest to the model of independent farmers. Women who have definite economic interests to advance or definite ideas on general policy make their voices heard through informal channels; they visit the treasurer, the secretary-general, or other members of the committee and talk with them privately.

Until recently, anthropologists and rural sociologists considered moshavim in terms of two models, the first emanating from the prototype established in 1921, and the second resulting from the so-called immigrant moshav settlement created during the 1950s. Without detailing all the characteristics of the two models, it can be said that the first—the ideal, classic model, according to which all prestate moshavim were established—was based on the ideology of both secular Zionist nationalism and agrarian socialism. Membership was accorded to all residents above the age of 18, regardless of gender or farm ownership. The second model was a compromise made to accommodate the immigrants who poured into the country from 1948 to 1958: survivors of the European holocaust, and emigrants from the Islamic countries of the Middle East and North Africa. These new immigrants lacked the ideology of the generation that had founded the collective and cooperative mainstream of Israel's rural sector, and the absorbing society thus searched for a new model for moshav settlements. Membership in the new cooperative villages was made contingent upon farm ownership—ownership that was established by sign-ing a contract with the settlement authorities.

Within a short period of time, many of the cooperative villages settled by Holocaust survivors resembled their veteran counterparts. The women, ap-proximating the Jewish female stereotype of the Eastern European townships, were no less involved than their husbands in making a living for the family. The women were usually signatories to the moshav contract and, conse-quently, moshav members in their own right. They worked on the farm and took part in moshav decision making. The demographic structure of these survivor families was a contributing factor to this pattern. Often the marriage was a second one for both partners; their comparatively higher ages and the presence of only one or two children who were too young to work necessi-tated the women's participation in economic activities. Nevertheless, I found that in only 9 percent of these moshavim was there a woman on the village management committee, as compared with 32 percent (still not 50 percent) in the veteran moshavim. The information concerning women's representa-tion on the management committees was compiled on a statistically viable sample (40 percent of all the moshavim in the country) and referred to the years 1977 to 1980 (Nevo and Solomonica, 1983). On the basis of updated information from the Registry of Cooperative Associations, I am able to sur-mise that there is a regression in this sphere but that it is so far statistically insignificant.

Of the 450 moshavim in Israel today, only 60 were established before 1948. The majority of the approximately 350,000 people presently living in the moshavim arrived after 1948; the largest contingent among them consists of settlers who are either themselves from Islamic countries or whose parents or grandparents came from Islamic countries.

While the moshav was certainly a voluntary settlement—anyone could leave at any time—in fact, immigrants who arrived during the period of mass im-migration were directed towards this type of settlement as well as towards specific geographical areas. As they had no experience and little desire to work the land, the moshavim on which they were settled or which they them-selves actually founded—out of necessity rather than ideological conviction—became administered communities, in which finances were handled by representatives of the Jewish Agency, who also planned their crops and taught them how to cultivate them. In accordance with the stereotype of the Orien-tal Jewish family as a patriarchal structure in which women had low formal status, settlement officials assumed that it would be appropriate only for heads of families to sign the contracts that established possession of the farm and bestowed moshav membership; they rarely bothered to ask the women to sign. Strictly speaking, according to the Registrar's rules for cooperative societies, a formal request for membership in the moshav had to be made to the Management Committee. In fact, this was honored in the breach rather than the observance. The cultural norms of Oriental Jews were thus "protected" and a possible reason for further opposition to settlement plans avoided. The women in these moshavim confined their work to the domestic orbit (house and farmyard). They never participated in moshav decision making. Their prevailing cultural and social norms as well as large families prevented their working outside the home; also, their labor was less critical, as there were usually a number of older children available to work the farm.

The fact that Oriental women were not signatories to the moshav contract created numerous problems, but only two will be mentioned here. First, if widowed or divorced, they were often at the mercy of surviving male relatives. There are still cases on record where pressure by the extended family forced a woman to leave the village with only a small amount of money as compensation. Her farm was then allocated by the moshav committee to another member of the family. Second, since membership in the corporate entity of the poststate moshavim is contingent on farm ownership, it is the man who is the farmer-owner, the moshav member, and, therefore, the one who has a vote in moshav affairs. There are, of course, exceptions: widows who stay on to manage the farm and claim voting rights. However, in 1980, only 1.4 percent of the moshavim established by immigrants from Islamic countries had a woman (never more than one) sitting on the seven-member Management Committee, the major decision-making body of the moshav.

The last five years have seen an increased awareness among Israeli women of their low social and economic status. A Ministerial Committee enquiry into the position of women in the cooperative rural sector resulted in a spate of activity: consciousness-raising and lobbying for legislative action. The former was conducted on the moshav level, and some success was achieved in obtaining the right of women to vote for their village institutions. I followed the process in two moshavim settled by immigrants from Islamic countries. Although the women had won their fight for suffrage, they still did not appear in the voting booths.

A new regulation has recently been instituted granting spouses in a moshav the right to claim membership by virtue of marriage to the farm owner and permanent residency in the village. (The term "ownership" of moshav farms must be qualified. The land is nationally owned and the farms are leased from the Jewish Agency for Israel—a quasinational land settling body. This arrangement restricts their deployment on the open market.) There is no waiting period; the claim is valid by virtue of having been made. Although the regulation refers to either spouse, clearly it is the wife who needs to legalize her status. However, she has to initiate the action. The number of women who have done so is negligible. It appears that women are not aware of the new regulation; it is not the women who must be blamed for apathy, then, but the moshav movement officials, who, in truth, would prefer not to rock the boat. They neither disseminate information about women's rights nor campaign for action, for they are content to see the men continue managing the moshavim.

The last decade has seen a deterioration in the economic situation of many moshavim. The new generation of moshav women have better educational qualifications than their men and work as teachers, nurses and social workers (traditional service occupations of women in Israel). A recent statistic (albeit unofficial) is that 70 percent of moshav women work outside their villages. Their salaries often provide capital for rehabilitating failing farms, but rehabilitation also necessitates women's labor. In at least one geographical area of Israel which I have been observing, the moshav women now have a triple burden: family, outside work and farm labor.

Gender equality necessarily involves political and managerial responsibility, but in the moshav, which emphasizes the family unit, this can only be achieved by the redefinition of the male as well as the female role. The family roles were not restructured in the past, not in the moshavim created after the establishment of the state and not in the prototypes founded during the pioneering period, and there is as yet no indication of its occurring in the present.

REFERENCES

Bejaoui, Sylvia (1990) *Mothers or Comrades? Women in the Kibbutz 1910–1986. A Historical Perspective.* Tel Aviv: The Open University (Hebrew).

Ben-Rafael, Eliezer (1988) *Status, Power and Conflict in the Kibbutz.* Aldershot: Avebury.

Galbraith, John K. (1975) *Economics and the Public Purpose.* London: Pelican Books.

Nevo, Naomi and Solomonica, David (1983) *Ideological Change of Women's Role and Status: Case Study of Family-Based Cooperative Villages in Israel.* Women in Development Series. East Lansing: Michigan State University.

Yaffe, Eliezer (1919) *Moshavim.* Sifriat Ha'aretz V'haavoda. Jaffa (Hebrew). Republished as *The Writings of Eliezer Yaffe* (1947) Tel Aviv: Am Oved, Vol. 1; 75–76 (Hebrew).

Section Seven
Feminism Israeli Style

Israeli Feminism New and Old

Barbara Swirski

EARLY FEMINISM

If equality among women and men in prestate Palestine is a myth, the struggle for equality was real, and it was informed by the vision of a new and better society for women and men. The ideology was socialist, not feminist; the context was nation-building, the task at hand was gaining a foothold on the land, and the immediate need was physical and economic survival. The women's struggle contained many of the elements associated with the new feminist movement: the perception of women as an oppressed group, the idea that personal transformation was necessary for social change, the creation of all-female political organizations, and the establishment of alternative institutions.

The achievements of the women who first fought for gender equality, reviewed in the following pages, were radical not only for their time, but also for ours. They established the right of women to work, and they proved that women were capable of doing what had hitherto been considered men's jobs. They created a model, however imperfect, for collective childcare. And they established a number of all-female institutions that did not exist anywhere else, including a women's political party.

The early Jewish women's struggles were part of the socialist Zionist vision of a "new man" or a "new Jew." The leaders were immigrants who came from Russia, educated women who had absorbed revolutionary ideas. They were members of socialist Zionist organizations, and they came to a Palestine the majority of whose residents were Palestinian Arabs, in the framework of Zionist immigration—about 30,000 immigrants in the first wave (1882–1903), 35,000 in the second wave (1904–1914), 30 percent of whom were women—and 35,000 in the third (1919–1923), 36.8 percent of whom were women. The women who struggled for equality constituted a very small revolutionary minority within a larger Jewish minority. All the events described below occurred among Jews and were not relevant for Arab women, nor did they have anything to do with Oriental or Orthodox Jewish women.

The women believed that Jewish national liberation would include women's liberation, and they viewed physical labor, especially farming, as the forge that would temper it. However, when they arrived in Palestine, they had to fight for the very right to work, whether in agriculture, road construction or the building trades. They found that both the "veterans" (the members of the first wave of immigration to Palestine who had preceded them), as well as their own male comrades, expected them to fit into traditional women's roles: cooking, cleaning, laundering, and taking care of the men. Most of the struggle was carried out within their own movement.

With the financial support of the Palestine Office of the World Zionist Organization, the pioneers organized communal farms (called *kvutzot*, and later, kibbutzim). However, few women were able to join these communes, and those who did were usually relegated to service jobs. As one of the women described the attitude of her own male comrades: "They also considered us absurd. Not only those of us who wanted to break down the so-called natural barriers and adopt the difficult occupation of agriculture, but also those of us who engaged in work that women seem to be especially suited for—they too were considered absurd" (Bernstein, 1987:19). While the men received wages for their labor from the Palestine Office, the women did not; they were viewed as employees of the men (Bernstein, 1987:19). A celebrated exception to the rule, the one that provided inspiration for women in other communes, as well as for the myth of the plough woman, was the Sejera Collective, established on the initiative of Manya Shochat. At Sejera, the women learned to plow, and later they clandestinely planted the first vegetable garden, an initiative that gave women pioneers a new option (Ben Zvi, 1989; Izraeli, 1981; Bernstein 1987). What was unique about the efforts of the early feminists in Palestine was their emphasis on physical labor as the force that would liberate them from the fetters of both Jewish and bourgeois society, transform them, and ensure their partnership in the building of a new, egalitarian society. But they soon discovered that even in the new land, the most important activity was "men's work"; if physical labor was the key to this particular chapter in history, women would have to fight to make it.

In 1914 there were no more than 14 communes in Palestine. Jews comprised about 12 percent (85,000) of the total population of 700,000, and Jewish agricultural laborers less than 2 percent (1500) of the Jewish population of Palestine during the formative time of the Women Workers' Movement (Bein, 1976: 115–117). In 1911, the women workers from the agricultural communes began to organize. Their first meeting, attended by seventeen women, was closed to men; they discussed the fact that their male comrades did not regard them as full-fledged laborers, that opportunities for women were limited, and that they lacked training in agriculture. That same year, the first women's agricultural training school was set up by Hannah Meizel, a member of the Sejera Collective. Leaders began to regard training as the key to equality. Ada

Maimon, one of the most prominent, and most radical leaders, later wrote: "At the dawn of the movement we thought that we had only to overcome the barrier of occupational training, and as for equality, it would all follow automatically" (Maimon, 1972: 121, in Izraeli, 1981: 97). Additional farms were established by the Women Workers' Movement. Their graduates were in high demand, but training alone did not give women equality.

Just as they were excluded from prestigious physical labor, women workers were also excluded by their socialist Zionist comrades from decision-making bodies. When they were not invited to an agricultural union conference held in 1914, they disrupted the meeting in protest. Later the same year, they called the first women workers' convention, attended by 30 delegates representing 209 women workers (Izraeli, 1981: 98). Annual conferences were instituted, and a Women Workers' Committee was created to coordinate activities.

During World War I, when unemployment in Palestine soared, especially among women, several groups of women organized themselves into all-female agricultural communes and were able to obtain land and financial assistance. However, when the war ended, financial aid was no longer extended to the women's collectives, and their plots were assigned to other uses (Bernstein, 1987: 22–23). Although the communes were short-lived, they constituted another "first" of the early women's movement, an alternative institution created when women could not realize their aspirations in male-dominated frameworks.

When the Histadrut (National Federation of Hebrew Workers) was created in 1920, most of the organizations and resources of the labor movement were subsumed under its roof and became dependent on it, including the Women Workers' Movement. The women's movement was not officially represented at the founding convention of the Histadrut, because representation was based on political party membership, and the women viewed their organization as nonpartisan. However, leaders of the movement attended as guests. The poor representation of women in the political parties and the neglect of the problems of the woman worker at the convention spurred Ada Maimon to announce that the women would form their own association, for which she demanded official representation on the Histadrut Council. Her demand was accepted, and two seats were reserved for women workers (Izraeli, 1981: 103). The founding conference of that association, the Women Workers' Council, was held in 1921, attended by 43 delegates representing 485 workers. An executive committee and representatives to the Histadrut were elected. At the second conference, held the following year, two major factions emerged. One advocated a strong, separate female organization that would be free of party and male control and would work closely with grassroots members to promote vocational training and secure employment for women. The other faction regarded a separate women's labor union as an unnecessary duplication and a manifestation of unwarranted lack of faith in male members of the labor movement. They argued that the Women Workers' Council should abandon the idea of trade union activities and focus on women's political education and activization (Izraeli, 1981: 105). The latter faction eventually prevailed. The Women Workers' Council came under the increasing control of the Ahdut HaAvoda Party (Workers United — later Mapai), the largest political party in the labor movement, and militant feminist leader Ada Maimon, Chairwoman of the Council, was replaced by party loyalist Golda Meir.

The Histadrut established a network of local labor councils in the cities and agricultural villages; these local branches included committees of working women, whose task was to activate women workers and represent them in local trade unions and labor exchanges. At first members of the women's committees were elected at a general meeting of local women workers, but by 1932 the system had been changed and they were appointed on the basis of proportional party representation.

Once it became part of the Histadrut, the Women Workers' Movement became divided against itself and fought a losing battle for power within a male organization controlled by a political party. The Women Workers' Council failed to achieve either economic or political power within the Histadrut. By 1926, it still had no budget. At first, a few women sat on Histadrut committees, but their numbers, too, decreased over time. Only one woman, Ada Maimon, was a member of the policy making body of any of the economic enterprises created by the Histadrut (Izraeli, 1981:112).

A new wave of socialist-Zionist pioneer immigrants came to Palestine after the First World War (between 1919 and 1923, some 35,000 men and women arrived, predominantly socialist Zionist pioneers). Like their sisters before them, the women immigrants were idealists, and they expected to be equal partners in the building of a "Jewish national revolutionary movement in Palestine" (Bernstein, 1987:28). Many came as members of the He-Halutz (Pioneer) youth movement; before immigrating they had received agricultural training in Europe on farms organized as communes, in which both men and women rotated at household chores and work in the fields. But upon arrival in Palestine, they, too, found that manual labor was considered improper for females (Bernstein, 1987:31). At the time, the main economic activity was road construction for the new British Mandate authorities, and the young women wanted to be a part of it. However, the same norms that had hindered their predecessors from working in agriculture prevented them from working in road-building. Still, a few hundred managed to break in: during 1922 to 1923, some 3,000 laborers were engaged in road construction; 400 of them were women, half of whom worked in the communal kitchens of the construction gangs (Bernstein, 1987:34–36). Working on a road gang, even as cooks, was a radical departure for the pioneer women, not to mention actual construction work. This was a breakthrough for its time, and impressive even by contemporary standards.

The majority of the Jewish immigrants who came to Palestine in the 1920s settled in the cities, where they lived either in rented rooms or (in the case of Tel Aviv) set up tents along the seashore. Jobs were not easy to find. The most prestigious and remunerative occupations were in construction, and then as now, the norm excluded women. Still, a small minority of determined women managed to obtain construction jobs, notably in floor tiling, by joining collectives or even forming all-female collectives that competed for job contracts. This was another radical departure from women's past economic activity; not only did women work at the building trades, occupations unheard of for women, but they created alternative forms of organization for themselves. In 1922, women comprised 16 percent of the membership of construction collectives; half of these women provided domestic services (Izraeli, 1981:102). The women workers made a number of policy gains, although these were not translated into action: the Tel Aviv-Jaffa Workers' Council resolved that every workers' collective engaged in construction was to accept two women into its ranks, the Federation of Construction Workers made a decision to increase the employment of women, and the Women Workers' Council organized training for women workers in tiling, bricklaying and plastering. A 1926 workers' census found 51 women tilers, 19 painters and 13 plasterers (Bernstein 1987:49–51). While their numbers were small, these women constituted the vanguard of urban workers, the women who trained and organized to enter new occupations and created new frameworks for women.

Yet another innovation of the Women Workers' Movement were the women workers' collectives called "havurot," temporary organizations the purposes of which were to give women immigrants training and employment and "to prepare [them] for an honest and cooperative life of work, to inculcate in [them] the idea that work is the content of life, and to develop [their] consciousness and [their] self-confidence" (Bernstein, 1987:101). The first was begun in 1926: A great economic crisis had begun, the fourth wave of Zionist immigration was in progress, and there was no employment for women. Unlike their predecessors, the immigrants of the new wave (82,000 Jews arrived between 1924 and 1931) were not committed to gender equality and the liberating value of labor. Mostly members of the lower middle class, they were not socialist; their motivation for immigration was economic distress in Poland. For them, work was simply a necessity. The Women Workers' Movement persuaded the Labor Department of the Zionist Executive to advance the funds for five women's collectives, two of them in Tel Aviv and the others in Rishon Le-Tzion, Petah Tikva, and Binyamina. In 1927, five more women's collectives sprung up in Hadera, Afula, Haifa, Tiberias and Ramat Gan. The original plan had been for the women to engage in vegetable gardening, as well as to produce manufactured goods like cement, cloth, shoes and handicrafts. However, the workshops that were to provide economic diversity never materialized for lack of funds. Half the members of the collective (comprised of 20 to 25 members) worked in the collective gardens, and the others were employed outside. The collectives were run by committee, and housework and cooking were done by rotation. Despite its own positive report on the economic and absorption activities of the women's collectives, the Zionist Executive cut back its allocations in 1927. With the cutbacks in funds and the burn-out of veteran members, the collectives fell apart. Although the idea had originated with Hanna Tchizik, a movement leader, the individual "havurot" were grassroots initiatives (Bernstein, 1987: 101, 107). While the collectives never provided an employment solution or a means for personal transformation for the masses of women as envisioned by their founders, they constituted a significant chapter in the history of the women's movement, for they not only provided employment and housing based on principles of equality for several hundred women; they also advanced the idea of women's full participation in the new Jewish collective.

Although the Russian social movements provided the Zionist women workers with an ideology that included the right to work and the idea of labor as a liberating force, there was no ideological alternative to the idea of the Jewish family. When the pioneers married and bore children, they usually stopped working, for caring for the family took up all of their time. Living conditions were primitive, sanitation was poor, health care was not readily available, and illnesses were frequent. There was nothing to challenge the traditional division of labor within the family; the women had sole responsibility for child care. As they had left their families behind, there were usually no members of the extended family to help out. In the kibbutzim, however, child care became a collective task rather than an individual one. This was a significant departure from the past, although the responsibility devolved exclusively on female members.

Upon marriage, the majority of the pioneer women became economically dependent on their husbands. They ceased to be regarded as workers, which meant a regression in their own definition of the struggle for equality. Still, the Women Workers' Movement made several attempts to preserve the status of the married woman as a worker in her own right. In the 1930s, when unemployment was high and the Histadrut (which was becoming a major employer) began to dismiss married women, movement leaders campaigned against these dismissals; they were not successful. At the same time (mid-1930s), the Women Workers' Movement succeeded in obtaining separate Histadrut membership cards for married women who did not work outside the home; previously, the women had been listed on their husbands' cards as "workers' wives." This was a far cry from the earlier achievements of the movement. The Women Workers' Movement, the Federation of Hebrew Workers, and the employers had all become part of the same apparatus. In such a situation, the former could hardly be expected to agitate for far-reaching changes.

In 1930, the Women Workers' Movement established a network of local "Associations of Mothers Working in Their Homes," the purpose of which was to give married women a sense of belonging, to activate them, and to prevent the development of a "petty bourgeois" way of life that might enervate the labor movement (Bernstein, 1987: 142–143). Activities offered to married women by the Associations of Mothers resembled those of traditional, philanthropic women's organizations and were designed neither to raise women's consciousness nor to change the structure of employment for women.

The Women Workers' Movement was created to give women the right to work in jobs that involved building a new society of "new Jews," first farming, and later, road and house construction. As these aims lost their relevance, because the immigrants who came after 1925 had no interest in agriculture, because in the wake of the financial crisis there was no work to be had in either road or house construction, or because motherhood removed women from the labor market, the movement was bereft of its primary message. By the 1930s, when nearly half of the women in the labor market were employed in services, many of them in domestic work, and the local women's councils were engaged in securing cleaning jobs for women, the movement had lost its radical vision.

By that time, the Labor movement had gained supremacy within the Palestinian Jewish community and its energies were devoted to the maintenance of that supremacy, vis-a-vis the center and right wing opponents, as well as to leading the national struggle for statehood, vis-a-vis the Arabs and the British. The labor hierarchy had "much more important" matters to contend with than gender equality.

The Women Workers' Movement was not the only feminist force in the Jewish community in Palestine; there was a women's suffrage movement as well. Like their sisters who founded the Women Workers' Movement, the leaders of the suffrage movement were members of the second wave of immigration to Palestine (Bejaoui, 1981). While they came from the same urban, bourgeois backgrounds, they were inspired by different ideologies; the workers believed productive labor would make women equal to men, and the suffragists, who became members of the urban bourgeoisie, believed that legislative reform, and above all, the vote, would lead to equality.

The women who created the suffrage movement also found that the new society in the making did not live up to their expectations for equality. The Jewish community in Palestine was self-governing, but women had no part in the decision making. The story of the suffrage struggle is recounted in a book written by one of its leaders, Sarah Azariyahu, entitled *The Union of Hebrew Women for Equal Rights in Eretz Israel*. (The work was rediscovered by feminists in the 1970s, who reprinted it and later translated it into English.) Azariyahu's account preserves one of the first voices raised for women's suffrage, that of Hannah Zahavi: "My son, whom I educated and raised, is permitted to manage the affairs of Petah Tikva, but I, his mother, who have given all my strength and energy and the best years of my life to this settlement—I am excluded from doing so" (Azariyahu, 1980:3).

The issue of women's voting rights first reached the local agenda in 1903, in the agricultural village of Zichron Ya'acov, where the local governing body decided against women's suffrage. In 1917, a group of women organized a Women's Society for the purpose of obtaining the right to vote in the Tel Aviv-Jaffa city council. This time the struggle was not an internal one, between socialist women and socialist men, but between bourgeois women, later joined by socialist women, and men of various and sundry ideological persuasions. In a pattern that continues to this day, the women had to fight religious Orthodox opposition, as well as a tendency on the part of the labor parties to abstain or compromise when it came to a vote, in order to placate religious elements. The Tel Aviv women won the vote in 1917, followed by the women of Haifa and Rishon L'Zion, who had also organized in Women's Societies.

The suffrage movement, which was based in the cities and agricultural villages, put more stress on organization than the Women Workers' Movement (Bejaoui, 1981; Izraeli, 1981). In 1919, the women established a national nonpartisan organization, the Union of Hebrew Women for Equal Rights in Eretz Israel; the local Women's Societies provided the organizational base. The purpose of the new body was to obtain the right to vote and be elected to the Jewish national, self governing bodies which were being organized. When the first steps were taken to create a Jewish Representative Assembly, the Union of Hebrew Women made a decision that was unprecedented among women's movements anywhere: to run an independent women's list in the elections for delegates to the Assembly. By so doing, the activists hoped both to encourage women to be politically active, and to spur the parties to give more places to women candidates on their lists. They were successful. Elections were held in 1920, with women participating, and 14 women were elected as delegates (out of a total of 314), five from the Union of Hebrew Women, two from the Progressive Party, and seven from the two workers' parties. Still, women's suffrage was yet to be formally ratified by the Representative Assembly.

The first national convention of the Union of Hebrew Women was held in 1922. It was also attended by leaders of the Women Workers' Council, including Ada Maimon. According to Azariyahu, the two feminist groups worked together to assure ratification of women suffrage by the Representative Assembly, after which no further cooperative actions were taken (1980:22). The joint effort achieved its goal in 1925. After numerous debates and delays, due to the opposition of the religious parties, the Representative Assembly ratified the principle of women's suffrage, then nullified it under pressure from the religious parties, whose last resort had been to demand a referendum on the question. Just before the referendum, one of the religious parties, Agudat Yisrael, announced that it would boycott the referendum. This move, taken without consultation with the other religious party, Mizrachi (later the National Religious Party), prompted the latter to withdraw its demand for a referendum and to assent to women's suffrage in elections to the Representative Assembly. When elections to the Second Assembly were held, 13 delegates were elected from the Union of Hebrew Women, as well as 13 women from other parties (out of a total of 221 delegates), so that women comprised 12 percent of the Second Representative Assembly (compare this with 5.8 percent after the 1988 Knesset elections). The Union of Hebrew Women ran its own list in three subsequent elections. Despite the women's attempt to pass a resolution obliging local governments to grant women suffrage, the matter was left to the discretion of the locality. The Union of Hebrew Women had to refight the same battle in each local community, until Petah Tikva, the first Jewish agricultural village established in Palestine, became the last to grant women the vote in 1940.

Concurrent with these struggles, the Union for Hebrew Women founded a feminist magazine called *Woman*. It also published a handbook on domestic rights for women (1930) and established legal aid bureaus on family matters for women.

By the end of the thirties, both struggles had petered out. Some victories, like the vote, and some crises, like unemployment, brought the two groups of activists to what appeared the end of the road. Meanwhile, the general movements or sectors to which they belonged had taken over the helm of the Palestinian Jewish community. During the 1940s, the burning issues were the World War, the Holocaust, the struggle against the British Mandate, and the war with the Arabs. In 1948, once the state was established, the scene changed once again, in the face of a mass immigration of Jews, many of them in distress, and a new minority of Arabs under Jewish domination. The veteran women activists had become a part of a new "ruling elite," as the labor parties had come to dominate political institutions and their husbands and comrades were now the managers of the state apparatus. The suffragists were part of the sector that managed private and government enterprises, as well as the army. The women themselves were not predisposed to reach out and recruit new allies among the new groups. Instead, they slowly took on a "social service" orientation, in keeping with their new class positions. The new orientation also suited the priorities of the state apparatus, which, faced with massive welfare and social service needs, found in activist women a convenient solution. A massive inflow of financial aid from Jewish communal organizations abroad, among them Hadassah, Women's International Zionist Organization (WIZO), and Pioneer Women, also pushed in the same direction, as the activist women of the new local elite were the "natural" counterparts of the middle and upper class Jewish philanthropists from abroad. Thus it was that like the Women Workers' Council, the Union of Hebrew Women gradually shifted its focus to philanthropic and social work activities, until it was absorbed by WIZO. Efforts at liberation would not be resumed until the new women's movement spread to Israel in the 1970s.

THE NEW WOMEN'S MOVEMENT

The new women's movement did not originate in a civil rights or student movement as it did in the United States and Western Europe, but was the result of the direct influence of new immigrants from the United States and other English-speaking countries. The nurturing ground this time was not a socialist Zionist movement, but rather a new middle-class: University-educated, mostly Ashkenazi young women who, like the rest of the middle and upper classes of Israeli society, had become identified with American culture. The post-Six Day War prosperity, the massive influence of the United States in the Israeli military, economy and culture, as a result of increased financial aid and the introduction of television, with its many United States' programs created a fertile ground for the acceptance of the "American way of life," that is, the middle class lifestyle, by its Israeli counterpart. However, the private home or spacious apartment in the suburb or a plush urban neighborhood and the private car were easier to accept than feminist ideas.

The beginnings of the movement can be traced to 1970 and Haifa University. Israel's unprecedented prosperity and expanding economy included new universities and growing student enrollments. At Haifa University, new faculty were recruited: lecturers from American and European universities as well as Israelis returning from advanced studies abroad. These lecturers, together with other elements unique to Haifa University at the time: new immigrants from South and North America, Arab students, and kibbutzniks, made provincial Haifa the most cosmopolitan university in Israel.

The Women's Movement had its beginnings in two seminars—which evolved into consciousness-raising groups—on women's issues given at Haifa university by two immigrants from the United States: Marcia Freedman, a philosophy lecturer, and Marilyn Safir, a psychology lecturer. The interest generated was considerable, and, following the universal pattern of the movement, new consciousness-raising groups were formed in Haifa, facilitated by students and instructors who had participated in the seminars. The organizers and some of the participants of these seminars continued to meet on a regular basis and decided to attempt to create a women's movement. Their first projects were designed to uncover the hidden agendas in hiring practices at the Technion and renting practices in Haifa. They also staged a demonstration at the Haifa Rabbinic Court. Another notable action taken by the Haifa women was a successful campaign in 1972 to persuade the University to open a daycare center for students and employees. Before long, Marcia Freedman emerged as the dominant figure and was besieged with requests for information from women around the country. In 1972, Haifa women consolidated in a movement they called *Nilahem,* acronym for Women for a Renewed Society (Finkel, 1981). The next year the group began to publish a newspaper of the same name. An examination of the group's "Principles and Purposes" reveals a radical analysis of the oppression of women and of male-dominated society, though the term "patriarchy" was not mentioned (Finkel, 1981:22–3).

The movement soon spread to Tel Aviv, where a group of women, among them Esther Eilam, Ruth Rasnic and Joanne Yaron, set up a feminist organization that stressed equality and legislative reforms, and resembled the American NOW or the French Choisir, eventually calling itself "The Israel Feminist Movement." Independently, another feminist group formed in Jerusalem. The initiators, among them Leah Zemel and Ofra Kamar, came from groups on the left; their ideological emphasis was on oppression in general rather than on women's oppression (Finkel, 1981). The first actions of the Jerusalem group were demonstrations against "Woman of Valor" and beauty contests. The Tel Aviv group began by petitioning for passage of the Law of Community Property, which stipulates that the property accumulated by a couple in the course of their marriage be equally divided upon divorce, and for abortion on demand.

In 1973, a group of Palestinian Arab women in Israel, students and university graduates, led by Mariam Mar'i, began a consciousness raising group in Acre, the outcome of which was the creation of *Dar e-Tifl el-Arabi,* a preschool teachers' training institute. There was no interaction between this group and the Jewish groups.

When Shulamit Aloni formed the Citizens' Rights Party in 1973, she turned to the women's movement to help her obtain the requisite number of signatures to enter the Knesset elections; in return, Marcia Freedman was allotted third place on the party slate. The Yom Kippur War gave Aloni an unexpected victory—three seats in the Knesset—and the new feminist movement a spokeswoman in the Knesset (Shulamit Aloni did not identify with the movement). During her four years in the Knesset, Member of Knesset (MK) Freedman raised the key issues (among others) of abortion on demand and wife battering (Freedman, 1990). Tensions arose over Marcia Freedman's allegiance to the Citizen's Rights Party vs. the women's movement. Immediately after the elections, Aloni had tried, through emissaries, to persuade Freedman to relinquish her Knesset seat; when she refused, Aloni punished her with five years of cold shoulder. The women's movement did not appreciate the precariousness of Freedman's position as the only declared feminist in the Knesset and an upstart in her own party, and it failed to give her the support and backing she needed (Freedman, 1990; Finkel, 1981).

The fourth issue of *Nilahem,* published in September 1974, dealt mainly with the Yom Kippur War, a source of frustration for many women, not because of the political or military issues involved, but because the war marginalized women and sharpened the divisions between the sexes. When the war broke out and every able-bodied man appeared to have been mobilized, a group of Haifa women went to military and local authorities to volunteer whatever vital services might be needed. They, too, wanted to serve their country in its hour of need. However, they were advised to go home, bake cakes, knit woolen hats, pay visits to wounded soldiers, and not worry their heads about men's work. *Nilahem* was the only feminist forum that dealt with this issue; the subject of women and war would not be raised again until the Lebanon war in 1982.

During the years that followed, feminists set up women's centers in Haifa and Tel Aviv, did extensive lecturing in schools, army bases and kibbutzim, supported striking nurses and social workers, and held demonstrations for the liberalization of the abortion law. However, the centers did not succeed in attracting many women, and the abortion issue failed to mobilize large numbers of women. There were publishing ventures, too, most significant of which was an anthology of translated feminist writings entitled *Woman, Women, and Womanliness,* published by the Tel Aviv group, including passages from *Our Bodies Ourselves, The Dialectic of Sex, Free and Female, The Feminine Mystique,* and *Sisterhood is Powerful.* It sold out, was reprinted, and gave impetus to two members of the group to start The Second Sex Publishing Company. In 1975, the feminist movement spread to Beer Sheba, where a group of women established a health collective and published a report on conditions in the gynecology department of the Soroka Medical Center.

From 1975 to 1977, attempts were made to coordinate activities in Haifa, Tel Aviv, and Jerusalem. Committees were set up for this purpose, but conflicts and dissensions could not be overcome, and a national organization never emerged.

Marcia Freedman's Knesset term was to end in 1977. With the aid of her share of campaign monies from her party (she had left the Citizens' Rights party and formed another party with a Labor party dissident), the women's movement organized a Women's Party to run in the coming elections. The campaign attracted many women to the movement (including the writer) and gave it an unprecedented opportunity to bring feminist issues to the public. The party platform, printed in the color purple, was entirely devoted to women's issues and included a demand for remuneration for housework. The party did not succeed in obtaining a mandate. Nevertheless, the women regarded the results as a victory, not a defeat, for the 6,000 who had voted for the Women's Party were not concentrated in the big cities, but distributed throughout the country. Having achieved its major aim, a public hearing, the party was disbanded after the elections.

In 1978, the first feminist conference was held in Beer Sheba, attended by about 150 women. The first of four national conferences, it foreshadowed the future development of the Israel Feminist Movement: the concentration on specific, local feminist projects rather than the attempt to develop a national, mass movement. Representatives of existing projects reported on their activities: the first shelter for battered women, in Haifa (1977); the first rape crisis intervention center, in Tel Aviv (1977); the Second Sex Publishing Company; and "Aleph," an organization of Lesbian feminists, who came out at the Beer Sheba conference.

In the following years, feminist bookshops and centers were organized in Haifa, (*Kol Haisha* [Woman's Voice], later *Isha L'Isha* [Woman to Woman]), Jerusalem (*Kol Haisha*) and Tel Aviv (*Kol Haisha*, later *T'zena U'rena*, and still later, the Israel Feminist Movement center). Additional shelters for battered women were created in Herzliya and Jerusalem; and additional rape crisis intervention centers in Haifa, Jerusalem, Raanana and Eilat. And Arabic-language rape crisis services were organized by and for Arab women in Jerusalem and Haifa as part of the existing services. The major issue for feminists in the late seventies was a fight against repeal of the abortion law clause that permitted abortion under certain "social" circumstances. As in previous years, feminists were not able to generate mass support for their protest activities; the "social clause" was repealed, in accordance with the new coalition government agreement.

Following the pattern of development in other countries, especially those of the Third World, women's issues came to be promoted not only by grass-roots organizations calling themselves "feminist," but also by the political establishment: what women's movement historians call "feminism from above" (Mies, 1986:9). In 1975, the United Nations Decade of Women prompted Prime Minister Yitzhak Rabin to appoint a committee to examine the status of Israeli women. Their report, published in 1978, is still the definitive statement on the status of Israeli women. Israel sent official representatives to the United Nations Conference on Women in Mexico (Leah Rabin, the Prime Minister's wife, rather than Marcia Freedman), Copenhagen and Nairobi, and "the status of women" took on the patina of respectability.

The 1980s have been marked by the development of "feminism from above," with the focus on "the status of women." New departments, committees, and "advisors on the status of women" have proliferated in local and national bureaucracies. Another result of the new-found respectability of the "status of women" was that the two largest establishment women's organizations, WIZO and Na'amat (the descendant of the Women Workers' Movement), began to compete for a piece of the action. At Na'amat, the "status of women department," first created to assist war widows, took on renewed life, opening a counseling center for battered women (and batterers, too, in accordance with their family orientation) and expanding legal aid activities. The organization also provided funding for the first Women's Studies courses, at Haifa University, in 1983. WIZO opened its own shelter for battered women in Ashdod (1984), followed by a Tel Aviv hot line for battered women (1988). Feminism provided these organizations with a new agenda and new content; local chapters of WIZO and Na'amat began to engage in discussions that resembled consciousness-raising. After a new chairwoman took office and publicly declared herself a feminist, Na'amat began to initiate intensive campaigns on women's issues.

In the early 1980s, a small group of feminists from the secular kibbutz movements persuaded their federations to create "departments for the advancement of sexual equality." These departments, which consist of rotating coordinators with very small budgets, have become the focus of feminist activity in the kibbutzim.

Other feminist projects created in the course of the last decade include Women's Studies Programs; *Noga*, a feminist magazine; *Breirot* (Alternatives) Publishers; the Agunot Organization, a support group for spouses (mainly women) of divorce refuseniks, which also engages in public education and lobbying; *Lahan*, a group that promotes women's sports; women's health and birth education centers; a women's therapy collective; and the Israel Women's Network, whose main activities to date have been lobbying for legislative reforms, providing legal aid for cases with precedent setting potential, and encouraging women to run for political office.

During the 1980s, feminists were especially active in the Israeli peace movement. Following the invasion of Lebanon, a group of feminists formed Women Against Occupation. And since the outbreak of the *Intifada* (1987), feminists, many of whom were active in male peace organizations or supported their activities, have also organized all women peace groups to demand an end to the occupation and negotiation with the Palestine Liberation Organization (PLO), and to aid women political detainees and expose abuses against them. The women's peace movement, whose initiators and most active members are feminists, represents a departure from past feminist activity; prior to the outbreak of the Palestinian *Intifada*, most Jewish feminists in Israel did not view peace issues as legitimate feminist concerns. Moreover, there has been increasing cooperation between Israeli Palestinian Arab and Jewish women, as well as between Israeli women (both Palestinian Arab and Jewish) and Palestinian women in the occupied territories.

The 1980s also saw some organization by Orthodox Jewish women, whose activities included study groups, all-women prayer groups, and most recently, Women of the Wall, organized to literally and metaphorically break down the barriers to women's prayer at the Wailing Wall in Jerusalem. Most of the initiators and participants in these activities have been immigrants from English-speaking countries.

The most recent development was the organization of a group of Oriental Jewish women, in 1987. The initiators, Tikva Levi and Elana Sugbaker, are university students; most of the members are also students or college graduates who are Oriental activists. Over the last three years, members of the group have been exploring the connection between gender and ethnic oppression.

The new Israeli feminism is essentially an elitist movement. It originated in a university; its leaders were faculty, and their first converts were students. It then spread horizontally, attracting primarily university-educated women, which in Israel constitute a much smaller group than in the United States or Europe. In 1974 to 1975, there were 50,000 students in Israel, 42.9 percent of whom were women (Central Bureau of Statistics [C.B.S.], 1987:640). They constituted only 9.5 percent of their age group (C.B.S., 1987:616). From there, it spread "upward," to university faculty, leaders of established women's organizations, and officials in various state bureaucracies. Thus far, the movement has failed to become relevant to the majority of Israeli women, whether they live in urban centers, development towns, moshavim or kibbutzim. One of the reasons for this is the lack of political efficacy among Israelis in general and women in particular, due to the centralization of a wide range of social and political activities in political party and state institutions. There is no tradition of acting in the framework of voluntary organizations, and no ethos of "organizing for change." The political parties, at least until very recently, had a near monopoly on local organizing. Na'amat, as a party organization, helped to preserve that monopoly by co-opting new organizational efforts, or, more frequently, refusing to cooperate or lend its support to any activity that did not originate inside its own head offices.

Another reason for the movement's limited relevance has been its general failure to recognize or relate to other glaring inequalities in Israeli society: between Ashkenazi and Oriental Jews, and between Jews and Arabs. Yet another is activists' tendency to design activities for the like-minded, in locations convenient for the same, that is, its middle-class social base and its neglect of outreach. This, of course, is related to many feminists' own narrowness of perspective, as well as to their distrust of organization; the movement has failed to develop organizational structures that would enable it to increase the scope of its activities. Israeli feminists have also been hampered by the distrust of leadership endemic to feminist activity, a distrust that has prevented them from empowering sisters with vision or political acumen.

The agenda of the feminist movement at the beginning of the 1970s included issues that might have cut across class and ethnic boundaries, abortion and violence against women, but the potential was never realized. This was due not only to the social background of the activists and their organizational limitations, but also to the form of action chosen. Abortion activities were aimed at power centers rather than at powerless women: demonstrations in major city squares, disruption of a conference of gynecologists, and lobbying, rather than, for example, neighborhood campaigns designed to inform women of their options. Shelters for battered women were created in major cities. While their founders envisioned them as feminist centers that would generate a variety of feminist actions, over time, the focus of activity became narrower, more and more devoted to the day-to-day running of the institution—albeit an alternative one—and to taking maximum advantage of government bureaucracies in order to benefit the shelter or its residents, rather than all women or even all battered women. While shelters reach women that other feminist organizations do not reach—Arab women, Oriental Jewish women, poor women, women from development towns and other peripheral areas—their impact has been limited by routinization.

Over the last decade the agenda of the major feminist organizations has become even more middle class and less relevant to the majority of Israeli women. The employment issues raised, like equal opportunity, income tax reform, replacing maternal benefits with parental benefits, and removing protective legislation, affect mainly the better educated and higher paid. While the issue of laws of personal status has universal relevance, at the present juncture, change is regarded as an unattainable goal by most feminists as well as by the majority of women and men in Israel. Pornography is an issue that has received considerable attention; yet for women without a feminist consciousness, the message invariably falls on deaf ears. Women's health issues, which are essentially consumer issues, have no tradition of consumerism to build on, and have nothing to offer women who have no access to alternative services. Lastly, in Israel, as in other societies, running for political office is an option reserved for elites.

The assumption behind the above critique is that feminism is in essence a radical movement, the aim of which is to enable women to become makers of history. If the term "patriarchy" means anything, it means that women are dominated and exploited by men, not merely discriminated against, and that it is not enough to give women more education, or more rights, or even higher wages; the problem is not some kind of cultural lag or wage disparity, but that men (and women in the service of men) are defining culture and controlling the economy. The present assumption is that feminism is a politics that aims at basic change and addresses every aspect of life, not simply a shopping list of women's issues like more shelters for battered women or more women in the Knesset. While these are important, feminism is not perceived here as a new ghetto where women concern themselves only about a select list of topics, with no connection with the general civilizational, social and economic context.

At the present juncture (1990), however, Israeli feminism is more often than not reduced to a list of reforms, especially, but not only, by "feminism from above." This type of enterprise, concerned with adding "the women's component" to existing institutions, has no vision of a society or world in which the relations between women and men are basically different and in which women participate in history, but rather is devoted to improving things so that women have a little more of this and a little more of that.

It has been noted that feminism differs from past women's struggles not only in its revolutionary aim and global scope, but also in its method of organization. Rejecting bureaucratic procedures of party or trade union politics, the prototypical feminist group is nonhierarchical, and conscious efforts are made to share rather than monopolize power (Bunch, 1986: 122–133). The mode of action is "politics in the first person," women taking direct action (Mies, 1986: 28). These principles do characterize the more "grassroots" Israeli feminist groups, like the shelters, rape crisis intervention centers, cultural centers, and health projects; however, they do not hold for Na'amat or for the newer Israel Women's Network.

Like everyone else in Israel, feminists and feminist organizations have tended to view the state as the embodiment of the patriarchy and to address most of their demands to it. They have directed the greater part of their energies to meetings with officials—Barbara S. Deckard (1983) calls the phenomenon "feminism as business"—rather than to meetings with women. One reason for this style of action may be that despite their notorious inaccessibility, for persons of a certain background (Jewish, Ashkenazi, educated, upper-middle class), state officials are more accessible than people of different ethnic origin and lower socioeconomic status.

Perhaps we are coming closer to the crux of the matter. It is possible that despite the theoretical universality of its ideology, translated into practice, feminism is something for the upper-middle class, and that this limitation is not confined to Israel. The difference is that which North Americans refer to as the middle-class-life-style; it is relevant to less than a third of the Jewish population of Israel, most of it Ashkenazi, and a much smaller segment of the Arab population. Feminism is rather like a car; for those whose standard of living allows them to make the purchase, the car can change their lives, giving them far greater freedom and control; but for those who cannot afford it, the advantages of the motor vehicle are simply irrelevant. Perhaps feminism is literally and metaphorically just too expensive for most Israeli women. If this is the case, feminists must be aware that the changes they are working to effect, however liberating they may be for themselves, may not influence the majority of their sisters. If this does not concern them, and it seems to me that it does not, there is no problem. But if at some point it should become of concern, then a way must be found to combine present efforts with actions designed to change the basic socioeconomic structure of Israeli society so as to make what is presently defined as feminism relevant to all women and all men.

REFERENCES

Azariyahu, Sarah (1980) *The Union of Hebrew Women for Equal Rights in Eretz Israel*. Haifa: Women's Aid Fund.

Bein, Alex (1976) *History of the Jewish Settlement in Israel*. Ramat Gan: Massada (Hebrew).

Bernstein, Deborah (1987) *The Struggle for Equality: Urban Women Workers in Prestate Israeli Society.* New York: Praeger.

Ben Zvi, Rachel Y. (1989) *Before Golda: Manya Shochat.* New York: Biblio Press.

Bejaoui, Sylvia (1981) "Du Côté de Chez Eve: Les Femmes Juives de Palestine, 1881–1948." Doctoral Dissertion, Notre-Ecole des Hautes Etudes en Sciences Sociales.

Bunch, Charlotte (1986) *Passionate Politics: Feminist Theory in Action.* New York: St. Martin's Press.

Central Bureau of Statistics (1987) *Yearbook.*

Deckard, Barbara S. (1983) *The Women's Movement: Political, Socioeconomic and Psychological Issues.* New York: Harper & Row.

Finkel, Gilberte (1981) "A History of the Women's Liberation Movement in Israel." M.A. Thesis, University of Paris, Women's Studies, English Institute, Paris.

Freedman, Marcia (1990) *Exile in the Promised Land: A Memoir.* Ithaca: Firebrand.

Izraeli, Dafna N. (1981) "The Zionist Women's Movement in Palestine, 1911–1927: A Sociological Analysis." *Signs* 7(1) Autumn: 87–114.

Maimon, Ada (1972) *Along the Way.* Tel Aviv: Am Oved (Hebrew).

Mies, Maria (1986) *Patriarchy and Accumulation on a World Scale: Women in the International Division of Labour.* London: Zed Books.

Feminist Identity vs.
Oriental Identity

Vicki Shiran
(Translated by Sharon Ne'eman)

Sexual identity—like national or ethnic identity—is not a personal, but a collective identity imposed upon the individual by society. The fact that I identify myself as a woman, an Israeli, a Jew, or an Oriental does not necessarily transform these identities into personal identities, despite their being integral parts of my self.

Collective identities are inherently political. Even when a person changes her or his content for herself or himself, the personal act does not personalize the collective identity; rather, the new identity negates the content of the previous identity and strives to replace it. Until the new identity succeeds in representing the entire collective, it characterizes a small and revolutionary part of it.

"Feminism" refers to a revolutionary sexual identity. Thus, in contrast to her sisters of the past, the contemporary woman has the possibility of choosing between two alternatives: She may adopt the gender identity known as "feminine," or the identity known as "feminist." The former cooperates with the oppressor; the latter rebels.

There is no other possibility. Still, it is not uncommon to hear women presenting variations on one or the other of these two gender identities, in a pathetic attempt to swim without getting wet. Women who declare that, while they are not feminists, they support equality for women, are actually stating that they are not opposed to sex inequality, but are, rather, in favor of fairy tales—will the prince rescue poor Snow White?

Other women claim that they are feminists, but at the same time, they reject political struggle on the part of women. Such women share the common misconception that gender identity is a personal matter, and that each woman can select the components she prefers. This notion implies that feminism is "something" from which one chooses what she likes. Yet gender identities are never personal, simply because no identity common to a collective is personal. A collective identity is a "whole," including interrelated behavior codes, feelings, and beliefs.

In a way, collective identities resemble territories. Pursuing the analogy, the feminist struggle is a struggle for autonomy—for the restitution of women's control over themselves, and the creation of a new code. Hence, women's movements for changes in gender identity are no different from national liberation movements. They call for a new form of self-determination, represent new interests, and demand a different political structure. Any woman who claims to oppose the revolutionary political organization of women is not a feminist. In fact, such women actually support the status quo, whether they admit it or not. They, too, are waiting for Prince Charming.

Gender identity, like national identity, serves specific interests. If women in Israeli society are discriminated against, compared to men—and Arabs, compared to Jews; and Orientals, compared to Ashkenazim—then the very acceptance of the content of these collective identities makes me an integral part of society, and, as such, a party to the perpetuation and preservation of its present form. Like other collective identities, gender identity can only be changed by the new content which women are presently injecting into the mold imposed on them from without. The introduction of new content is a political act, a protest challenging the existing order.

As a political activist for over a decade, I have been involved in many struggles. Nevertheless, although my voice rang out from numerous public platforms, I must confess that I was impressively silent on every issue concerning the situation of women in general, and in Israeli society in particular.

It is strange, since I define myself as a feminist and am no stranger to political struggle. Yet I contented myself with making new rules of behavior only within a restricted, personal circle; I never initiated any consistent action aimed at feminist change, nor did I participate in such action. In fact, I was a "personal feminist," that is, something which does not exist, except as a convenient female lie.

I will try to explain why. In so doing, I may be able to answer a much more disturbing question: why so many women take no part in the struggle; and why so many publicly prominent women are not feminists, that is, do not oppose women's oppression.

I was born female, to Jewish parents, who immigrated to Israel when I was an infant. During the first four years of my life, the following identities were imposed upon me: "feminine," "Jewish," "Israeli." A short time later, my Israeli identity was negated and replaced by an ethnic identity—a process which, in fact, was perpetrated by Israeli society on all those Jews born and raised in Moslem countries. Israel imposed the "Oriental" identity on those immigrants in order to set them apart from those citizens perceived as entitled to the "Israeli" identity, the Ashkenazi Jews; and also, to a certain degree, to set them apart from the Palestinian Arab citizens, who were entitled to almost nothing. The "Oriental" identity meant discrimination, and the "Arab" identity, even greater discrimination. The force which determined the pecking order was "society," that is, that sector that had a monopoly on power and social resources. "Society" was first and foremost the Ashkenazi male Jews; their women supported them wholeheartedly, whether out of love for their own privileges, or merely because they had been brought up to obey.

Obviously, I hated my "Oriental" identity. From the day I learned to tell the difference, I yearned to assume the identity of an "Israeli"; naturally, I longed to resemble its true representative, the Ashkenazi male. In this context, my womanhood was a privilege that might relieve my inferior "Oriental" status: by marrying an Ashkenazi, I could rise in class. Among many Oriental families, marriage to an Ashkenazi male was considered a formula for success, the breaking of a social barrier; as elsewhere, women were viewed as no more than mirror images of the men they had managed to "catch." Similarly, Ashkenazi families perceived Oriental women as warm and subservient creatures, whose assumed capacity for serving Ashkenazi males compensated, to some degree, for their inferior ethnic status. A common Yiddish proverb illustrates this point: "A Frenk is a chaye; a Frenkina, a mechaye" ("an Oriental is a beast; an Oriental woman is bliss"). Reality, then, showed me that by being more feminine, I could become less "Oriental." No doubt, at that stage, my feminine gender identity did not bother me one bit; on the contrary, I was about "to make it."

When I finally attained "Israeli" status, however, I realized that an identity is not merely a trapping—like a first name or a veil—but an array of behaviors, thoughts, and feelings supporting the interests rooted in that identity. Thus, as an "Israeli," I was supposed to discriminate against Arabs, Orientals, and women; to believe that such discrimination was "natural," "vital," or "nonexistent"; to feel that it was "all right," or "not all right, but there's no choice"; and to construct a logical edifice to explain why it was "essential," or "objective," or "not the best thing in the world, but that's the way it is." The most problematic aspect of this process at the time was the need to despise Orientals—to despise my parents, my grandmother, many people whom I loved—and to view them as directly responsible for their inferior status in Israeli society. After all, I was about to join the ruling class, which is never responsible for anything bad, and whose members achieve their goals by virtue of their wisdom, beauty, and energy.

By the time I could be considered "Israeli," I had already begun to reject that dubious distinction. As Israeli society is composed of three ethnic groups (with class and ethnicity overlapping)—Ashkenazi Jews, Oriental Jews, and Palestinian Arabs—it was obvious that I and others like me would have to go on being "Orientals" for a long time, with all that this implied. Accordingly, my first challenge was to infuse new content into my "Oriental" identity, to build new behaviors, thoughts, and feelings. This process included an effort to dredge up from the past various illustrious forefathers (not foremothers); to rehabilitate memories; to construct symbols; and, most important, to understand (with a certain amount of regret) that I would have to renounce the privileges devolving on me as an Israeli Jew, even one who was also an Oriental woman.

The change in my "Oriental" identity gave me the right—a right which did not depend on the Ashkenazim—to an "Israeli" identity, even though I had come to realize that that identity, too, would have to be changed. Such a change meant imposing on Ashkenazim their own ethnic identity and negating their "Israeli" identity, in order to create an identity with room for Arabs and Jews, Orientals and Ashkenazim alike. The process would be both individual and collective. Without individual effort, I could not change my own inner ethnic and national identities; without a political struggle, I could not press for change in the collective identities and the interests they served. At that point, I consciously stopped using my femaleness as a ploy to make life easier for myself. I began to demand rights, rather than beg for favors; and the first thing I looked for was comrades-in-arms.

I had all kinds of odd partners—chauvinist Oriental men, antifeminist women, nationalist and liberal Ashkenazim. Each of them had his or her own reasons and interests for changing the existing "Oriental" identity. Yet, when later I went on to struggle for change in the national identity, many of my erstwhile comrades dropped out. For example, Orientals who wanted to be just as "Israeli" as the Ashkenazim were not interested in granting "Israeli" identity to Palestinian Arab citizens; nationalist Ashkenazim who deigned to admit the Orientals into "their" identity refused to concede that Palestinian Arabs could also be unreservedly "Israeli." Even liberal Ashkenazim, who were prepared to incorporate Palestinian Arabs into the national identity, had difficulty confronting their own "Ashkenazi" identity, as this would have necessitated changing the content of that identity and renouncing the interests and privileges reserved for them alone. In short, it became clear that many Israelis face an internal conflict of identities—partners in any one stage of the struggle were liable to disappear en route to the next.

With women, too, my experience of support was brief—but instructive. The great majority of Israeli feminists are Ashkenazi. In the few opportunities I had to meet with them, I noted that they called for the liberation of women from male oppression, but refused to fight discrimination against Orientals or Arabs, whether because they saw no oppression (in the case of discrimination against Orientals by Ashkenazim), or for tactical reasons (in the case of discrimination against Arabs by Jews). The scarcity of Oriental and Arab women among their meager ranks admittedly bothered them; yet, they accepted it as they would a chronic eye infection. Moreover, as they could not even reach the thousands of women of their own ethnic and class affiliation, they felt no need or impulse to contend with their "Ashkenazi" identity and its privileges. The Oriental struggle was alien to them.

Basically, their approach was no different from that of the Oriental and Palestinian movements. Orientals argued that for tactical reasons, it was not prudent to come out against male oppression of women, since the Oriental struggle for liberation was still in its infancy and could not (yet) open another front and risk losing supporters. To the best of my knowledge, this hesitancy also characterizes Palestinian revolutionary movements. As the great majority of my comrades in the Oriental movement were men, this approach—if and when it ever reached the point of discussion—was adopted without objection.

Fighting oppression is not poetry. Rather than fine distinctions, it requires rough outlines and crass generalizations. Its initial stages must be marked by "us" against "them"; "oppressed" against "oppressors"; "justice" against "injustice." Only after the struggle reaches mass proportions and achieves a certain legitimacy can the social analysis take nuances into account. This being the case, who were the "us" with whom I was to struggle? With the feminists, who fought against the oppression of women, but were not prepared to fight against that of Orientals; or with the men, who opposed the oppression of Palestinian Arabs or Orientals, but were not prepared to oppose that of women? And if that wasn't enough, the feminists' "them" included my Oriental comrades-in-arms, and the Orientals' "them" included Ashkenazi feminist women (not to mention that the Palestinians' "them" quite rightly included Jews of both sexes and all ethnic origins). Members of all these groups acted both as oppressed and as oppressors. As oppressed, they were right; as oppressors, they were blind.

The lesson I learned is by no means new. Changing the oppressive content of one identity does not necessarily lead to a change in the content of another, privileged identity; and while no group likes to be oppressed, it may not really mind being oppressors. As the saying goes, the foot hurts only where the shoe pinches.

The question is not which of the oppressed groups is "more right," or with which of them to empathize (as, from both the intellectual and the emotional standpoint, one can empathize with all oppressed collectivities without distinction), but with which group to ally oneself in the actual struggle. I chose to join the Orientals, rather than the feminists. This may have been because I considered the class element, the Orientals' belonging to the lower class, as crucial; or because I had not yet exchanged my "feminine" identity for a "feminist" one. Nonetheless, in the process of changing my gender identity, my inability to identify with the Ashkenazi feminists, and my lack of trust in their sincerity, became an obstacle. I was not prepared to join their collective struggle. I could not ignore their refusal to fight for change in the situation of Orientals in Israeli society, although I could resign myself to the similar refusal of Orientals to oppose the oppression of women.

It would be wrong to assume from the foregoing that ethnic identity is stronger than gender identity. When collective identities are in a process of change, the transition from the stage of individual change (affecting the collective identity within myself) to that of collective change (affecting the collective identity in society) depends upon existing agents of social change. If these agents pose a problem for the individual, the process of change in the collective identity is liable to come to a halt. I am speaking of a problem that stems from basic conflict of interests, not one that originates in disagreement over tactics or misgivings over negative stigma that may attach to participants of the struggle.

The Ashkenazi feminists, and this is no less true of white feminists in the West, are an integral part of the dominant ethnic group. They are, in fact, fighting against their oppression by Ashkenazi or white men, and not by Oriental or black men; they are not married to the latter, are usually not exploited by them, and they do strive for the types of dominance that the latter cannot obtain. By contrast, the circles of oppression surrounding the Oriental and Palestinian Arab women are much wider than the space occupied by their men. Oriental and Arab men are not policy-makers and do not control the economy or the media; thus, in their wretchedness, they oppress only their own women. While the women must certainly fight against them, they must also struggle against the Ashkenazi men and women who keep Orientals and Palestinian Arabs, irrespective of sex or age, from an equal share of the resources of the society in which they live. The Ashkenazi feminists (and the white feminists of the western world), who have not stood up against their own ethnic group and class and joined the fight against its dominance, are not natural allies in the collective struggle of women from lower ethnic classes, as they do not oppose the existing social order as a whole, but only one dimension of it.

Finally, I cannot omit another, embarrassing observation. I did not protest against the oppression of women—not even Oriental women—because it was not convenient. Just as many women artists refuse to be "women's artists," and women in politics often refuse to deal in "women's affairs." Artists and politicians alike want to reach the summit, the tip of the pyramid built by men. At that summit, all things involving "women" are considered trivial; we, the women at the summit level, want to deal in "universal" matters, even though we know them to have been defined as "universal" by men. And if "women's affairs" are not a "universal" matter and women's art is "sectoral," we tend to avoid dealing with or identifying with these issues. Therefore, many women in prominent positions prefer to preserve their own status in the masculine ivory tower by ignoring the condition of women. This supposed ignorance is pleasant and convenient, not to mention the fact that it enables women to remain grateful to the men whose prodigious assistance got them up there in the first place.

Furthermore, any struggle against the oppression of women threatens men and male privilege. Since the object is to strip men—especially those at the top—of power, they will fight any woman colleague who demands her due. In a very subtle way, women learn that a great deal of discomfort can be avoided by careful phrasing and intonation. This is the soil which nurtures "personal feminists": Those women universally respected for having "made it on their own"; those women who are, "of course," in favor of women's equality, but who (even if unconsciously) always manage to turn the oppression of women into an intellectual, ethical, noncontroversial, and extremely marginal subject on the public agenda. In this way, they have the best of both worlds. If asked directly, they will express feminist attitudes; at the same time, any concrete action they take in this area will be limited and sporadic. I hate to admit it, but I've been there.

Several years ago, when I began my activity on behalf of the party [TAMI, the "Israel Tradition Movement," a short-lived Oriental party that was a member of the government coalition 1981–1984—Trans.], the party leaders asked me to organize a women's movement. I refused, because I felt they were trying to reduce my status, as if I had been asked to set up a kindergarten while they, the men, dealt with affairs of state. At a certain point, I changed my mind and agreed to meet with women at local branches, in order to recruit them for party activities. After two meetings in two development towns, I received no further invitations, because the men heading the party branches were stunned at the nature of the encounters. They had intended for me to come to the women and encourage them to "help out" in branch activities: to send letters, make telephone calls, prepare refreshments. What I had done, however, was to spur the women to act as branch managers and local party heads; I also showed them techniques for achieving a majority vote, or for finding time for political activity ("Take a baby-sitter for the kids," "Leave your husband with them," "Set up a playroom in the party offices," etc.).

At those two meetings, the male party members in attendance felt profoundly insulted. They had invited some 30 women to each meeting, and had treated me with considerable deference. As soon as we began to talk, I asked them politely to serve the refreshments, so that the women could all be present at the discussion. To help them over the shock, I even encouraged them to joke about it. Within a few minutes, however, when I realized that the very presence of men was preventing the women from speaking freely, I asked them to leave the room. Feeling that I was undermining their authority, they tried to protest or to poke fun at me. When they returned, they found the women highly critical of party activities and full of new ideas. At that point, the men could no longer conceal their rage. They had treated me as "one of their own," and I had betrayed them by challenging their status.

I was not invited to any more development towns, nor was I ever again asked to organize a women's movement. I could have tried to change the decision, to fight their tendency to put women down. I did not do so, because I wished to avoid conflicts, to be "just like a man," to deal in "important" matters, and to be appreciated by the men. It was much easier for me to forget my obligation toward the women whom I had met in the two development towns, as I had no further contact with them, in contrast to my daily encounters with the men, during our discussions of "affairs of state."

For years, then, I tried to resolve all the above conflicts by defining myself as a "personal feminist." As I now see it, such a definition is foolishness at best, tantamount to acceptance of the status quo and, therefore, passive cooperation with the oppression of women. The commonly suggested solutions for this dilemma are the establishment of a universal movement against all forms of oppression, or joint struggle by an umbrella organization. These, unfortunately, are not real solutions: not only because they have not been effectively implemented, but also because they do not present the critical analysis necessary for any serious consideration of the problems raised.

For the sake of illustration, let us assume that I get up tomorrow morning and found a humanist movement, with a general platform opposing all oppression. What would happen? The number of people prepared to fight for overall social change and abolish all forms of oppression, including any and all of their own personal privileges, would probably not exceed two dozen. All of them would be decent people whose financial situation enabled them to be decent. After three "ideological" meetings, a dozen of them would tire of the game; when we reached the problem of financial resources, the others would also drop out. It is, of course, possible that no one would quit, and that we would remain a united group, meeting once a month for ideological discussions, funding a small newspaper, and incessantly debating the question of how to reach the masses. There are such groups in New York and Tel Aviv; they remain tiny for years. Despite the attractiveness of the idea, such groups lack the strongest motive for struggle—organization around a burning issue specifically defined by the members themselves. Yet when this occurs, the principle of "the foot hurts where the shoe pinches" and its implications are bound to narrow the perspective of the struggle once again.

Another strategy is the formation of an alliance of organizations opposing various forms of oppression, within which each movement continues to strive for its specific goals, while maintaining "strategic" contact with the other groups, cooperating in the organization of occasional mass demonstrations. This, too, is an attractive idea; in practice, however, it is nothing but an illusion. During a 3 year stay in New York, I found that this type of cooperation resulted in no more than one march per year, with many participants and colorful signs, something resembling a carnival. During the same period, I witnessed a number of vehement protests against racial incidents—protests at which, to my astonishment, whites were conspicuously absent. And in the 1989 march against changing the abortion laws in the United States, the proportion of Black and Hispanic women participants was negligible.

What basis is there for such an alliance in Israel? While intellectually opposed to the oppression of women, many Oriental political activists are chauvinists in practice; most of the Ashkenazi feminist women are against the oppression of Orientals, only they do not really believe that Orientals are, in fact, oppressed. As for the Palestinians, they are not sure they need to devote even a moment's thought to the oppression of women or Orientals, when their own children are being shot in the streets every day. Not to mention the fact that not a few of the men are proud chauvinists.

The problem is not alliances and strategy, but old identities that act as nets of oppression, from which most people — including political activists involved in the struggle against oppression — have not managed to free themselves, if indeed they wish to free themselves.

The feminists' contribution to solving this problem should be by concentrating on critical social analysis, which is sorely lacking in feminist discussions. Their tendency to content themselves with analyzing one aspect of society — the oppression of women — obscures the obvious connection with other forms of oppression, and leaves the feminist struggle detached from, and occasionally opposed to, other liberation movements. Without a critical analysis of the society in which women live, the feminist struggle is liable to take the form of an internal elitist conflict, and thus to lose its great revolutionary potential.

Rape and Rape Survivors in Israel

Esther Eilam
(Translated by Sharon Ne'eman)

Over the last decade, important amendments have been made to the laws pertaining to rape in Israel and special instructions have been issued to the police and hospitals regarding the investigation of rapes and the treatment of rape survivors. Much of the credit for these changes goes to the Rape Crisis Centers, which provided the starting point for breaking the "conspiracy of silence" and shattering the prevailing myths about rape.

Whereas in the United States, the last two decades have witnessed a constant increase in the number of reported rapes (some view this as indicating a rise in the actual number of rapes), there has been no change in the extent of reported sexual offenses in Israel over the same period. The number of sexual offenses reported during the 1980s has, in fact, decreased. In 1988, the number of reported sexual offenses was 44 per 100,000 residents, or 1,970 for the 4.5 million residents of the state of Israel. The number of complaints recorded in that year for each of the eight crimes classified as sexual offenses is as follows: rape by force or by threat—295; rape and statutory rape—331; unnatural offenses (sodomy)—45; forcible indecent acts—463; nonforcible indecent acts—598; indecent acts in public—230; spreading venereal diseases—6; attempted sexual offenses—2. Police report identifying the perpetrators of 1,335 of the total of 1,970 complaints, (Israel Police, 1988).

In 1987, 1,930 complaints of sexual crimes were recorded, and the figure in 1988 was similar. However, the number of rape complaints in 1988 was nearly double that of 1987: 626 compared with 330; the estimate for 1989 is 476 (Israel Police, 1989). One reason for this increase may be the broadened definition of "rape" in Amendment 22 to the Criminal Code, passed in 1988 (Israel Criminal Code, 1988) which defines rape not only as penetration of the female sex organ by the male sex organ, but also as penetration by various objects or forcible fellatio. In addition, the amendment gave legislative status to a 1980 Israel Supreme Court ruling that a woman may sue her husband for rape. It should be noted that the 1988 Amendment deleted

312

the term "unnatural act" in its reference to sodomy, which is now considered as serious as rape, if committed under the conditions defined by law as rape.

The only existing statistical data on rape survivors come from police records and those of the Rape Crisis Centers. In 1988, approximately 850 women—some 700 Jewish women and about 100 Arab women, the latter including residents both of Israel and of the occupied territories—contacted the country's five Rape Crisis Centers to request assistance following rape or other sexual assault. About one-half of all requests for assistance were made to the Rape Crisis Center in Tel Aviv, which serves the most densely populated area in Israel.

The number of calls to the Rape Crisis Centers increases each year; the growth rate for 1989, relative to 1988, is forecast at between 50 percent and over 100 percent (Tel Aviv Rape Crisis Center, 1989).

There is a certain overlap between the calls to the Rape Crisis Centers and the complaints filed with police. Whereas only 16 percent of the total calls to the Haifa Rape Crisis Center are also reported to the police (Haifa Rape Crisis Center, 1988), the figure in Tel Aviv exceeds 40 percent (Solomon and Winter, 1988). According to data furnished by the Tel Aviv Rape Crisis Center, 70 percent of all calls of this type were reported to the police before being handled by the Rape Crisis Center. This may be explained in either of two ways. The first possibility is that the investigators in Tel Aviv police stations are aware of survivors' needs, and therefore refer them to the Center. The second is that poor treatment encountered by survivors in Tel Aviv police stations, prompts them to seek the assistance of the Center. In any case, there are differences in the extent of contact between the Rape Crisis Centers and the police in various parts of Israel. For example: in Eilat, a national and international tourist resort town, the overwhelming majority of calls to the Rape Crisis Center are police referrals.

In the Tel Aviv Rape Crisis Center, some 60 percent of calls concern survivors up to age 18; 24.7 percent concern girls and boys up to age 12. In the Haifa Center, 44 percent of the calls were with regard to sexual assault of children. These figures represent a steep rise in the number of calls dealing with assault on children. At the same time, a sharp rise has also been noted in the number of calls concerning incest. In 1988, the Israel Ministry of Labour and Social Welfare opened 1,343 files on sexual offenses involving children; in 83 percent of these, children were the victims, about 25 percent of them boys.

The authorities in Israel did not become aware of the unique problems of rape survivors until the late 1970s. Two events helped alert them to the issue. The first was the publication of a report by the Government Commission on the Status of Women, which included recommendations for the provision of assistance to rape survivors. The second was an individual case which shocked the nation: the suicide of a young woman of "good family" who had complained to the police of rape, and who had a traumatic experience upon being sent unaccompanied to the Institute of Forensic Medicine for an examination. Following this incident, in the early 1980s, the Departments of Investigation in Israel's police stations were issued special instructions regarding the taking of statements from rape survivors. A special arrangement was made with the Ministry of Health whereby 18 hospitals throughout the country were authorized to examine rape survivors by means of a special kit, and to give them medical treatment as required.

The principal shortcoming in the instructions issued to police investigators regarding rape complaints is that the items supposedly intended to provide for rape survivors' needs are "contingent upon the requirements of the investigation." An additional shortcoming is that the rights granted to the complainants, such as nonexposure in identification line-ups, are to be implemented "at the request of the complainant" only, rather than automatically. The instructions appear in a document classified for internal use, and are not accessible to the complainants. Senior police officials have recently issued general instructions to investigators concerning "survivors' and witnesses' rights"; nonetheless, only after pressure by the Rape Crisis Centers did the police agree to draft special information leaflets, to be published in early 1990 and then distributed to all rape complainants in the police stations throughout Israel.

Unfortunately, investigators tend to have a mythical, idealized conception of rape, which has been termed "classical rape," that is, rape by a stranger, preferably at night and in a location unfamiliar to the survivor. A woman complaining of rape which does not fit this conception is often suspected of submitting a false complaint. This idealization also enables investigators to dismiss accounts of "classical rape," merely because one fact or another in the survivor's account does not correspond to the investigator's concept of the act. Each police station has its own policy concerning the proper attitude toward and treatment of rape survivors; even within a particular station, the attitude toward rape complainants may vary from investigator to investigator.

Police investigators tend to take full statements from rape complainants even if they are in poor physical and mental condition. In various investigative procedures—identification of the suspect, confrontation with the suspect—survivors not infrequently encounter lack of understanding and consideration on the part of the investigator, including disregard for privacy. In one case, in the course of a Tel Aviv Police manhunt for a rapist-burglar who systematically raped women alone in their homes at night, the home of a woman who had been raped was visited, not only by investigators, but also by journalists and press photographers. Israeli law forbids the publication of rape survivors' names.

Police sexism is expressed in investigators' skepticism regarding women who complain of rape, especially rape by an acquaintance; the accuser then becomes the accused and is subjected to humiliation and insult. If an arrest is made, in 50 percent of the cases, the suspected rapist is released on bail within a short time, after which he is free to harass the survivor. Following the police investigation, the complainant must undergo a gynecological examination. Despite the fact that a number of hospitals are authorized to perform such examinations, the police continue to send rape survivors to Israel's Institute of Forensic Medicine, in Tel Aviv. There, in a special room known as the "living room" [a macabre pun on "dead room," the Hebrew word for "morgue" – Trans.], the survivor is examined by a pathologist, whose routine occupation is the performance of autopsies. Survivors examined by pathologists at the Institute of Forensic Medicine, as well as those examined by male gynecologists in hospitals, report a lack of understanding on the part of these doctors.

As might be expected, there is no typical rapist in Israel. Based on their acquaintance with thousands of rape survivors, volunteers at Rape Crisis Centers can attest to the fact that rapists come from all strata of society. Relatively few are punished; even if the survivor complains to the police, the chances of conviction are not high. Out of 2,077 cases handled by the Attorney General's office in 1988, 55.4 percent were closed for reasons unrelated to the judicial process, such as "lack of public interest," or "mental illness." Only 8.1 percent of cases ended in conviction.

When the case does come to court, the positions of the complainants and the accused are not equal. The accused come to court well prepared, with the assistance of their own attorneys, whereas the survivors are dependent upon a State-appointed prosecuting attorney to represent their interests. Some cases reaching the Attorney General's office never come to trial because the prosecution does not consider them sufficiently "strong." In others, "deals" are made with the accused, without consultation with the survivor. During the trial itself, the survivor is exposed to cross-examinations designed to undermine her reliability. In addition, judges are often biased. In one case, for example, a young woman was taken by a young man to a cemetery, where he threatened that if she did not comply with his demand for sexual relations, she would join the dead. In his verdict, the judge noted that: "The accused apparently belongs to the category of persistent suitors who must have recourse to ruse. It seems to me that this type of courtship is not appropriate to a cultured man, but does not constitute a criminal offense." The accused was acquitted.

The maximum penalties stipulated by law for rape and sexual offenses are severe – up to 20 years for rape; nevertheless, the imposition of the maximum penalty is very rare. There is no stipulated minimum penalty, and many convicted assailants receive light or even suspended sentences. For example, a father convicted of having intercourse with his daughter over a 13-year period, beginning when she was 11 years of age, was given 4 years' imprisonment; in practice, the time he had already spent under arrest was deducted from that term, and a further one-third was taken off for "good behavior." In Israel, very few suits for civil damages are filed by rape survivors. Only in rare cases do the judges rule that the accused is also liable for payment of compensation for damages to the survivor. At the same time, it should be noted that rape trials are conducted by three judges, rather than by a single judge, or by a jury and that rape trials are held *in camera*.

The five (soon to be six) Rape Crisis Centers in Israel are "grassroots" organizations based on volunteer work. They operate emergency hot lines 24 hours a day; they do not specialize in any specific kind of assistance, but provide whatever is required by rape survivors. This assistance may include telephone consultation; face-to-face meetings; escort to the police station, the hospital, or the court; meetings with relatives or guardians; and contacts with other helping agencies in the community. The Centers also engage in public relations, education, legal defense, and reaching-out to potential rape survivors. The Tel Aviv Rape Crisis Center, established some 12 years ago, is the oldest; the Center in Eilat is the most recent. Hot lines in Arabic were opened in Jerusalem in mid-1987, and in Haifa in mid-1988. Similar hot lines are planned in Tel Aviv and in the Center now being set up in Beer Sheba.

Calls to the Jerusalem hot line come in from Arabic-speaking women from both Israel and the occupied territories. Generally speaking, the callers are between 13 and 30 years of age. Most of the rapes they report are committed in places considered safe—in the survivors' homes or yards—and by men acquainted with the survivor: fathers, brothers, relatives, neighbors. Some 70 percent of calls come from survivors between the ages of eight and 15, half of them involving incest.

The loneliness of Arab rape survivors is especially striking, due not only to the absence of services but also to the lack of support from their environment. The stigma of rape plays a central role here, via feelings of shame and guilt. In addition, the fear regarding loss of virginity is an important factor. The very fact of lost virginity through rape often endangers Arab rape survivors' lives. They cannot approach the community gynecologist, for fear of damage to their reputation (especially if the survivor is unmarried, as unmarried women are not expected to have any reason to visit a gynecologist). Yet another isolating factor is the lack of economic independence: many Arab women do not even have the possibility of paying for transportation to meet with a Rape Crisis Center volunteer, or for a visit to a gynecologist outside their place of residence.

In most cases, Arab rape survivors identify themselves by pseudonyms, at least in the initial stages of contact. Survivors generally make contact in the morning hours, when their families are not at home. They are pressed for time, and are liable to hang up suddenly in the middle of the conversation if anyone enters the room. Callers expect immediate, practical solutions, and are not capable of dealing with feelings when they call. They maintain contact with volunteers over long periods of time, sharing the distress which caused them to call the Center in the first place and other problems which develop.

The number of sexual assaults on women soldiers in the Israel Defense Forces is classified information. It may, however, be assumed that the official number of rape complaints does not reflect the true extent of the phenomenon. As in civilian society, and even more so, the military hierarchy is ranked by sex, with women generally subordinate to men. The day-to-day interaction of women soldiers with men soldiers, and especially with their male commanders, is based on sexist norms of behavior which are not even defined as sexual harassment. As most women soldiers are subordinate to men and must submit their complaints via those men—who are themselves liable to be the assailants—the submission of complaints against them or their comrades-in-arms is liable to result in sanctions, such as the revocation of passes. The following example made its way to the Israel press: a woman soldier severely molested by her young male commander tried to complain to a senior male officer, whose reaction was to assault her sexually. In despair, the woman attempted to poison the young commander (using a nonlethal quantity of poison), was tried by court-martial and sentenced to military prison.

By contrast, military personnel have considerable awareness of the possibility of women soldiers being raped on the roads. For many years, the Israel Defense Force (IDF) authorities waged a campaign against hitchhiking by women soldiers. An arrangement was finally reached between the IDF and Israel's public transportation cooperatives, whereby women soldiers received free transportation on inter-city roads. In addition, instructions were issued stating that any woman soldier caught hitchhiking at night would be tried by court-martial. In this connection, it is impossible not to mention a well-known statement by Golda Meir. Following the increase in rapes in Jerusalem, it was suggested that Golda instruct women to stay at home after dark. Golda replied: "We'd do better to instruct the men to stay at home—they're the rapists!"

The military have special instructions for the handling of complaints by sexually assaulted women soldiers. However, investigations are generally conducted by men. Concern for survivors' welfare is reflected in instructions obligating the treatment of sexually assaulted women soldiers by helping elements within the IDF. In practice, these elements—generally young, inexperienced women officers—cannot always effectively support the survivors.

A group of women from the Tel Aviv area have recently undertaken to raise women soldiers' awareness of the subject of sexual harassment. In cooperation with the Chief of the Women's Corps, they assembled an educational kit, which they circulated among women officers. This activity leaves room for hope that sexually harassed or assaulted women soldiers will find greater support and more legitimacy in registering complaints. At the same time, lower-echelon women officers frequently invite women from the Rape Crisis Centers to hold lectures and discussions on rape with women—and sometimes men—soldiers.

The Rape Crisis Centers are founded on the concept of women's autonomy, on women's right to say "no," and on women's solidarity, which breaks the social isolation forced upon us. In the framework of assistance to rape survivors, women create a model for a nonsexist society, whose human relations are "'womanly," not in the stereotyped sense, but as an antithesis to the masculine "death culture," as Susan Griffin (1982) and Mary Daly (1978) define patriarchal society. Personally, the establishment of contact with every rape survivor is a reaffirmation of life. In such contacts, I feel that the survivor and I are working together to recreate the world in which we wish to live.

REFERENCES

Daly, Mary (1978) Gyn-Ecology: The Metaphysics of Radical Feminism. Boston: Beacon Press.

Griffin, Susan (1982) Made From This Earth. New York: Harper & Row.

Haifa Rape Crisis Center (1988) Annual Report.

Israel Criminal Code, Amendment 22, 1988 (included in Israel Criminal Code 1988, "Sexual Offenses," Codex 1246, 31 March 1988) (Hebrew).

Israel Police (1988) Annual Report (Hebrew).

Israel Police (1989) Department of Statistics.

Solomon, Alison and Winter, Ruth (1988) Action Approaches and Evaluation, January 1988–December 1988, Special Report Commemorating a Decade for the Rape Crisis Intervention Center (Hebrew).

Tel Aviv Rape Crisis Center (1989) August. Internal data.

Jews Don't Batter Their Wives: Another Myth Bites the Dust

Barbara Swirski

It appears that Jewish religious law has always given a husband the right to "moderately chastise his wife" for misconduct (Amram, 1968:70); for Jews living in modern-day Israel, it is Jewish religious law or *halakha* that governs relations between spouses. The following is limited to Jewish (as well as Palestinian Arab) women living in Israel. For Jewish battered women in the U.S., see Spitzer (1985), Scarf (1988), deBeer (1988), and Levy (1988).

Evidence of the existence or prevalence of wife abuse in different historical periods and among different peoples is scant; until the development of the shelter movement, battering of women was hardly mentioned in historical chronicles, literature or philosophical treatises, with the notable exception of John Stuart Mill's *The Subjection of Women* (1980). One of the few sources available are the various codes of law. However, a problem of interpretation arises: How do we determine the significance of what appears—or does not appear—in these sources? For example, if wife battering is not mentioned at all (it is not mentioned in the Old Testament), are we to conclude that the phenomenon did not exist, or that it was uncommon? Or should we entertain the possibility that it was prevalent, but the status of women was so low that violence against them was taken for granted and not considered worthy of mention. Conversely, when we find a law forbidding a husband to beat his wife, are we to conclude that wife abuse was rampant in the period under study, or should we assume that the law reflected an accepted norm, and that wife abuse was actually rare? Moreover, we could also ask who the lawmakers were, and what societal group they belonged to. Without this information, we have no way of knowing if a particular law against wife abuse, or the absence of such a law, reflected a widely accepted social norm or merely the attitude of the group to which the lawmakers belonged. We should also have to know whether the law was an effective one; the fact that a law has been enacted does not tell us whether it is honored in the breach or the observance.

With these reservations in mind, it should be noted that there are a number of references to wife abuse in the body of writings that make up Jewish law—the *Talmud*, the *Responsa*, the *Code of the Law*, and the *Shulhan Arukh*. A computerized search for judgments recorded between the 8th and 20th centuries identifies 160 that refer to wife beating (*Responsa Project*, 1983). To cite but a few of the better known ones: the first, an opinion of Babylonian scholar Rabbi Yehudai (8th century) stated that a woman should never raise her voice; "even if [her husband] beats her she should remain silent, as modest women are wont to do" (*Otzar Geonim*). In another judgment, he declared, "Whoever strikes his wife and inflicts injury upon her (and she wants a divorce and he doesn't) he is to be fined in accordance with his ability to pay, and the payment is to be given to his wife, who may do with it whatever she pleases as long as she does not give it away without his consent. And peace should be made between them; he should not be forced to divorce her" (*Otzar Geonim*). Maimonides, one of the greatest interpreters of Jewish law (12 century—Spain, Morocco, and Egypt), stated that there were situations in which a husband might beat his wife. He listed the duties incumbent upon married women. All women were to act as their husbands' personal servants; they were to wash his face and feet and fetch him whatever he asked for. If a wife had maidservants, they could do the housework; if not, she was to do the cooking, baking, laundry, flour grinding, and livestock feeding. "If a woman refuses to carry out one of her duties, she should be forced to do it, even with a whip." And a commentary in the *Shulhan Arukh*, or *Book of the Law* (1554) by Rabbi Isserles, a well-known Polish Jewish scholar (1525–1572), also suggested that a man was justified in beating his wife under certain circumstances.

Jewish religious authorities generally differentiated between "justified" and "unjustified" beatings. "Unjustified" beating was a transgression and often considered grounds for divorce. As Jewish spiritual leaders regarded their religion as more cultured and advanced than those of surrounding peoples, they sometimes argued against battering in these terms. Rabbi Shlomo Ben Abraham Aderet (13th century—Spain) opined that if a husband hit his wife without her having been at fault, the Rabbinic court should rebuke the husband and warn him that if he persisted, he would be forced to divorce her and give her the amount stipulated in her *Ketuba*, or marriage contract (*Responsa Harashba*: 168). A well-known commentary by Rabbi Isserles in the *Shulhan Arukh*, referred to above, states: "A man who beats his wife commits a sin, as though he had beaten his neighbor (!), and if he persists in his conduct the court may castigate him and excommunicate him and place him under oath to discontinue this conduct; if he refuses to obey the order of the court, they will compel him to divorce his wife at once (though some are of the opinion that he should be warned once or twice) because it is not customary or proper for Jews to beat their wives; it is a custom of the heathen. This is the law where he is at fault; but if she curses him or insults his parents, some are of the opinion that he may beat her, and others say even if she is a bad woman he may not beat her; but I am of the first opinion" (*Shulhan Arukh*).

Mention of the phenomenon of wife abuse can also be found in the Geniza documents, a large collection of papers dating from 700 to 1200 A.D., preserved by Jews who lived in Egypt and other Mediterranean lands, discovered in the geniza or storage room of a synagogue in ancient Cairo. The foremost Geniza scholar, S.D. Goitein, reported that among the Geniza papers were many divorce suits brought by wives against violent husbands. According to Goitein, the Rabbinic courts usually reproached the husbands; occasionally, they also fined them; however, they did not recommend divorce (1978: 184–189).

The first public mention of woman beating in the state of Israel occurred more than a decade before wife abuse became a feminist issue. In 1962, Member of Knesset Beba Edelson (a woman) put a parliamentary question to the Minister of Police. Edelson asked whether Israeli police were aware of the phenomenon of wife beating, and what the Minister intended to do about it. His reply was that the police were aware of the problem, were coping with it, and saw no need for any further action (Knesset Protocol, Vol. 33). The matter was quickly forgotten.

In 1976, fourteen years after Edelson's parliamentary question, the subject of wife beating was once again raised in the Israeli Knesset. Member of Knesset (MK) Marcia Freedman moved that it be placed on the agenda. No sooner had she begun to address the house, than she was interrupted by laughter and heckling from the floor. One MK, Mordecai Ben-Porat, interjected, "And what about the second motion, husband battering by wives?" While Freedman asked those present not to joke about the matter, another MK, Pesach Groper, repeated the same question. And then Minister of Health Victor Shem-Tov commented, "MK Groper, you don't look like your wife beats you." The Minister of Police joined the fray, "How do you know, you haven't seen his wife!" (Knesset Protocol, Vol. 77).

Freedman persisted, unsure whether her well-researched speech was even being heard. Not only was it heard, it was broadcast on the evening news; and since there was only one TV channel, millions watched and listened. When Freedman finished speaking, Minister of Police Shlomo Hillel (Alignment) declared that wife beating was not as serious as Freedman described it and moved to table Freedman's motion. However, his motion was killed; the majority were in favor of referring the matter to parliamentary committee. In a rare breach of party discipline, all the female MKs from the Alignment, the Knesset faction comprised of members of the two Labor parties, as well as a few of the men, had voted against Hillel's motion (Freedman, 1990:104). Subsequently a subcommittee on police affairs was charged with investigating the phenomenon of battered women in Israel.

When the subcommittee began its work, it discovered that the police had no record of complaints filed by women against their husbands. As a police officer at the Haifa station had told Freedman, "The Arabs beat their wives, but the Jews don't" (Freedman, 1988). At the request of the Knesset subcommittee, the police appointed a special committee of their own to investigate police handling of battering complaints. The monitor found that in the first half of 1976, 2,000 Israeli women filed assault complaints against the husbands. Freedman presented the Knesset with other figures as well: the legal aid bureaus of the Women's International Zionist Organization (WIZO), the second-largest women's organization in Israel, reported that 55 percent of the 1,500 women who had turned to them in the first half of 1976 had been systematically battered by their husbands. Most of these women had never filed a complaint with the police.

The Knesset subcommittee estimated that between five and ten percent of Israeli married women were battered: that is, in 1976 — 30,000 to 60,000 women. Despite the enormity of the problem, and contrary to usual parliamentary procedure, no report or conclusions were ever published by the subcommittee (Freedman, 1990). Thus, the Israeli public was not to perceive woman battering as a social problem until the establishment of the first shelter for battered women, in Haifa in 1977. Marcia Freedman was the driving force among the founders.

The first Israeli shelters were created by feminists, and like their sisters living in other parts of the globe, they forced existing institutions to change their attitudes and practices with regard to woman battering. Before the first shelter opened its doors, social service agencies had had no name for either the phenomenon or the victim; they tended to view battering as part of "the dynamics of interaction" between spouses, and to blame the woman for being "too" or "not enough" — whatever — to satisfy their husbands' needs. Battered women were usually referred to mental health clinics, where they inevitably received prescriptions for tranquilizers. In some cases, social workers gave women welfare payments or subsidized daycare (not that these benefits could end the violence, but they were what the social workers had to offer); in others, they referred women to marital counseling services. Like their cohorts in other parts of the world, Israeli batterers tended to refuse counseling. If they did cooperate, it was the woman who was expected to change her behavior. There was no feminist counseling and no Batterers Anonymous. Not all battered women turned to state social service agencies, of course; a study of clients of the Na'amat family violence counseling service revealed that 73.9 percent of them had had no prior contact with social workers (Lev-Ari, 1986).

The legal system had no provisions for battered women either. A 1977 law defined assault as "striking, touching, pushing or applying physical force in some other way, either directly or indirectly, without consent or with consent acquired by deception" (Criminal Law-1977, Article 378). The absence of any mention of the assault of a husband against his wife left the police broad discretionary powers in applying the law to marital violence.

When the first shelter opened in 1977, the police had no regulations for dealing with complaints brought by wives against their husbands. Often they did not even register the complaint. In other cases they would ask the woman, "What do you want me to do—warn him or arrest him?" thus transferring responsibility to the woman herself. As they had no knowledge of criminal law, most women were intimidated by the officer's tone, which implied that he expected them to say that a warning would suffice. If the husband was summoned to the station, the investigation took the form of "a man-to-man" talk, and the husband understood he had nothing to fear; the police would not prosecute. Arrests were made only if there was blood, broken bones, or other visible signs of "serious injury."

In the few cases in which police did open a criminal file on the husband, little effort was made to bring the case to trial. For one, there was no evidence. Police did not give women medical certificates to be completed by their physicians, nor did they bother to explain the necessity for an immediate medical examination for the sake of evidence. Second, Israeli police, like their cohorts the world over, perceived husbands' assaults as "family quarrels" entirely lacking in "public interest."

It was only after a battered woman by the name of Carmela Nakash was murdered by her husband in the courtyard of the Herzliya shelter in 1979 that National Police Headquarters issued regulations for dealing with complaints filed by battered women. These regulations required police to register every complaint and to issue a warning to every husband. They also mandated them to open a criminal file on the violent husband—unless it was his first offense, or he expressed remorse, or the injury was "not serious." However, the regulations did not define "serious injury," nor did they offer any guidelines with regard to arrest. The decision to arrest a husband or to ask the court for a stay of arrest was still left to the discretion of the officer in charge.

The courts were also lenient towards woman batterers. The story of Carmela Nakash is, again, a case in point. On April 12, 1978, Carmela filed a complaint against her husband at the Petah Tikva police station. He had beaten her in the past. This time he hit her with a steel pipe, causing a visible head injury. Five days after filing the complaint, Carmela fled to the Haifa shelter. There she began a long correspondence with the Petah Tikva police station. Eight months later, on December 21, 1978, the shelter received a letter from the Petah Tikva police stating that the criminal file opened for Carmela's husband had been transferred to the legal department "a few days ago."

The trial was eventually set for July 19, 1979—a year and a quarter after Carmela first filed her complaint. During most of the interim, she remained in the Haifa shelter. At one point, she moved to a rented room, but her husband uncovered her address and forced her to return home. She fled once again, this time to the Herzliya shelter. It was not long before her husband discovered her whereabouts. The day before the trial, he slit her throat.

On the rare occasions in which assault cases against violent husbands came to trial, the maximum sentence was (and still is) 3 years' imprisonment (Criminal Law-1977, Articles 379,380). Under the Israeli legal system, criminal cases are tried not by jury but by a court of three judges. Often the judges, most of whom are male, took into account the "extenuating circumstances" — namely, the fact that the plaintiff and defendant were husband and wife — and imposed a small fine or suspended sentence. When the offense was repeated, and it usually was, the judges still preferred suspended sentence to imprisonment.

Judgments in battering cases were, and often still are, tainted with male prejudice, for example the following judgment from the Haifa magistrate court: "Concerning the testimony of a wife against her husband when there is a serious quarrel against the background of a divorce suit; in such circumstances it is difficult to rely solely on the testimony of the woman, and the defendant should be found innocent." This statement was made in a case in which the woman's complaint was supported by other evidence: a medical certificate which described the injuries sustained, the testimony of policemen, previous complaints filed by the woman against her husband, and the absence of any denial on the part of the husband himself (Salomon, 1980).

In the religious courts, the situation was (and still is) much worse. Unlike their predecessors, contemporary Jewish religious judges are not spiritual leaders of the community, but low-level bureaucrats who lack a broad education. Like all bureaucrats, they tend to "stick to the rules," that is, confine themselves to a narrow interpretation of the law. The guiding principles of the religious judges are "keeping the family together" and "shalom bayit," or peace in the household. Thus, in a study of battered women who had taken refuge in three Israeli shelters, 55 percent of the women reported that when they sued their husbands in a Rabbinic court, they were told to return home to make "peace in the household" (Epstein and Marder, 1986:70).

A basic principle of Jewish law is that marriage and divorce are by mutual consent. Only a man can actually perform the divorce ceremony, but the woman must agree to take part in it. If one of the parties objects, there is no divorce. But what if the man beats his wife and refuses to give her a divorce? This is a knotty problem, but as we have seen, past judgments compelled men to divorce their wives. In contemporary Israel, however, Rabbinic judges do not perceive this as an option; in fact, the Orthodox religious establishment has vigorously opposed all efforts on the part of religious leaders in the Jewish diaspora to find halakhic solutions to the problem (Falk, 1973).

By creating the first shelter for battered women, in Haifa, in 1977, Israeli feminists paved the way for a number of changes in social institutions and social policy. The most obvious development was the establishment of services for battered women: feminist groups founded two additional shelters, one in Herzliya (1978: "No to Violence Against Women") and another in Jerusalem (1981: "Woman to Woman"). The issue of violence against women and shelter work soon became a major focus of feminist activity in Israel. Before long, the cause had become respectable, probably because it was generally perceived in humanitarian rather than feminist terms, and the two largest women's organizations, Women's International Zionist Organization (WIZO) and Na'amat, opened their own services. In 1983, Na'amat established a counseling center for the prevention of "family violence," and in 1984, WIZO opened a shelter in the town of Ashdod, followed in 1988 by a hot line in Tel Aviv. The Herzliya municipality's Community Affairs Department initiated a program for batterers, and Na'amat offered treatment for violent men as part of its counseling services. During 1987, a total of 461 women and 713 children took refuge within the four Israeli shelters (Steiner, 1990), and an estimated additional 200 women received counseling from the shelters. The same year, about 1,250 women were serviced by the Center for the Prevention of Family Violence (Lev-Ari, 1989). While the first shelter residents were Jewish women, all Israeli shelters and services are open to and have been used by Moslem, Christian and Druze women as well. In recent years, 15 percent of the women in the Haifa shelter have been Israeli Palestinian Arab women.

The shelters were accorded almost immediate official recognition by the Ministry of Welfare and provided with an annual budget. A new department was eventually created to develop services for battered women, and to administer allocations to the shelters. It worked with other government ministries, notably Housing and Health, to obtain housing subsidies and medical insurance for battered women and to sensitize social workers and public health personnel to the problem of wife abuse. Social workers began referring battered women to shelters and counseling services rather than to mental health clinics.

The police instituted new procedures for dealing with complaints by battered women. Today every complaint is registered, and most police stations keep a special file on violent husbands. In a 1986 study, 37 percent of the battered women in the sample reported that their husbands had been arrested following assault complaints (Epstein and Marder, 1986:64). However, the majority of batterers still escape arrest and prosecution, and there are still no clear guidelines for officers on duty. In 1986, the Attorney General appointed a committee to look into the police policy concerning investigation and prosecution in cases of family violence. New legislation was drafted by a number of bodies, but no new laws have been passed. In some cases, civil courts impose heavier sentences than in the past, but the law itself remains lenient. Rabbinic courts have become increasingly hostile to women suing for child support, custody or divorce, so that shelters and counseling services advise

them to avoid the religious courts and adjudicate in the civil courts whenever possible.

A new concept, *isha muka* (battered woman) has entered the Hebrew lexicon; newspapers periodically present features about battered women and
shelters, court reporters cover wife abuse cases as a matter of course, and
radio and television, which are national, not private, have aired a number
of programs on the battering of woman. Wife abuse is now studied in Israeli
universities, and research has been conducted on the subject. The findings
support those of research in other societies. For example, after studying battered women in the lower socioeconomic classes (Lev-Ari, 1979), Lev-Ari surveyed the clients of the Na'amat counseling service and found evidence that
battered women and batterers come from all ethnic groups and all levels of
education (Lev-Ari, 1986:7; Walker, 1979). Other studies found that battered
women often have more education than their batterers (Epstein and Marder,
1986; Steiner, 1990; Pinton and Selei, 1986); Hornung, McCullough, and
Sugimoto, 1981). The history of the battering relationships of Israeli women
was reported to be remarkably similar to that of women in other parts of the
world (Swirski, 1984, Dobash and Dobash, 1979; Walker, 1979); the same
is true for the pattern of abuse that includes a combination of physical battering, mental cruelty, sexual abuse, and the imposition of social isolation and
economic dependence (Swirski, 1984; Walker, 1979). Like their sisters in other
societies, battered women in Israel exhibit low self-esteem, (Swirski, 1984;
Steiner, 1990); they also report feelings of being alone and of not belonging
(Steiner, 1990), which has led social work practitioners to recommend support groups and group therapy rather than individual therapy (Epstein and
Marker, 1986; Steiner, 1990).

Israeli research has shown that shelters help to reduce violence. In a preliminary study of the Ashdod shelter, 23 out of the 27 women surveyed reported
that the violence decreased after they left the shelter (Pinton and Selei, 1986:4),
and a follow-up study of 100 women who had stayed in the Haifa, Herziliya
and Jerusalem shelters found that after leaving the shelters, 61 percent of the
respondents ceased to be abused. Of those who separated from their husbands, 74 percent reported no longer being subject to violence; of those who
returned home, 53 percent stated that their husbands had stopped beating
them (Epstein and Marder, 1986: 46). The same study also found a significant correlation between the amount of time spent in the shelters and the
cessation of violence (Epstein and Marder, 1986: 53).

Despite attempts to change them to fit the social work model (Schechter,
1982), Israel's three feminist shelters have retained their original feminist orientation. If there is no less woman battering in Israel than there was ten years
ago, it is no longer ignored or joked about. The shelters are there to proclaim
that battering is a crime and that women have an alternative.

REFERENCES

Amram, David W. (1968) *The Jewish Law of Divorce According to the Bible and the Talmud.* New York: Hermon Press.

deBeer, Elizabeth (1988) "Wife Abuse, Drugs and Silence." *Lilith,* No. 20, Summer, 6–7.

Dobash, Rebecca and Dobash, Russell (1979) *Violence Against Wives: A Case Against the Patriarchy.* New York: Free Press.

Epstein, Maxine and Marder, Reggie (1986) *Shalom-Bayit.* Haifa: Breirot (Hebrew).

Falk, Ze'ev (1973) *Israeli Law Concerning Women Who Sue for Divorce.* Jerusalem: The Institute for the Study of Legislation and Comparative Law (Hebrew).

Freedman, Marcia (1990) *Exile in the Promised Land: A Memoir.* Ithaca: Firebrand.

Goitein, S. D. (1978) *A Mediterranean Society: The Jewish Communities of the Arab World as Portrayed in the Documents of the Cairo Geniza,* Vol. 3. Berkeley: University of California Press.

Hornung, Carlton; McCullough, B.; Sugimoto, Taichi (1981) "Status Relationships in Marriage: Risk Factors in Spouse Abuse." *Journal of Marriage and the Family* 43 (3): 675–692.

Knesset Protocol (No date) Jerusalem: Government Press: 77: 3537–3541 (Hebrew).

Knesset Protocol (No date) Jerusalem: Government Press: 33: 1123 (Hebrew).

Lev-Ari, Ronit (1979) "Battered Wives in Israel." M.A. Thesis, Institute of Criminology and Criminal Law, Tel Aviv University (Hebrew).

Lev-Ari, Ronit (ed.) (1986) "Violence in the Family." Tel Aviv: Na'amat (Hebrew).

Lev-Ari, Ronit (1989) Personal communication.

Levy, Naomi (1988) "Two Shelters, One Threat." *Lilith,* No. 20, Summer:8.

Maimonides *Mishneh Torah* (No date) "Women, Conduct, Domestic Law," Chapter 21, Paragraphs 4–10. (Hebrew).

Mill, John S. (1980) *The Subjection of Women.* Arlington Heights: AHM Publishing Corporation (first published in 1869).

Otzar Geonim. Cited in Morris, Nathan (1964) *The History of Jewish Education,* Vol. 2, Book 1. Tel Aviv: Omanut (Hebrew).

Pinton, Naomi, and Selei, Yehudit (1986) "The Battered Women's Shelter in Ashdod." Jerusalem: the National Insurance Institute and The Research, Planning and Training Department of the Ministry of Labor and Social Welfare (Hebrew).

Responsa Harashba. Cited in Morris, Nathan (1977) *The History of Jewish Education,* Vol. 2, Book 2. Jerusalem: Reuven Mass (Hebrew).)

Responsa Project (1983) "Battered Women." Bar Ilan University (Hebrew).

Salomon, Atalia (1980) "Wife Beating." Unpublished manuscript (Hebrew).

Scarf, Mimi (1988) *Battered Jewish Wives.* Lewiston, New York: Edwin Mellen Press.

Schechter, Susan (1982) *Women and Male Violence: The Visions and Struggles of the Battered Women's Movement.* Boston: South End Press.

Shulhan Arukh (No date) "Even Ha-ezer," Chapter 156, Paragraph 3 (Hebrew).

Spitzer, Julie (1985) *Spousal Abuse in Rabbinic and Contemporary Judaism.* New York: The National Federation of Temple Sisterhoods.

Steiner, Yosepha (1990) *The Needs and Self-Concept of Battered Women.* Tel Aviv: Breirot (Hebrew).

Swirski, Barbara (1984) *Daughters of Eve, Daughters of Lilith: On Women in Israel.* Givatayim: Second Sex Publishing Company (Hebrew).

Walker, Lenore (1979) *The Battered Woman.* New York: Harper & Row.

Author Index

Subject Index

About the Editors
and Contributors

ABOUT THE EDITORS

Barbara Swirski (M.A., sociology, Michigan State University, M.A.T. Harvard) is managing director of Mifras Publishing House and coowner of Breirot Publishers. She is one of the founders of the first shelter for battered women in Israel and served as a coordinator for 5 years. She is also author of *Daughters of Eve, Daughters of Lilith: On Women in Israel; Legal Guide for Women in Domestic Matters,* as well as "Israeli Women on the Assembly Line," in Annette Fuentes and Barbara Ehrenreich, *Women in the Global Factory* (Hebrew).

Marilyn P. Safir (Ph.D., Syracuse University in clinical psychology) is director of women's studies at the University of Haifa and associate professor in the Department of Psychology. She has coedited: *Women's Worlds: From the New Scholarship* (with Martha S. Mednick, Dafna Izraeli and Jessie Bernard); *Sexual Equality: The Israeli Kibbutz Tests the Theories* (with Michal Palgi, Joseph I. Blasi, Menachem Rosner), plus numerous chapters and articles. Professor Safir was one leader of the new Feminist Movement of the early 1970s and led one of the first consciousness-raising groups. She organized and chaired the First International Interdisciplinary Congress on Women in 1981 at the University of Haifa and served on the organizing committee of the Second International Congress held in Groningen, The Netherlands in 1984, the Third held in Dublin in 1987, and the Fourth held at Hunter College in New York in 1990. M. P. Safir is a Fellow of the American Psychological Association. (Society for the Psychological Study of Social Issues, SPSSI & Division of Psychology of Women) She is also a fellow of the American Psychological Society. She was appointed director of the National Commission for the Advancement of the Status of Women in 1986 by then Prime Minister Shimon Peres.

ABOUT THE CONTRIBUTORS

Saniya Abu Rakba was born in Acre and lives in Haifa. She is a graduate of the Haifa Arab Teachers' College and taught elementary school for 7 years before returning to study for a B.A. in education and sociology at Haifa University. She currently is employed at the Dar e-Tifl el-Arabi Center for early childhood research on the Arab child.

Judith Buber Agassi was born in Germany and immigrated to Palestine in 1938. She holds a Ph.D. in government from the London School of Economics. She currently is adjunct professor, Division of Social Sciences, York University, Toronto, specializing in sociology of work and of gender, dividing her time between Israel and Canada. She is the author of: *Women on the Job* (1979), *Comparing the Work Attitudes of Women and Men* (1982), and numerous other books, monographs, and papers.

Deborah S. Bernstein is a senior lecturer in the Department of Sociology and the Women's Studies Program at Haifa University, which she helped found. She is the author of: *The Struggle for Equality—Urban Women Workers in Pre-state Israel,* the first thorough analysis of the Women Workers' Movement in prestate Israel, and numerous articles on women and work. She was born in the United States and immigrated to Israel with her parents when she was three. She received her Ph.D. in Sociology from Sussex University.

Shoshana BenTsvi-Mayer was born in Czechoslovakia and is a survivor of the Holocaust. She came to Israel in her teens. She worked as a teacher and later as principal of the Experimental School at Haifa University. She obtained her Ph.D. in Education from the University of Connecticut at Storrs. Currently teaching at Oranim Teachers' College (Educational Thought and Psychology), she has researched and published widely on gender-issues, including directing and writing programs for nonsexist education.

Anne R. Bloom received her Ph.D. from Bryn Mawr College in developmental psychology. Born and living in the United States, she is a frequent resident in Israel. She is a senior research associate in the Center for Advanced Studies in Education at the Graduate Center of the City University of New York. She researches personality and social structure including family, school, and military institutions, with a particular emphasis on the psychology of women.

Naomi Chazan was born in Jerusalem and received her Ph.D. from the Hebrew University. She is an associate professor of political science and African studies and chair of the Harry S. Truman Research Institute for the Advancement of Peace at the Hebrew University of Jerusalem. She is the author and editor of seven books on African and comparative politics. Between 1985 and 1987, she was the Matina Souretis Horner Radcliffe Distinguished Visiting Professor at Radcliffe College. Together with Galia Golan, she is conducting a comprehensive research project on "The Attitudes and Behavior of Israeli Women on Issues of War, Peace and Conflict Resolution."

Esther Eilam was born in Tel Aviv. She is one of the founders of the Israel Feminist Movement, and a founder of the Tel Aviv Rape Crisis Center, where she served as coordinator and has been active as a volunteer. She is presently working on a book on rape in Israel.

Nabila Espanioly was born in Nazareth. She has a B.A. in social work from the University of Haifa and a B.A. and M.A. in psychology from the University of Bamberg in West Germany. She is on the faculty of the Friends' World College Middle East Israel Center and has taught in Women's Studies at Haifa University. She directs the Nazareth Pedagogical Center and is co-chair of "Partnership." She is active in feminist and peace circles.

Marcia Freedman, who has an M.A. in philosophy, immigrated to Israel in 1967. She was the driving force behind the reemergence of feminism in Israel in the 1970s and a Member of Knesset on the Citizens' Rights List from 1973 to 1977. She founded the Israel Women's Party, which ran in the 1977 elections (but did not achieve a mandate), and was one of the founders of the first shelter for battered women. She now lives in Berkeley, California, and is author of *Exile in the Promised Land: A Memoir.*

Nurit Gillath (M.A.) is a Ph.D. candidate at the Department of Political Science of Haifa University, where she was also one of the first graduates of the Women's Studies Program. Active in the feminist movement since its reestablishment in Israel in the early 1970s, she is director of the Haifa Office of the Citizens' Advisory Service. She was born in Jerusalem.

Avirama Golan, who was born in Givatayim (near Tel Aviv), is a journalist for the daily newspaper *Davar* and an editor for Zmora Bitan Publishing House. She is the author of a book of interviews entitled *Women About Themselves* (Hebrew).

Eveline Goodman-Thau was born in Germany in 1934. In 1939 she fled to Holland, where she survived the war in hiding. She immigrated to Israel in 1955, where she studied Bible and Jewish Philosophy and lectured on Jewish theology. Founder, and for many years director of the Institute for Research of Dutch Jewry, her publications include text and source books for the teaching of the Holocaust, Jewish tradition, and feminist theology in the Jewish tradition.

Manar Hassan was born in the village of Mashhad (near Nazareth) and now resides in Jerusalem. She is a registered nurse, a feminist and peace activist, and, currently, a typesetter.

Hannah Herzog was born in Tel Aviv and received her Ph.D. from Tel Aviv University. She is a senior lecturer in the Department of Sociology at Tel Aviv University. Her main interests are political ethnicity, minor parties, women in politics and political communication. She is author of *Political Ethnicity— The Image and the Reality* and *Contest of Symbols— The Sociology of Election Campaigns Through Israeli Ephemera.*

Dafna N. Izraeli is Canadian-born. She immigrated to Israel in 1963. Her Ph.D. is from Manchester University. She is an associate professor of Sociology and past chairperson of the Department of Sociology and Anthropology at Bar Ilan University. Izraeli cochaired the First International Interdisciplinary Congress on Women—Women's Worlds: the New Scholarship. She edited a special issue of the *Israeli Social Science Review* on Women in Israel (1989). Her works include: *Women's Worlds: From the New Scholarship* (with Marilyn P. Safir, Martha S. Mednick, and Jessie Bernard), *Women in Management Worldwide* (with Nancy Adler) and *Dual Earner Couples: A Cross National Perspective* (with Susan Lewis and Helen Hootsman).

Ruth Katz received her Ph.D. from Tel Aviv University. She is a sociologist who has specialized in the family and has made extensive studies of working mothers. She teaches in the Department of Sociology, Women's Studies, and the School of Social Work at Haifa University. She was born in Haifa.

Fatima Shaloufeh Khazan was born in Nazareth. She has an M.A. in cognitive and research psychology. She has run consciousness raising and assertiveness groups and writes about the status of Arab women. She teaches high school psychology at Kufir Yassif.

Amia Lieblich (Ph.D.) is Jerusalem born. She served as dean of students and is professor of psychology and teaches in the Program of Gender Studies at the Hebrew University in Jerusalem where she directs the center for Research on Gender Roles in Society. Some of her books are: *Kibbutz Makom, Tin Soldiers, On Jerusalem Beach,* and *Transition to Adulthood During Military Service.*

Mariam Mar'i has been a lecturer in the School of Education and in the Women's Studies Program at Haifa University, and school counselor of the Orthodox College in Haifa. She is the director of Dar e-Tifl el-Arabi (Arab Preschool Education Project). She has a Ph.D. in cross-cultural counseling from Michigan State. Mar'i lectures widely on the status of the Arab woman in Israel. She was born in Acre.

Sami Kh. Mar'i, was born in Kufir Kabri. He received his Ph.D. in educational psychology from the University of Wisconsin and was director of the Counseling Division at the University of Haifa. He is the author of *Arab Education in Israel*. He died in 1986 at the age of 46.

Naomi Nevo received her Ph.D. from the University of Tel Aviv. She is a social anthropologist researching rural communities. She has presented her research at congress venues as varied as Mexico, Hungary, and Italy and has published numerous articles in journals and books. Formerly scientific director of the Jewish Agency Rural Settlement Department Team of Sociologists, she is presently an independent consultant on social planning. She is a research associate of the Women's Studies Program at Haifa University and is deputy-chairperson of the Israel Women's Network. Born in London, she came to Palestine in 1946.

Jo Oppenheimer was born in Chicago. She received her M.A. in clinical psychology from Trinity University in San Antonio, Texas, where she worked at the Bexar County Women's Center for 2 years. She has been in private practice in Israel as a feminist psychologist since immigrating in 1985. She lectures frequently on lesbian issues in Israel and abroad.

Michal Palgi was born in Haifa. Her Ph.D. is in sociology from Hebrew University. She is currently the director of the Institute for the Study and Research of the Kibbutz and the Cooperative Idea and a lecturer in sociology and in women's studies at Haifa University. She is senior author (with Joseph Blasi, Menachem Rosner and Marilyn Safir) of *Sexual Equality: the Israeli Kibbutz Tests the Theories,* and has published widely on gender-roles in the kibbutz.

Juliet J. Pope lives in England and is engaged in postgraduate research in Middle-East studies at St. Anthony's College, Oxford. She is writing her thesis on political discourse among Arab and Jewish women in Israel. Between 1987 and 1989 she was a Lady Davis Graduate Fellow at the Hebrew University of Jerusalem.

Frances Raday received her Ph.D. from Hebrew University. She was born in London and immigrated to Israel in 1969. She holds the chair in labor law at the Hebrew University. She has been active in employment discrimination litigation, and is author of *Adjudication of Interest Disputes: The Compulsory Arbitration Model* (1983). She directs the Israel Women's Network's Legal Bureau.

Vicki Shiran was born in Cairo and immigrated to Israel with her parents at the age of four. Active in the Oriental movement since 1970, she was one of the founders of the Israel Traditional Party, an Oriental political party that became a member of the government coalition in 1981. She served as spokesperson for the party and as spokesperson and advisor to the Israel Ministry of Absorption. She is presently writing her thesis for a Ph.D. degree in criminal justice from the John Jay College of Criminal City University, New York.

Ella Shohat was born in Petah Tikva and is currently assistant professor and coordinator of the Cinema Studies program at the Department of Performing Arts, The City University of New York, Staten Island. She is on the editorial board of *Social Texts* and the author of *Israeli Cinema: East/West and the Politics of Representation*. Her Ph.D. is from the City University of New York.

Vivian Silver was born in Winnipeg, Canada and immigrated to Israel in 1974 with a group that established Kibbutz Gezer. She now lives on Kibbutz Beeri. She established the Department for the Promotion of Sex Equality in the United Kibbutz Federation in 1981 and served as its coordinator for 2 years. She is author of *Male and Female Created He Them* (Hebrew).

Alison Solomon was born in England and immigrated to Israel in 1978. She has served as coordinator of the Tel Aviv Rape Crisis Center, is the representative of FINNRAGE in Israel, and is currently studying for her masters degree in social work at Bryn Mawr College in the United States.

Regine Waintrater has an M.A. in clinical psychology from the Sorbonne. She is a senior psychologist at the mental health clinic of the Histadrut Sick Fund in Ramat Gan and has taught postgraduate courses in the departments of psychology at Haifa and Tel Aviv universities. Coauthor of a book on women and war in Israel, with Danielle Kriegel, *Cette nuit encore, Golda ne dormira pas,* she is presently pursuing doctoral studies in Paris.